# Religion, Violence, and Local Power-Sharing in Nigeria

Why does religion become a fault line of communal violence in some pluralistic countries and not others? Under what conditions will religious identity – as opposed to other salient ethnic cleavages – become the spark that ignites communal violence? Contemporary world politics since 9/11 is increasingly marked by intra-state communal clashes in which religious identity is the main fault line. Yet, violence erupts only in some religiously pluralistic countries, and only in some parts of those countries. This study argues that prominent theories in the study of civil conflict cannot adequately account for the variation in subnational identity-based violence. Examining this variation in the context of Nigeria's pluralistic north-central region, this book finds support for a new theory of power-sharing. It finds that communities are less likely to fall prey to a divisive narrative of religious difference where local leaders informally agreed to abide by an inclusive local government power-sharing arrangement.

Laura Thaut Vinson is an Assistant Professor of International Affairs at Lewis & Clark College, Portland, Oregon.

# Religion, Violence, and Local Power-Sharing in Nigeria

**LAURA THAUT VINSON**
*Lewis & Clark College, Portland*

CAMBRIDGE
UNIVERSITY PRESS

CAMBRIDGE
UNIVERSITY PRESS

University Printing House, Cambridge CB2 8BS, United Kingdom

One Liberty Plaza, 20th Floor, New York, NY 10006, USA

477 Williamstown Road, Port Melbourne, VIC 3207, Australia

4843/24, 2nd Floor, Ansari Road, Daryaganj, Delhi – 110002, India

79 Anson Road, #06–04/06, Singapore 079906

Cambridge University Press is part of the University of Cambridge.

It furthers the University's mission by disseminating knowledge in the pursuit of education, learning, and research at the highest international levels of excellence.

www.cambridge.org
Information on this title: www.cambridge.org/9781107179370
DOI: 10.1017/9781316832110

© Laura Thaut Vinson 2017

This publication is in copyright. Subject to statutory exception and to the provisions of relevant collective licensing agreements, no reproduction of any part may take place without the written permission of Cambridge University Press.

First published 2017

Printed in the United States of America by Sheridan Books, Inc.

*A catalog record for this publication is available from the British Library.*

ISBN 978-1-107-17937-0 Hardback

Cambridge University Press has no responsibility for the persistence or accuracy of URLs for external or third-party internet websites referred to in this publication and does not guarantee that any content on such websites is, or will remain, accurate or appropriate.

*For the unsung Nigerians who have borne the costs of conflict but have nevertheless chosen to believe in and stand for peace.*

*In memory of Papa, who intensely valued knowledge of the world.*

# Contents

| | | |
|---|---|---|
| *List of Figures* | | *page* viii |
| *List of Tables* | | x |
| *Preface* | | xiii |
| *Acknowledgments* | | xxiii |
| 1 | Deterring Religious Violence | 1 |

    PART I  THE IMPORTANCE OF THE POLITICS OF RELIGIOUS CHANGE AND LOCAL GOVERNMENT

| | | |
|---|---|---|
| 2 | Pattern and Politics of Religious Change in Nigeria | 41 |
| 3 | Tenuous Unity: Federalism, Local Governments, and Politics in Nigeria | 84 |

    PART II  MAKING THE CASE FOR POWER-SHARING: THE EMPIRICAL EVIDENCE

| | | |
|---|---|---|
| 4 | A Theory of Local Government Power-Sharing | 109 |
| 5 | Power-Sharing Data and Findings | 132 |
| 6 | Case Studies and the Power-Sharing Mechanism | 166 |
| 7 | Case Studies and the Origins of Power-Sharing | 196 |
| 8 | Considering Competing Hypotheses | 232 |

    PART III  CONCLUSIONS

| | | |
|---|---|---|
| 9 | Conclusion | 259 |
| *Appendices* | | 289 |
| *References* | | 306 |
| *Index* | | 328 |

# Figures

| | | |
|---|---|---|
| 1.1 | Northern and north-central Middle Belt states | *page* 4 |
| 1.2 | Representation of power-sharing argument and factors | 27 |
| 1.3 | Sites of power-sharing analysis: Kaduna and Plateau state LGAs | 33 |
| 2.1 | Total number of affiliated Christians, 1900–2025 (millions) | 44 |
| 2.2 | Muslim and Christian affiliation in Africa, percent of population, 1900–2010 | 45 |
| 2.3 | Percentage of Pentecostal-charismatic Christians, 1900–2025 | 46 |
| 4.1 | Rotating seat-based power-sharing model | 126 |
| 4.2 | Static seat-based power-sharing model | 127 |
| 5.1 | Cases of ethno-religious and ethno-tribal violence, 1979–2011 | 138 |
| 5.2 | Outline of Nigerian States, Kaduna state and Plateau state emphasized | 143 |
| 5.3 | Frequency of communal violence in Middle Belt states (1979–2011) | 144 |
| 5.4 | Relationship between inter-religious violence and power-sharing, Plateau state | 148 |
| 5.5 | Relationship between inter-religious violence and power-sharing, Kaduna state | 155 |
| 6.1 | LGAs included in comparative case studies, Plateau state and Kaduna state | 168 |
| 7.1 | Pattern of power-sharing adoption in the pluralistic Middle Belt | 200 |

*List of Figures*

### APPENDIX FIGURES

| | | |
|---|---|---|
| D.1 | Muslim and Christian affiliation in Asia, percent of population, 1900–2010 | 293 |
| E.1 | Percent affiliated Christians in Africa, Latin America, and Asia, 1900–2025 | 294 |
| F.1 | Number of cases in which *any* religious group is noted as party to communal violence | 295 |
| K.1 | Types of precipitating events in cases of *ethno-religious* violence | 303 |
| K.2 | Types of precipitating events in cases of *ethno-tribal* violence | 303 |

# Tables

| | | |
|---|---|---|
| 2.1 | Percentage of Affiliated Christians in Select Northern Nigerian States over Time | *page* 55 |
| 2.2 | Major Christian Denominations in Northern Nigeria, Percentage of Growth/Year | 55 |
| 2.3 | Percentage of ECWA Congregations/Churches Established in Northern Nigeria Pre-1970 and Post-1970 | 56 |
| 5.1 | Pattern of Power-Sharing and Violence, Plateau State | 147 |
| 5.2 | Plateau State LGAs: Power-Sharing and Count of Ethno-Religious and Ethno-Tribal Violence | 150 |
| 5.3 | Pattern of Power-Sharing and Violence, Kaduna State | 154 |
| 5.4 | Kaduna State LGAs: Power-Sharing and Count of Ethno-Religious and Ethno-Tribal Violence | 157 |
| 6.1 | Similarities between Chikun and Jos | 170 |
| 6.2 | Similarities between Kanam and Shendam | 172 |
| 6.3 | Similarities between Bassa and Zangon-Kataf | 173 |

### APPENDIX TABLES

| | | |
|---|---|---|
| A.1 | GINI Index Measure, Urban/Rural | 290 |
| B.1 | GDP per Capita by State (2007), ($US) | 291 |
| C.1 | Real Income Growth, GINI Change, and Poverty Incidence, 1998–2004 | 292 |
| G.1 | Ethno-Religious Cases and Religious Precipitating Events, $\chi^2$ | 296 |
| G.2 | Ethno-Religious Cases and Religious Precipitating Events, Test of Proportions | 297 |

## List of Tables

| | | |
|---|---|---|
| H.1 | Ethno-Tribal Cases and Economic/Tribal Precipitating Events, Test of Proportions | 299 |
| I.1 | Ethnic Violence and Religious Precipitating Events, Test of Proportions | 301 |
| J.1 | Population and Communal Violence Figures, Middle Belt States (1979–2011) | 302 |
| L.1 | Kaduna LGAs Population Total | 304 |
| L.2 | Plateau LGAs Population Total | 305 |

# Preface

When I arrived in Nigeria at the beginning of February 2011 for a year of fieldwork, it was with some trepidation. The presidential election, scheduled for April, created potential for instability and violence, depending on the outcome; an emergent terrorist threat loomed in the northeast, raising new security concerns; and inter-religious communal violence was ongoing. This last, however, was precisely what I had come to study, seeking to better understand why religious identity becomes the fault line in some pluralistic communities of northern Nigeria and not in others. Unfortunately, then, these concerns validated my reason for choosing to study Nigeria in the first place.

Arriving in Jos, Plateau state – a four-hour drive north from the capital of Abuja in the center of the country – I had hardly alighted from the vehicle when my husband and I were told there had been an incident downtown. As we crossed the road to reach the place we would call home for about the next year, a truck went by carrying a few dead bodies. There had been a stabbing in the marketplace that threatened to reignite communal violence, and already the streets were emptying. Such was my welcome to Jos.

### NIGERIA'S SECURITY CHALLENGES

Since my fieldwork in 2011, the security challenges facing the Nigerian state and its people have only increased. The 2011 election emphasized the national dimensions of Nigeria's regional and ethnic tensions. The election risked fueling the flames of Muslim–Christian violence since the election pitted Muhammadu Buhari, a Muslim from the North and former military ruler turned champion of democracy and anti-corruption, against Goodluck Jonathan, a Christian from the south and the incumbent. There were particular concerns about instability and insecurity in the Middle Belt or north-central Nigeria, since this is the region of the country where the predominantly Christian south meets the predominantly Muslim north. The candidacy of Jonathan was a hotly contested issue, in particular, because the elected president in 2007 – Umaru Musa Yar'Adua – became critically ill after taking office, leaving Jonathan temporarily with the reigns of power during Yar'Adua's medical treatment and then permanently after he passed away in 2010. Some brief context is necessary to explain the contentiousness of the election.

For those familiar with Nigeria's history, the regional tensions over political control surfaced immediately after independence in 1960, in no small part a product of the structure of governance under British colonial rule. To manage the competing regional ethnic interests, Nigeria pursued an ethno-federal model of national governance, a consociational or power-sharing mechanism. One informal mechanism of inclusion that emerged from Nigeria's "federal character" was the implicit understanding that the presidency should rotate between the north and south. Although it was not ultimately written into the constitution, parties are expected to adhere to this principle to keep the lid on regional fears of northern or southern domination of the country. Hence, although Jonathan was propelled into the presidency unexpectedly in 2010, many felt that it was now time for a northerner to lead the country in keeping with the informal principle of rotation (Paden 2012; Lewis and Kew 2015). With the powers and advantages of incumbency on his side and the popular (at least in the south) People's Democratic Party's decision to put him forward as their main candidate, the prospect of Jonathan's reelection raised concerns about a possible violent reaction in the north.

These concerns were not unfounded. After the presidential election results were announced, news quickly spread of violent protests. Although Jos, where I was based, remained more or less peaceful (my fieldwork continued uninterrupted except for the occasional curfew), other areas of the Middle Belt and north experienced rioting and violence that took on the coloration of Muslim–Christian communal conflict. Human Rights Watch (2011) estimated that hundreds of churches were destroyed, upwards of 800 people killed, and 65,000 displaced across Nigeria's 12 northern states. Nonetheless, although irregularities were certainly present, international observers deemed the election to be largely free and fair, a vast improvement on the previous election. Although the victory was challenged in court, Jonathan was ultimately declared the winner and the West was hopeful that his presidency would lead to the strengthening of democratic institutions and stem rampant corruption.

These expectations were sadly disappointed. While to some degree it was "politics as usual" from 2011 to 2015, a number of significant challenges to national stability emerged (or intensified) during Jonathan's presidency. One of these is the continuing threat of Jama'atu Ahlus-Sunnah Lidda'Awati Wal Jihad, better known as Boko Haram. The world seemed to wake up to the reality of the Boko Haram threat in 2011 when a suicide bomber rammed a car through the gate of the United Nations Headquarters in Abuja, killing at least 18 people. Boko Haram veritably rocketed to international media attention in April 2014 with the widely reported abduction of over 200 school girls in Chibok in the northeast state of Borno and the subsequent #BringBackOurGirls campaign. Suddenly this extremist cell in the corner of northeast Nigeria was a far more virulent threat. And indeed, Nigeria Security Tracker data collected by the U.S. Council on Foreign Relations estimates that more than 20,000 people have been killed by Boko Haram attacks since 2009 and as many as two million displaced (Campbell 2016). The Nigerian army has struggled to stem the security threat, waging battles against Boko Haram in the north while also falling under international criticism for extrajudicial killings and pervasive human rights violations (Amnesty International 2014).

At another level, violence between nomadic Fulani cattle-herders and farming communities in the Middle Belt also seems to have become a deeper problem, particularly in Barkin Ladi and Riyom local government areas of Plateau state. These clashes have spread to other states and as far south as the Niger Delta, the product of the shrinking availability of grazing land in northern Nigeria due to desertification, population growth, and the expansion of farming activities into wetlands traditionally used for cattle grazing. The rise in cattle thievery and decline in the peace mediation ability of traditional rulers has increased the scale of the problem (Stein 2016; Baca 2015; Blench 2004). The religious identity of these communities – predominantly Muslim Fulani herders and predominantly Christian farmers – also risks aggravating perceived religious cleavages and tensions.

There are calls for the government to address this increasingly ominous security issue before clashes become even more widespread. There is no consensus, however, on how to address the problem. During a return visit to Jos in summer of 2016, talk of the government passing a bill that would set up grazing reserves (and/or ranches; the terminology and its implications are part of the debate) to address the problem was at the forefront of local conversation about political problems. News of this possible political "solution" sparked an outcry earlier in the year and widespread opposition to the passage or implementation of any such bill by the government. One fear is that if state governors support such a policy, it could spark renewed violence in communities whose land might be affected, communities already worn thin from previous communal violence.

To add to the challenges, economic troubles have hit Nigeria's economy hard in recent years, following on the heels of the 2008 recession and the decline in global oil prices since 2014. Acquaintances in Jos bemoan the more than doubling in the prices of basic food staples in the market. Rice is no longer affordable. An indicator of the weakened economy, in mid-2016, the value of the Naira was pegged to around 197 naira to the dollar, but the going rate on the black market hovered as high as 360 naira. With the economy seeing its worst growth figures in years in the first quarter of 2016, a doubling in the price of fuel and basic food items, and the lack of foreign exchange, the government caved to the pressure to devalue the currency.

Related to these economic problems, the Niger Delta region continues to be a significant security challenge for the Nigerian state after a peaceful lull of four or five years. A program of amnesty initiated under Yar'Adua's administration in 2009 and continued under Jonathan's administration helped to put a stop to destabilizing violence hamstringing the oil industry. The program offered militants job training (domestically and abroad) and a living stipend in exchange for putting down their weapons and stopping attacks against oil installations and kidnapping of oil workers. A 2013 United States Institute of Peace special report on security in the Niger Delta warned, however, that the relative peace and renewed oil production as a result of the amnesty could reverse in the coming years if deeper issues were not addressed (Sayne 2013).

The warning proved prophetic. In the first part of 2016, a newly emergent militant group that calls itself the Niger Delta Avengers began regularly blowing up oil installations or pipelines, wreaking havoc on Nigeria's already hard-hit oil economy, cutting oil production by as much as a quarter or one-third in May and June 2016. The militants condemn the government for failing to bring development to the poverty-stricken region from which the majority of Nigeria's national revenue derives (Ewokar 2016; "Niger Delta Avengers" 2016). The main actors are unclear, and the hypothesized factors contributing to their mobilization include anger at the Buhari regime for ending some of the amnesty benefits accruing to ex-militants; former militants disillusioned with the empty promises of amnesty, or politicians siphoning funds intended for the program; an effort to extort benefits from a new peace process; anger at the increasing poverty with a shrinking economy; and continued development concerns and pollution (Ebiede 2016; Searcy 2016; Fick 2016; Sayne 2013). Locals in Jos also placed blame on former president Jonathan, accusing him of failing to lend a helping hand in calming tensions among his co-ethnics in the Niger Delta – perhaps because it reflects poorly on President Buhari, Jonathan's former political rival. Whatever the case, the attacks have only worsened the economic crisis and created another significant economic and security challenge for the Buhari administration.

To make matters worse, the troubles in the Niger Delta region come on the heels of renewed agitation for the formation of an independent Biafran state. In October 2015, when the government arrested Nnamdi Kanu, a leader of a Biafran separatist movement, it sparked protests in the southeast and further raised the profile of the movement (Gaffey 2016). Although it is unclear whether the agitation will develop into anything beyond just that, this at least low-level resurgence of separatist sentiment is another political worry, as it harkens back to the devastation of the Biafran Civil War from 1967 to 1970 that nearly split the country apart. While it is unclear how widespread sentiment and support are, the agitation is the product of similar feelings of political disenfranchisement and economic woes.

This is just a snapshot of a number of complex security challenges facing the Nigerian state. It remains to be seen how Buhari, who this time won his election bid against Jonathan in 2015, will fare in managing these challenges. On the one hand, Buhari's election victory was a landmark and widely heralded event since it marks the first time an opposition party in Nigeria has defeated the incumbent ruling party in an election. Jonathan's immediate peaceful concession also forestalled considerable violence expected throughout the north if he contested the results (see Lewis and Kew 2015). Also, Buhari made strong initial strides in reducing Boko Haram's control in the northeast, and he came into power on a popular platform to fight corruption. On the other hand, the Boko Haram challenge is ever-present, and there are concerns that the targets of Buhari's anti-corruption campaigns are primarily members of the defeated PDP party, rather than known corrupt figures in his own All

Progressive Congress (APC) party. Unlike previous administrations, Buhari also must navigate the host of socio-economic and security challenges highlighted here without the massive oil revenue that has buoyed the economy in the past.

To say that Nigeria is a complex country borders on the superfluous or trite. But for the political scientist and the comparativist, in particular, this complexity presents a rich field of study. Nigeria is a country, in many senses, of contrast. It is a state with massive ethnic and cultural diversity that weathered a civil war at the end of the 1960s, and yet a state that continues to face ethnic cleavages and militant movements that threaten to fracture it. It is a state that, for much of its post-colonial history, was ruled by successive military regimes with short-lived stints of civilian rule, but in 1999, returned to civilian rule and has generally adhered to the basic institutions of democracy, with fits and starts. (Note that its experience of colonialism, like many African states, left little in the way of strong or representative institutions upon which to build.) It is a state that, since the 1970s, has reaped bountiful wealth with the discovery of major oil resources, but the lived reality of the vast majority of Nigerians is deep poverty. It is a state with a massive population and one of the biggest economies in Africa, but whose full potential is also hobbled at many levels by corruption. It is a deeply religious country where both Islam and Christianity have flourished side-by-side, but religion has also become a tool of political mobilization and, in recent years, lent its mantle to inter-religious communal violence. And, as stated at the outset, it was specifically to study this last puzzle that I went to Nigeria in 2011.

### FOCUS AND FRAMEWORK OF THE BOOK

This book therefore tackles only a slice of the security questions that Nigeria has faced – the rise of inter-religious communal violence since the 1980s – but it is an important one. As stated by Paden (2012, 105–106), a long-time scholar of Nigerian politics, "the national implications are clear: if ethnoreligious conflict is allowed to fester in the middle of the country, it may eventually destabilize the entire 'Nigerian project.'" Exploring the dimensions and subnational variation in ethno-religious violence, therefore, I propose a new theory of power-sharing. For, despite the upsurge in inter-religious violence and sacralization of politics over the past 40 years, I argue in this book that inter-religious violence is not the bane of Nigeria's pluralistic communities everywhere. Indeed, even in the Middle Belt – hit hardest by Muslim–Christian violence since the

1980s – a number of pluralistic communities have managed to maintain inter-religious peace and cooperation. Considering the ease with which inter-religious disputes in one area of the Middle Belt or north can spark retaliation among co-religionists elsewhere, what explains this? Why are some local government areas – the third tier of Nigeria's federal structure – less prone to inter-religious violence than others? Although Osaghae (1998, 249) observes that weaknesses of the Nigerian state, failed economic policies, the failure of civilian rule to take root in the 1980s and 1990s, and the increasing ethno-religious tensions of various types following the 1978 national Sharia issue all contributed to "religious, ethnic, and regional conflicts," he notes that the "Muslim-Christian conflicts … manifested themselves chiefly in the religious uprisings and riots in the North and in more localized ethnic or so-called communal conflicts." Hence, the pattern of Muslim–Christian conflict requires further exploration of the nature of local government politics and institutions. It requires attention, I argue, to the role of informal power-sharing institutions at the *local* government level in defusing ethnic and, in particular, religious communal violence.

The book is therefore structured around this puzzle and my answer to it. Chapter 1 introduces and frames the puzzle itself. It also outlines the main arguments: the role of power-sharing at the local government level in explaining variation in inter-religious communal violence in Nigeria's pluralistic north-central region. The chapter then proceeds by defining the study's key concepts and briefly discusses prominent theories of civil conflict and their inability to explain Nigeria's puzzle of subnational variation in inter-religious communal violence. Finally, Chapter 1 lays out the methodology of data collection and case study work.

Providing critical background for understanding the rise of divisive identity politics and inter-religious violence in Nigeria, Chapter 2 addresses the subject of religious change. Not unique to Nigeria, the rapid post-colonial growth of Christianity in Nigeria – particularly the new, more politically mobilized Pentecostal-charismatic variant – and the radicalization of Islam are fundamental to the story of how religious identity became a repertoire for collective mobilization and communal violence. While other political and socio-economic grievances affect the likelihood of communal violence in northern Nigeria, the politics of religious change is a critical factor shaping the political identities, perceptions, and interests of actors. In particular, this chapter highlights the events and new forms of mobilization that have led to the sacralization of Nigerian politics over the past four decades. This discussion emphasizes the importance of taking seriously the changing boundaries or forms of religio-political practice propelled by this religious change.

Chapter 3 provides important background for the theory and analyses presented in subsequent chapters. It explores the role of ethno-federalism as a tool of creating a strong, centralized state that could balance ethnic and regional interests, but highlights the significance of reforms adopted in the 1970s creating local governments as a third tier of federal administration. I argue that these decentralization reforms, while creating institutions closer to the people, also increased contestation and the importance of rights and representation at the local level.

Having laid the groundwork for understanding the context of governance, Nigeria's federal structure, and the history of religious change in Nigeria, chapters 4–6 discuss the bulk of the support for the theory of local power-sharing, including case study evidence from the three paired comparisons of violence-prone and peaceful local government areas. Chapter 4 outlines the theoretical argument and hypotheses regarding the role of informal and local-level power-sharing in defusing identity-based communal violence. It discusses the existing literature on power-sharing, the major critiques, and makes the case that, as a local-level mechanism of more inclusive representation, power-sharing is less prone to the weaknesses scholars associate with the national-level variant.

Chapter 5 presents the findings of power-sharing data collected for the 17 and 23 local government areas of Plateau state and Kaduna state, respectively. My research focuses on the local government areas in these two states because of their comparative value; while they have a similar colonial history and ethnic pluralism, some of the local government areas are prone to recurrent inter-religious violence, while others are largely peaceful. The power-sharing data presented in this chapter confirm that pluralistic communities with power-sharing institutions – e.g., rotation of ethno-tribal leadership in the governing councils – are less likely to be major sites of inter-religious violence.

Elucidating the *causal* link between power-sharing and communal peace, Chapter 6 explores the mechanisms through which informal local government power-sharing provides a foundation for inter-religious peace. It does so drawing on insights and examples from three paired comparison case studies. The case study evidence shows how power-sharing reduces perceptions of inter-ethnic marginalization and competition, providing a foundation and incentives for local leaders to cooperate and build stronger inter-ethnic ties across the tribal, religious, and political spectrum.

Chapter 7 takes up an important question that arises out of the analysis – why, if power-sharing is a key institutional constraint on communal violence, did elders in only some communities opt for power-sharing following decentralization reforms in the 1970s while others did not? This chapter presents findings from case studies and interviews with local community leaders and representatives, revealing that there is no one path to power-sharing. Rather, the routes to power-sharing – the incentives or disincentives affecting decision-makers – have varied based on the divergent social, political, and economic changes affecting communal relationships in LGAs since independence. Patterns of colonial-era assimilation and integration are important, but a range of post-colonial changes shaped the various strategic incentives or disincentives for tribal elite to adopt power-sharing in any one local government area. Where local government leadership does not rely on an institutional foundation of inclusivity, however, there is greater risk that local grievances or disputes will breed inter-religious violence in Nigeria's current sacralized political climate.

Finally, before concluding, Chapter 8 addresses a series of counterarguments or competing hypotheses, including the possibility that power-sharing is endogenous to some other factor (e.g., prior colonial history, a history of violence or peace). I find that the evidence for these counterarguments is weak. The argument does not presume that local government councils characterized by a power-sharing arrangement are impervious to inter-religious tensions; rather, they are better able to dispel claims of exclusion or unequal representation.

The final chapter summarizes the main findings and contentions of the book, and it draws on the experience of Indonesia to discuss the broader generalizability and applicability of this study to other democracies in the Global South that have also seen an increase in inter-religious violence in recent years. Recapping the main argument and findings, this chapter highlights a number of important implications for how scholars think about the relationship between local government institutions, identity, and subnational communal violence.

### PURPOSE AND NATURE OF THE BOOK

It may be fairly asked: is this a book about Nigeria? It is, but its theoretical assumptions and analyses go beyond Nigeria. In line with the purpose and methods of comparative politics research, my goal is to explore an important puzzle at the intersection of identity, violence, and institutions.

I address lines of inquiry and research central to the civil war and ethnic conflict scholarship – designing institutions (e.g., consociationalism or power-sharing) to prevent conflict in pluralistic societies – and I explore the limited explanatory power of dominant instrumentalist accounts that overlook or marginalize the role of religious identity in conflict.

In this vein, like major scholars of ethnic conflict in the comparative politics field, I focus on within-country comparative analysis at the subnational level to test my theory in relationship to other competing theories of identity and conflict. Careful selection of subnational cases allows one to control for other competing theories while testing one's own theory. This is what this book does. As outlined above, it begins by framing the politics of religious change, federalism, local politics, and communal violence in Nigeria writ large, and then, to test its power-sharing theory, delves more deeply into the pattern of representation in two pluralistic Middle Belt states and a handful of local government areas with either a history of peace or violence. In this sense, the project is consistent with comparative politics work that looks at a single country and uses case study analysis and data to test a larger theory about conflict and identity.

The findings, however, have implications for how scholars understand the role of local institutions in the prevention of subnational communal violence. I expect the analysis to be of interest to scholars who study Nigerian politics and are interested in the relationship between identity and politics, the rise of inter-religious violence over the past few decades, and what Nigeria's experiences can teach us about broader patterns of politics and conflict; but more broadly, the book also speaks to the scholarship on civil war and ethnic conflict, religion and politics, and the role of institutions in divided societies. It is my hope that this study will contribute to the discussions among academics, government actors, community leaders, and peace activists on how to build institutions in conflict societies that can mitigate ethnic cleavages and defuse the divisive politicization of religion, reclaiming the religious narrative for the task of peacebuilding rather than violence.

# Acknowledgments

This book would not have seen the light of day without the guidance, support, and generosity of a host of individuals in the U.S. and Nigeria. It developed out of my dissertation research at the University of Minnesota (UofM), and I was fortunate to have the guidance of my dissertation committee members David Samuels, Kathleen Collins, Michael Barnett, and Dara Cohen. Their feedback and advice helped me refine my ideas and chart my path forward. I am particularly grateful to my advisor David Samuels, who went above and beyond to support my fieldwork, offer critical feedback at every stage, and encourage me to keep going despite the hurdles. To Michael Barnett, for his constant support and faith in this research, I am grateful. Thanks are also due to Bud Duvall, who strongly supported the fieldwork during his time as chair of the political science department at the UofM. Departmental fellowships and University support in the form of the Doctoral Dissertation Fellowship and Graduate Research Partnership Program also enabled the research.

My thanks, as well, to the John Sloan Dickey Center for International Understanding at Dartmouth College and its director Daniel Benjamin for supporting my research and writing during a year-long post-doctoral fellowship from 2013 to 2014. This gave me the freedom and time to refine the manuscript and to do so in a stimulating intellectual environment. I am very grateful, in particular, to William Wohlforth, Nelson Kasfir, Simon Chauchard, and Jeremy Horowitz from the Government Department for generously taking the time to read a draft of the manuscript and provide extremely helpful suggestions for its improvement.

Additionally, my warm thanks to the two anonymous reviewers who provided some of the best critical and constructive feedback I have ever received, helping me to make considerable revisions and improvements to the manuscript. I am grateful to Robert Dreesen at Cambridge University Press for finding such excellent reviewers and guiding the manuscript through the review process, and to Cassi Roberts for guiding the book through the production process.

On the Nigerian front, I am indebted to many people. In particular, assistance from Dr. Danny McCain at the University of Jos helped make my time in Nigeria possible. Without his legwork over various bureaucratic hurdles, it is highly questionable whether I would have made it to Nigeria at all. For his advice, encouragement, and help all along the way, I am grateful. Dr. McCain's colleagues at the Nigeria Pentecostal and Charismatic Research Centre in Jos – Rev. Dr. Yusuf Turaki, Dr. Musa Gaiya, and Dr. John Brown – also offered wonderful insights and assistance. And I am endlessly indebted to Dr. Katrina Korb at the University of Jos for her help navigating local customs and organizing follow-up data collection. More importantly, I gained a wonderful friend.

The University of Jos and the Political Science department graciously hosted me during fieldwork. Dr. Galadima of the Political Science department and Dr. Audu Gambo of the Centre for Conflict Management and Peace Studies were welcoming and provided valuable assistance. Other faculty in various departments were also generous in their insights. My deep thanks also go to my research assistants from the University of Jos and the Centre for Conflict Management and Peace Studies: Luther Gaiya, Nelson Iheanacho, Ardo Sam-Jackson, Samuel Obiora Okoye, Ashley Chundung Dauda, Jonathan Lar, Friday Haruna Fyammang, Ethelbert Lawrence, and Samuel Maiwada. These students worked hard with me for two months in dusty (and worse) libraries, helping me go through thousands of newspaper editions to identify cases of ethno-religious and ethno-tribal violence. I will never forget their kindness to this *bature*, their laughter and jokes, and the little bit of their lives that they shared with me, even if I did fail in my attempt to cook them real Nigerian food. Ashley Chundung Dauda and Samuel Obiora Okeye, in particular, I consider friends who went above and beyond in their effort to help me complete data collection from various local government areas. I am also grateful to Yakubu Ibrahim Ali, Danlami Mortal, and Daniel Datok Dalyop, who interrupted their own work to assist me in the final phases of data-gathering in local government areas of Plateau state and Kaduna state.

My heartfelt thanks also go to members of Serving in Mission (SIM), Nigeria, and the Evangelical Church Winning All (ECWA) staff. ECWA staff were generous in sharing church data, and SIM director Phil Andrew was gracious in agreeing to provide housing to my husband and me on an SIM/ECWA compound during our ten months living in Jos. Chris and Helen Cowie were overwhelming in their kindness and care (i.e., surrogate parents), our neighbor Dee Grimes was a great source of encouragement and laughter during the challenges of fieldwork, and Lami – one of the caretakers of the compound – brightened our days with her unwavering joy even in troubled times.

To Anari, Michael, and Andrew, I must also extend thanks for always getting me safely from point A to point B on Nigeria's nerve-wracking roads, and for putting up with my many curious questions about life in Nigeria. These wonderful drivers helped me avoid any number of *faux pas* along the way, and got me safely through some unnerving checkpoints without incident.

My interest in the intersection of the sacred and secular was planted during undergraduate studies at Whitworth University, and so I would be remiss in not thanking Dr. Michael LeRoy (my dear advisor and mentor), Dr. John Yoder (who introduced me to African politics), and Dr. Julia Stronks who all inspired my love of research and global politics. This book is in many senses their fault. Their encouragement and investment in my life meant more to me than they will ever know.

My family has been a constant source of encouragement through the various phases of the research journey. My parents, Steven and Catherine Thaut, taught me the importance of discipline and hard work and have always had more faith in me than I have had in myself, even if they have not been particularly thrilled about my choice of research destinations. With a grateful heart, I say thank you to them and to my wonderful brothers Eric and Jason, and to my extended family, who always know how to jolt me out of research and writing sloughs. They fill my life with joy.

I lack sufficient words to thank my husband, Matthew Vinson, for his constant (patient) support. He married me just in time to join the fieldwork adventure. Little did he (or I) know how much I would come to rely on him for endurance during the daily grind of coding "yet another" case of communal violence, for navigating local living and staying safe, keeping the water system up and running, chasing down cockroaches and eliminating other unwelcome creeping critters, helping me talk through and think out all the conceptual and theoretical problems with my work, and for keeping me upright when I was more than once ready to call it quits. He has garnered the unfortunate "privilege" of becoming my pseudo-editor and advisor, reading multiple versions of manuscript chapters along the way and providing clarity when I could no longer see my own work.

Finally, I also owe a great deal of thanks to a host of traditional leaders, religious leaders, local activists, community organizers, and local government officials. They form a list far too long to include here, but the research benefited immeasurably from their openness in sharing their thoughts on the challenges of inter-religious violence in Nigeria or in allowing me to attend their meetings. The beauty and privilege of fieldwork is having the opportunity to be let into the lives of people half a world away, if only for a season, and to learn from them. I gained far more from this – on a personal level – than I will ever be able to repay. This book is ultimately dedicated to the Nigerians who continue to struggle every day to live with dignity and hope in the face of challenging circumstances, and who remain committed to peace and loving their neighbors at whatever cost.

# 1

# Deterring Religious Violence

On August 29, 2011, at the end of Ramadan during the Muslim Eid-ul-Fitr holiday, the city of Jos was quiet. Quiet streets are a bad omen when the indicators of normality in Jos are honking vehicles, the hum of business, and chatter of greetings on the streets. Soon enough, black smoke rose over a neighborhood not far from the city center, marring the city skyline. Rumors spread: *Muslims and Christians are clashing in the Jos North area.* Subsequent reports confirmed that a group of Muslims had apparently trekked into a predominantly Christian neighborhood to pray at an abandoned mosque – destroyed in previous inter-religious violence – against the warning of security personnel. Christian residents, questioning the intentions of the worshippers and threatened by the action, armed themselves. Which side attacked first remains unclear, but in the subsequent few hours, over 100 vehicles were set ablaze, at least 24 people were killed, and gruesome reports emerged that Christian youth had not only beheaded some Muslims, but also roasted and eaten their flesh. Reprisal attacks were predictably carried out in various neighborhoods around Jos over the next two days. Some later reports blamed the Muslim worshippers for provoking trouble, while others pointed to the provocative action of the armed Christians who surrounded the mosque and worshippers (see Human Rights Watch 2013, 71). Whatever the case, that it was a violent clash between Muslims and Christians was clear.

This is only one of a number of increasingly common stories of Muslim–Christian clashes in north-central Nigeria since the 1980s. Yet, this instance of inter-religious violence in an ethnically pluralistic region points to an important puzzle for the study of ethnic conflict in Nigeria and other pluralistic countries. In countries struggling to stem inter-religious tensions, why does violence occur in only some religiously pluralistic communities and not others? Further, why does the violence take an ethno-religious dimension when there are other overlapping and salient ethnic cleavages available for mobilization?[1] These are important questions for countries such as India, Indonesia, Nigeria, Myanmar, Egypt, Malaysia, and the Central African Republic, among others, as these countries have been or continue to be flashpoints of inter-religious violence, and inter-religious violence can carry great cost; such violence can lead to significant loss of life, refugee flows, and internal displacement, as well as devastate infrastructure and local economies or even destabilize the state. These questions therefore warrant further investigation.

Many scholars have noted the importance of studying identity-based conflict in one fashion or another. The uptick in intra-state conflict since the end of the Cold War has motivated scholars to explore the microdynamics of ethnic conflict – the actors, mobilizing mechanisms, and material and ideational conditions that seem to render ethnic violence more likely in some countries than others. Indeed, significant advances have been made in our understanding of the role of electoral incentives and the manipulation of identity politics by political entrepreneurs (e.g., Brubaker and Laitin 1998; Wilkinson 2004; Posner 2004; Brass 2006; Berenschot 2013), the level of civic associationalism or integration among ethnic communities (e.g., Varshney 2002; Fearon and Laitin 1996), and economic inequalities leading to greed- and grievances-based mobilization (e.g., Gurr 1993; 2002; Collier and Hoeffler 1998; 2001; Cederman, Weidmann, and Gleditsch 2011). Less attention, however, is given to the subnational variation in ethnic violence and the *local* political institutional dynamics that incentivize or restrain violent mobilization. As cases of communal violence in northern Nigeria highlight, not all religiously pluralistic communities characterized by limited resources and incentives for political manipulation of identity are prone to Muslim–Christian violence. Also, a number of communities that for decades lived peacefully side-by-side have become sites of recurring inter-religious violence, contrary to what one would expect. How do we explain this type of subnational variation in religious violence?[2] This puzzle

---

[1] Scholars generally refer to Horowitz's (1985) definition of ethnicity as the category to which racial, linguistic, religious, tribal, or caste-based identities belong.

[2] By "religious" violence, I am not making an essentialist argument that religious adherents are inherently prone to violence or that violence is more likely to be propagated on religious grounds or as a product of religious beliefs than secular ideologies, the "secular" state, or nationalism. Cavanaugh's (2009) the *Myth of Religious Violence* exhaustively

requires exploration of the *local* politics of conflict, exploration of subnational variation that structural or state-level analyses miss.

This study therefore focuses on the role that local government institutions and representation play in either exacerbating or defusing divisive religious narratives. Specifically, the study investigates the relationships among identity, violence, and local political institutions, ultimately finding that local power-sharing arrangements are critical to understanding patterns of inter-religious violence. Notably, and in contrast to work that examines *national* power-sharing institutions as a means of resolving conflict and sustaining peace between warring parties, I explore the effect of *informal local* government[3] power-sharing institutions on the likelihood of inter-religious violence. While scholars have identified a number of weaknesses associated with national power-sharing institutions (e.g., Cheeseman and Tendi 2010; Tull and Mehler 2005; Spears 2000; 2002; Sisk 1996), I find that the variation in inter-religious violence in the pluralistic region of Middle Belt (north-central) or northern Nigeria, broadly speaking (see Figure 1.1), can be explained by the presence or absence of local government power-sharing institutions. That is, local government councils that rotate or more broadly represent the tribal[4] and religious pluralism of their communities have been less prone to national and local politicization of Muslim and Christian identities and inter-religious violence. In this respect, the findings of this study contribute to and expand a major area of research and scholarly debate since the publication of Lijphart's work on consociationalism in the 1970s.

---

deconstructs any such claims. Rather, I use the term religious violence to refer to violence ensuing between two groups in which religious symbols, religious discourse, and/or religious actors are mobilized or targeted as the repertoire for collective action. Communities experiencing inter-religious violence may still debate the "religious-ness" of the conflicts, but the fact that this label is debated highlights its ascriptive identity, its social significance as a structuring characteristic or interpretive tool used to make sense of the violence that falls along religious lines. Furthermore, discussion of religious violence is not meant to exclude other political, social, or economic variables or factors in the construction of group differences and conflict. As should become clear, political representation and the political dimensions of religious identity cannot be separated from the story of inter-religious violence in Nigeria.

[3] Local governments are Nigeria's district- or county-level governing councils, the third tier of Nigeria's federal system, which have jurisdiction over a geographically delineated local government area (hereafter referred to as an "LGA").

[4] Note that I refer to kinship or ancestral groups as "tribe," "tribal," or "ethno-tribal" identities. This use of the word tribe is not meant to indicate anything primordial or backward about the ethnic category, but, rather, adopts the local parlance for kinship groups used daily by Nigerians when referring to their ethnic affiliation or heritage.

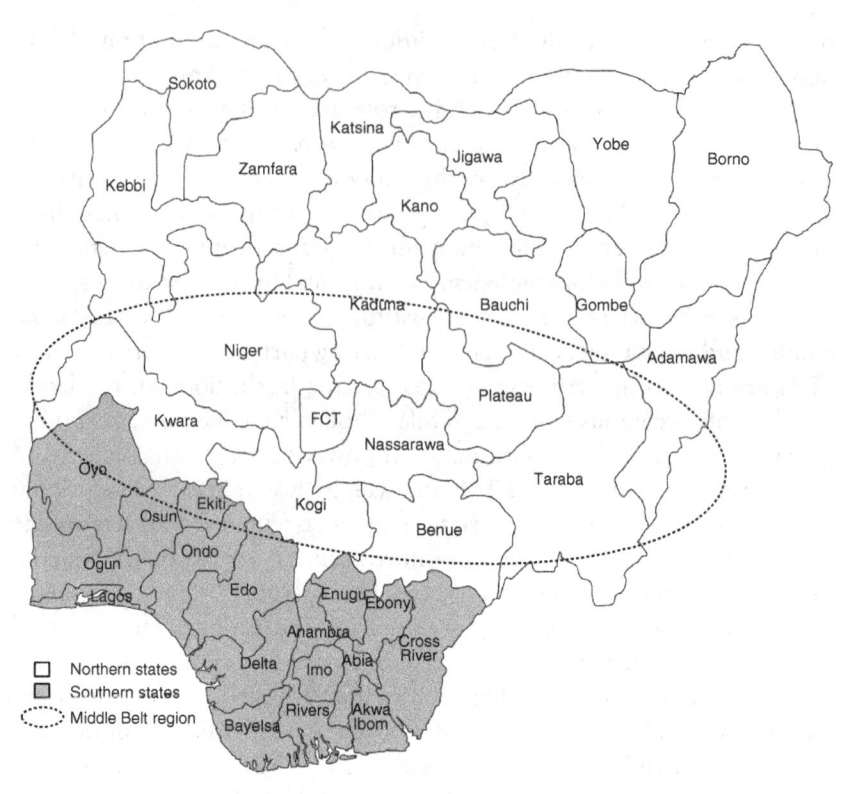

FIGURE 1.1 Northern and north-central Middle Belt states
* Note that the area designated as the Middle Belt is a geographical approximation.

This chapter is structured as follows. First, it provides context for this study, briefly highlighting the rise of inter-religious violence and tensions not only in northern Nigeria since the 1980s, but also globally. Second, it expounds on the theory of power-sharing articulated in this book along with specific *types* or expressions of local power-sharing. Third, it briefly addresses some of the main competing theories or counter-arguments to this theory of power-sharing, pointing to evidence of the theory's overall validity as developed in subsequent chapters. Finally, this chapter presents the methodology employed in the study – including the construction of an original dataset of communal violence, the collection of electoral data at the local government level, and case study or process-tracing work – which elucidates the causal relationship between communal inter-religious peace and local power-sharing.

## BROADER APPLICATION AND IMPORTANCE

Exploring these questions in the context of northern Nigeria is productive for a number of reasons. First, Nigeria is an important actor in both regional and global politics due to its economic clout and massive, growing population. Nigeria is one of the world's top ten crude oil producers and has one of the fastest-growing populations in the world (Suberu 2015, 34; Osaghae 2015, 73). As a United Nations Population Division (2013, 16) report notes, by the year 2050, Nigeria's population is projected to more than double from 173 million in 2011 to 440 million. For further context, nearly half the population of West Africa resides in Nigeria, and approximately one in six Africans is Nigerian – i.e., Nigeria accounts for 18 percent of the total African continent's population (World Bank 2011). Additionally, despite being one of the poorest countries in the world with abysmal performance in development indicators and rampant corruption, Nigeria's economy is one of the fastest-growing in Africa and globally, and it is one of the largest economies in Africa, despite a downturn in 2016 (World Bank 2013; African Development Bank 2013, 6; World Bank 2017). Instability and religious violence between Muslims and Christians, as well as the "terrorist" activity of extremist groups like Boko Haram in the far north, are, therefore, of concern not only to the Nigerian state and its efforts to ensure stability and security, but also to actors in the region and those with economic interests in Nigeria's oil economy. As a major oil producer, the most populous country in Africa and most rapidly growing in the world, Nigeria is not only a suitable site to test the propounded theory of identity and conflict, but also an important country in sub-Saharan Africa and globally.

Second, this study of northern Nigeria's experience of communal violence has broader implications for how scholars and practitioners understand the relationship between local institutions, politics, and prospects for peacebuilding in states threatened by ethnic conflict. Coinciding with rapid religious change in the Global South and transitions to democracy, other countries such as India, Malaysia, the Philippines, Indonesia, Thailand, and Myanmar are now also flashpoints of inter-religious violence. Since the 1990s, "ethnic divisions have replaced the cold war as the world's most serious source of violent conflict" (Lijphart 2002, 37). Formerly peaceful communities in Indonesia suffered a spate of Muslim–Christian violence from 1999 to 2002 that killed upwards of 10,000 people (Bertrand 2004, 32; see also Davidson 2008; Sidel 2006; Mohamed 2006). In early 2012, Egypt began making headlines over clashes between Coptic Christians and Muslims. Ethnic violence and retaliations in the Central African Republic have also fallen along Muslim–Christian lines. Since mid-2012, Myanmar has seen several ethnic/religious clashes between Buddhist Arakanese and Muslim Rohingya.

In other countries such as Kenya, Tanzania, and Ghana, although the lethal communal violence is minimal or absent, a vitriolic religio-political discourse infuses the public space, blurring the lines between the politics of church and state (Ranger 2008a, 237; Magesa 2007; Rukyaa 2007; Ammah 2007). In Ethiopia, tensions simmer between the large Muslim minority and politically dominant Christian majority. Furthermore, a survey by the Pew Research Center (2010, 44) indicates that fears of inter-religious violence are on the rise in a number of countries in the Global South (see also Fox 2004; Duffy Toft 2006). In 19 countries in sub-Saharan Africa, "sizable numbers (20% or more) of people in most countries surveyed see conflict between religious groups as a *very big problem*."[5] Religious extremism also concerns many; in "17 of the 19 countries surveyed [surveyed by the Pew Forum], 40% or more of the population says they are somewhat or very concerned about religious extremism within their country's borders."[6] In 2012, the Somali Al-Shabab Islamic extremist group targeted Kenyan Christian churches for the first time, and there are heightened religious tensions in Mombasa in the southeast of the country (Gettlemen 2012).

Yet, the riveting character of these events masks the same important subnational puzzle as exists in Nigeria. Inter-religious conflict only occurs in some otherwise similar religiously divided countries and only in some *parts* of those countries, and does not follow patterns of inter-*tribal* conflict, which is often rooted in struggles over land or other economic resources. In states prone to inter-religious communal violence or riots, why does the violence occur only in some religiously pluralistic communities and not others? That is, despite the cases noted above and the

---

[5] The Pew Forum (2010, 4) survey also notes that "in four countries, roughly half or more of the population sees religious conflict as a very big problem. These countries include Nigeria, Rwanda (58% each), Djibouti (51%) and the Democratic Republic of the Congo (48%)."

[6] A large number of people surveyed (upwards of four-in-ten in most countries) also express concern over religious extremism in their nation. In general, concern about Muslim extremism outweighs concern about Christian extremism. In addition, the Pew Forum (2010, 47) survey finds that "substantial minorities (20% or more of the population) in many countries consider violence in defense of one's religion to be sometimes or often justified."

religious dimension of many civil conflicts since the end of World War II (Fox 2004; Toft 2006; Toft, Philpott, and Shaw 2011), inter-religious violence is not inevitable in communities with different admixtures of religious groups. Despite this profound religious change and sacralization of politics and violence, religion does not become the flashpoint of violence or symbolic trigger of conflict everywhere there is ethno-religious pluralism. Rather, the variation points to the need for closer exploration of local political dynamics to explain why identity-based conflicts flare up in some areas of some countries and not others. While civil war – its causes[7] and duration,[8] peace-building after civil war,[9] insurgent actors,[10] mass violence, and genocide[11] – receives a great deal of attention, the prevalence and micro-dynamics of *communal* violence and the role of competing identities is understudied.

~

As this book contends, local-level – not just national-level – politics and institutions are critical for study if scholars and practitioners are to make sense of why some ethnically pluralistic communities are prone to communal violence, while others with similar characteristics are not. Particularly in the many federal states across Africa and Asia that have, like Nigeria, pursued decentralization or devolution policies since the 1970s, local politics and political institutions have become an even more important site of contestation. As the center of decision-making, local governments are entrusted with significant resources that shape economic, social, and political development in their communities. As Baba (2015, 121–122) notes, subnational politics "received scant scholarly attention … even though the subnational level is where most people interact with government on a daily basis, and where most of their needs and requests for state services that could improve their lives, for example, education, clean water, and health care are made, or not, as the case may be." He further notes, "It is at this level that most citizens' attitudes and

---

[7] See Justino 2009; Bakke and Wibbels 2006; Collier, Hoeffler, and Soderbom 2004; Collier and Hoeffler 1998; Miguel, Satyanath and Sergenti 2004; Fearon and Laitin 2003; Collier and Sambanis 2005; Sambanis 2001; Horowitz 1985; Wilkinson 2004; Gurr 1970; Kaufman 2001; Walter and Snyder 1999.
[8] See Bleaney and Dimico 2010; Escribà-Folch 2010; Hegre 2004; Collier, Hoeffler and Söderbom 2004; Wucherpfennig et al. 2012.
[9] See Walter and Snyder 1999; Hartzell, Hoddie and Rothchild 2001; Hoddie and Hartzell 2010.
[10] See Staniland 2012; Findley and Young 2012; Humphreys and Weinstein 2008.
[11] See Verdeja 2012; King 2012; Straus 2012; Fujii 2009.

preferences regarding democracy are formed" (Baba 2015, 122). Hence, representation in local government councils can affect which groups benefit more from local resources, gain access to education, and are accorded the basic rights that affect everyday lives and livelihoods. For this reason, study of the local dynamics and political institutions that affect the likelihood of communal violence in Nigeria can offer important lessons for thinking about the causes of and solutions to ethnic violence occurring elsewhere.

### THE NIGERIAN CONTEXT AND PUZZLE

The upsurge in inter-religious violence in northern Nigeria since the 1980s does not mean that Nigeria's immediate post-colonial history has otherwise been free of major intra-state violent conflict. Indeed, Nigeria is not a stranger to large-scale civil war engulfing major regional or ethnic blocs. From 1967 to 1970, the Biafran Civil War pitted the Eastern region of Nigeria with its secessionist majority Igbo ethnic group against the Yoruba and Hausa of the two other major regional blocs. The civil war paralyzed the country, killed an estimated one to three million Nigerians, and displaced or made refugees of around three million more (Osaghae 1998, 69).

Yet, the Middle Belt of Nigeria, with its mix of ethno-tribal groups and adherents of Islam, Christianity, and indigenous religion, was not a major site of ethnic violence prior to the late 1980s. Indeed, before 1987, inter-religious communal violence was largely unheard of in the Middle Belt and far north of Nigeria.[12] As Falola (1998, 48) notes, efforts at inter-religious dialogue characterized the 1960s and 1970s; "the Christian-Muslim rivalry did not degenerate into conflict or violence, and there were many southern Christians who were indifferent to the existence of Islam." The Sharia debates at the end of the 1970s certainly raised the specter of Muslim–Christian violence, but, as Laitin's (1986) study explores, it did not lead to major civil conflict due to the saliency of other identities that spanned religious cleavages.

What explains, therefore, this transformation in identity politics and conflict? A brief introduction here to the politics of identity in Middle Belt Nigeria and the evolution of post-colonial politics will set the stage for

---

[12] Note that I will use the designations ethno-religious and inter-religious interchangeably, but I am not referring to *intra*-religious violence unless otherwise specified. I use ethno-tribal and inter-tribal interchangeably as well.

better understanding the rise of inter-religious violence and its puzzling variation across the pluralistic Muslim–Christian communities of Middle Belt Nigeria.

### Pre- and Post-colonial Context

The absence of major violent conflict in the northern region of Nigeria prior to the 1980s should not be misconstrued as indicating that contentment and peaceful integration of ethnic groups characterized the region. To the contrary, political tensions between Middle Belt minorities and the politically dominant Hausa-Fulani majority predated British colonialism, extending back to when the Hausa-Fulani ruled the north under the Islamic Sokoto Caliphate. Although Hausa-Fulani were politically dominant – and thus the British choice for proxy rulers under the separately governed Protectorate of Northern Nigeria (prior to the north and south amalgamation in 1914) – minorities on the fringes of the northern region opposed subjugation to the religio-political basis of Hausa-Fulani rule and cultural assimilation or adaptation to Islam. The British deployed force as necessary to ensure minorities adhered to the system of proxy rule, but many Middle Belt ethnic minorities attempted to maintain what cultural and political autonomy they could, continuing to practice their own African traditional religion, rather than convert to Islam, for example. Although political elites at the national level did not heed demands for a Middle Belt Zone – a distinct region autonomous from northern political control – demands for demarcation of new regions and states accumulated in the 1950s and post-colonial period. Minorities in the north clamored for states in which they would form the majority, so as to gain a greater voice over their political futures.[13]

The major 1976 reforms creating local government councils, a third tier of the federal government, also sparked a massive number of demands by minorities for their own local government areas (LGAs). Rampant proclamation of new LGAs by minorities throughout Nigeria had to be reeled in. Hence, in the context of Nigerian federalism, political tensions prior to the 1980s were largely between the major regional ethnic

---

[13] As Osaghae (1998, 74) notes, the debates over the demarcation of new states and the initial 12 new states formed in 1987 by General Gowon "left many groups dissatisfied," and led to the "appearance of new majorities and minorities and new fears of domination." The subsequent formation of 19 new states under General Mohammed's initiative further sparked demands among minorities for states that reflected their geographical concentration (Osaghae 1998, 86).

blocs – Hausa, Igbo, and Yoruba – competing for national political influence or control, while minorities sought to take advantage of new opportunities for self-determination.

## Religious Change Context

How, then, did religious identity emerge as a major political cleavage in Nigerian national and local politics? Identity politics began to take on a new, threatening specter or mantle of religious conflict in Nigeria following independence due to significant religious changes with the rapid growth of Christianity and radicalization of Islam in some corners of the north. During the colonial era, the British agreed to the Hausa-Fulani demands to limit Christian evangelization in the predominantly Muslim north. Although conversion to Christianity among minorities in the Middle Belt was limited due to these barriers, adoption of Christianity signified resistance to Hausa-Fulani rule. Consequently, the subsequent removal of barriers to evangelization following independence created new religious freedom and constituted Christianity as a significant identity of resistance or non-assimilation – a powerful category of identity for groups in the Middle Belt to differentiate themselves from their politically dominant northern counterparts. Non-Muslim minority tribal groups in the Middle Belt had long been advocating for autonomy from the cultural and political control of the northern Hausa elite.

The argument here is not that the adoption of Christianity with the rapid increase in evangelization of the Middle Belt and north was simply instrumental, but, rather, that the spread of Christianity in the north threatened the religio-political basis of northern domination and emphasized a new political cleavage. A series of religio-political events and changes helped set the stage for the rise of inter-religious violence in parts of the Middle Belt: the spread of revivalist Pentecostal-charismatic Christianity in the region at the end of the 1970s, initial signs of Islamic radicalization with the Maitatsine riots at the beginning of the 1980s,[14] and the national debate surrounding adoption of Sharia in northern states. As Chapter 2 explores in more depth, the rise of religious conflict cannot be separated from a deeper exploration of post-colonial religio-political change.

---

[14] While the Maitatsine riots of the early 1980s resulted in loss of life among Christians, these riots are generally considered *intra*-religious communal clashes between the radical Muslim Maitatsine sect and other moderate Muslims.

Yet, this brief overview of events and changes associated with postcolonial identity politics only further *emphasizes*, rather than explains, the puzzle of inter-religious violence in Middle Belt Nigeria since the end of the 1980s; with the sacralization of politics in Nigeria, broadly speaking, and the religious pluralism of the Middle Belt, why have only some areas been prone to Muslim–Christian communal violence and not others? For example, Plateau state, of which Jos is the provincial capital, holds the title "Home of Peace and Tourism," a title now cited only for its sad irony in light of major clashes in 2001, 2002, 2008, and 2010, not to mention smaller scale communal violence in Jos and surrounding areas. In other parts of northern Nigeria, notably Kano, Kaduna, and Bauchi states, inter-religious violence has become the bane of communities, bringing cities and their business and educational institutions to a grinding halt.[15] Seemingly "small" cases of inter-religious violence can result in massive displacement of thousands of people. In affected cities, populations that formerly lived together peacefully, attending one another's religious celebrations and family events, are now segregated by religious identity – into their neighborhood "Jerusalems" and "Afghanistans."

Yet, even in the volatile Middle Belt region of Nigeria – the locus of the inter-religious violence – Muslims and Christians coexist peacefully. While some areas of Plateau state and Kaduna state have been hit hard, other pluralistic religious communities have been far less prone to inter-religious violence. For example, in the districts of Kanam, Bassa, and Chikun – despite their religious pluralism, colonial history similar to violence-prone areas, proximity to communities with tensions, and the incentives for political leaders and parties to exploit religious cleavages for political gains – the communities pride themselves on having avoided inter-religious violence. Religious identities do not take on the same intensity of political threat or conflict, much less violence, and efforts at inter-religious coordination and collaboration are present. To explain this puzzle, therefore, the following section turns to theories of civil war and ethnic conflict, exploring the weaknesses of existing theories in explaining this subnational variation.

---

[15] Although not limited to northern Nigeria or religious conflicts, Chukwuma (2009, vi) notes that "over 20,000 people have lost their lives and hundreds of thousands displaced in over 200 outbreaks of violence traceable to identity related disputes" in Nigeria. In Kaduna alone, the state estimates that they spent ten billion naira (66 million USD) on security from April to December 2011 in the aftermath of the post-election violence, and they spend approximately 200 million naira every month in this one state (Isuwa 2011).

EXISTING THEORIES AND POSSIBLE EXPLANATIONS

This book proposes a new institutional theory of identity-based conflict, showing how the presence or absence of informal local government power-sharing institutions shapes the likelihood of inter-religious violence. Before further specifying this theory, however, it is important to consider the explanatory power of competing theories of ethnic conflict – specifically structural, rational choice/instrumentalist, and state-level theories. Indeed, these theories are reflected in local discourse at peace and security meetings I attended in Jos and other communities during fieldwork in 2011 and during subsequent fieldwork in 2016. For example, some blame the weaknesses of the Nigerian state – its ineptitude in stemming issues of inequality and poverty or its inadequate or undisciplined security apparatus. Others point to the local socio-economic and political marginalization of members of some minorities. Still others blame local politicians who "everyone knows" exacerbate religious cleavages and, seeking some local political advantage, pay poor miscreants to cause trouble. Finally, others claim that there are insurmountable *religious* differences and fears that fuel the violence. In short, there is a confusing array of explanations for the rise of inter-religious communal violence since the 1980s that befuddles even local security experts, non-governmental organizations (NGOs), and peace activists working on peace and conflict resolution, academics, religious leaders, and the general citizens who are caught in the middle. How do these other explanations hold up under scrutiny?

## Structural Inequalities?

Issues of poor or unstable economic growth, high levels of poverty, and demographic issues are structural factors associated with vulnerability to civil war. Indeed, "the correlation between low per capita incomes and higher propensities for internal war is one of the most robust empirical relationships in the literature" (Blattman 2010, 4; see also Collier and Hoeffler 2000; Fearon and Laitin 2003; Sambanis and Hegre 2006). It is no surprise then that Nigeria is prone to intra-state violence. While Nigeria is an oil-rich country, wealth is largely concentrated in the hands of the political and economic elite, failing to raise living standards for the broader Nigerian population. Economic inequality is vast and the majority of the population lives in relative poverty. These conditions certainly feed group grievances and competition for scarce resources, particularly when one ethnic group is perceived as benefiting more from state patronage (or corruption) than another. Indicative of this is the mobilization of militant groups in the Niger Delta region in the oil-producing south of the country since the 1990s, attacking oil pipelines or installations in this main oil-producing region in protest against the lucrative extraction of crude oil at the cost of massive environmental devastation and pollution to the poverty-stricken region (Osaghae 2015, 71–95). Hence, it is perhaps no surprise that an ethnically heterogeneous country like Nigeria is prone to civil conflict or group rebellion since the costs of mobilization for the masses are lower (see Collier and Hoeffler 2000; 1998; Fearon and Laitin 2003; Alesina, Spolaore, and Wacziarg 2000).

Yet, structuralist explanations can tell us little about the subnational temporal and spatial dimensions of Nigeria's communal and inter-religious violence.[16] If economic inequality and insecurity are general features of Nigerian life, why do only some pluralistic communities experience inter-religious violence, while others remain peaceful? At the subnational level, states that suffer from higher levels of inequality or poverty are not necessarily more prone to communal violence. In the GINI index data for Kano, Kaduna, Bauchi, and Plateau states – where the majority of inter-religious violence is concentrated – the inequality levels tend to track very closely with those of surrounding states, and, according to the GINI index data, these four states often fare better than a number of other states in some years (Oyekale, Adeoti, and Oyekale 2006, 47). The story is similar with GDP per capita and change in GINI scores from 1998 to 2004 (see Appendices A, B, and C).[17] Vinson and Bunte (2016) also find that there are similar levels of inequality across both relatively peaceful and violence-prone communities in Kaduna state and

---

[16] See, for example, Cederman 2008, 243; Wilkinson 2008, 276; Boix 2008, 197–198; Kalyvas 2008, 402 for discussion of structuralist explanations.

[17] Again, the four states where the majority of cases of inter-religious violence are concentrated are not necessarily the worst performers. The GDP of Kaduna and Kano are middling, but they are better off than a number of other states in the north. Bauchi and Plateau states, in contrast, are among the states with the lowest GDP per capita. Regarding the *change* in a state's GINI score from 1998 to 2004, inequality in Kano declined somewhat, while in Kaduna, Plateau, and Bauchi, inequality increased. However, apart from Kano, *all* northern states showed increased inequality from 1998 to 2004, and these four states have fared better than a number of their neighboring states. Other measures, such as the percentage growth in real income and the poverty incidence scores from 1998 to 2004, also do not reflect a pattern in which the four Middle Belt/ north-central states are worse off than their neighbors (see Appendices A, B, and C).

Plateau state in the Middle Belt, and poor economic performance and competition alone do not explain individual incentives to participate in violence. As these data indicate, indices of inequality gloss over local variation in social, economic, and political rights – variation that shapes the subnational geographic and temporal dimensions of communal violence. Simply put, violent conflict does not erupt everywhere there is economic inequality, poverty, or grievances between groups (Boix 2008, 197–198). Specification of the causal mechanisms or conditions under which these factors lead to conflict is necessary (Kalyvas 2008, 402; Horowitz 2001; Fearon and Laitin 2003; Collier and Hoeffler 2000).[18]

## Motivated Political Entrepreneurs?

Moving beyond structural arguments, the wheeling and dealing of local politicians and poor leadership are often blamed for local conflicts and violence in Nigeria. Indeed, any explanation for the variation in ethnic or religious violence at a subnational level must take into account the factors that shape the individual incentives of actors to mobilize or participate in violence. It may be the case that the competitive political environment in some LGAs renders mobilization of ethno-religious identity frames useful for electoral purposes. Wilkinson (2004) finds, for example, that where local elections in India are more competitive, ethnic riots are more likely, as ethnic parties have incentive to rally their base by kindling ethnic antagonism and conflict (see also Posner 2004). Similarly, security dilemma analysis of ethnic conflict contends that in situations of material competition, information problems, and lack of credible commitments between contending parties, leaders have incentives to play on fears that one group could dominate resources to the exclusion of others (Posen 1993, Lake and Rothchild 1996, Roe 1999, Saideman et al. 2002). Indeed, a common refrain in Jos – a site of intermittent Muslim–Christian violence since 2001 – is that politicians are manipulating the population through appeals to identity, mobilizing poor unemployed youth to do their dirty work. Commenting on the causes of the 2008 crisis in Jos, the Sultan of

---

[18] The demographic composition of the population may affect the politicization of identities around certain cleavages (Posner 2004), but this factor alone does not explain the variation in Nigeria's communal violence as demonstrated in subsequent case study comparisons of LGAs that, while similar in their ethnic demographic balance, vary in their experience of inter-religious violence. For cross-national studies assessing the role of ethnic fractionalization and polarization in civil conflict, see Collier and Hoeffler 2000, Fearon and Laitin 2003, Ellingsen 2000, and Elbadawi and Sambanis 2000.

Sokoto observed, "It is not just politics, it is not just religion, it is total hunger and poverty in the land that you have a ready-made army anytime, anywhere, in their hundreds of thousands with just only one or two thousand naira and they are ready to form an army for you" (Abdulsalami, Ughegbe, and Okoronkwo 2008.) Under conditions of resource competition and greed, therefore, political entrepreneurs – intent on gaining power for themselves or looting resources – can mobilize the masses by framing the competition for scarce resources as an identity-based political contest (Mueller 2000).

At first glance, these rational choice or instrumentalist theories of ethnic conflict would seem to explain the Muslim–Christian violence in north-central Nigeria rather well. In Jos, events such as the appointment of a Hausa Muslim to a local administrative position[19] and accusations of vote-rigging after a contested local government election sparked protests and inter-religious violence in 2001. Religious cleavages were certainly prominent in the local 2011 election for the governorship as well; despite the Christian affiliation of the non-incumbent candidate, some in the Christian community disparaged her as the "Muslim" candidate for her willingness to engage more closely with local Muslims. Moreover, in the 2011 national presidential election, the victory of Goodluck Jonathan over former military ruler Muhammadu Buhari led to widespread violence in many states in northern Nigeria, clearly taking on a religious character. More than 350 churches were burned, 800 people killed, and 65,000 displaced (Human Rights Watch 2011; Lewis 2011, 70–71). Additionally, a common claim by locals and former youth participants in the violence is that politicians pay off local unemployed youth to cause trouble. For the troublemakers, it presents an opportunity to loot as well – a criminal element usefully playing into a narrative of inter-religious conflict (Brass 2006, Berenschot 2013).[20]

Despite these observations, the causal story of Nigeria's inter-religious communal violence cannot be fully explained by these instrumentalist arguments. First, apart from the events noted above, the data I collected on cases of inter-religious violence show that violence in *northern* Nigeria does not often occur in relationship to local or national elections.

---

[19] Chairmanship of the temporary Management Committee of Jos North, coordinator of the National Agency for Poverty Eradication in Jos North.
[20] Anonymous(Z), interview by Laura Thaut Vinson, Jos, Plateau State, Nigeria, March 29, 2011; Anonymous(G), interview by Laura Thaut Vinson, Jos, Plateau state, Nigeria, April 4, 2011.

The massive violence after the announcement of the 2011 election results was a new and worrying phenomenon, an aberration in the accounts of communal violence since the 1980s.[21] Based on the electoral competition model one would expect that the politicization of ethno-religious identity would be far more pervasive in the pluralistic communities of the Middle Belt. Yet, there are a number of tribally and religiously pluralistic LGAs where the violent politicization of religious identity is absent. The political saliency of the cleavage should incentivize greater politicization, work directly against cooperation, and spark significant Muslim–Christian violence for electoral gain in far more LGAs in southern Kaduna state and Plateau state. Why LGAs such as Chikun, Bassa, and Kanam are not flashpoints of Muslim–Christian violence, for example, is a puzzle for these instrumentalist theories of ethnic conflict. Instead, politicians and community members in these areas emphasize the cooperative and constructive relationship between Muslims and Christians. Some other factor or set of factors must be shaping the incentives to participate in identity-based violence.[22]

Second, considering the extreme levels of poverty in northern Nigeria, if the violence were simply a story of strategic actors mobilizing poor, uneducated youth for political gain, one would also expect the violence to

---

[21] This is not to say that election violence in the form of politically motivated attacks against opposition party members by hired rabble-rousers or party thugs does not occur. However, unless such cases noted an ethnic dimension in the identities of the actors, these cases are not recorded in the data, since the focus of data collection was on cases of ethnic violence (e.g., pitting members of groups defined by their religious or tribal identity against one another). If a reported incident of violence did not report anything other than, for example, members of one political party attacking the headquarters of another political party or suspected party members murdering a political candidate or leader (incidents I came across in newspaper reports), such cases were not included in the dataset. Granted, one possible limitation of the data collection is that there may be an underlying religious or tribal dimension to political protests or violent attacks carried out by party members (due to the affinity of ethnic groups with certain political parties in Nigeria) that are not reported in newspaper stories, and thus not coded as a case of communal violence. While I discuss the data-collection strengths and limitations in more detail in Chapter 5, these are cases that I argue would fall better into the category of political riots or targeted political killings, unless they specifically mention a local ethnic dimension to the violence. One would also expect the data on precipitating events to be far messier than it is if local communal violence coincided often, at least tangentially, with election-related events (e.g., speeches, announcement of electoral outcomes). Rather, communal ethno-tribal and ethno-religious violence – the focus of this study – is rarely *precipitated* by local and national elections.

[22] An instrumentalist argument would also have to address why politicians or elite appeal to one salient identity dimension (e.g., religion), as opposed to another salient category (e.g., tribe).

be far more prevalent. Issues of political inequality and competition over scarce resources are not uncommon in northern Nigeria, particularly as it is a region with deep poverty; 90 percent of the population lives on less than two dollars a day (Campbell 2011, 12). Hence, local conditions would seem to over-predict violence in an instrumentalist account; that is, it is unclear where we should expect *not* to see violence. Again, there are plenty of grievances to go around and many opportunities to politicize religion, but the violence only erupts in some LGAs and not others.

### The Meddling and Malaise of the State?

Finally, any analysis of the crisis of politics, identity, and violence in Nigeria cannot overlook the weaknesses of the Nigerian state.[23] Scholars consistently find that weak states – indicated by poor economic development, dependence on natural resources, lack of strong democratic institutions, or semi-democracy – are more prone to intra-state civil war or ethnic conflict (e.g., Fearon and Laitin 2003, Elbadawi and Sambanis 2000, Ellingsen 2000, Hegre et al. 2001, Sambanis 2001). One could attribute, therefore, the problems of insecurity in Nigeria to the weaknesses of the state. The lack of legitimacy, effectiveness, and credibility is reflected in its failure to provide the stability and security necessary to defuse local tensions and combat the politicization of religion. Further, different forms of violence have found room to flourish in the country – inter-religious communal violence, electoral violence, violent land disputes, militant violence against the state, and terrorism by Jama'atu Ahlis Suna Lidda'awati wal-Jihad (i.e., Boko Haram) and its splinter groups. Indeed, international observers such as Human Rights Watch implicate the Nigerian state in the intensification of Boko Haram violence since 2009, due to the state's overly militarized responses, extra-judicial killings, and disregard for the distinctions between civilians and terrorists (Human Rights Watch 2009; 2012; Pérouse de Montclos 2014a; 2014b).

---

[23] Lack of state legitimacy can make it difficult to obtain the consent of the governed, and weak states lack the institutional capacity and organization to prevent groups from mobilizing, providing greater opportunity for groups to seek redress for grievances or assert demands through violence (see Jung, Lust-Okar, and Shapiro 2008, 141; Fearon and Laitin 2003, 75–90; Chester 2008; Gurr 2000; Quinn, Hechter, and Wibbels 2004; Collier and Hoeffler 2000; Collier and Hoeffler 1999). Another variant of the weak states thesis argues that states' divergent policies toward different ethnic groups explain the likelihood that religious or ethnic identity differences will spiral into conflict (Wilkinson 2008; see also Wilkinson 2004, Hechter and Kabiri 2008, Philpott 2007).

So too, prior to the reorganization of security in Jos after major Muslim–Christian violence in 2010, locals viewed security personnel as partial to their local kin or co-religionists (Human Rights Watch 2009). The lack of an effective and well-disciplined security apparatus, as well as accusations of human rights abuses, reflects one dimension of Nigeria's weak state problem.

Another dimension of the weakness of the Nigerian state is the corruption and economic competition stemming from a combination of an oil revenue-dependent economy and the lack of strong institutions and accountability. Consequently, these conditions can enhance ethnic competition for resources and political office not only between regional ethnic blocs at the national level, but also at the local level. Claims of vote-rigging and nefarious local politics can antagonize ethnic and religious divides, and go beyond simply local political conditions and contestation. Local and national party machines and patron-client politics cannot be so easily disentangled. For example, Nigeria's federal system mandates that approximately 24 percent of national revenue go to its 36 states, and the national government stipulates that the 20 percent of national revenue allocated to Nigeria's 774 local government councils be distributed by the states on behalf of the federal government (*Nigerian Constitution*, 1999, Art 7, Sec 1).[24] These funds enable (at least in theory) the local elected councils to run the day-to-day development projects and agricultural, educational, and social programs in their communities. In the distribution of these funds, however, arises many opportunities for elites to manipulate local politics for their own monetary and political gain consistent with clientilistic, prebendal[25] politics (Suberu 2015, 45). State officials are known to misuse their control over these funds for political advantage or to punish opposition politicians by blocking distribution to local government councils (e.g., Rivers state in southern Nigeria) (Fashagba 2015, 104–105).[26] Alternatively, corrupt officials can also siphon off the funds to pad their own pockets or enhance their political standing through patronage (Human Rights Watch 2007, 33; Afrobarometer 2008). This dynamic of Nigerian politics only enhances the competition for resources at the local level and may feed into the incentives for elites to politicize

---

[24] Previously, local government areas were allocated 10 percent of federal government revenue, and states 32.5 percent under the 1982 Revenue Allocation Act (Osaghae 1998, 171).

[25] For discussion of prebendalism, see Joseph (1987) and Adebanwi and Obadare (2013).

[26] The same can occur between those who hold the purse strings at the federal level and their state counterparts.

religion and for local communal groups to take up arms against one another.

As this brief discussion highlights, state weakness – and all that it entails – can contribute to ethnic politics and competition for state and local government political seats, as well as generate national interest in who controls these seats.[27] The country's transition to civilian rule in 1999 after a number of coups (or attempted coups) and 16 years of successive military rule has evidently not solved the state's crises of corruption, legitimacy, and security. In contrast to a story about local institutions, therefore, the causes of ethno-religious and ethno-tribal violence may be rooted in this larger story of a weak Nigerian state.

Yet, while Nigeria certainly falls into the category of a weak state according to the Failed States Index and the State Fragility Index, this status does not explain why communities with similar ethno-religious diversity and a shared colonial history in northern Nigeria reflect such different trends – inter-religious peace versus violence. These "weak state" characteristics are all too common features of Nigeria's national and local politics that, while important, would seem to over-predict violence rather than explain its variation. While state-level factors increase opportunities for politicization of ethnic and religious identity, some LGAs are less prone to this type of manipulation and identity-based violence. The messy politics of a weak Nigerian state, therefore, only further emphasizes the puzzle of why the latent identities of some pluralistic LGAs are not successfully exploited (despite clear efforts internal and external to the LGA) and *do not* become central and violent cleavages. Instead, state-level theories raise a subsequent question: what are the local political dynamics that distinguish these communities and render them less susceptible to the politicization of identity or sacralization of politics?[28]

A second critique of a thesis that gives prominence to national politics and weak institutions is the fact that even in cases where the

---

[27] National-level manipulation of local politics may exacerbate conflict in any number of forms. Party elite, for example, have a clear interest in ensuring that their party candidates or incumbents achieve or maintain positions of state and local influence, as they may be better able to derive patronage and political benefits. Additionally, since a portion of the senators to the National Assembly is elected from "senatorial zones" within states, party control in the National Assembly is affected by who achieves local electoral support. Hence, national political figures or party machines presumably have incentive to stir up ethnic and religious antagonism in state and local elections in order to influence the results.

[28] For further critiques, see Sambanis 2001; 2004; Cederman 2008.

national government has sought to defuse local tensions or violence, the nature of the disputes on the ground and their local identity dimensions can thwart these efforts. Consider, again, the case of Jos in Plateau state. Due to criticism of local police and security forces – e.g., failing to intervene promptly in violence, violating rules of engagement during states of emergency, and favoring co-ethnics or co-religionists (Human Rights Watch 2009; 2005; 2012) – the national government made an effort to enhance the provision and credibility of security in Jos. In 2010, the Nigerian Ministry of Defence deployed a military Special Task Force (STF) under the title "Operation Safe Haven" to keep the peace, drawing STF soldiers from areas outside Plateau state. Thus, prior to the 2011 election, an estimated 15,000 STF were "keeping the peace" in the communities of Jos. Although perceived more favorably by the population, better managed, and more disciplined, the STF on its own has not been sufficient to ensure complete calm in Jos. Security is certainly essential in discouraging mobilization and preventing the escalation of violence, but the underlying incentives for violent mobilization and identity-based politics do not simply disappear with better security. Mistrust rooted in issues of local political representation in Jos North and other LGAs remains at the core of the tensions and occasional violence. Despite enhanced security since 2011, one would be hard-pressed to find members of the segregated Muslim and Christian communities who believe that the tensions and underlying conflicts have been resolved and religion is no longer a divisive cleavage.

~

Ultimately, while a weak Nigerian state, issues of economic inequality, and the interests of political entrepreneurs may be *contributing* factors to the diffusion of identity politics, a theory that does not consider how the local political context and institutions filter these conditions will fall short. To explain the variation in inter-religious violence across pluralistic LGAs in Middle Belt states like Kaduna and Plateau, I explore how *local* government institutions – the level of government and representation closest to the people – either constrain or exacerbate local identity politics and shape incentives for violent mobilization. That fact that some LGAs – whether majority Muslim or Christian – have avoided the inter-religious violence experienced by Jos and other areas in recent years suggests that some LGAs have a system of local representation that helps defuse or mediate divisive identity politics.

## A NEW THEORY OF POWER-SHARING

To explain the variation discussed above, this book makes the case for a new theory of identity, politics, and conflict that builds on or challenges current explanations in the ethnic conflict and power-sharing literature.[29] Based on original data gathered from nearly 40 LGAs in two Middle Belt states, along with comparative case studies of conflict and non-conflict LGAs, this study finds that the presence or absence of local government power-sharing institutions shapes whether pluralistic communities experience ethnic and, in particular, religious violence.[30]

Power-sharing helps to reduce inter-religious violence in two specific ways. First, in communities characterized by tribal *and* religious pluralism, power-sharing institutions that rotate the tribal leadership of a local government also rotate religious representation. For example, a power-sharing arrangement between the Gbagyi (largely Christian) and the Hausa-Fulani (largely Muslim) groups in Chikun LGA means that both a Muslim and Christian generally share executive authority. Under this type of power-sharing system, the main ethnic groups in the area are represented in the most influential seats in the local government, helping to dispel claims of marginalization and ethnic discrimination that otherwise render communities vulnerable to politicization of religious identity.

The second key function of power-sharing at the communal level is that it creates the precedent for collaboration and coordination among those of different tribal and religious affiliations. Power-sharing provides a foundation for leaders to build trust across ethno-tribal and ethno-religious divides and to more effectively appeal for calm and understanding where tensions threaten to ignite violence. For example, in Bassa LGA, which neighbors the volatile Jos North LGA, ethnic groups have rotated leadership positions in the local council since its formation, providing the

---

[29] I do not distinguish between communal *violence* and communal *riots*, as both involve conflicting communal groups. This is in accord with Horowitz's (2002, 1) study of ethnic riots, which he defines as "an intense, sudden, though not necessarily wholly unplanned, lethal attack by civilian members of one ethnic group on civilian members of another ethnic group, the victims chosen because of their group membership." He continues, "So conceived, ethnic riots are synonymous with what are variously called 'communal,' 'racial,' 'religious,' 'linguistic,' or 'tribal' disturbances." I do, however, distinguish communal violence from civil war and genocide, the former used to refer to conflict between insurgents and the state and the latter used to refer to an organized campaign to exterminate a particular group of people.
[30] I am particularly interested in lethal violence, but the original dataset of communal violence I will introduce also includes cases of injuries, displacement, or property destruction.

community's religious, traditional, and youth leaders, as well as peace activists, a political precedent for information-sharing, collaboration, and peacebuilding that downplays ethnic categories. Consequently, communities like Bassa are more effective in fostering peaceful relations between their tribally and religiously defined ethnic groups and in counteracting divisive religious narratives. In contrast, the original conflict in neighboring Jos North was fueled by disputes over local government leadership (i.e., in the absence of power-sharing), which intensified and took on the volatile guise of a Muslim–Christian religious conflict. Overall, I find that in heterogeneous LGAs where the ethno-tribal elite abide by an informal power-sharing arrangement, the broader representation of the local ethno-tribal and -religious groups reduces the saliency of an antagonistic sacralized politics and provides a framework for greater collaboration, trust, and coordination.

This focus on the politics of local government councils is justified for a number of reasons. Local governments are critical to communal ethnic relationships, since, as the third tier of the federal government, they are tasked with overseeing and implementing development projects and mediating the day-to-day social, economic, and political concerns of their respective local communities. Constituted of members of the community – both elected and appointed – local government leadership is important, since special favors or benefits may go to family members, friends, or members of the ethno-tribal group whose representative heads a local government council. A council's degree of representation, therefore, is of primary concern to local ethno-tribal groups of Muslim and Christian persuasion, even if local politics is not entirely free of national- and state-level political skullduggery. For this reason, local power-sharing creates conditions that de-incentivize both the politicization of local identity by elites or political entrepreneurs, as well as reduces perceptions among the population that local disputes are the consequence of religious cleavages and competition.

This case for power-sharing departs from long-standing articulations and analyses of power-sharing in two key respects. First, it focuses on local government power-sharing institutions rather than those at the national level. Second, it emphasizes implementation through informal rather than formal mechanisms. The importance and novelty of the findings are underscored by the otherwise general consensus across a broad range of cross-national analyses and comparative case studies that power-sharing is not the hoped-for path to sustainable peace. Despite power-sharing mechanisms' centrality in international peace agreements – intended to broadly represent warring parties in a nationally representative institutional arrangement to end intra-state civil conflict – many scholars find that the various mechanisms of political inclusion (e.g., proportional representation, mutual veto, federalism, broader cultural autonomy) do not tend to be sustainable conflict resolution mechanisms. As Chapter 4 discusses in more detail, critiques of power-sharing institutions include the disincentives the institutional arrangement creates for long-term cooperation between elites, security dilemma problems (e.g., lack of credible commitment), the counterproductive rarefication of ethnic categories, and the rigidness of the institution, to name a few.

Despite these negative findings, this book makes the case that power-sharing theory is not defunct; rather, its mechanisms of inclusion are more suitable for stemming local-level conflict in pluralistic communities. Unlike national-level power-sharing agreements, the local government variant can represent the groups and grievances specific to a local district. Also, the benefits of power-sharing agreements at this level can be more easily observed, and defectors more easily punished through the local electoral system. For example, in a pluralistic country like Nigeria with more than 250 ethnic groups, a single national political arrangement cannot represent the various grievances or disputes that surface across the swath of ethnically pluralistic Nigerian communities.

## Forms of Power-Sharing

The forms of LGA-level power-sharing identified in this study are of two primary variants. The first type *rotates* local government council leadership consistently among the ethno-tribal groups based on a pre-electoral power-sharing arrangement between ethnic elite. So, for example, political parties only select candidates to run for the chairmanship who come from the designated group whose turn it is to lead the local government. The candidate for chairman then runs on a ticket with a deputy or vice-chairman selected from one of the other main ethno-tribal groups. In some cases, the rotation may be a de facto function of an agreement to rotate representation among the various wards of the local government settled by different majority ethnic groups. Due to the religious pluralism of the LGAs, this type of rotational system is also representative of the religious diversity of the LGAs.

The second type of power-sharing follows a *fixed* representation model. That is, the principle of shared representation is the same, but, according to the agreement, the top seats of the local government council – chairman, deputy chairman, and secretary – are consistently held by members of different ethnic groups according to the ethnic composition of the LGA. For example, the Christian Gbagyi – the majority indigenous group – always takes the chairmanship in Chikun LGA, while the deputy seat is designated for the Muslim Hausa-Fulani, and secretary post for the Christian Kabilu minority. Again, a slight variation on this arrangement may draw candidates from among certain wards in accordance with the principle.

### EXPLAINING ADOPTION OF POWER-SHARING

As with any institutional theory, a fundamental question raised by the argument above is where the power-sharing institution came from. Why is it that, if power-sharing institutions have such apparent benefits, leaders in only some LGAs in Kaduna state and Plateau state adopted power-sharing institutions? These questions suggest an issue of endogeneity – that there is perhaps some other fundamental condition that shaped why some LGAs adopted power-sharing and others did not. If this is the case, then it is not power-sharing itself that begets peace, but another underlying causal factor, such as the demographic balance of an LGA, a history of non-violence, or prior colonial relationships. I address these ulterior explanations briefly in turn and more thoroughly in Chapter 8.

#### Demographic Balance?

While official ethnic demographic data are not available for LGAs – since the Nigerian government stopped collecting this census information after 1967 due to its sensitivity – local estimates gathered in the course of research reveal that the adoption or success of power-sharing does not depend on a particular ethnic population balance. LGAs with and without power-sharing are not characterized by a certain ethno-tribal or -religious balance. For example, in Kanam LGA, Muslims constitute the religious majority. Regarding the ethno-tribal balance, the Bogghom (mixed Muslim and Christian) and Jahr (predominantly Muslim) ethnic groups are the majority ethnic groups, while the Muslim Hausa-Fulani constitute the minority. In Bassa LGA, Christians of three main ethno-tribal groups comprise the vast majority of the population. In Chikun, Christian ethno-tribal groups hold a slight majority. Despite the variation in the ethno-tribal and ethno-religious demographics of these areas, all three are cases of power-sharing, with both Muslims and Christians generally represented in key positions of local government leadership. This finding goes against the expectations of an electoral competition model in which the majority status of an ethnic or religious group would incentivize the violent politicization of religious identity in deeply contested or competitive elections, thereby working against incentives for power-sharing (e.g., Wilkinson 2004; Posner 2004). Power-sharing councils identified in this study run the gamut – some are majority Christian, others majority Muslim, and others more evenly split in their communal identity. The reasons for adoption of power-sharing go beyond a simple demographic explanation.

## Peace Begets Power-Sharing?

Why then did elite or tribal elders in some areas adopt power-sharing following decentralization of rule in the mid-1970s? Is it simply the case that the more "peaceful" communities were most likely to adopt power-sharing, while those with a history of conflict between the local ethno-tribal groups did not pursue a power-sharing option? The historical evidence suggests otherwise. Decentralization in the 1970s – which introduced representative local government councils – and the formation of local government power-sharing arrangements took place largely *before* the rise of inter-religious violence in Nigeria.[31] Indeed, it was not until 1987, more than a decade after official decentralization reforms, that major Muslim–Christian violence rocked the nation. National religio-political disputes surfaced in 1979, but religion was not seen as a major and violent cleavage in Nigerian politics until the late 1980s. Rather, tribe was the main political cleavage (Laitin 1986).[32] Hence, it was not simply that areas without religious violence adopted power-sharing while those with violence did not. Instead, the pluralistic areas with local government power-sharing institutions implemented these informal arrangements generally *before* the rise of inter-religious violence in the north, ensuring broader tribal and religious representation and creating a foundation for

---

[31] Some power-sharing arrangements were adopted later, since a number of LGAs were carved out of existing LGAs in Kaduna and Plateau state in the 1980s and 1990s. Hence, the negotiation of power-sharing will coincide with the official creation of an LGA, rather than 1970s decentralization.

[32] The devastating 1967–1970 Biafran Civil War most strongly illustrates the degree of ethno-tribal political cleavages in the country, splitting the country mainly along the lines of the powerful Yoruba, Hausa, and Igbo political blocs.

the mediation of religious conflicts that would threaten local peace in the future.

Further addressing this endogeneity concern, Bunte and Vinson (2016) find in their analysis of conflict data from the Social, Political, and Economic Event Dataset (SPEED), covering the years 1955–1985, that prior ethnic violence is not a significant predictor of the likelihood of adopting power-sharing institutions. Communities affected by ethnic violence prior to the 1980s were no less likely to adopt power-sharing institutions than those characterized by ethnic peace.

## Prior Colonial Institutions Key?

One might still argue that there must be *something* about the relationship between the ethno-tribal groups or their inherited colonial institutions that rendered power-sharing feasible and desirable in some areas and not others. Indeed, the history of colonial rule is important in one key respect. During the colonial period from 1900 to 1960, ethno-tribal cleavages in northern Nigeria were primarily a product of patterns of cultural conquest or assimilation and political integration (forced or by gradual assimilation). Colonial rule elevated the Hausa-Fulani Muslims to proxy ruler status, furthering both cultural *assimilation* (e.g., spread of Islamic religion and Hausa language) and political *integration* (e.g., adherence to traditional rule of Muslim emirs and political elite) in large parts of the non-Muslim[33] northern region. Some non-Muslim communities were able to avoid or resist full assimilation and integration due to factors such as their distance from the center of the northern colonial establishment, a prior history of organized resistance, or the more lenient policy of local Muslim emirs. This colonial legacy, therefore, tells us what kinds of ethno-tribal relationships were likely to matter upon independence in 1960 and in the face of post-colonial political, socio-economic, and religious changes.

The colonial history of the region, however, provides only general and not specific insight into subsequent power-sharing decisions, as discussed in detail in Chapter 7. While the colonial legacy of assimilation and integration is important for understanding the ethno-tribal cleavages in particular communities at the end of the colonial period, this legacy does not *predict* power-sharing at the end of the 1970s and thereafter. Both

---

[33] At this point in time, the non-Muslim population was largely animist or adhered to African Traditional Religion.

colonial *and post-colonial* events shaped a) the degree of cultural assimilation among local ethno-tribal groups and b) their degree of political integration. Consequently, depending on how post-colonial events – exogenous or endogenous to an LGA – affected the relationship between communities along these two dimensions, the incentives for or feasibility of power-sharing varied. Specification of one particular historical institution, colonial dynamic, or ethnic grudge that predetermined the likelihood of power-sharing would offer simplicity and elegance, but it would be an oversimplification and incorrect. Case study evidence reveals that the decision to institute power-sharing in any one area derived from elites' assessments of the various costs and benefits of shared representation across ethno-tribal divisions. These assessments were shaped by the impact of exogenous post-colonial political, social, and religious changes on local ethnic relations (Figure 1.2). The rise of a politically activist and radical form of Islam, a new politicized form of Christianity, the failures of the Nigerian constitutions to adequately define citizenship and indigenous rights, the politics of new LGA and state creation, and patterns of

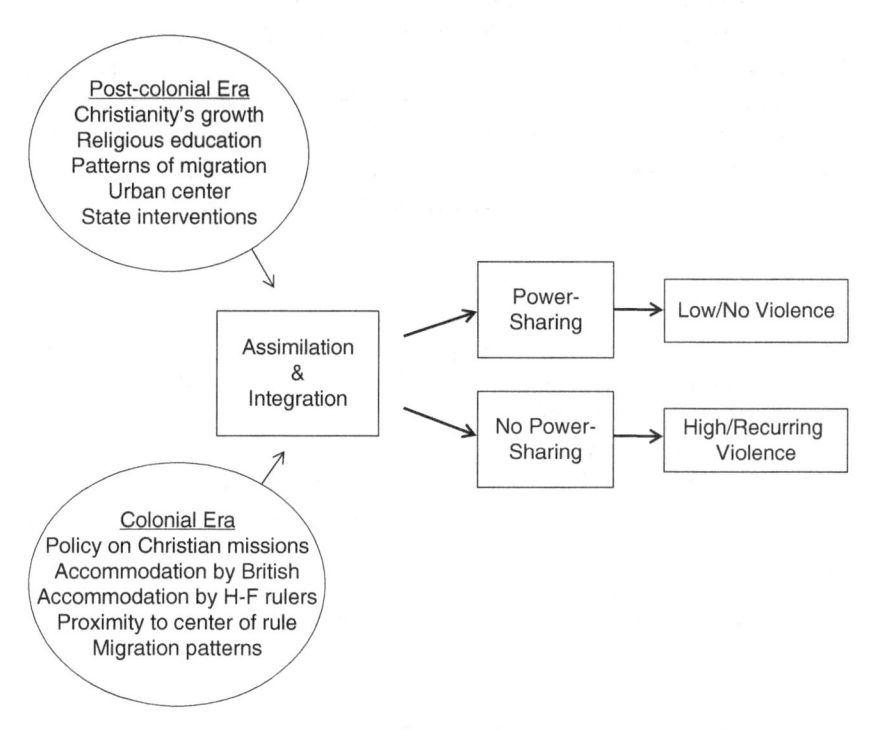

FIGURE 1.2 Representation of power-sharing argument and factors

migration represent a few of the major post-colonial factors that shaped the evolution or iterations of local politics and ethno-tribal relationships in any one area and perceptions of the costs and benefits of power-sharing.

In short, a lack of power-sharing was not inevitable in any one of the now violence-prone LGAs. While the historical legacy provides a framework for understanding subsequent group relationships, it does not tell us how these relationships were transformed and evolved into a communal politics of ethno-tribal and religious significance. To understand why some LGAs adopted power-sharing while other similar LGAs did not, one must explore the particular socio-economic, political, and religious changes that occurred after independence.

## Examples of the Argument

A case of "no power-sharing" such as Jos North, discussed in detail later in this book, elucidates this argument. The inability of leaders to establish power-sharing in Jos North was not predestined during the colonial era. In fact, the former Jos LGA[34] was long known as one of the most peaceful local governments in the north – a popular vacation destination, the supposed "Home of Peace and Tourism" – even with its considerable Muslim Hausa-Fulani minority population living intermixed among the indigenous Christian ethno-tribal groups. While religious identity became increasingly politicized in Nigerian national politics from the end of the 1970s onward and major Muslim–Christian violence occurred in surrounding states in the 1980s and 1990s, Jos remained peaceful. Due to the re-drawing of state boundaries in the 1960s and 1970s, the Hausa-Fulani had argued for some time that that they were marginalized in the new Plateau state and deserved greater political representation. Debate occurred, but non-violently.

Yet the peace would not last in Jos. During a period of local government creation in the early 1990s, General Babangida, the military leader at that time, made the decision to "resolve" the long-standing dispute between the ethno-tribal groups living in the larger Jos LGA by carving out a new local government called Jos North in which the Hausa-Fulani would constitute at least half, if not the majority, of the LGA

---

[34] Present-day Jos North, Jos South, and Jos East were encompassed in a single Jos LGA prior to 1991.

population. The politics of identity and local government representation suddenly shifted as a result of this change, providing more political autonomy to the Muslim Hausa-Fulani population living in the area, to the chagrin of Christian ethno-tribal groups or "indigenes." Consequently, these policy decisions coming from the national level exacerbated identity cleavages, made the costs of power-sharing too high for all parties, and sparked the beginnings of communal violence in the Jos area.

This case demonstrates how exogenous political events exacerbated tensions and transformed a peaceful community into one driven by a narrative of irreconcilable politico-religious differences. Although colonialism certainly shaped ethno-tribal relationships in Jos – as it had elsewhere – ultimately the colonial legacy proved irrelevant to the question of whether power-sharing would be established.

The same is true elsewhere. In some cases, such as Chikun LGA in Kaduna state, post-colonial politics and socio-economic changes helped foster the political incentives for power-sharing. The current territory of Chikun is home to a large Hausa-Fulani Muslim population and was near the center of and politically integrated with Hausa-Fulani political rule during colonial times. The majority of the local population is Christian, however, as the non-Muslim adherents of African Traditional Religion largely converted to Christianity in the post-colonial period, offering a clear cleavage around which identity groups could mobilize. Relations in this LGA have nonetheless remained relatively peaceful due to local power-sharing agreements. Ethnic group leaders, both Christian and Muslim, arrived at a power-sharing agreement between the three main ethnic groups for a number of reasons: the ethnic composition of the population (both Christian and Muslim tribal groups of "indigenous" status), their urban context, and the expectation of future demographic changes. Power-sharing post-1970s in Chikun was subject to different sets of incentives or hurdles than in Jos, evolving in tandem with socio-political and religious changes specific to the area. I find that the *routes* to power-sharing were at least smoother in those cases where these changes did not aggravate the relationship between local ethno-tribal groups over time.

In sum, the colonial legacy does not tell us anything about the inevitability of power-sharing or the costs and benefits elites considered. There is no one colonial institution or legacy from 1914 to 1960 that predicts why power-sharing was or was not adopted in any particular area in the

1970s and later. In fact, factors that varied across LGAs, occurred after independence, and that *cannot be traced back to colonization* powerfully shaped how local elites perceived the relative costs and benefits of power-sharing. These include the rapid growth of Christianity, the radicalization of Christian and Muslim politics, missionary education of previously politically marginalized populations, the adjustment of state and local government boundaries, land pressures bringing groups into closer proximity/tensions with one another, and constitutional changes affecting indigenous status. The colonial-era historical context, while an important part of the story, does not present a uniform explanation as to why power-sharing institutions were deemed more feasible or desirable in some places and not others.

~

Ultimately, the findings hold out hope – not only that religious violence is not an inevitable feature of strongly religious communities in weak states – but that there is no one path to power-sharing and no one historical experience that can definitively eliminate the possibility of religious peace. Despite the saliency and acrid nature of religion in Nigerian national and local politics, the data and comparative case studies presented in subsequent chapters show that local elites in power-sharing LGAs are less likely to exploit religious cleavages, and they are more conciliatory in their actions and rhetoric. Similarly, the local population is less likely to perceive local issues of inequality and political competition through the lens of religion or to see religion as a basis for violent mobilization.

## THE FORCE OF RELIGION

These findings should not imply that religious identity and religious change are merely epiphenomenal and ancillary to the story of interreligious violence. As in many other countries experiencing a religious resurgence since the 1970s, the religious change that occurred in the latter half of the 20th century in Nigeria is central to understanding the construction of religious identity as the locus of political contention and communal violence. This religious change involved not only growth in the number of Christian adherents, but also the emergence of a more educated and politically influential Christian political class among denominations shifting toward active political engagement. This doctrinal shift coincided with the rapid spread of Pentecostal-charismatic Christianity.[35] The religio-political lines were further drawn when, in reaction to the organized political efforts of Islamic leaders, Christian leaders formed the Christian Association of Nigeria (CAN) in the 1970s, a major Christian umbrella body, to advocate on behalf of Christian political interests. A series of post-1970s religio-political disputes – including quarrels over Nigeria's membership in the Organization of the Islamic Conference (OIC) and the implementation of Sharia in northern states – also served to reify political identities along religious lines.

Whereas identity disputes had in the past coalesced around major ethno-tribal blocs, religious identity emerged as a primary form of ascriptive political identity useful not only for making sense of socio-economic poverty and inequality, but also political inequality, exploitation, and deficits in representation at the communal and national level. The saliency of religious identity vis-à-vis tribal identity is demonstrated by the violence in southern Plateau state in 2004 that spread from Shendam LGA; the perceived Muslim-versus-Christian religious dimension of the violence put members of the same ethno-tribal groups and even family members on different sides of the conflict. What started out as a dispute rooted in political and socio-economic inequalities quickly morphed into a religious conflict of deadly proportion. Religion is now, like ethno-tribal identity, a potent symbol of group belonging, a politicized category in national and local politics, and a significant rallying point for violent mobilization in pluralistic communities – hardly epiphenomenal.

As Chapter 2 will explore in more detail, the politics and discourse of religious difference became both more prominent and rigid concurrent with the rapid expansion of Christianity in northern Nigeria and new forms of radicalized Islam. Beyond Nigeria, the resurgence of Christianity has reshaped the landscape of identity politics in countries across the Global South, presenting a narrative of beliefs that can both fuel and constrain inter-religious violence. While one might argue that religious identity only becomes a relevant cleavage when used as a tool of interested actors who can mobilize adherents at their whim for political ends, this argument overlooks how changes in religious teachings can create or close off space for the politicization of religion (e.g., Miller, Sargeant, and Flory eds. 2013; Marshall 2009; Philpott 2007; Jenkins

---

[35] Note that the Pentecostal-charismatic revival is also referred to as the renewalist, Neo-Pentecostal, and "Born Again" movement.

2002; Casanova 1994). Hence, broad changes in Nigeria's religious landscape, as well as in many countries where Islam and Christianity are experiencing a revival, have been pivotal in shaping both the political debate and the terrain upon which community disputes and identities are negotiated, even if the "root" causes of inter-religious violence are not always overtly religious. Where power-sharing institutions at the local level are absent, politicized religious identity can more easily become a fault line of violence.

## METHODOLOGICAL OVERVIEW AND APPROACH

To assess the relationship between the pattern of communal violence and local governance – the absence or presence of power-sharing – the primary fieldwork for this study took place over a ten-month period (Feb–Dec 2011) and involved the construction of a wholly original dataset of communal violence in northern Nigeria (1979–2011), collection of data on patterns of representation in local government councils, and in-depth controlled case study comparisons. The north-central or Middle Belt states are an ideal site for comparative study; they are characterized by ethno-tribal and ethno-religious diversity, a shared colonial history, rapid growth of Christianity, and an increase in Muslim–Christian violence since the 1980s in a context of national politicization of religious identity. In particular, I focus on tribally and religiously diverse Kaduna state and Plateau state (see map in Figure 1.3). These two states were not selected because of prior knowledge of the existence of power-sharing institutions, but due to the interesting variation observed in their experience of inter-religious violence – a high number of cases of inter-religious violence in some LGAs and the absence of violence in other similar LGAs. Kaduna is also a Muslim-majority state while Plateau is a Christian-majority state.

### Original Ethnic and Religious Violence Dataset

In light of the problems with extant data on communal violence for Nigeria and other countries, as I discuss in Chapter 5, I present analysis of an original dataset of communal violence for northern Nigeria, drawing on the methodology employed by Varshney (2002) and Wilkinson (2004) in their construction of a communal violence dataset for India. With the help of research assistants, I reviewed 32 years (1979–2011) of *The Guardian*, an independent Nigerian national daily newspaper,

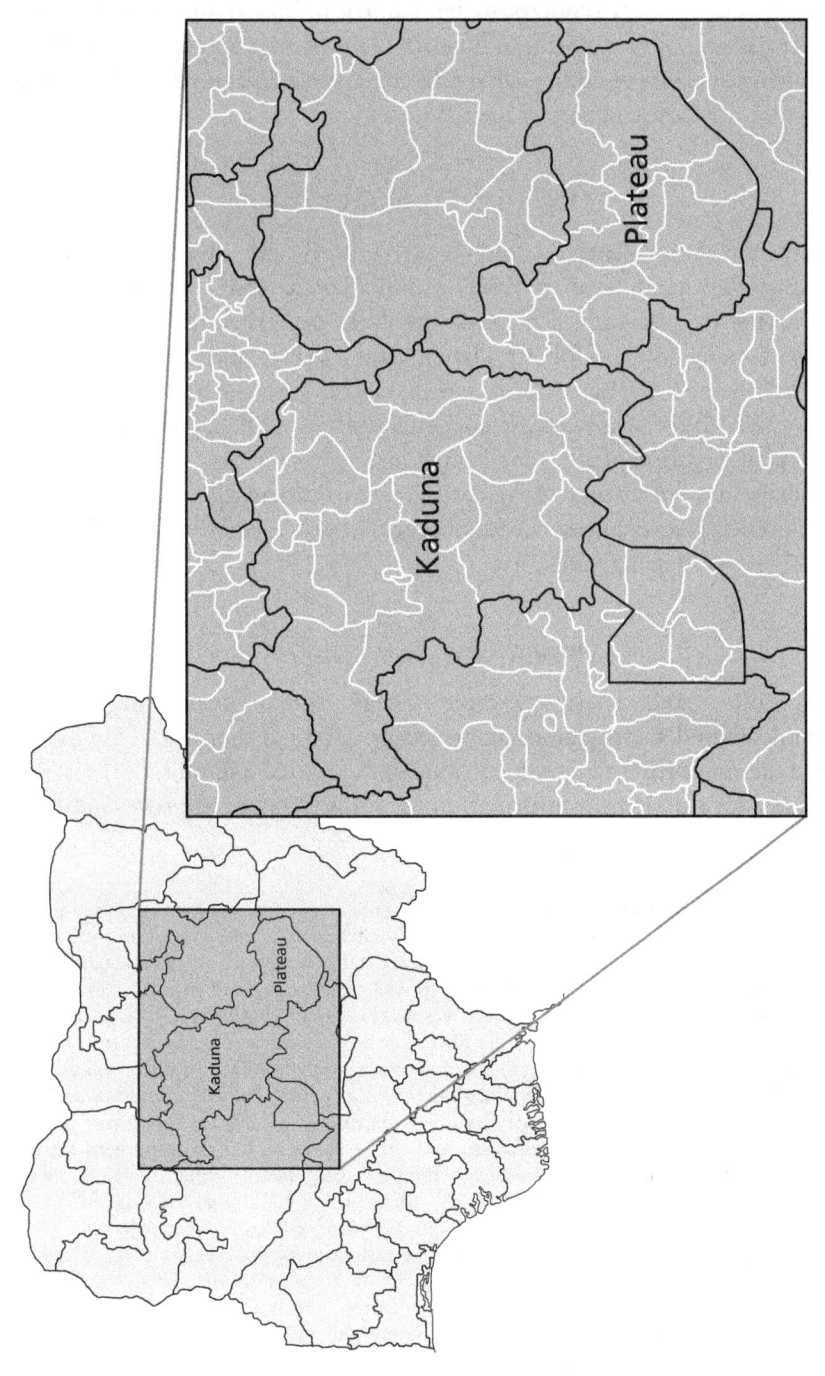

FIGURE 1.3 Sites of power-sharing analysis: Kaduna and Plateau state LGAs

considered by local scholars to be a fairly unbiased source with good coverage of events in northern Nigeria.[36] I analyze the scope and pattern of over 500 cases of ethno-tribal and ethno-religious communal violence coded in the construction of the dataset.

### Original Power-Sharing Data

Chapter 5 also presents the original data gathered on power-sharing at the local government level in Kaduna and Plateau states, controlling for a variety of factors.[37] This task involved gathering the election and appointment records for 17 Plateau state LGAs and the majority of Kaduna state's 23 LGAs (see map in Figure 1.3). Since hard copies of these records for past years are not generally maintained, the task required the reconstruction of records through interviews with current and former officials in some cases. These data confirm information gathered from local officials on the presence (or absence) of power-sharing, as well as the *form* power-sharing takes.

### Original Church Growth Data

To confirm and assess the rapid spread of Christianity in Nigeria, I implemented a data-gathering project with one of the largest and oldest churches in northern Nigeria – Evangelical Church Winning All (ECWA). These data supplement information from the *World Christian Database*

---

[36] The number of newspaper editions across the 32 years amounts to over 13,000 editions. Currently, the dataset is based on an approximately 90 percent completion rate of the total number of editions (i.e., I and research assistants reviewed 13,759 daily editions in the construction of the dataset). Prior to 1987, inter-religious violence was largely unheard of and intra-Muslim violence was more common, but I select 1979 as the start date for coverage as a buffer in order to capture any cases that were perhaps overlooked prior to 1987. Note that during the years (1979–1983) when *The Guardian* was not yet publishing, I gathered data from two other newspapers – *The New Nigerian* and the *Nigerian Standard*. I selected these two newspapers for balance, as the former is considered more Muslim/northern-biased and the latter more Christian/southern-biased. Note that while research assistants were trained to help identify potential cases, I coded each case myself. For 1994 and 1995, in which sparse editions of the Guardian were available, I also used the *New Nigerian* and the *Nigerian Standard* to supplement.

[37] Generally, I was able to obtain the religious and ethnic identities of each local government representative for the LGAs, but in some cases, only some of the top officials – chairman, deputy chairman, and secretary – could be acquired. This is not a major issue, however, since these top three positions are the most important seats in local government councils. Hence, the most important evidence of power-sharing is at this level.

and *World Religion Database* on the growth of Christianity and Islam in Nigeria. They ultimately support the broad claim that Christian churches significantly expanded in number in the post-1970s period as part of a process of rapid religious change.

## Qualitative Case Studies

Finally, the qualitative portion of the fieldwork for this study adopted a controlled comparison case study approach combined with historical process tracing. I adopt Mill's method of difference, or a "most similar case design," in that I compare LGAs that are similar in as many theoretically relevant ways as possible, but that have different outcomes on the dependent variable – inter-religious violence. From interviews with traditional tribal chiefs, local government officials, peace activists, religious leaders, and youth leaders, I explore the selected communities' histories of ethnic group settlement, group relations, representation, and pattern of peace or conflict. Two of the case studies relied more on extensive secondary sources. In a series of three paired comparisons – presented as part of the analysis in Chapters 6 and 7 – I test my theory in each pair against one community where there has been endemic inter-religious violence and another where violence has been largely absent.[38] A number of other LGAs are also referenced in the course of this study for their theoretical insight or illustration.

## CONCLUSION

This research has implications not only for how scholars conceptualize the role of institutions and federalism in pluralistic societies, but also for how policymakers approach the task of designing institutions sufficient to prevent or resolve inter-group violence in conflict states. As the discussion of consociational and power-sharing institutions in Chapter 4 shows, much of the scholarship on institutional design is focused on how national institutions can best be structured to avert ethnic conflict or civil war. Yet, the effectiveness of consociational or power-sharing approaches, adopted in countries around the world, has, as much of the literature highlights, failed to be the panacea to intra-state conflict. In countries beset by intra-state group conflict, however, this book emphasizes the importance of

---

[38] Note that this is similar to the "most tightly controlled" case selection methodology adopted by Varshney (2002) in his study of Hindu–Muslim violence in India.

local government institutions in structuring incentives for group violence. That is, in countries beset by subnational ethnic or communal conflict, local-level institutions are central for understanding the causes of and conditions for inter-group violence, an area of study that generally goes overlooked not only in the institutional design and conflict literature, but also in the scholarship on group mobilization or radicalization. Further, exploring the representative nature of local political institutions helps to shed light on the conditions under which personal grievances, motivations, or incentives for violence are more or less likely to take violent form or, in contrast, be channeled into political dialogue and conflict resolution.

Second, this research emphasizes the importance of *informal* locally grown institutions in reinforcing local peace and more equitable democratic electoral outcomes. The power-sharing institutions studied in this book are not exogenously imposed, but are birthed in local communities between local elite who come to a shared understanding of the importance of broader representation in local governance. While the incentives for adopting such institutions vary depending on the community in question, the case studies highlight the centrality of informal rules, locally rooted conceptions of fair representation, and local authorities in initiating and sustaining forms of power-sharing outside of the traditional scholarly focus on formal rules and institutions.

Third, this research calls for greater attention to studying the dynamics of communal non-state ethnic violence. While scholarship on civil war and ethnic conflict, in which the state is a party to the conflict, has shed important light on the conditions for or drivers of violence, the extent to which these explanations apply to inter-group violence (in which the state is not a main target or initiator) is less clear. Large-$n$ studies, in particular, with high death count thresholds for case inclusion, exclude countless cases of intra-state violence that nonetheless have significant ramifications for the security and stability of states. While a case can be made for studying civil war and non-state ethnic violence separately or as distinct types of violence, the point rather is that "low-scale" non-state or communal conflict should *also* be a critical area of attention and study for conflict scholars and policymakers, whatever the methodological challenges.

In sum, the main thrust of this research is that forms of representation in local government bodies at the subnational level can powerfully shape the prospect of communal inter-religious clashes. This is particularly the case where decentralization has rendered local governments sites of greater contestation for power and influence. In countries where the politicization of religious identity infuses political and communal space, local government patterns of representation are all the more critical in shaping communal relationships and either intensifying or quelling the politics of identity and religious conflict through the pattern of representation.

Despite the similarity among the LGAs compared in this study, the analyses in subsequent chapters show that local government power-sharing reframes the politics of identity at the local level in a vital way, helping to prevent the spillover of inter-religious violence and instability in Nigeria. When it comes to peace-building and conflict-prevention, cooperation among youth, religious leaders, tribal elders, and government officials of different tribal and religious identities are easier to coordinate in communities with local government power-sharing institutions. From both a series of case studies and original empirical data, the findings are clear and highlight the significance of power-sharing at the subnational level as an important determinant of communal peace or conflict.

Of course, Nigeria is not the only country where ethnic or inter-religious violence is now a major security challenge. Indeed, reports of religious communal violence or riots in many countries frequent the headlines, coinciding with the global resurgence of religion and its politicization and radicalization. Countries such as India, Indonesia, Nigeria, Myanmar, Egypt, Malaysia, Ethiopia, the Central African Republic – to name a few – have been or continue to be flashpoints of inter-religious violence. Other countries such as Ghana, Tanzania, and Kenya face increasing tensions among their religious groups, and religious cleavages are present in major conflicts in the Middle East, such as in Iraq and Syria. In many of these cases, a vitriolic religio-political discourse infuses the public space, blurring the lines between the politics of church and state. The rapid transformation of the religious composition of many countries in the Global South since the 1970s, the increase in *intra*-state conflict, and watershed events such as the Iranian Revolution in 1979 and the U.S. 9/11 attacks have raised the specter of a world increasingly characterized by religiously motivated violence.

Before delving deeper into the theory of local power-sharing and the empirical findings, the next two chapters first provide some context, exploring the story of religious change in Nigeria and the nature of its federal and local government structure and politics. Without an understanding of the dimensions of and reasons for the politicization of religion in Nigeria, power-sharing's importance in ameliorating inter-religious crises would make little sense. The religious change in Nigeria, particularly with the rapid growth of Christianity since the end of the 1970s, was central in constituting Muslim–Christian religious identity as a salient political narrative of difference and conflict.

PART I

THE IMPORTANCE OF THE POLITICS OF
RELIGIOUS CHANGE AND LOCAL GOVERNMENT

# 2

# Pattern and Politics of Religious Change in Nigeria

Over the past half-century, there has been a revival or resurgence of religion in countries across the Global South. Christianity and Islam are the two fastest-growing world religions, accounting for an estimated 32 percent and 23 percent of the global population in 2010, respectively, or about 3.8 billion people (Pew Research Center 2012, 9; 2015). Despite Christianity's waning presence in the West, it is the fastest-growing religion in the Global South, with its Pentecostal-charismatic variant the driving force. The fact of this resurgence – increasing rather than declining religiosity – has prompted scholars who previously adhered to secularization theory or the modernization thesis to abandon or marvel at assumptions that religion would decline as countries modernized (Berger 1999; Bellin 2008; Philpott 2009; Toft, Philpott, and Shah 2011; Thomas 2005; Snyder 2011). Indeed, Peter L. Berger (1998) who, like many sociologists, had advanced the argument that modernity would lead to secularization of societies, revoked this thesis in *The Desecularization of the World* (see also Berger 2008, 23–27). Now, the standard opening refrain in academic literature on religion and international politics begins with the requisite summary of how religion was expected to disappear from the modern repertoire of personal and political life, that the scholarly predictions of modernization and secularization failed woefully, and that events such as the 1979 Iranian Revolution and September 11, 2001, have forced this realization upon all. Now, scholars are newly interested in, on the one hand, the relationship between democracy and religious change,[1]

---

[1] See Lumsdaine 2009; Ranger 2008b; Woodberry 2012; Freston 2008; 2004; Philpott 2007; Steigenga and Cleary 2007; Patterson 2005; Woodberry and Shah 2005; Gill 2002; Hallum 2002; Marostica 1998; Gaskill 1997.

the role of religion in global humanitarianism,[2] religion and the international human rights regime,[3] and, on the other hand, the role of religion in fueling and responding to terrorism,[4] sectarian violence, and civil war.[5] The global "War on Terror," the religion-fueled sectarian conflicts occurring globally, and the increasing public attention in the West on religious persecution all raise concerns that the supposed wars of religion in the 17th and 18th centuries have not truly been left behind, but threaten the social and political stability of countries in the modern era.

This global religious resurgence sets the stage for understanding the process and politics of religious change in Nigeria as well. As noted in the previous chapter, religion is perceived to be central or a contributing factor to conflicts in a number of countries; in Nigeria, Muslim–Christian communal violence in the Middle Belt and north, broadly speaking, has been on the rise since the late 1980s. Thousands have been killed in the violence, countless displaced, livelihoods destroyed, and villages and homes wiped out. The relationship between religious identity or change and civil conflict is not well-understood, however. Is religion or religious change the direct cause of conflict – something about religion in particular that renders it more conducive or susceptible to politicization and violence? Or is religion merely epiphenomenal, a latent identity that only matters when selectively manipulated by political elite?

The most direct answer is that religious change or difference is clearly not the primary explanation for the pattern of inter-religious violence in Nigeria. If it were, there would be no puzzle to explore – why only some religiously pluralistic communities experience inter-religious violence while others do not. However, without understanding the process and politics of religious change in Nigeria, the explanation for the pattern of inter-religious violence will be truncated or incomplete. The construction of political power is intrinsically bound up with the story of religious power in Nigeria. While political and socio-economic grievances affect the likelihood of communal violence, the politics of religious change critically shapes actors' political identities, perceptions, and interests. This chapter explains

---

[2] See Thaut, Gross Stein, and Barnett 2012; Benthall 2012; Barnett and Gross-Stein 2012; Thaut 2009; de Cordier 2009; 2008; Barnett and Weiss 2008; Benedetti 2006; Bellion-Jourdan 2005; Ferris 2005; Bornstein 2003.
[3] See Hertzke 2013; Grim 2013; Grim and Finke 2011; Lauren 2011; Freston 2011; Donnelly 2007; Gill 2005; Woodberry and Shah 2005.
[4] See Marsden 2012; Piazza 2009; Hoffman 2006; Wiktorowicz and Kaltenthaler 2006; Atran 2003; Crawford 2003; Elshtain 2003; Esposito 2002.
[5] See Hassner 2013; Svennson 2012; Fox 2004; Duffy-Toft 2006; 2007; Cavenaugh 2009.

how the resurgence and radicalization of Christianity and Islam has reshaped national and communal politics, and, where local power-sharing institutions are absent, contributed to the rise of inter-religious violence.

The following two sections discuss the dimensions of this global resurgence of Christianity and Islam, respectively, helping contextualize the religious and political transformation in Nigeria. The subsequent section briefly introduces the general pattern of Nigeria's religious change with the growth of Pentecostal-charismatic Christianity and the rise of radical Islam over the last four decades. The chapter then places these recent events in their historical context, examining the shifting relationship between religion and politics during the pre-colonial, colonial, and post-colonial periods and the effect on inter-group relationships in northern Nigeria. Finally, the last section highlights the events and new forms of mobilization that have led to the sacralization of contemporary Nigerian politics. This discussion explains why religion has become such a salient category of identity and conflict in Nigeria, helping to frame this puzzle of why, despite the political saliency of religion in the Middle Belt, only some communities have been prone to major Muslim–Christian communal violence.

## RELIGIOUS CHANGE: THE GLOBAL CONTEXT

The global influence of religious ideas and religious movements is becoming increasingly evident in states that are experiencing rapid economic growth *as well as* those that are falling further behind. Prophecies within academia that religion declines as societies secularize or modernize have not been fulfilled and cannot explain the rapid growth of Christianity outside the West (Berger 1999; Jelen and Wilcox 2002; Casanova 1994; Esposito 1998; Marshall 2009). Further, the geographical saturation of Christianity has shifted southward. By 2025, experts predict that there will be more Christians in the Global South than the North, with the most in Latin America (640 million) followed by Africa (633 million) and Asia (460 million) (Jenkins 2002, 2–3; see also Jenkins 2011).[6] In contrast, there have been "massive losses in the Western world over the last sixty years ...

---

[6] See also Barret et al. (2001, 5), as well as Johnson and Chung (2004, 171). In contrast to Jenkins' projection, Johnson and Chung (2004, 173) observe that the number of Christians in the South surpassed the North in the early 1980s. Authors' calculations of the World Christian Encyclopedia figures may vary depending on the denominational categories that they include under the term "Christian."

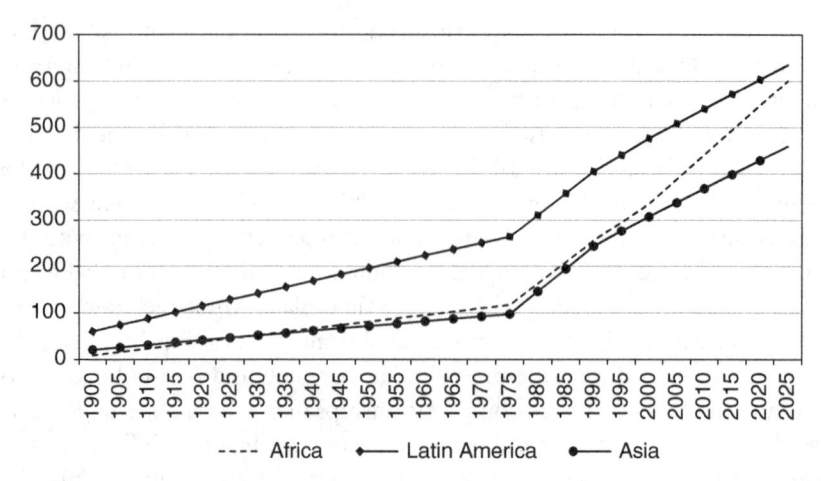

FIGURE 2.1 Total number of affiliated Christians,[7] 1900–2025 (millions)
Source: Johnson (2007). Interpolated by author.

an average of 7,600 [adherents] every day" (Barrett et al. 2001, 5). Figure 2.1 highlights the upsurge of Christian adherents in the latter part of the 20th century across Africa, Asia, and Latin America (see Appendices D and E for the percentage change in Africa and Asia).

At the same time, Islam is also growing rapidly and is expected to outpace Christianity's rate of growth over the next few decades. Indeed, based on Pew Research Center (2015) projections, the total number of adherents of Islam and Christianity may be equal by 2050 if the current trend holds. Currently, there are about 1.6 billion Muslims, 23 percent of the global population (Pew Research Center 2015). Population growth rates in Africa and the Middle East will be particularly important drivers of this trend.[8] Figure 2.2 shows the percent increase in Muslims and

---

[7] Note that "affiliated Christians" refers to "Church members: all persons belonging to or connected with organized churches, whose names are inscribed, written or entered on the churches' books, records, or rolls" (Barrett et al. 2001, 27). This includes the six main blocs of Christians: 1) Roman Catholics, 2) Protestants, 3) Independents, 4) Orthodox, 5) Anglicans, and 6) Marginal Christians.

[8] Both natural increase and conversion have driven the rapid growth of Christianity and Islam in these regions to varying degrees over time. Presently, conversion is driving the growth more strongly in some regions and countries than others. For example, the *World Christian Database* calculates that from 2000 to 2010, conversion accounted for 5.3 percent and 3.7 percent of the increase in Christians and Muslims in Africa, respectively. In Asia, conversion accounted for 50.7 percent and only 3.9 percent of the increase in the number of Christians and Muslims, respectively (Johnson 2007).

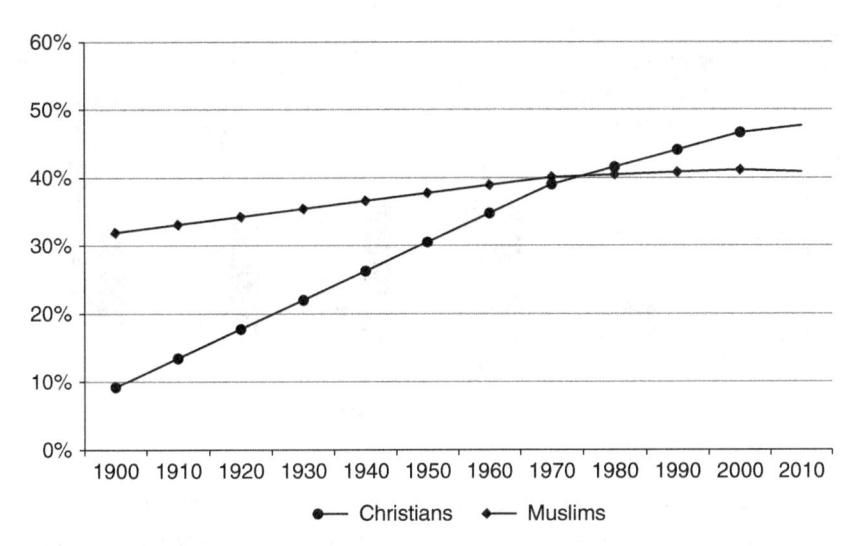

FIGURE 2.2 Muslim and Christian affiliation in Africa, percent of population, 1900–2010
Source: Johnson (2007). Interpolated by author.

Christians over time on the African continent (see Appendix D for Asia). While the growth of Christianity has been more limited in northern Africa, it has grown rapidly across the rest of the continent, appealing in particular to former adherents of African Traditional Religion.

Within Christianity, it is Pentecostal-charismatic Christianity, in particular, that has seen unparalleled growth since the 1970s and 1980s, rendering it "the most dynamic and demographically dominant force" in Christianity in the Global South (Shah 2009, x-xi). Of the total number of Protestant churches in Latin America, for example, around two-thirds of them are Pentecostal (Chesnut 2007, 83; see also Freston 2008, 15, 18–19).[9] Figure 2.3 shows the increase in the percentage of adherents who identify as Pentecostal-charismatic across the three regions (see Appendix E for percentage of general affiliated Christians in the three regions over time). "By 2100, over three fourths of all Christians will be living in the South," note Johnson and Chung (2004, 171).

As noted previously, although Christianity is the fastest-growing religion and accounts for the largest share of the global population, Islam's growth is

---

[9] Freston (2008, 15, 18–19) also notes that "Perhaps two-thirds of Latin America's fifty million or so Protestants are Pentecostals" and that "[i]n Brazil alone, the number of evangelicals has tripled in the last thirty years."

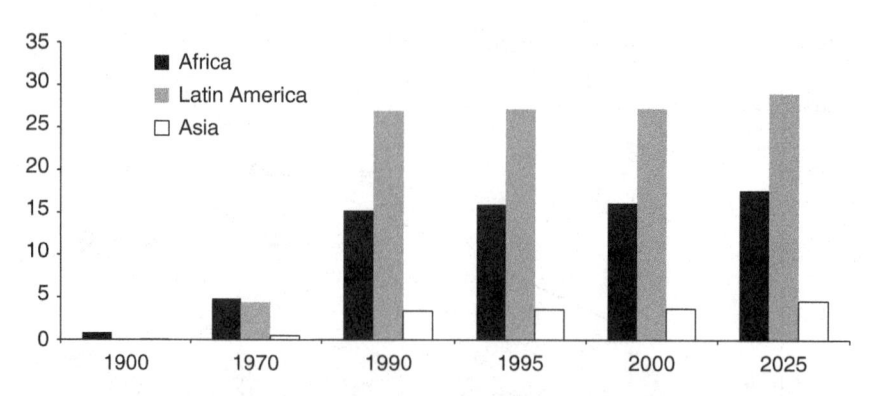

FIGURE 2.3 Percentage of Pentecostal-charismatic Christians,[10] 1900–2025

now expected to outpace that of Christianity in the coming decades. Although this growth may largely be due to natural population increases, the Muslim world is not a stranger to periods of reform and revival. These revivals are driven by a re-thinking of the role of Islam in personal and political life in reaction to the geo-political and social conditions affecting Muslim populations, leading to calls for a return to Islamic tradition and teaching or to new forms of religio-political adaptation or mobilization. Islam's political resurgence has varied both in its driving rationale and types of mobilization over time and within different periods of revival and reform.

In short, with the rapid growth of Christianity and Islam in non-Western countries, the dominance of the secularization thesis and modernization theory has waned recently in both political science and religious studies, unable to fully explain the phenomenon.[11] As Esposito (1998, 19) contends, since the end of the Cold War, "[r]eligion has become a major ideological, social, and political force, appealed to by governments,

---

[10] This graph refers to the percentage of Pentecostal and Charismatic Christians across the Christian "mega-bloc"; that is, the six "major ecclesiastico-cultural subdivisions of affiliated Christians and their churches" (Barrett et al. 2001, 29).

[11] During the 1950s and 1960s, the secularization thesis and modernization theory in academia diminished the relevance of religion as an independently significant political force. This "dominant paradigm" of secularization, notes Gaskill (1997, 74), "suggests that as societies become increasingly pluralized and 'modern,' non-religious meaning systems emerge and largely replace religious systems of meaning – in short, secularization occurs." For example, as Pippa Norris and Richard Inglehart (2004, 5) argue, the "importance and vitality of religion, its ever-present influence on how people live their daily lives" gradually erodes with economic development. Hence, the Iranian revolution and the terrorist attacks of September 11 came as a surprise, as the discipline had long dismissed the independent significance of religion as a force for political change or conflict.

political parties and opposition movements alike, a source of liberation and violent extremism."[12]

## EXPLAINING THE REVIVAL OF RELIGION

### Christianity's Resurgence and Political Consequences

Identifying the cause of Pentecostal-charismatic Christianity's rapid growth not only in Nigeria but also across Latin America, Asia, and Africa more broadly is difficult. This difficulty is not necessarily due to geographic and historical dissimilarities, but, rather, to the challenge of substantiating any one theory to explain the similar trend across these three continents. Some scholars point to the dislocation produced by globalization and modernization (Marshall 2009; Gifford 1998). That is, people turn to religion to find comfort in their material struggles, since other avenues have not helped to improve their conditions.[13] Others point to disappointment with political systems – the corruption, mismanagement, and failed or failing democratic experiments since the 1970s. Religion serves as a rallying cry for the transformation of political systems (Snyder 2011, 3). Similarly, Gifford (1998, 328) observes that people are abandoning mainline Christian churches for Pentecostal-charismatic churches because the latter engage with the socio-political, material, and spiritual reality of people's struggles in the face of dashed modernization hopes. Or as Norris and Inglehart (2004) contend, in politically or economically dilapidated circumstances, the church may represent a moral community to which people appeal for stability and "existential security." Alternatively, Gill (1998) highlights the success of Pentecostal-charismatic churches due to the stronger appeal over their competition, the mainline churches. Pentecostal-charismatic churches are winning in the religious marketplace with a decentralized model of leadership and church growth, vibrant worship, possibilities for women's empowerment, and a message of social regeneration and spiritual power over earthly suffering (Miller, Sargeant, Flory 2013). Finally, other scholars point to the material and status benefits that derive from being associated with the Pentecostal-charismatic churches, as well as

---

[12] See also Gill 2002, 217; Norris and Inglehart 2004, 5; Marshall 2009; Bellin 2008, 316; Gaskill 1997, 74; Gill 2004, 44.

[13] Pippa and Norris (2004) present a version of modernization theory advancing this perspective.

their links to Western money and religious figures (Marshall 2009; Gifford 1998).[14]

One should note, however, that the expansion of Pentecostalism in the Global South, including Nigeria, is widely considered a strongly indigenous phenomenon whose *success* is not a product of Western imposition or driven by foreign missionaries or religious organizations (Freston 2004, 22–23; Dixon 1995, 479–492; Steigenga and Cleary 2007; Cleary and Stewart-Gambino 1998; Gill 2002). As Cleary and Stewart-Gambino (1998, 7) point out regarding Pentecostalism's rise in Latin America, "It did not begin with a pervasive outside missionary effort, nor are major groups sustained by personnel or money from the United States or Europe." Although Gifford (1998, 308) argues that transnational ties between African Pentecostal-charismatic churches and U.S. churches or evangelists have increased the prominence of African churches, it is a stretch to argue that their growth or stunning success is *primarily* dependent upon these ties between a few prominent local church leaders and Western churches.[15]

Concurrent with this religious change in the Global South, Christians have become increasingly participatory in the political sphere over the past 30–40 years in new forms of religio-political engagement. Mainline and conservative Christian denominations, especially those within the Holiness tradition, have generally emphasized the "eternal" and spiritual as the all-encompassing concern of Christians, necessitating a "turning away" from the world's corrupt influence. This disdain for politics has been upturned by the revival of Pentecostal-charismatic Christianity since

---

[14] As Gifford (1998, 334) notes, "Today in Uganda and Zambia, becoming born-again actually brings one close to power; elsewhere, though it may indicate some turning against the political elite, it can be a way of linking into other material benefits." Similarly, Marshall (2009, 215) contends, "From the strict rejection of participation in political activities or seeking of political office, from the early 1990s pastors have increasingly used their status as spiritual authorities and the wealth thus acquired not only as a means of access to the state and channels of accumulation, but also as means of political influence."

[15] See Gifford's (1998, 308) analysis of Pentecostal and Charismatic Christianity's success in Africa, in which he argues that "[t]hrough these [external] links the churches have become a major, if not the greatest single, source of development assistance, money, employment and opportunity in Africa." Furthermore, he observes, "history indicates that the growth of Christianity in Africa was never unrelated to its relations with the wider world; externality has always been a factor in African Christianity" (318). At least in its initial stages, Steigenga and Cleary (2007, 8) also note that the rapid growth of Pentecostalism in Latin America starting in the 1960s was "related to intensified missionary movements from North America."

the 1970s and 1980s. By and large, the shift is accompanied by the belief that it is incumbent upon Christians to pray for, participate in, and provide godly council and leadership in politics (Freston 2004, 16). As Gifford (1998, 334) notes, "the idea of turning one's back on the world, as we have seen, is rarely involved at all ... these churches are one of the best available means of linking into the outside world." Active participation in political life is no longer anathema. Pentecostal-charismatic Christianity, Kalu (2008, 223) observes, "challenges the doctrine of the *l'etat theologique* by revisiting the state's modes of organizing power, its institutionalized domination, its general principles of state and norms of behavior." The church is no longer simply focused on the "kingdom come," but now on temporal concerns, in hopes of providing a transforming, prophetic voice to redeem and heal countries' socio-political ills.

This merging of Christian teaching with political imperatives is evident in Pentecostal-charismatic Christianity's emphasis on the collective transformation and redemption of society and politics, particularly through an individual conversion project. In Nigeria and many other countries, this political theology of conversion concerns, as Ruth Marshall (2009, 13–14) notes,

the projection into collective, public space of a highly political agenda. The image of the invading army, sweeping all unbelievers in its path, expresses the political ambition of replacing a corrupt regime with a new form of righteous authority that presents itself as the unique path to individual and collective salvation. This ambition does not take the form of the creation of a theocracy, where spiritual authority underwritten by institutionalized religion would constitute the basis for political authority. Rather, conversion is represented as a means of creating the ideal citizen, one who will provide a living incarnation of the *nomos* of a pacified and ordered political realm.

Although the teachings of such churches may not be directly politicized or preached from the pulpit (though in many cases this is undoubtedly true),[16] the emphasis on socio-political regeneration takes various forms. New forms of political engagement – such as the formation of evangelical political parties, the organization of ecumenical councils on political issues, the grassroots organization of previously marginalized poor or indigenous people, the participation of Christians in political campaigns and contestation for office, and the formation of representative councils or civic associations – characterize the Pentecostal-charismatic movement

---

[16] See Paul Gifford's (1998) analysis of Ghana, Uganda, Zambia, and Cameroon.

(Lumsdaine 2009; Ranger 2008b; Steigenga 2007; Martin 1990; Freston 2008; Gifford 1998; Cleary and Stewart-Gambino 1998; Marshall 2009). From Nigeria and Kenya to Brazil and Nicaragua, Pentecostal-charismatic Christians seek political office or attempt to organize politically. Evangelical political parties claim divine leadership to address social ills and bring about socio-political transformation, although they have achieved little success due to their inability to mobilize more than a narrow constituency (Brazil being the exception) (Freston 2004, 27). In other instances, religious leaders or believers run for office and draw on the language of faith to legitimize their leadership or bolster their appeal, especially since to do otherwise could distance them from powerful Christian churches and harm their political chances (Gifford 1998, 191–245). Churches have also rallied around secular leaders or parties to increase their appeal among a wider audience (Freston 2004, 4).

In short, the entry of Pentecostal-charismatic Christians more overtly into political life is evident in a range of political activity and expression. Pentecostals are "immensely adaptive and pragmatic" in the orientation of their beliefs to social or political conditions (Cleary and Stewart-Gambino 1998, 145). The spread of Pentecostal-charismatic Christianity in the Global South reflects a new political theology that is increasingly oriented around the temporal plight of social conversion. The sacralization of contestation is the rising and attendant phenomenon, and it is reflected in a variety of political expressions. The beliefs or faith emphasized in Pentecostal-charismatic churches, therefore, tend to be oriented toward a politics of "kingdom come," moving away from a theology that abstains from or shuns temporal politics. Consequently, as Thomas (2005, 26) observes, "What is increasingly being challenged is an idea that is part of the political mythology of liberal modernity. This is the idea that religion is, or should be, privatized, restricted to the area of private life in domestic and international politics."

## Islam's Resurgence and Political Consequences

The Muslim world has experienced a number of revival and reform movements over the past few centuries, all with significant social and political consequences. The relationship between religion and state has been rearticulated by various reformers in reaction to the socio-economic and political plight of Muslims in various countries, such as during subjugation to Western colonial rule in the late 19th century and in subsequent efforts to articulate an Islamic approach to modernity in the early 20th century.[17] The post-1970s revival and reform movements, coinciding with Christianity's resurgence, had significant political consequences. With the end of colonial rule and newly gained independence for many Muslim-majority countries, expectations were high. Yet, the post-colonial adoption of secular, modern institutions did not lead to vast improvements in the political and socio-economic well-being of Muslims everywhere. Increasing poverty and inequality, unemployment, political repression, and civil wars dashed expectations. In place of colonial rule, oppressive authoritarian Muslim regimes took power, perceived by their populations as merely puppets of the secular West (Esposito 2011, 188–190). Efforts to adapt to modern conditions and reinterpret liberal values within an Islamic framework left people disillusioned, as their lot in life did not seem to improve. The subsequent revival and reform movement ignited in the 1970s again involved a rethinking of the principles of Islam in relation to the social, economic, and political struggles in the Muslim world.

The new round of soul-searching triggered by these events resurrected calls for a return to Islamic values, tradition, and an Islamic system of government (Esposito 2011, 190–191; Esposito 1999b, 667; Nasr 1999, 656–668). Consequently, many throughout the Muslim world met the 1979 overthrow of the Western-backed Shah in Iran and the establishment of a strict Islamic state with euphoria, inspiring similar grassroots

---

[17] The late 19th- and early 20th-century reform movements led by figures such as Jamal al-Din al-Afghani, Muhammad Abduh, Sayyid Ahmad Khan, and Muhammad Iqbal responded to the apparent socio-economic decline and political subjugation of Muslims under colonial rule (Esposito 2011, 152–184; Nasr 1999; Voll 1999, 530–531, 547). Challenging the conservativism of the *ulama*, reformers contended that Islam is a dynamic faith and its principles, laws, and values contain within themselves the rationale for reform that could accommodate socio-political changes and modern institutions (Esposito 2011, 165–167; 1999b, 646–650; Nasr 1999, 561–562). However, the reforms advocated and envisioned by Muslim intellectuals and scholars were not fully accepted, as conservative religious scholars or *ulama* saw these re-interpretations as a capitulation to the West and secularism, and "neorevivalist" or modern reforms feared the moral and social decline of adaptation (Esposito 2011, 171; Esposito 1999b, 653, 656). Reacting to the post-colonial failed experiments with Western secularism and models of development and major political defeats, neorevivalists called for a return to Islam as a comprehensive way of life. Modern reformers such as Hasan al-Banna, founder of the Muslim Brotherhood, and Mawlana Mawdudi in southeast Asia, founder of Jamaat-i-Islam, although they agreed to the need for reform, were harsh critics of Western culture and institutions. These movements were more successful, drawing lower, middle, and upper-class adherents to their ranks and establishing effective broad-based social organization, outreach and assistance to the poor, and spiritual training (Esposito 2011, 173–183).

mobilization against regimes in places such as Saudi Arabia, Egypt, and Afghanistan (Esposito 2011, 192). In this new era of revivalism, modernity is not considered anathema, but it must be "Islamized," or kept consistent with Islamic principles and values. This reformist movement found fertile ground across the Arab world, northern Africa, and Asia, mobilizing new social and educational reforms and independence movements and bringing Islamists into power in a number of countries (Nasr 568–570).

Part of the successful appeal of this modern revivalism is the sociopolitical composition of the resurgence of Islam inside and outside of the Arab world since the 1980s; it has largely been driven by a moderate majority. In contrast to the early 20th century, this Islamic resurgence is driven not by a small handful of intellectuals and Islamic scholars, but has been internalized by both educated elite trained in the West, as well as lower- and middle-class populations in the Muslim world possessing a "renewed awareness and concern about leading a more Islamically informed way of life" (Esposito 1999a, 104). New grassroots organizations have multiplied to provide legal aid, fight poverty, provide services to women and children, and offer a vast range of other social services in response to this call to live an exemplary Muslim life based on the example and teachings of the Prophet Mohammad (Esposito 2011, 233; Esposito 1999b, 667–668). As with the resurgence in Christianity, the emphasis is not merely on personal piety and spiritual observance, but rather on a faith that is "comprehensive," offering rules and principles for right living that inform all aspects of political and social life. The political expressions and calls for Islamization, therefore, have also taken many forms – e.g., pressure for change through mass protests, the advocacy of ideas through the formation and platforms of new political parties, and service in elected assemblies or parliaments (Esposito 2011, 194, 233–234).

The moderate majority, attempting to reform society and politics from the bottom-up through a return to Islamic principles and values, has not been the only expression of the revivalism in the Muslim world. Rather, perspectives on the proper understanding and application of Islam continue to be debated across and within conservative, fundamentalist, and modernist camps (Esposito 2011, 256–260; Esposito 1999b). Post-1960s events inspired more radical or extremist forms of mobilization in some cases. Encouraged by the Iranian revolution, the quick defeat of Arab states in the Arab-Israeli war, and the writings of radical extremists, a minority have interpreted the return to Islamic teachings as a call to violent mobilization against not only Western interests, but also against "moderate" Muslims or unbelievers, and Muslim governments whose adherence to Islamic law is questioned (Esposito 2011, 191–195). The vast majority of Muslims condemn the activities of groups such as al-Qaeda, Boko Haram in Nigeria, and the Islamic State (also known as ISIS and ISIL) in Iraq and Syria. The common denominator in the modern Islamic resurgence, however, is the perceived failure of modernism and Western secular institutions, values, and capitalism. Westernization and liberal reforms are seen as the cause of, rather than solution to, problems in the Muslim world. The effects of both the broader Islamization as well as the radicalization among a minority have been widely felt across both Muslim majority and minority countries. Nigeria is no exception.

~

This brief sketch of the revivals within Christianity and Islam in recent decades across the Global South provides the broader context for making sense of Nigeria's religio-political transformation since the 1970s. Although the specific actors, events, and politics of religious change are unique to each country, the broader phenomenon of religious change in the Global South is not unique. To further illustrate the puzzle of inter-religious peace and violence represented by the Middle Belt states, the remainder of this chapter turns to the particular form this religious change and political sacralization has taken in Nigerian, the related actors and events, and the relationship to religious conflict.

## RELIGIOUS CHANGE IN NIGERIA

### Christian Religious Change

As in many other countries in the Global South, Christianity has grown rapidly in Nigeria. At the beginning of the 20th century, the population of Christians in Nigeria was almost non-existent in the northern region of the country. Christian missionaries had not yet made significant inroads into Nigeria's interior, and disease and death kept them at bay. Instead, the population was predominantly Muslim or adherents of African Traditional Religion. In less than 50 years, however, the religious landscape of Nigeria altered significantly. By 1953, Christians constituted approximately 21 percent of Nigeria's population (Pew Research Center, "Religious Demographic Profile, Nigeria"). By 1963, Christians constituted just over 34 percent of the population, and, by 1990, approximately 48 percent of Nigerians were affiliated Christians. In the north-central Middle Belt states, which are now a mix of Muslims and Christians, Christianity made significant gains in the post-colonial era. Currently, with the rapid growth of Christianity and decline in the number of adherents of African Traditional Religion (largely due to conversion), Nigeria is home to nearly an equal portion of Muslims and Christians, with Muslims concentrated in the northern half of the country and Christians predominant in the South (Barrett et al. 2001, 549).

The rapid religious change since the 1970s is largely due to the flourishing of the "renewalist" or Pentecostal-charismatic variant of Christianity. In 2001, the renewalists constituted approximately 20 percent of the Nigerian Christian community (35 million people out of 110 million) (Barrett et al. 2001; Gaiya 2004, 354; Awolalu 2001, 18; Nwafor 2002; Uzoma 2004).[18] These burgeoning renewalist groups include not only those of the Pentecostal variant, but also Charismatics within the Catholic Church and other Protestant groups. According to a Pew Research Center (2006, 86) survey, this bloc accounts for "approximately three-in-ten Nigerians," and "roughly six-in-ten Protestants are either Pentecostal or charismatic, and three-in-ten Catholics surveyed can be classified as charismatic" (see also Nwafor 2002, 58). The change in the number of affiliated Christians overall is also highlighted in Table 2.1. States in northern Nigeria where Christianity was virtually non-existent in 1931, such as Benue and Plateau, are now Christian majority. While the "core" northern states remain strongly Muslim, many Middle Belt states experienced a rapid religious transformation in the post-colonial period.

Another indicator of the rapidity of 20th-century religious change in Nigeria is the rate of church growth among the various denominations. From 1990 to 2000, Nigeria's churches grew 6.6 percent *per year* (Johnson 2007). While different denominations are stronger in certain parts of the country, the following four Pentecostal-charismatic churches are most prevalent in the north: Living Faith World Outreach Ministries, Redeemed Christian Church of God, Deeper Life Bible Church of Nigeria, and Mountain of Fire and Miracles Ministries. A smattering of other Pentecostal/Neo-Pentecostal charismatic churches such as the Assemblies of God are also among the major Christian denominations.

---

[18] Gaiya (2004) and Awolalu (2001) note similar though slightly lower figures for the Christian population in 2001 (at approximately 30 percent) and a higher percentage as adherents of traditional religions. Based on World Christian Encyclopedia data, Jenkins (2002, 167) also notes that neither the Muslim nor Christian adherents predominate in Nigeria. Similarly, Nwafor (2002, 25) estimates that 43 percent of the population are Christians and only 7 percent are adherents of traditional religions.

TABLE 2.1 *Percentage of Affiliated Christians in Select Northern Nigerian States over Time*

| Province | 1931 | 1952 | 1963 | 2010 |
|---|---|---|---|---|
| Adamawa | 0 | 3.2 | 14.3 | 25.0 |
| Bauchi | 0.1 | 1.6 | 3.2 | 15.0 |
| Benue | 0.2 | 6.9 | 41.2 | 73.0 |
| Borno | 0.0 | 0.6 | 2.0 | 20.0 |
| Kaduna | 0.0 | 7.8 | 25 | 35.0 |
| Kano | 0.0 | 0.4 | 1.0 | 8.0 |
| Katsina | 0.0 | 0.3 | 0.3 | 7.0 |
| Niger | 0.0 | 3.0 | 3.5 | 25.0 |
| Plateau | 0.5 | 12.9 | 20.0 | 60.0 |
| Sokoto | 0.0 | 0.5 | 0.3 | 5.0 |

Source: World Christian Database (Johnson 2007) and Crampton (2004).[19]

TABLE 2.2 *Major Christian Denominations in Northern Nigeria, Percentage of Growth/Year*

| Denomination | No. of Adherents (2010) | % Growth |
|---|---|---|
| Redeemed Christian Church of God | 1,451,000 | 23.94 |
| Living Faith World Outreach Centre | 622,000 | 20.25 |
| Deeper Life Bible Church | 1,147,000 | 10.07 |
| Evangelical Churches of West Africa | 5,410,000 | 7.68 |
| Assemblies of God in Nigeria | 2,900,000 | 8.86 |

Source: Johnson (2007).

Table 2.2, derived from the *World Christian Database*, highlights the rapid growth of these churches in Nigeria.

Among the traditional Protestant denominations, the Church of Christ in Nigeria (COCIN) and the Evangelical Church Winning All (ECWA) remain very strong in the Middle Belt and north.[20] These two denominations stem from missionary efforts that began in the first decade of the twentieth century. While they are still considered mainline evangelical

---

[19] Census data figures for 1931, 1952, and 1963 derived from Crampton (2004).
[20] ECWA was formerly the Evangelical Church of *West Africa*, but this name was changed in light of the denomination's expansion in church planting beyond West Africa.

denominations within the Protestant tradition, the Pentecostal-charismatic movement has heavily influenced them as well. Thus, the emphasis on being born-again can be found in these churches, with both charismatic and traditional forms of worship. However, these Protestant churches are less likely to run miracle/healing crusades or emphasize demon possession and prophecy, and they do not encourage speaking in tongues during services.

The data in Table 2.3, collected in cooperation with the ECWA headquarters in Jos Nigeria in 2011, offer a clear picture of the recent expansion of Christianity in 14 northern states within this one major northern Nigerian Protestant denomination alone. The data highlight very clearly that church planting grew far faster in the post-1970 period than prior, with 79 percent of ECWA congregations established since 1970 and accounting for over 2,000 churches.[21] Kaduna, Nasarawa, Plateau, and

TABLE 2.3 *Percentage of ECWA Congregations/Churches Established in Northern Nigeria Pre-1970 and Post-1970*[22]

|  | Total No. | Pre-1970 | Post-1970 | Unclear |
|---|---|---|---|---|
| Bauchi | 99 | 6 | 85 | 8 |
| Benue | 32 | 1 | 29 | 2 |
| FCT | 105 | 29 | 72 | 4 |
| Gombe | 130 | 28 | 82 | 20 |
| Gongola* | 12 | 0 | 8 | 4 |
| Jigawa | 19 | 4 | 13 | 2 |
| Kaduna | 789 | 174 | 520 | 95 |
| Kano | 41 | 1 | 26 | 14 |
| Katsina | 41 | 3 | 36 | 2 |
| Kogi | 49 | 18 | 31 | 0 |
| Kwara | 143 | 52 | 80 | 11 |
| Nasarawa | 426 | 85 | 297 | 44 |
| Niger | 243 | 24 | 150 | 69 |
| Plateau | 356 | 21 | 264 | 71 |
| Sokoto | 11 | 3 | 7 | 1 |
| Total N | 2,496 | 449 | 1700 | 347 |
| % of total | – | 21 | 79 | – |

* Gongola state was split into present Adamawa and Taraba states in 1991.

[21] This includes ECWA Evangelical Missionary Society (EMS) churches (i.e., established in Nigeria by Nigerian ECWA missionaries) and Prayer Houses.
[22] This congregation establishment data include establishment of EMU and Prayer Houses. Although there is some missing data, the above congregation data is likely close to full figures, as ECWA estimates that it has around 5,000 congregations in all of Nigeria. For just 14 states in northern Nigeria, I have accounted for 2,496 of the overall total.

Niger states reflect the most activity in ECWA church planting. I do not include the congregations for which church officials did not report their year of establishment, but it is likely that the percentage of congregations established since the 1970s would be even higher if these data were known.

In short, data collected in the field along with data from the *World Religion Database* and *Religion in the World Database* show clear evidence that not only has the number of adherents of Christianity in Nigeria rapidly expanded, Christianity has also grown rapidly in the pluralistic Middle Belt region between the predominantly Christian south and Muslim north where much of the inter-religious communal violence has been concentrated since the 1970s.

## Islam and Religious Change in Nigeria

The Muslim share of Nigeria's population, as evidenced in the data, has stayed fairly stable, since it was already the predominant religion among the tribes of the north prior to the arrival of Christianity and active evangelization. As the next section explains, Islam preceded the arrival of Christianity and gained preeminence in the north with the establishment of the Sokoto Caliphate and the rule of Usman dan Fodio. Indeed, Islam and the political rule of the Fulani went hand-in-hand, as conversion to Islam was one of the primary ways smaller tribes were assimilated into the political establishment. Yet, Islamic practice and belief has not been static in Nigeria over the past century. While the majority of Nigeria's Muslims are moderate in their religio-political orientation, some minority sects have adopted more radical teachings popularized by the global reform movements of the early and late 20th century. The Maitatsine movement, well-known for the intra-Muslim violence in northern states such as Kaduna and Bauchi in the early 1980s, adhered to a stricter interpretation of Islam and condemned the moderation of fellow Muslims and religious elite (Adesoji 2010; Campbell 2011, 52; Laremont 2011, 167–169; Falola and Heaton 2008, 206). Other radical groups or precursors of Maitatsine or Boko Haram have gone by the names Izala, Kala Kato, the Islamic Society of Nigeria (under El-Zakzaki), and the Nigerian Taliban (Adesoji 2011; Laremont 2011, 154–169; Falola 1998, 227–246). Gaining prominence since 2009, Boko Haram, the extremist terrorist organization based in the northeast, and breakaway sects such as Ansaru, also hold to a radical interpretation of Islam, increasingly employing more violent and larger-scale tactics in their efforts to purge Western secular influence and achieve "pure" Islamic rule in Nigeria. Although Christian sites or populations are occasionally targeted, it is Muslims who have faced the brunt of Boko Haram attacks. The tactics and goals of Boko Haram and offshoot movements have changed dramatically over time, but Muslims deemed "too moderate" have borne the brunt of the terrorist violence in states in the northeast such as Borno, Yobe, and Gombe. Although factors like political corruption and state weakness contribute to the conditions for Boko Haram's successful mobilization – e.g., the inability of the state to project security effectively throughout the country – the formation of Boko Haram is also directly tied to and clearly influenced by Islamic radicalization beyond its borders (Adesoji 2010, 101; 2011; Walker 2012; Perouse de Montclos 2014a; 2014b). This is most evident, for example, by Boko Haram's 2014 declaration of an Islamic caliphate in northeast Nigeria and its 2015 pledge of allegiance to the Islamic State, or ISIS.

In short, although Islam is the majority religion of ethno-tribal groups in the core northern states, competing over time with Christianity in the Middle Belt, Muslims in Nigeria do not comprise a homogeneous religious category. There are intra-religious divisions and debates that have sometimes spilled over into intra-religious violence, particularly with the mobilization of radical groups like the Maitatsine and Boko Haram. Before addressing contemporary religio-political divisions between Muslims and Christians generally speaking, however, the next two sections place recent inter-religious clashes in their historical context, addressing the politics of religion and religious change in Nigeria in the pre-colonial and colonial eras.

## POLITICS AND RELIGIOUS CHANGE IN THE PRE-COLONIAL PERIOD

The construction of religious identity as a category of belonging and political identity is not new in Nigerian history. The religious cleavages and conflict of the past three to four decades must be understood within a larger history of ethnicity and political competition. A brief foray into northern Nigeria's history is therefore necessary to begin to explain the puzzle of the Middle Belt – why some mixed Muslim and Christian communities have experienced inter-religious violence while others have remained peaceful.

## Arrival of Islam

The arrival of Islam in Nigeria during the Fulani conquest of Usman dan Fodio in the first decade of the 19th century ushered in profound sociopolitical change. Although Islam first came to Nigeria in the 13th or 14th century, it did not make significant inroads until much later (Crampton 2004, 7; Falola 1998). Its real ascendency began with the Jihad of dan Fodio in a region dominated at the time by forms of African Traditional Religion. With the subsequent establishment of the Sokoto Caliphate in the far north, the branches of Muslim Hausa and Fulani[23] rule extended over a large swath of northern Nigeria, gradually expanding and subduing the smaller northern ethno-tribal groups through Islamic religion and political power (Voll 1999, 535–536).

Spreading the Islamic faith served as the holy cause that justified the expansionist project and subsumed ethnic divisions during this period, and it did so rather effectively. Under dan Fodio, religion and rule went hand-in-hand, conquering and pacifying populations. In turn, the formation and solidification of the Sokoto Caliphate empire through conquest and assimilation elevated the Hausa-Fulani ethnic amalgamation and majority bloc to elite status. The Caliphate installed regional leaders or emirs in the various regions, who then paid homage to the Sultan of Sokoto. In turn, the political elite appealed to the Islamic faith as an authoritative force to legitimize Hausa-Fulani rule. Although, as Kukah (2003) argues, the Islam of the Sokoto Caliphate was more or less a veneer over underlying political and economic interests, it served its purpose. Political and economic imperatives were key motivations for the Caliphate's expansion, but religion was presented as the holy cause or justification, and it effectively overcame ethnic divisions. Islam was a powerful basis for political rule during this time, since it "served as a fulcrum for uniting the various people that it had converted in a way that transcended the ethnocentric confines of pre-Islamic relations in these diverse polities" (Kukah 2003, 2).

---

[23] Usman dan Fodio was a Fulani religious scholar. The Fulani and the Hausa became integrated over time, hence I generally adopt the "Hausa-Fulani" designation when referring to the empire of the Sokoto Caliphate and the dominant population in the largely Muslim north. As Adebanwi (2009, 354) notes, "The majority Hausa ethnic group and several minority ethnic groups in these areas were subsequently converted to Islam under the rule of the Fulani. The Fulani aristocrats adopted the Hausa language and Hausa culture in general, inter-married and related closely with the majority Hausa so much so that, even though a minority, they became identified with the Hausa as an ethnic-amalgam called, Hausa-Fulani – thus transforming them to a part of a majority group."

## Cohesion and Fragmentation

The religious change ushered in under the Caliphate thus served to unify much of northern Nigeria under a single political regime. The impact of the "Jihad" on the identity of northern Nigeria cannot be overstated. Religious identity and political imperatives constituted a single logic of governance. As Falola and Heaton (2008, 72) observe, "Culturally, local populations across the Sokoto Caliphate increasingly came to identify themselves primarily as Muslims and only secondarily as citizens of their local emirates" and this "left the impression on many that they lived in an Islamic state and therefore they were all unified by a common religion." Although there were cracks in the unity of northern Nigeria under the Sokoto Caliphate, the religio-political combination of Islamic rule brought about – either by force or willing conversion/submission – a level of cultural assimilation and political integration that rendered northern Nigeria "more culturally united than at any other time in its history, and this unity was based heavily on a shared experience of life in an Islamic state" (Falola and Heaton 2008, 73).

In parts of the Middle Belt region of the north, however, religio-political domination was not entirely achieved, and the foundation of the Caliphate began to show weaknesses in its ability to maintain effective control and governance. While the religious goals of the original Jihad may have been strong and driving, "[i]n seeking to expand its economic and political hegemonic spheres of influence, the caliphate leaders soon began to sacrifice the spiritual fervour that had necessitated the Jihad," as they "seemed more preoccupied with slavery, economic, and political expansionism than the spread of the faith" (Kukah 2003, 2). Further, although the area of the core north known as Hausaland was conquered by 1808 during the Fulani Jihad, the Hausa-Fulani did not completely pacify the ethno-tribal groups of the entire Middle Belt or north of present day Nigeria. "Right up to the 1820s," Crowder (1978, 78) notes, "there were pockets of resistance to Fulani rule." In the areas on the fringes of the north, adherents of African Traditional Religion and smaller ethno-tribal groups attempted to maintain their cultural and political autonomy, warding off Hausa-Fulani domination to the extent possible in occasional clashes. By the time of the colonial conquest, therefore, some areas of the north-central region (present day Middle Belt) were less culturally/religiously assimilated and less integrated into the Caliphate's political structure.

In sum, both cohesion and fragmentation characterized northern Nigeria by the beginning of the 20th century and the start of the British colonial pacification. The Sokoto Caliphate had successfully used its political acumen, structure, and religious creed under the Hausa-Fulani majority to assimilate or pacify many of the small ethno-tribal groups of the north. Pockets of resistance during Caliphate rule, however, persisted and required pacification under British colonial rule as indigenous ethnic groups continued to seek autonomy or some form of cultural independence. In 1900, the British defeated the Sokoto Caliphate and declared the British Protectorate of Northern Nigeria, but rather than change the administration of Hausa-Fulani rule in the north, the British system of Indirect Rule ultimately served to entrench rather than retract Muslim Hausa-Fulani rule. This British colonial strategy profoundly impacted the political and inter-tribal relations in northern Nigeria and the political wrangling and developments since.

## POLITICS AND RELIGIOUS CHANGE IN THE COLONIAL PERIOD

With the British defeat of the Sokoto Caliphate by 1900, the administration of the northern region fell to High Commissioner Sir Fredrick Lugard. Lugard oversaw the system of Indirect Rule after he "subdue[d] the Emirs and eliminate[d] the more distasteful features of their rule, warfare and slave-raiding," seeking out local elites or chiefs who could administer territory on behalf of the British (Crampton 2004, 28; Falola and Heaton 2008, 116–128; Mamdani 1996). The selection of chiefs, however, was not necessarily in keeping with local structures of authority, imbuing authority in many cases to a local figure who did not necessarily garner the respect of his local community and who, as both prosecutor and judge, did not always act in the community's best interests. As Mamdani (1996, 61–62) observes regarding this system of Indirect Rule or Native Authority,

> Its personnel functioned without judicial restraint and were never elected. Appointed from above, they held office so long as they enjoyed the confidence of their superiors. Their powers were diffuse, with little functional specificity ... Native Courts, Native Administration, and a Native Treasury – together crystallized the ensemble of powers merged in the office of the chief.

Under the British policy of Indirect Rule, it was ultimately the Hausa-Fulani or the Muslim emirs who continued to rule the northern region. Surveying the Caliphate's institutional political and administrative structure, the British deemed proxy rule through the Hausa-Fulani majority the most conducive strategy for maintaining their hold on northern Nigeria. Proxy rule avoided the otherwise acute challenge of creating a completely new system of rule without the necessary institutional gestation period, one that would be foreign to the socio-political and cultural context of the region. By working within the existing framework of ethno-tribal groups, the British could keep violent resistance and the drain on resources to a minimum, so the logic went. "Finding the Muslim states had centralized and bureaucratic socio-political institutions," notes Turaki (1993, 54), "Lugard decided to incorporate them into his system of Native Administration, if only modified and developed." The British, therefore, worked primarily with the Hausa-Fulani elite, viewing their social and political system as more advanced and civilized than that of the many "pagan" ethno-tribal groups in the north. In short, it was in British interest to build a good relationship with northern Muslim emirs, protecting their proxy rule from subversion and guaranteeing respect for the dominance of Islam in the north.

## Consequences of Indirect Rule

The British policy of Indirect Rule had far-reaching consequences for the relationship between the Hausa-Fulani and other ethno-tribal groups in the north. Areas of the north that had not previously been subject to or had long resisted Hausa-Fulani rule now suddenly came under the rule of the Muslim emirs whom the British placed in authority over the non-Muslim groups of the north. For example, the people of Southern Zaria (now southern Kaduna state) had been fighting to retain independence from Hausa-Fulani rule prior to British arrival and were "in a state of war with the Fulani rulers of Zaria and Jemaa" (Turaki 1993, 97–98). Through British Indirect Rule, then, Hausa-Fulani elite solidified their authority over the local ethno-tribal and non-Muslim groups in this area and other non-assimilated and integrated areas of the north. The local populations perceived this as an affront, elevating and bestowing upon an ethno-tribal Muslim group political power that they did not previously hold over other local groups (Turaki 2010, 169). Indeed, Indirect Rule dismissed the traditional forms of rule and chieftaincy long adhered to by local ethno-tribal groups. Nonetheless, resistance by these groups was kept at bay by the peril of British guns. As Turaki (1993, 108) notes,

What kept down the uprisings of the non-Muslim groups was the fear of the ruthless British punitive patrols. Hausa-Fulani rule was seen by British political officers as a 'divine rule' which must be supported and protected ... The British concept of law and order was strongly attached to Fulani rule and any self-determination was viewed as rebellion and lawlessness. Thus, the colonial political system did not permit self-determination or practical expressions.

## Christian Missions and the Protection of Muslim Rule

Regarding its policy on religious expansion and conversion, British colonial rule was paradoxical. To promote commerce and civilization, the British government often supported Christian missionary activity in its colonies. In the case of northern Nigeria, however, it adopted a different tack in order to protect the stability of governance under the majority Hausa-Fulani Muslims; the British limited or prohibited Christian evangelization in the north. Some background regarding the pre-colonial and colonial era expansion of Christianity in Nigeria will provide context for understanding this colonial policy.

Christian missions first arrived in Nigeria not with the British, but, rather, during the mid-19th century under the auspices of the Anglican Church Missionary Society. These missionary "expeditions" by the Anglican Church, and later by other missionary societies, earned this west coast region of Africa the less-than-welcoming title "White Man's Grave" due to the high mortality risk (Crampton 2004, 19). Generally, missionary expeditions into the interior of present-day Nigeria were more effectively led and staffed by indigenous converts, such as Samuel Crowther, a freed slave and returnee who worked with the Church Missionary Society (CMS). As Crampton (2004, 89) recounts, "Africans themselves dominated missionary activity in the Nigerian region, communicating with local chiefs and leaders about the benefits Christianity could bring to their societies."

Toward the end of the 19th century, other major missionary operations such as the Sudan Interior Mission (SIM) arrived, which later formed the Nigerian-led ECWA denomination – a major Protestant presence in the north today.[24] SIM set up operation in 1893 and was "among the first pioneering Christian missions in Northern Nigeria and, in later years, it

---

[24] SIM now goes by the name "Serving in Missions," to reflect a non-regional focus. Other missionary organizations that eventually came to northern Nigeria include the following: Sudan United Mission, Church of the Brethren Mission, United Missionary Society, Roman Catholic Church, Dutch Reformed Church Mission, and the Lutheran Mission (see Turaki 1999, 3).

became one of the largest, covering a wider geographical territory than any other single Mission in Northern Nigeria" (Turaki 1999, 3). Church of Christ in Nigeria (COCIN) churches stemmed from the Sudan United Mission (SUM), another organized missionary effort that began work in Nigeria around 1904 and subsequently became one of the major Protestant denominations in the north. According to a minister in COCIN leadership, the sole reason the missionary organization was established was to "prevent Islam from sweeping across the whole of Nigeria."[25] Similarly, one local historian explained that

> the various groups of missionaries that came to Northern Nigeria had a common agenda, which was to check the further advance of Islam in the Sudan. Okay? It doesn't matter whether they were the American branch, or the British branch, or the Danish branch, and so on. They served a common purpose. And the protection of this region and the fear of Islam became a strong, if you like, ideology, among the Christians. This is what they imbibed – the fear of Islamic domination. And so on. So, [as] much as they cooperated with the government, much as they accepted northern region and so on and so forth there was this basic tension beneath the apparatus of government.[26]

Like the initial arrival of Islam in Nigeria, however, these Christian missionary efforts did not take a strong foothold in the northern part of Nigeria initially, and this was due to the colonial policy that deliberately limited Christian missions in an effort to maintain a stable system of British Indirect Rule through Muslim elites in the north.

What was the nature of these restrictions? Although Lugard maintained a good relationship with the missionary community, political expediency demanded that he limit missionary work in northern Nigeria, to the chagrin of the missionaries. In exchange for the cooperation of the newly installed Muslim rulers, he promised them that the "Government would not interfere with the Muslim religion" (Crampton 2004, 45). Christian missions were only encouraged or allowed by the colonial authorities under certain conditions, and, at other times, were explicitly prohibited in the north. One exception was missionaries who were allowed to work in the leper colonies in the north toward the mid-1930s, but this was contingent upon them not attempting to proselytize the population (Crampton 2004, 64). Missionaries often faced resistance, if not from the Muslim emirs, then from the British authorities who feared that allowing Christian missionaries to evangelize in predominantly

---

[25] Anonymous(D), interview by Laura Thaut Vinson, Jos, Plateau State, April 15, 2011.
[26] Anonymous(E), interview by Laura Thaut Vinson, Jos, Plateau State, September 7, 2011.

Muslim areas would jeopardize the political agenda of the British and their relationship with the northern emirs.

There was, nonetheless, some limited space allowed for missionary work in the north. Missionaries made some inroads among adherents of African Traditional Religion on the fringes of the Hausa-Fulani area of rule, primarily in what is now the Middle Belt of Nigeria. Indeed, "[g]enerally the entry of missions into the purely 'pagan' independent areas was welcomed by the government," as a civilizing force, undertaking civilizing efforts that the British administration could not afford (Crampton 2004, 64). In the non-Muslim areas under Muslim rulers, however, the tensions were starker between the missionaries, the administration, and local rulers. With some exceptions, Christian missionary evangelization made Muslim rulers nervous, as it was seen as a threat to their expansion and rule. This should come as no surprise, since the pre-colonial rule in northern Nigeria was founded on religio-political authority. British policy – the proscription against Christianity spreading in the non-Muslim areas subject to Muslim emirs – thereby gave a tacit go-ahead for Islamization. The Hausa-Fulani political establishment was able to elevate its system of law and courts, for example, over the non-Muslim population. Thus, as Crampton (2004, 67) concludes, "This policy of upholding the authority of the Fulani District Heads undoubtedly gave great prestige to Islam and assisted in its spread in areas where the 'pagans' were not especially hostile to the Fulani."

~

In sum, while Christianity and colonialism are often spoken of as two sides of the same coin, the history of colonialism in Nigeria dispels this notion. Religious imperatives were secondary to the British political agenda in the north. Although missions and commerce worked together to create inroads in the north in the first part of the 19th century, missionaries were restricted and few in number up until the 1960s when Nigeria achieved independence and the British policy against evangelizing the north ended.

In general, the pre-colonial sacralization of political rule and the colonial maintenance of the precedent integrally shaped ethno-tribal and inter-religious relationships in Nigeria. This historical antecedent did not determine the religious change and rapid growth of Christianity in the latter part of the 20th century, and it did not cause the emergence of inter-religious violence in the pluralistic Middle Belt. It explains, however, how religious identity was integral in constituting political identity in prior periods and how it shaped the boundaries of religio-political identity in Nigeria as a whole by independence in 1960.

## POLITICS AND RELIGIOUS CHANGE IN INDEPENDENT NIGERIA

Religious change in the latter half of the 20th century in Nigeria is central to understanding the construction of Muslim–Christian identity as the locus of political contention and communal violence since the 1980s. This religious change involved not merely growth in the number of adherents, but also the emergence of a more educated and politically influential Christian political class, as well as a doctrinal about-face among denominations toward active political engagement, particularly with the rapid spread of Pentecostal-charismatic Christianity and the establishment of the Christian Association of Nigeria (CAN). A radical and violent strand of Islam also emerged with devastating consequences by the beginning of the 1980s. Finally, as this section elucidates, a series of religio-political disputes since the 1970s – including disputes over Nigeria's membership in the Organization of the Islamic Conference[27] (OIC) and the implementation of Sharia in northern states – served to reify political identities along ethno-religious lines.

### Barriers Removed: Missions and Christian Education

The removal of a restrictive evangelization policy in the post-colonial period ushered in significant religious change in Nigeria. Christianity made greater inroads in the north among the non-Muslim population as missionaries (particularly indigenous ones) took the Gospel to the north and also brought new education opportunities. Northern Nigerians trained in missionary schools came into positions of leadership in their local communities and in national administration. As Crampton (2004, 67) notes,

> In the early days it is doubtful if many people ever thought that the results of this missionary activity would constitute a threat to the authority of the rulers. The Missions made converts very slowly and the first Christian groups seemed small and insignificant ... In some areas the 'pagans' were so difficult and dangerous that the areas were declared 'closed' and missionaries were not

---

[27] The name was changed and is now the Organization of Islamic Cooperation.

allowed to enter. As these gradually become [sic] 'open' missionaries were anxious to enter them so as not to come after Muslim emissaries.

Over time, Christian missionaries did make inroads, and this, in combination with the political ambition of the northern Nigerian Muslim elite, created new incentives for religio-political competition and fear-mongering. Both Christianity and Islam began to grow, ethno-religious identity took on political significance as a tool of political loyalty and belonging, and ultimately, Muslim–Christian identity became a symbol of cleavage and fault line of communal violence.

Prior to independence, Christian identity was not a form of social mobilization or political empowerment in northern Nigeria, and what little Christian missionary education there was in the non-Muslim areas was largely oriented toward evangelization, church-planting, and spiritual training, spurning political or non-spiritual education. The majority of non-Muslims also did not have access to the better, largely Muslim-dominated and British-supported northern schools. While the northern Muslim political elite already feared the political consequences of the growth of Christianity as early as the 1940s, those concerns were quelled by the fact that the non-Muslim populations did not have the means to challenge their status, especially since the British forces could easily quell any sort of uprising.

With the expansion of education by the 1950s to the non-Muslim population and the change in the educational approach of the mission schools, greater social and political awareness and opportunity for advancement came to non-Muslim groups. Enhanced access to education led to increased social mobility and the possibility to escape from the marginalization associated with non-Muslim or traditional African religious identity.[28] The articulation and mobilization of greater political demands and rights followed. As Turaki (1993, 119) notes,

Christianity and education were instrumental in the development of political consciousness and self-determination. The people became awakened to the oppressive and autocratic rule of the Fulani rulers ... Their silence, passivity, submission and acquiescence soon gave way to open protests, rebellion and agitation for self-rule and independence. Their social development through

---

[28] As Turaki (1993, 117) notes, "It must be borne in mind that the rapid growth of education in Southern Zaria and the non-Muslim areas in general should not be interpreted to mean that the [non-Muslim groups] had a head-start in education than the Muslim groups ... a good secular education did not really start in the non-Muslim areas until the 1950s."

Christianity and education had resulted in the development of a new ethnic identity, which could no longer tolerate their prescribed subordinated role and status under both colonial and Fulani rule.

Indeed, as Turaki (1993, 110) further observes, increased education, adoption of Christianity, and new political awareness led to greater agitation, since the political marginalization of the non-Muslim groups did not also change in tandem; rather, their aspirations were kept in check by the British colonial authorities.

This gradual shift in the religious contours of the Middle Belt region following independence, therefore, represented a threat to the power of the Muslim northern establishment vis-à-vis the south during the debates about the regional lines of authority in Nigeria. A historian at the University of Jos explains that

> the missionaries then used all sorts of facilities – dispensaries ... schools, carpentry work, artisan institutions and so on, which quickly attracted people to them, such that by independence, a core educated group had emerged in these minority areas that [were] Christian. And, inevitably, this core group was at once the political elite. They were the politicians of the lower minority groups.[29]

The response of the north and colonial regime was to co-opt the Middle Belt and non-Muslim areas of northern Nigeria with promises of greater rights and representation. These promises proved empty, however, and reinforced fears in the post-colonial period of an Islamization of northern Nigeria to the detriment of the increasingly Christian population. The political activism of some educated in the restricted Christian missionary schools created tensions in areas such as southern Zaria even prior to independence, as the "rise of new identity, political consciousness and aspirations imposed a serious threat to the legitimacy of Hausa-Fulani rule and hegemony" (Turaki 1993, 97). In another example, Christian indigenous leaders instigated the Movement for a Middle Belt Zone – known at its creation in 1949 as the Non-Muslim League and then in 1950 as the Middle Zone League – that pressed for a Middle Belt region autonomous from the Northern Region (Barnes 2009, 242). Such efforts threatened the political superiority and power of the northern elite, and the British sought to quell such movements through a policy of co-option in some cases, assuring religious freedom to the non-Muslim Christian groups that feared Islamization.[30]

---

[29] Anonymous(E), interview by Laura Thaut Vinson, Jos, Plateau State, September 7, 2011.

[30] One example of the attempted cooption is that of Sir Ahmadu Bello, the first premier of northern Nigeria and the Sardauna of Sokoto, whose speeches were meant to re-assure Christian groups that they would have social and religious rights within a Northern

Ultimately, shifts in the religious and political terrain of northern Nigeria did not slow following independence. The about-face by Ahmadu Bello, the Sardauna or Sultan of Sokoto, in the 1960s from a policy of preaching religious tolerance and respect to preaching the necessity of conversion to Islam was none too reassuring to non-Muslims and Christians. At the same time, the expansion of missionary work brought to the fore a new Christian political elite with new demands. The Pentecostal-charismatic Christian revival that gained significant religious ground in the north in the 1970s and 1980s (following the devastating Biafran ethnic civil war), as well as a series of religio-political events, only enhanced the perception of a Muslim–Christian identity cleavage in Nigerian politics.

## The Pentecostal-Charismatic Revival

In post-colonial Nigeria, the removal of restrictions on Christian missionary activity in the north along with the Pentecostal-charismatic revival of the 1970s and 1980s opened a space for the politicization of ethno-religious identity in national politics and raised the specter of inter-religious conflict. The increased political presence of Christians (and the politicization of religion in general) sacralized political contestation in Nigeria as a whole. Religious identity could now span and unite different ethno-tribal divisions, particularly among the formerly non-Muslim groups of the Middle Belt and far northern states. The religious change of this period enhanced the perception that political conflict in Nigeria is a battle between religious kingdoms.

The beginning of the major Christian religious surge in Nigeria occurred not long after independence when a new Christian movement began to sweep the south. The Pentecostal-charismatic movement found fertile ground in southern Nigeria in the 1960s and subsequently began to spread to the north in the 1970s. As Falola and Heaton (2008, 14) observe,

This period witnessed a resurgence of global Islamism and Charismatic and Pentecostal growth worldwide, leaving significant influence in Nigeria. These trends affected the religious terrain and gave great impetus to identity consciousness and protestations as most religious adherents became radicalized

Region. His tune changed, however, after the political movement had been co-opted and pacified. In the 1960s, Ahmadu Bello went on religious preaching campaigns proclaiming the necessity of conversion to Islam.

and easily mobilizable. This period witnessed the emergence of radical and politically motivated religious groups and fellowships across Nigeria, particularly in Northern Nigeria.

In the south, the movement took a different form from that in the north, however. The revival started among university students who were said to have experienced an "outpouring of the Holy Spirit," and it became so widespread that the movement infused the more conservative mainline evangelical denominations. "The Christian revival in the early 1960s [New Life for All]," according to a local Nigerian scholar, "cut across *all* Christian denominations," such that people "came together in the evening in wards for praying and evangelism; outreach teams went door to door, village to village, town to town, region to region."[31]

While the movement attracted large followings from other denominations in the south and was primarily student-led, it was treated with suspicion and rejected by the mainline Protestant denominations. In the north, however, the revival in the 1970s broke out *within* the more conservative mainline denominations. The emphasis was not on Pentecostalism *per se*, but on becoming "Born Again," a new experiential revelation of Jesus Christ. One local religious scholar recounts how Eternal Love Winning Africa (ELWA) Radio, a station run by SIM – one of the oldest missionary organization in Nigeria – was instrumental in instigating the movement in the north. A scholar of religion in Nigeria described the radio's impact as "powerful ... It brought about revival in the Middle Belt ... there were large conversions – non-believers, Muslims, traditional religious adherents converting."[32] Subsequently, northern leaders and students formed organizations such as the Fellowship of Christian students, furthering the advance of what came to be known as the Pentecostal or Pentecostal-charismatic movement. Even among young people in the Anglican and Catholic churches, a Pentecostal-charismatic movement emerged. In terms of Pentecostalism's lingering influence on the Anglican Church today, it is "very evangelical."[33]

Not all of the denominations welcomed the revival in the north, but it profoundly influenced them. Reflecting on the emergence of the Pentecostal movement in northern Nigeria, one expert on the COCIN churches noted, "COCIN was scared." "A strange thing happened in 1972," he continued, "Gindiri, normally considered the Jerusalem of COCIN," experienced a "sudden outpouring of the Holy Spirit. People

---

[31] Anonymous(F), interview by Laura Thaut Vinson, Jos, Plateau State, March 1, 2011.
[32] Ibid., Anonymous(F), interview.   [33] Ibid., Anonymous(G), interview.

were led by the Holy Spirit, and God was speaking to a number of people. And the movement spread from Gindiri to Bauchi area, to Jos area, to parts of the Middle Belt."[34] Although mainline churches became suspicious of the movement, the Pentecostal-charismatic revival continued to strongly influence traditional Protestant churches.[35]

## The Revival Spurs Christianity's Expansion

Whatever the mainline hesitancy toward Pentecostal-charismatic Christianity, a number of new churches sprung from the movement in the 1970s and grew at enormous rates in both southern and northern Nigeria. The revival spread across all denominations, particularly in the south, and led to the emergence of new indigenous-led churches, such as Redeemed Christian Church, Deeper Life Church, and other mega-church movements that spread to the north. Religious entrepreneurs founded more than thirty Pentecostal-charismatic denominations, and some have established thousands of church congregations throughout the country.[36] For example, according to the World Christian Database, Deeper Life Bible Church – one of the fastest-growing independent denominations in the north and south since 1970 – has around 11,000 congregations. The Redeemed Christian Church of God, established in the 1950s and also strong in the north, boasts approximately 1.4 million members even with only 1500 congregations. Living Faith World Outreach, founded in 1980, has over 1250 churches and more than 620,000 members (Johnson 2007).

---

[34] Ibid., Anonymous(D), interview.
[35] While the initial sentiment of COCIN toward the movement was positive, believing that the hand of God was moving in some way among their churches, feelings soon changed. "By the end of 1972," a COCIN leader noted, "it was misused" (Anonymous D). That is, the church soon found that pastors or congregants were falsely claiming things in the name of the Holy Spirit or God, falsely speaking in tongues, or falsely demonstrating the Spirit's power. In general, "the mainline response was suspicion. All of them were suspicious of the movement except for the organized African churches" (Anonymous F). Note that the African organized churches are also called African Independent Churches and strongly influenced by African traditional religious practices. Within COCIN churches, the movement had more or less fizzled out by the end of 1974 and there was "not much presence of Pentecostalism in COCIN" (Anonymous D). Yet, despite the denomination's suspicion of the movement, the Pentecostal-charismatic influence can still be found in up to one-fourth of the urban COCIN churches, estimates this COCIN leader.
[36] The Aladura church, although still witnessing strong growth, is mainly concentrated in the southwest and its growth has declined since its heights in the 1930s. The new Pentecostal/charismatic churches have outpaced the Aladura church.

One of the innovations of the movement is that anyone who feels inspired by God to start his or her own church or to take the Gospel to a new area can do so without seeking the permission of a hierarchical authority or following a cumbersome process. The spread of the Gospel, through whatever means, is the goal. Thus, it is not surprising to see new "churches" suddenly springing up on street corners on a daily basis – with tacked-up signs, loud and charismatic music, and effusive preaching striking up at any hour, day or night. One of the more unique features of this phenomenon is the innovation and creativity of the pastors in distinguishing or naming their upstart churches. Some of the more notable ones that researchers of the Pentecostal and Charismatic Research Centre in Jos have come across include: Satan in Trouble Ministries, Holy Ghost Earthquake Commotion Ministries Inc., Guided Missiles Church, Real Fire Ubiquitous Ministries, Last Battle Prayer War Ministry, and His Battle Axe Foundation Ministries.[37]

The trend is remarkable, considering that prior to the 1960s, there were less than ten official and independent Pentecostal-charismatic denominations functioning in Nigeria, and these tended to be classical Pentecostals; that is, their emphasis was on individual holiness and strict moral living, and they did not reflect the emphasis on divine healing, speaking in tongues, prosperity, and charismatic worship that emerged with the revival of the 1960s and 1970s. The fastest-growing and largest Pentecostal-charismatic churches are by and large far outstripping their more conservative Protestant counterparts in terms of growth rates. The Assemblies of God, ECWA, Baptist conventions, Methodist, and Apostolic churches have more than a million members each, but they have had more than half a century's head-start on the Pentecostal churches in some cases.

Finally, international influence, although important in furthering the revival, was not the cause of the religious phenomenon and its rapid growth. Indeed, as one local religious scholar explains, "It didn't start as 'Pentecostal;' the name Pentecostal came later" once it was realized that the revival exhibited characteristics or the "style" of Pentecostalism as found in other countries.[38] Following the revival's outbreak, leaders made the connection with the Pentecostal movement outside of Nigeria. Because the mainline churches reacted with suspicion toward the movement, leaders of the new movement appealed to Pentecostal leaders in other countries for their leadership. Consequently, "the Western Pentecostal

---

[37] Courtesy of the Nigeria Pentecostal and Charismatic Research Centre, University of Jos.
[38] Ibid., Anonymous(F), interview.

church leaders started interacting with Nigeria. They provided the leadership, structure, style, and form which was adopted."[39] When the Western evangelists came to Nigeria, Nigerians then adopted their preaching and teaching style. The "crusade," for example, a Christian event usually held at stadiums or other large parks, is a Western import designed to attract and covert thousands of people at one time through open-air sermonizing.[40] Thus, "when this wave of Pentecostalism came in, people already were prepared to accept it. The Student Union and the [Fellowship of Christian Students] easily accepted the message, style, and emphasis. [Their revival movement] was no different from Pentecostalism."[41] The arrival of Pentecostalism, or the "Born-Again" movement, therefore, was not a Western imperial import. It was an indigenous Nigerian movement that then merged with the international Pentecostal-charismatic revival and subsequently connected with and benefited from the Pentecostal leaders in the West.

### Explaining the Growth and Success of the Movement

What explains why this religious movement took root? Was it, as adherents claim, due to the "outpouring of the Holy Spirit" among the population at this particular point in history, or did the new Christian movement provide answers to the dire socio-economic and political plight of the average struggling Nigerian? The assumptions underlying one's ontology will influence the response, but a number of factors shaped the strong appeal of the Pentecostal-charismatic movement in Nigeria.

As scholars of the global Pentecostal-charismatic resurgence have noted, the wave of Pentecostalism that took root at the beginning of the 1970s in many countries and the Neo-Pentecostalism that emerged in the 1980s provided, or at least *claimed* to provide, answers to the socio-economic and political trials faced by Nigerians and others (Marshall 2009; Duffy-Toft, Philpott, and Shah 2011; Miller, Sargeant, and Flory 2013). Furthermore, the charismatic style of worship and the beliefs regarding spiritual and physical life fit well within the spiritual worldview and practices of African Traditional Religion (Stinton 2004). Both

---

[39] Ibid., Anonymous(F), interview.
[40] Note, however, that the conversion results of such crusades are unclear – whether there have actually been "thousands" of conversions at Nigerian crusade events or whether the attendees are primarily Christians even when hosted in cities with a large or majority Muslim population, such as Kaduna or Kano.
[41] Ibid., Anonymous(F), interview.

personal spiritual and social transformation can be achieved through the "re-birth" that the movement preaches, and the supernatural can also be tapped for power over everything from invisible demons to the ever-present and gut-wrenching poverty faced by the average Nigerian.

In a cultural context in which the spiritual is intimately bound up with people's understanding of their daily struggles, it is not surprising that a message of hope and promise of God's power to overcome harmful spiritual forces and life trials would find reception among a vast segment of Nigerians. When oil prices stagnated at the end of the 1970s, the Nigerian economy and people suffered severely, and political leaders failed to deliver the socio-economic and political stability Nigerians expected. These socio-economic and political travails continue today. As Falola and Heaton (2008, 221) note, "The charismatic movement offers an alternative path to social and spiritual well-being, and attracts members by addressing people's needs for community development, physical, mental, and spiritual healing, and the hope of prosperity in this life and the next, all of which the Nigerian state has been unable to provide." What is perhaps most interesting is that this phenomenon of Pentecostal-charismatic revival is not unique to Nigeria; across Africa, Latin America, and the Global South, this brand and message of Christianity has grown or been rapidly "poured out" since the 1970s.

## Politics of the Religious Change

The early Pentecostal churches in Nigeria prior to the "Neo-Pentecostal" or new Pentecostal-charismatic wave largely emphasized personal holiness and individual salvation, eschewing a political agenda or political involvement. Christian leaders taught that conversion, prayer, individual transformation and holiness would result in social transformation that would infuse the conduct of politics. This "holiness" emphasis characterizes what is now referred to as the "traditional" or classic Pentecostal denominations, but the Pentecostal-charismatic wave introduced a theological shift. A new, more political face of Christianity emerged in combination with an emphasis on personal prosperity – the "health and wealth" or "name it and claim it" gospel. "While the charismatic movement remained largely apolitical throughout the 1970s," notes Falola and Heaton (2008, 221), "by the 1980s charismatic churches were beginning to take an active part in Nigerian civil society, lobbying the Nigeria government to be more responsive to the needs of the Christian community."

And, it seemed, there was good cause for the reformulation of the Christian's role in politics and the abandonment of an apolitical view of church and politics. Corruption, poverty, unemployment, and political scandal were rife, especially with the fall in oil prices in the 1970s and the ensuing economic crisis that Nigeria and many other developing countries experienced. Hence, many Nigerians turned to a gospel that claimed to hold the answer to their problems and that went beyond an individualistic spiritualism to call for godly transformation of politics and society as a whole. It was during this period, therefore, that both Muslim and Christian leaders began to form religio-political organizations and that religious identity became a salient and useful national and local *political* category, politicized by both religious and political elite. In tandem with the religious changes and sacralization of politics, inter-religious or ethno-religious communal violence began to shake northern Nigeria in the latter part of the 1980s.

This politicization is evident on any given Sunday in Nigerian churches. Not only is the church claiming a political voice, it is actively pressing for and equipping Christians to participate in politics. Attending a Sunday worship service early in 2011 at a prominent Protestant church in Jos, Plateau state, this dynamic was evident. The special speaker was a former pastor and local political representative who spoke on the topic of Christians and politics. After briefly noting the calling of God for him to be in politics, he highlighted the binary between the way of God and the way of evil outlined in Scripture. "The Bible is so much a book of conflict," he noted, wherein the "most basic conflict of life is a conflict between God and evil ... armies are arrayed on both sides ... you are either in one or the other," and, "if you don't have the spirit of God, you are on the side of the devil." Politics, he argued, is the arena in which this struggle between God/good and evil is played out.

The crux of his message was that it is the duty of the church to raise up Christian leaders who can go into politics. One of the failures of the church, he noted, is that it "has never been successful in taking over the power, privilege, resources, and commanding heights in our land ... Let's not deceive ourselves that God is not interested in what happens in Jos, in political parties ... God is not here to take sides, He is here to take over." Otherwise, he emphasized, the church risks the danger of being "over-run." The connection between a thriving church and political activism was clear from his message: "When God raises [people into politics] we are at the threshold of a great revival," he urged, since "God's purpose is to establish and defend godly rule in Plateau State and all of the world."

"I am convinced that the biggest resource God has for transforming this country is the local church," he concluded.

Similarly, pastors emphasized the political role of the church during a March 27, 2011, Sunday service at another prominent Protestant church in Jos. At the end of the service, a pastor announced the ongoing "political education sessions" the church was hosting and instructed congregants to pick up the manual "The Christian Becoming a Political Leader," written by Rev. Dr. Pandang Yamsat. The foreword to the manual, written by Nde Alexander Molwus of the People's Democratic Party (PDP) in Plateau state, reflects on the religio-political change that has taken place in Nigeria and infused churches since the 1970s – the shift from a "kingdom-come" and holiness-oriented theology to a "this kingdom" orientation that preaches active Christian engagement in this-world politics. He argues the following:

> In the past, the Church was lukewarm in elections and electioneering campaigns in Nigeria. However, the ever growing destruction of li[fe] and property and Church building at any electioneering, has made the church to be focused and interested in what the State and its statutes are doing, so as not to get more churches burnt and more members dying on such unnecessary clashes! The Church and its leadership cannot involve itself in partisan politics, but it cannot shy away from what happens in the political arena and in the corridor of government since they affect the church for good or bad. (Yamsat 2011, v)

To further illustrate the major shift in the orientation of Christians to politics in Nigeria, it is worth quoting at length the introduction written by Rev. Yamsat (2011, 1, 2–3). He notes,

> In spite of the significance of politics and political leadership in the life of a people, right from the time of the Colonialists until the seventies, politics was not thought to be for Christians but for unbelievers. Very few Christians ventured to go into politics then and those who did were not thought to be true Christians ... However, if the church would impact the globalized world of the twenty first century, it must take politics and political leadership seriously ... It is for this reason that the Holy Bible says that political leadership is instituted by God for the purpose of caring for his creation, of which human beings are the chief beneficiaries. That is why the church can no longer shy away from politics ... To change the trend of politics for good in Nigeria, the church leaders must encourage faithful Christian men and women that God has bestowed with the gift of political leadership to go into partisan politics, while the church leaders participate in non-partisan politics by speaking in favour of the rights of their members, their rights to vote and be voted for and by speaking against any form of injustice and oppression in the land. It is the responsibility of church leadership to sensitize Christians on politics and political leadership so as to enable them [to] play politics according to the teaching of the word of God, without which they will never succeed in the world of sin. Failure to do so, the church will

wake up one day to see that it can no longer worship in its beautiful and gigantic cathedrals and preach the gospel on the streets and villages of its land freely ... The handwriting is already clear in Muslim dominated States.

Regarding the question of whether Christians should elect non-Christians (i.e., Muslims), Yamsat also argues, "They must first of all know him or her to have a good record of fighting for the unity of the country and that such a person is not linked to the Islamic terrorism that has been a thorn in the flesh of this country since the eighties and not linked to the constant movements to turn Nigeria into an Islamic State" (Yamsat 2011, 35). Apart from this, he directs Christians to vote for whoever has the best interests of the country and its people at heart without discrimination on the basis of ethnic or other identities.

A similar message was preached from the pulpit at another prominent Protestant Jos church on April 3, 2011. Regarding the upcoming elections, the pastor instructed his congregants that "whosoever the Holy Spirit lays it on your heart to vote for, vote." Yet, he then quickly added, "But He cannot tell you to vote a Muslim. He can't." In other words, congregants were instructed to vote for whoever they want based on their assessment of his/her merits, except that they are clearly voting against God if they vote for a Muslim.

This trend of Christian leaders encouraging active political participation and organization, as well as educating church members, is not unique to Nigeria. It is a trend that would have been unheard of in church circles prior to the 1970s, however. Further, as the above examples illustrate, the emphasis on the role of churches in doing battle against the spread of Islam and Islamic political power in the country is now rampant and a central political goal. Fears of the religious other, well-founded or not, are common on both sides of the religious divide. From the perspective of the Muslim community in the north, the growth of many independent Pentecostal-charismatic churches gives the impression of an advancing Christianity that is intent on converting Muslims and claiming more political rights and power in the north. On the other hand, the rise of radical Islamic sects in northern Nigeria (e.g., Boko Haram) and the expansion of Sharia to 12 northern Nigerian states conveys the impression that a new Jihad is being waged, intent on overwhelming the Middle Belt, pushing south, dominating national politics, and instituting Islamic law in the whole of Nigeria. These views are both at extreme ends of the discourse, but they are not uncommon. A series of events in Nigeria since the 1970s enhanced the perception of a war, or at least fierce competition, between Islam and Christianity for the religious and political domination of Nigeria. Although the causes of Muslim–Christian communal violence may be rooted in non-religious socio-economic and political dynamics, the violence is increasingly characterized by a Muslim-versus-Christian narrative.

## RELIGIO-POLITICAL EVENTS AND THE MUSLIM–CHRISTIAN CLEAVAGE

By the 1980s, both Christianity and Islam constituted nearly an equal portion of the population. The percentage of the population ascribing to African Traditional Religion declined to single digits, and Christianity flourished in parts of northern Nigeria (and Middle Belt states in particular) where missionaries and churches targeted their evangelism efforts. A series of events and political disputes heightened tensions and encouraged the politicization of religion.

### The Issue of Sharia

One of the most significant issues that sparked tension between the Muslim and Christian communities occurred in the late 1970s when Muslim majority northern states began to press for the inclusion of a federal-level Sharia appeals courts in the 1978 constitution. These efforts raised the ire of Christian political leaders and concern, especially in the Middle Belt, about the "Islamization" of the country (Falola and Heaton 2008, 205). The debate over Sharia did not end in 1978, however. After the death of General Abacha and with the return to civilian rule in 1999, Sharia was again back on the table when Governor Sani of Zamfara state proclaimed a constitutional basis for the adoption of Sharia criminal law in the state's judicial system. Prompted by Zamfara's example, 11 other northern states followed suit from 2000 to 2001 (Laremont 2011, 178–181; Campbell 2011, 53).

These events and the debate galvanized the Christian community. In their view, this move directly challenged the constitutional guarantee that "[t]he Government of the Federation or of a State shall not adopt any religion as State Religion," which was put in place to protect the religious rights and ensure the equal treatment of a nearly evenly split Muslim–Christian Nigeria (*Constitution of the Federal Republic of Nigeria*, Ch. 1, PII, Sec. 10; see also Gaiya 2004, 370). The marginalization of Christians in the north was at stake, in the view of Christian elite.

Muslims, by contrast, argued that Sharia would not apply to or affect Christians, and Muslims' desires for the free practice of their religion should be respected.

Whatever the case, the adoption of Sharia criminal law in the north drew the outrage of the Christian religious community and resulted in violent protests and significant loss of life in what became known as the deadly Sharia riots (Paden 2008, 58). Emphasizing the significance of these events, Gwamna (2010, 32) notes that "the Shariah *re-introduction* from 1999 created strong consciousness along religious divides that polarized inter-religious relations to unprecedent[ed] heights than prior to this period." Ultimately, this dispute and ones that followed incentivized religious groups to organize politically to defend their interests, intensifying a narrative of us-versus-them that fed subsequent Muslim–Christian communal clashes.

## The OIC Dispute

Along with these concerns over Sharia, an event in the late 1980s also caused anger to flare and sparked violent clashes between Muslims and Christians. In 1987, Christian leaders accused Ibrahim Babangida's military regime of going behind everyone's backs when he sought and was granted Nigeria's membership in the Organization of the Islamic Conference (OIC). This move produced an outcry among the Christian population and subsequent violence, as it appeared that Islam would then dominate the state in contravention of the constitutional provisions on religious freedom. As one major Christian peace activist noted recalling these events, "Because clearly the Christians said it is unacceptable – Nigeria is a secular state, Nigeria is not an Islamic state – they saw it as [a] first step toward Islamizing the country using political means. What [the Muslims] could not get through the Jihad, they were now trying to use political power."[42] Indeed, disgruntled by this event, six Christian military officers attempted to overthrow the Babangida regime in a 1990 coup (though they ultimately failed) (Paden 2008, 22).

Again, despite formal respect for religious freedom, actual government policies and initiatives increased tensions and fears that either Muslims or Christians would dominate state power to the detriment of one or the other ethno-religious community. Such conditions created a volatile social and political environment. Where a single ethno-religious community is

---

[42] Anonymous(H), interview by Laura Thaut Vinson, Jos, Plateau State, June 3, 2011.

identified with or dominates a regime to the detriment of other ethno-religious communities, this increases the danger of inter-group violence or a "permanent situation of domestic political instability" (Philpott 2004, 43).

## Creation of Religious Organizations/Political Bodies

In response to these events, religious bodies formed to lobby for their respective political interests, further sacralizing politics. Religious leaders came together to establish the Christian Association of Nigeria (CAN) to represent the voice of the Christian community in the halls of politics. As one Christian leader and activist explained, "The simple reason CAN was formed was to preserve the voice of the Christian minorities in the North. That's the real reason. And to give them a platform in which they would speak to political issues ... If you had not had groups like CAN in existence, Christians would have been shut out completely from the political arena."[43]

CAN is an example of the organizational capacity and political influence of Christian churches in Nigeria. Despite the non-hierarchical structure of Protestant churches and the variation among them, CAN symbolizes the "political unity" of Christians, contending on their behalf since the late 1970s. For example, to organize opposition to Sharia, membership in the OIC, and violence against Christians or church property, CAN helped to mobilize Christian politicians to oppose and bring pressure on the national government to contravene these apparent violations of religious freedom and worship (Gaiya 2004, 369; Paden 2008, 45). CAN sought to prevent the "Islamization" of Nigeria while also lobbying the government for greater employment opportunities for Christians, as well as state-sponsored pilgrimages for Christians to complement the state sponsorship since 1975 of the Islamic *hajj* (Falola and Heaton 2008, 221–222). Other Christian organizations, including the Association of Hausa, Fulani, and Kanuri Christians and the Pentecostal Fellowship of Nigeria (PFN), are also active on issues affecting the religious freedoms of Christians, particularly in response to the perceived fears of radical Islam.

In entering the political arena, Christian organizations came into direct conflict with Islamic organizations also engaged in politics since the 1970s. Organizations such as the Supreme Council for Islamic Affairs

---

[43] Ibid., Anonymous(H).

(SCIA) and the Jama'atu Nasril Islam (JNI), although moderate religious bodies, had long been pushing the Nigerian government to adhere to more Islamic norms of governance.[44] These included, among other things, changing the weekly day of rest from Sunday to Friday, removing symbols of Judeo–Christian traditions from public spaces, and, above all, allowing the spread of Sharia and Islamic courts.

While Islamic and Christian organizations clashed politically on a number of issues, mobilization was not restricted to elite politics. Muslim Student Society (MSS) groups and Fellowship of Christian Students (FCS) groups formed in universities all over the country, mobilizing the youth around issues of religious devotion and also to protect themselves against perceived threats from their religious counterparts (Falola and Heaton 2008, 221–222). It is important to note, of course, that some of the Muslim and Christian organizations are more or less politicized or "extremist" than others. In general, however, these groups were established as umbrella organizations to encourage religious faith as well as to express and advocate for their political concerns.

~

In the decades following colonial rule, religious identity became a salient political category around which elites mobilized on a number of divisive questions affecting the future of Nigeria. The events described above occurred in a context of Nigerian elites' failure to create a stable system of governance, the massive conflict and loss of life during the Biafran civil war from 1967 to 1970, disappointments with the failure of successive military regimes to create conditions for economic growth, the harsh crack-down on dissent, the emergence of a new brand of Christianity that promised hope and political transformation for a large swath of Nigerians, and the perceived religious threat this brand of Christianity represented to the Muslim religious and political elite (particularly in the north). Taken all together, post-1960s events and religious changes emphasized a latent but potentially volatile religious fault line in the country that spanned ethno-tribal categories and began to coalesce in communal violence that pitted Muslims and Christians against one another from the mid-1980s onward. Highly respected religious leaders on both sides have spoken out against the violence. Following the 2008 Jos violence in northern Nigeria, the Sultan of Sokoto appealed for peace, stating,

---

[44] See Paden (2008, 27–37; 2005) for further discussion of various Muslim identities and organizations in Nigeria.

we cannot fathom how individuals will just get up one night and tear apart all that Almighty God declared holy and sacrosanct, claiming people's lives in the name of religion or in the name of ethnic background or whatsoever, destroying people's property in the name of religion, in the name of ethnic background. This madness must stop."[45]

Similarly, Archbishop John Onaiyekan, the former president of the Christian Association of Nigeria, reminded the faithful at the same gathering,

We have come here as religious leaders and not as security agents. Both Christianity and Islam preach peace, and reconciliation is not possible without peace. Play your role very well by embracing peace.[46]

Nonetheless, fears of marginalization or domination on both sides of the religious aisle have been exacerbated at a local and national level through the series of religio-political events discussed above, as well as others. In this mistrustful atmosphere, Muslim and Christian religious identities – across many ethno-tribal divides – became salient political opposition forces.

## CONCLUSION

This chapter highlighted the dimensions and degree of religious change that has re-fashioned the politics of religion in Nigeria over the past 50 years. As with many countries in the Global South, the Pentecostal-charismatic wave of Christianity led to new forms not only of religious observance, but also political engagement. Attention to this process of religious change and the attendant religio-political disputes is essential for understanding how Muslim–Christian identity became a major fault line and symbolic trigger of communal violence in northern Nigeria. The rapid expansion of Christianity in northern Nigeria among both mainline and Pentecostal-charismatic churches, the conversion of denominations away from an isolationist stance toward politics, and the socio-political dimensions and consequences of Christianity's growth raised its specter of importance in communal relationships. The debate over Nigeria joining the OIC, the dispute over the expansion and implementation of Sharia in northern states, the formation of politico-religious umbrella organizations like CAN and

---

[45] Speech quoted in Abdulsalami, Isa, Lemmy Ughegbe, and Kelechi Okoronkwo. 2008. "Sultan Cites Hunger, Poverty in Jos Crisis." *Guardian* (Lagos), December 17, 2008, pp. 1–2.
[46] Ibid.

JNI, the emergence of a more radical form of Islam in the north with expansionary political demands, and the continued growth of indigenous-led Christian churches intent on evangelizing and winning souls among the Muslim-dominant north are all factors that have sacralized political debate and been a catalyst for inter-religious violence since the 1980s.

As the beginning of this chapter highlighted, this process of religious change also has a longer history. Unlike the far northern states, the non-Muslim (now predominantly Christian) minorities in the Middle Belt states were much less assimilated and integrated into the socio-political and religious order of the Hausa-Fulani Muslim political establishment. It is not surprising, therefore, that the inter-religious violence of northern Nigeria is largely concentrated in those states that were less assimilated and less integrated into the religio-political arrangement under the Sokoto Caliphate and under subsequent Hausa-Fulani proxy colonial rule. These were the areas where missionaries concentrated their evangelism and made the greatest conversion success following independence, as well as where the establishment of Christian missionary educational institutions reached a population of marginalized ethno-tribal groups that led to the emergence of a new "enlightened" Christian political class that threatened northern Muslim political domination.

This is not to say that religious change is *the* cause of the havoc and upheaval of inter-religious violence occurring at various times in some communities of the north or Middle Belt. The argument, rather, is that religious change has been pivotal in shaping both the political debate and the terrain upon which community disputes and identities have been constituted and negotiated, even if the "root" causes of inter-religious violence are not entirely, per se, *religious*. The following chapter lays further groundwork, shifting to a discussion of Nigeria's federal structure and local government politics – another theme essential for readers to understand before delving into the power-sharing theory propounded in this book to explain the puzzle and pattern of inter-religious violence in Nigeria.

# 3

# Tenuous Unity: Federalism, Local Governments, and Politics in Nigeria

The proceeding chapter provides a foundation for understanding the emergence of religious identity as a significant ethnic cleavage in Nigeria, particularly since the 1970s. Yet, religious change, although a necessary part of the story, can only shed partial light on the incidence and recurrence of Muslim–Christian violence since the end of the 1980s; it is not sufficient to explain the subnational variation in communal violence. Instead, as I contend in subsequent chapters, the politics and pattern of representation at the local government level is critical to explaining the conditions under which identity cleavages become the basis for communal conflict. To understand the significance of local government institutions in Nigerian politics, a broader introduction to the politics of federalism, decentralization, and ethnic politics in Nigeria is necessary. The process of political decentralization through local government administration is not unique to Nigeria or Africa in the postcolonial era, however. During the 1980s and 1990s, governments pursued decentralization policies to encourage democratization and put greater control of development in the hands of local leaders (Boone 2003; Crook and Manor 1998; Olowu and Wunsch 2004; LeVan, Fashagba, and McMahon 2015).[1] Development driven from the bottom up, leaders hoped, would spur overall national development, but the implementation of decentralization policies has been uneven with mixed results (Boone 2003, 356). Nonetheless, local governments have become important sites of contestation and representation, rendering power-sharing institutions that militate against the use and abuse of identity politics all the more important.

---

[1] See Mead (1996) and Mukoro (2003) for discussion of decentralization and local government in Nigeria.

Nigeria's adoption of a federal system of government dates back to the late 1950s in the lead-up to independence and debates between Nigeria's political elites about the structure of the state following independence. Decentralization reforms in 1976 were a major turning point, democratizing local governance in the north through the establishment of local government councils and regular elections for local executive and councilorship posts. Although the politics of military rule interrupted the democratic process at various times, this chapter unpacks the importance of local government in relationship to the rise of inter-religious violence in Middle Belt Nigeria. As perhaps the African state that has gone the furthest in pursuing decentralization, the issues and challenges Nigeria has faced can be particularly instructive for other states.

This chapter first provides an overview of the significance of Nigeria's adoption of a federal model in the attempt to maintain a cohesive, stable, and democratic multi-ethnic state following independence in 1960. As the chapter highlights, however, the other competing forces of regionalism and ethnic rivalry that the federal model both attempted to ameliorate but also *generated* ultimately gave rise to instability and military rule until the country's eventual return to civilian rule in 1999. Like many post-colonial states, Nigeria inherited weak institutions and a system of colonial rule that rarefied and elevated certain ethnic groups, creating the perception of a zero-sum game between ethnic majorities, as well as minorities, that could not be easily adjudicated even through consociational or power-sharing mechanisms at the national level. While federalism and decentralization – redirecting conflict away from the center – have been necessary for the survival of a unified state, Nigeria's experience also elucidates why these mechanisms are insufficient to stem subnational intra-state violence as groups compete for representation and their share of the national pie.

Also, as the second part of this chapter highlights, while the discussion of Nigeria's weak post-colonial state and the forces generating ethnic competition for power at the center have provided conditions for ethnic conflict and violence, these factors are not sufficient to explain the subnational *variation* in communal ethnic conflict. To get to the root of this puzzle, the second part of the chapter turns to the importance of *local* political representation and competition in Nigeria's third tier of the federal system – local government councils. Understanding the evolution of local government authority in Nigeria and subnational competition for political rights and representation, as I argue and show in subsequent chapters, is critical for explaining the variation in communal ethnic and, in particular, Muslim–Christian violence in Nigeria. Ultimately, this chapter makes the case that the local level is now a major arena in which communal competition and demands for rights and resources play out in the daily lives of Nigerians. Consequently, it is an arena in which the politics of religious identity can be a source of cleavage and conflict. The centrality of power-sharing institutions among local government councils becomes clearer with this background in place.

## FEDERALISM AND ETHNIC POLITICS

The discussion of federalism, a key component of a consociational or power-sharing approach to governance, is not novel to studies of Nigerian politics. Indeed, Nigeria's "federal character," enshrined in the 1979 constitution, is central to the story of its post-colonial political struggles. Debates between leaders of the country's various regional ethnic blocs over the balance of power within a federal structure date back to the mid-1950s and the negotiations with the British over the post-colonial political arrangement (Paden 2005, 40). A brief foray into the discussion of Nigeria's federal system leading up to and following the Biafran Civil War will not only help to contextualize Nigeria's current political cleavages, but also the emergence and significance of local government autonomy, politics, and conflict.

### The First Republic 1960–1966

When colonial rulers granted independence to their former colonial subjects from the late 1950s through the early 1960s, the euphoria and expectations associated with self-rule were high in newly independent African countries. The high hopes were short-lived in many cases, however. An inheritance of weak institutions, economic distortions, patterns of ethnic domination and exclusion, and clientilistic identity-based politics was a difficult legacy upon which to build strong states. Nigeria, like many other multi-ethnic post-colonial states, adopted a federal model, as elites considered this the best means of representing the interests of the country's major ethnic blocs and quelling fears of exclusion. At the time of independence, Nigeria was divided into the three major administrative regions (in 1947) that generally mapped on to its three largest and politically dominant ethnic groups – the Yoruba in the Western Region, the Hausa-Fulani in the Northern Region, and the Igbo in the Eastern Region (Albert 1998, 51; Cheeseman 2015, 218). A three-region federal model, therefore, was seen as the only way to accommodate the interests of these politically powerful groups at the time of independence (Tamuno 1998, 22). As Suberu's (2001, 20) in-depth exploration of federalism in Nigeria highlights, federalism "developed as an institutional response both to the federal character of the society (with its sharp territorial ethnolinguistic divisions) and to the explosive demographic configuration of the ethnic structure, which pitted three major nationalities in fierce competition with one another." From the beginning, however, a number of factors inhibited the federal structure of the First Republic (1960–1966) from stabilizing the state and mediating the competing interests of its powerful ethnic blocs.

First, political elite and parties affiliated with the southern and western regions were pitted against the politically powerful northern region. Due to its greater size and population, the north was able to demand a larger share of parliamentary seats and thereby wield greater parliamentary influence, advantaging the north in the allocation not only of national revenue, but important government jobs, including the appointment of military leaders (Osaghae 1998, 11, 25–28, 36; Suberu 2001, 28–29). This is why the 1963 national census became the focus of such intense debate, as the population size and growth in the north had significant ramifications for allocation of political power and revenue within the federal structure. In general, the three major regions coalesced around three main political parties, pitting the political interests of the regions against one another in mutual fear and suspicion (Albert 1998, 51).

Second, because the regional leaderships were loathe to give up too much authority, this federal model granted significant autonomy to the regions, and, in this sense, failed to decentralize conflict away from the political center. Strong regional autonomy with powerful political parties led to what Osaghae (1998, 35–36) refers to as "extreme regionalism," empowering regional political powers and elites to pursue their interests and political power at the expense of other regions (see also Osadolor 1998, 42–44). Federalism exacerbated political cleavages and competition, as political parties from Nigeria's other regions attempted to balance against the Northern People's Congress (along with its coalition partners), which dominated major political appointments and seats and, thereby, the purse strings of the state. Federalism, in this sense, failed to create cohesive governance or inspire shared vision and purpose among the political elite. Rather, politics remained a competitive ethno-regional political game.

Third, the large size of the four regions (three until 1963) did not eliminate long-standing minority tensions or grievances against their regionally and politically dominant counterparts. Rather, minorities *within* the major regions attempted to use or manipulate the larger ethno-regional party cleavages to their own advantage, throwing their hats in with the party that could best advance their own interests. Minorities also agitated for the creation of more states that mapped onto areas where they predominated. Indeed, minorities in the Northern region advocated for the creation of a Middle Belt state after the adoption of Nigeria's initial federal framework in 1954 (Osaghae 1998, 35–36; 2015; Osadolor 1998, 44). While larger ethno-political competition and disputes characterized this immediate post-colonial period, local political contestation and competition was also an important feature of post-colonial politics – a feature reinforced by and carried over from colonial era dynamics.[2]

The brief discussion of these three dynamics emphasizes the tenuous unity of the newly independent Nigerian state. Efforts of these major ethno-regional blocs to achieve or, in the case of the northern elite, maintain political advantage led to political impasses exemplified by major attempts at vote-rigging, census distortion, and violent protests and riots (Osaghae 1998, 38–47). The Biafran Civil War from 1967 to 1970 was the devastating result of these impasses. General Gowon, the military leader of Nigeria from 1966 to 1976, attempted to offset interest in secession among minorities in the Igbo-dominated Eastern region by creating 12 new states – six in the north and six in the south. These efforts failed, however, as the fears of northern domination, exclusion of Igbo from political power, and the massacre of thousands of Igbo living in the north propelled the country toward civil war. Additionally, although General Gowon's state creation efforts kept the minorities in the midwest region on board with the federal system and addressed their concerns about lack of political voice, disputes about political control did not simply subside, as the majorities "demanded more states ... to reflect the population differences," and the resulting "new majorities and minorities" in the various regions led to "new fears of domination" (Osaghae 1998, 74). In this sense, efforts to address fears of domination through state creation also created *new* fears and perceptions of an unfair political balance and competition.

---

[2] As Osaghae (1998, 25) aptly notes, "The elite in Nigeria is factionalised mainly along ethnic, regional, religious and institutional lines, being the product of the uneven development and rivalry which British colonial administration fostered among the different segments."

## Centralization and Decentralization Paradox, Post-1960s

Changes to the structure of the federal government under General Gowon's regime and subsequently with the reforms introduced and carried forward by General Murtala Mohammed (1975–1976) and General Olusegun Obsanjo (1976–1979) had significant implications for the locus of political conflict that speak more directly to the focus of this study – subnational ethnic violence. On the one hand, reforms led to greater centralization of power and resources under the control of the central government and military regimes, and, on the other hand, also shifted the locus of political conflict with political decentralization.

First, regarding the centralization of power, the military regimes in the 1970s adopted reforms that reduced the political power of the regions and enhanced the powers of the federal government. For example, reforms introduced from 1967 to 1979 "ended the reallocation of major public revenues (export, mineral, and custom revenues) on the basis of regional derivation," and revenue formerly collected in or allocated to the regions shifted to a Federation Account (Suberu 2013, 86; 2015, 38). With the massive revenues derived from crude oil production pouring in to the coffers of the now more powerful central government from the late 1960s onward, this was no small shift.[3] The federal government's enhanced control over the collection and allocation of Nigeria's resource wealth in tandem with the creation of more states – expanding to 19 in 1976 and to 36 by the return to civilian rule in 1999 – reduced and dispersed the political power and autonomy of the states and former regions. Prior to these reforms, states depended on the federal government for around half of their revenue. States then became dependent on the federal government for around 70–80 percent of their revenue. Hence, among other centralizing moves made under the military administrations, the federal government made states more dependent on the central government for the allocation of revenue and development (Suberu 2001, 33). Indeed, states became the "administrative agents and distribution outlets for federal resources" (Osaghae 1998, 86–87).

Second, the creation of more states changed the locus and nature of political competition. The centralization of political authority in tandem with decentralization through the creation of new states made political competition more diffuse and thereby less likely to threaten the integrity of the Nigerian state. State creation became a politicized and competitive game as groups and political parties lobbied for their own politically

---

[3] See Osaghae (2015) for more in-depth discussion.

autonomous geopolitical units (Suberu 2001, 79–110; Tamuno 1998, 21). Additionally, not only did state creation shift the political terrain of Nigeria's federal system, but the process of decentralization also included reforms in 1976 that instituted local government councils as a new third tier of the federal government (enshrined in the 1979 constitution and subsequently reinforced). The local councils were imbued with administrative and fiscal responsibilities to promote local development and represent the interests of their communities.

Despite the expressed aims of Nigeria's adoption of a federal model of government – with provisions to include the various politically important ethnic groups in the national decision-making structure so as to reduce political competition at the center – federalism in practice reoriented, not quelled, political conflict. The reforms and centralizing efforts of the military governments certainly shifted the locus of political competition and conflict away from the central government, but the act of balancing regional, state-based, ethnic, and religious interests has been a source of intense and ongoing debate. For example, decentralization created the incentives for regional majorities and minorities to demand more states so as to claim a sliver of the national revenue generated by the major oil economy (Osaghae 1998, 73, 100; 2015; Suberu 2001, 131–133). Indeed, the creation of 12 new states in 1967 was itself intended to reduce regional competition between the major ethnic blocs, but the reforms led to a proliferation of demands for new states to either reinforce the political influence of regional majorities or to give new voice to minorities. Political parties took advantage of this political card, making state-creation part of their political platforms. Hence, during the short-lived return to civilian rule from 1979 to 1983, major political parties became strongly aligned with certain states and continued to cultivate ethnic majority/regional interests while courting the necessary support of ethnic minorities (Osaghae 1998, 126–127, 138, 152). State-creation in the 1980s and 1990s, then, became a tool of political control (or punishment) and ethnic politics. As Osaghea (1998, 115–116) observes, the "federal character principal" enshrined in the 1979 constitution was an "inadequate instrument to ensure democratic stability," since it gave ethnic majorities the advantage and had the "unintended consequences of accentuating minority marginalisation and heightening demands for greater political and economic autonomy by the minorities."[4]

---

[4] Hence, although the adjudication of demands for new states was supposed to be subject to certain criteria concerned with achieving a demographic and ethnic balance in

Beyond debates about the creation of states and local councils, disputes about the proper balance of representation of northern and southern regions in political appointments, the civil service, the military, and other key political bodies has been a source of ongoing debate that, since the 1980s, has also taken a "religious turn" with calls to equitably represent Muslim and Christian interests as well (Suberu 2001, 111–140).[5] Arguably, however, Nigeria's commitment to a federal character has been a key source of stability at the national level since the 1970s. The constitution requires, for example, that any candidate for the presidency obtain at least a quarter of the votes cast in two-thirds of Nigeria's 36 states, and political parties therefore are compelled to seek broader cross-regional backing in order to propel their candidate into office. The People's Democratic Party (PDP) has as part of its party platform a commitment to rotating its candidate for the presidency between the north and south every election cycle (though this commitment was called into question in the 2011 election) (Paden 2012, 14–16). In an attempt to broadly represent the country's ethnic and regional pluralism, the 1999 Constitution also stipulates provisions for members of the National Assembly – the Senate and House of Representatives – to be drawn from Nigeria's 36 states.[6] While federalism is one of the pillars of consociationalism advanced by Lijphart to provide a broadly inclusive and stable government, the Nigerian experience highlights one of its potential weaknesses – the diffusion of political conflict to the local level. This is one of the potential risks of a

---

representation and development aims, the effect of the military regimes' "arbitrariness in the choice of new states and localities, their areas or composition, and their seats of government ... has been to undermine the legitimacy of state and local boundaries and to fuel pressures for further territorial reforms by aggrieved or disadvantaged segments of the population" (Suberu 2001, 80).

[5] As Suberu (2001, 138) aptly summarizes, "although the federal character principle was intended to promote national integration, its politics have proved to be extremely divisive in regional, ethnic, and religious terms. The absence of any definitive, comprehensive, and widely accepted guidelines for actualizing the federal character and the intensity of sectionally based distributive pressures on public offices and resources have combined to ensure that the federal character has operated more to expose and exacerbate Nigeria's divisions than to contain them."

[6] See *Constitution of the Federal Republic of Nigeria*, Ch. 5, PI, A, Section 47–49, which notes that "The Senate shall consist of three Senators from each State and one from the Federal Capital Territory, Abuja," and "the House of Representatives shall consist of three hundred and sixty members representing constituencies of nearly equal population as far as possible, provided that no constituency shall fall within more than one state."

power-sharing system – that it "creates new challenges for every problem it resolves" (Cheeseman 2015, 213).[7]

~

While the focus of this discussion is on Nigeria's experience of federalism as a means of balancing competing regional and subnational ethnic interests, it speaks more generally to the challenges faced by weak, pluralistic states in designing institutions to effectively give voice to and calm the fears of various national and subnational competing interests (see Kuperman 2015). In particular, the changes made to Nigeria's "federal character" generated conflicting forces of both centralization and decentralization, heightening political and identity-based contestation between states, political parties, and ethnic groups. Depending on the constitutional model, federalism can create a new locus for competition, contestation, and clientlistic prebendal politics, as Nigeria's experience suggests (Suberu 2013, 91; Cheeseman 2015, 218–221; Kuperman 2015). Reforms to the federal system rendered Nigerian states more dependent on the central government, but also created new focal points of political contestation, corruption, ethnic politics, and, ultimately, conflict.

The post-colonial political conflicts briefly discussed here are not meant to condemn Nigeria's adoption of federalism or blame it for ethnic politics, religious conflict, and the other list of symptoms associated with Nigeria's political malaise. Rather, the adoption and evolution of the federal principle through various political conflicts and struggles reflects an effort to *preserve* the Nigerian state from collapsing under the weight of regional and ethnic majority and minority interests. Federalism has not been able to perfectly balance the competing interests of the various parties, but it provided the institutional structure for ethnic and regional balancing in a highly pluralistic state. On the one hand, Cheeseman (2015, 220) notes, "In terms of conflict management at the national level, the arrangements introduced from the late 1960s onward have clearly been a success. Nigeria is one of the only countries in Africa to have had avoided a second civil war after suffering a first." On the other hand, as Suberu (2013) grimly observes, "much of Nigerian political history can be interpreted as an unfulfilled and convoluted struggle to establish and enhance federalist institutions for self-rule,

---

[7] Among the other perils of power-sharing Cheeseman (2015, 213) highlights, he notes that "federalism may help to deflect competition away from the political centre, but does so at the risk of relocating conflict to the local level."

shared rule, and limited rule in a context of debilitating ethnic fragmentation and neopatrimonial politics." While the efficacy of Nigeria's federal structure in balancing competing regional and ethnic interests is vigorously debated both by Nigeria's political elite and scholars of Nigerian politics (e.g., Adebanwi and Obadare eds. 2013; Suberu 2001; 2013; Paden 2012; Osaghae 2015; LeVan, Fashagba, and McMahon 2015; Alapiki 2005; Joseph 1987 [2014]), the purpose of this discussion is, rather, to situate the emergence and importance of local government councils in the history of Nigeria's adoption of a federal structure and its evolution.

## ESTABLISHMENT AND REFORM OF LOCAL GOVERNMENT

This broad-brush stroke introduction to the strengths and weaknesses of Nigeria's federal structure emphasizes the significance of decentralization reforms in shifting the locus of ethnic politics and group conflict to the local level. An important consequence of the 1970s decentralization and constitutional restructuring was the enshrinement of local government administration as the third tier of the federal government. The establishment of local government areas and councils was a product of the central government's efforts to respond to minority groups' demands for greater say in their affairs and to reduce grievances that could destabilize the state. As the previous section highlighted, however, the creation of more states and local government areas had the unintended effect of *increasing* demands for more states and more local government areas among Nigeria's many ethnic (non-majority) groups, as no group wanted to lose out on the country's bountiful oil wealth. The fragmentation of governance across these different tiers promulgated new concerns about domination by one group or another at this subnational level.

The remainder of this chapter, therefore, delves more deeply into the politics and the evolution of *local* government administration in the postcolonial period. That is, to make sense of the subnational puzzle – the variation in inter-religious violence since the 1980s – it is necessary to understand the significance of local government representation as a site of contestation. Within the context of Nigeria's federal model and decentralization efforts, it is the politics and transformation of local governance that, as I will argue, best explicates the issues of representation and identity fueling inter-religious communal violence in Nigeria since the 1980s.

## Colonial Era Rule and Reforms

The evolution and current contour of Nigeria's local government system is a product of a series of reforms dating back to the colonial period. The British colonial administrators first established a formal system of local government under the Native Authority Ordinance of 1916, which prescribed a Native Administration for governance of Nigeria. This system of Native Authority, also known as Indirect Rule, meant that the British ruled through select local elites – a system designed to save the colonial rulers the trouble and cost of directly overseeing the local populations. In northern Nigeria, it elevated and entrenched the traditional authority of Hausa-Fulani Muslim chiefs and emirs. These powerful political figures, endowed with colonial authority, oversaw the day-to-day functions of colonial administration. The people they ruled, however, did not always look kindly on their rule, since individuals chosen by the British as community leaders were in many cases not in fact respected locally; instead, many were seen as corrupt, exploiting their own people for personal gain (Mamdani 1996, 104–105). In subsequent reforms, such as the Native Authority Ordinance of 1933, Galadima (2009, 239) notes that the "law enhanced the duties of the local authorities, although only for those traditional leaders recognized by the colonial administration."

Little changed in practice with reforms in the 1950s and 1960s as well. As part of an "aggressive subnationalism," the Nigerian government established regional governments and then instituted a federal, state-based system of governance (Elaigwu and Galadima 2003, 124). A federal system, however, did little to change the culture of Native Authority in the north. Instead, governance remained blighted by corruption and mismanagement, hierarchically structured with traditional leaders wielding the power to maintain peace and order in their communities (Galadima 2009, 239; Oyediran and Gboyega 1979, 175). Although military governors were supposed to oversee the appointment of local councils, the traditional authority of the Hausa-Fulani Muslim emirs and chiefs was still extremely influential, as these religio-political figures had long exercised significant local political control (Ukiwo 2006, 7–8). Thus, despite expectations that an effective system of local government would contribute to the development of the country, the reality in the northern region was a system characterized by corruption, misuse of power, and the persistence of colonial forms of local authority (Oyediran and Gboyega 1979, 175). Southern Nigeria, meanwhile, moved the route of a liberal British model of local administration with an emphasis on popular participation and decision-making by majority vote (Ndam 2001, 15).[8]

## Post-colonial Landmark Reforms and Decentralization

In 1963, three years after independence, the national government began local government reforms, initiating elections for some members of the Native Authority councils. In response to these reforms, along with the divvying up of the northern region into more states in 1967, Plateau state and Benue state in the Middle Belt were quick to assert greater popular participation in local government elections.[9] By 1970, the north as a whole began to move toward greater popular representation with the goal to weaken the authority of traditional rulers. This fundamental shift in local governance, for example, meant that chiefs could no longer wield veto power over council decisions, but were subject to majority vote (much to the chagrin of the chiefs). Further, district heads were required to be indigenous to the districts they represented (Oyediran and Gboyega 1979, 187; Osaghae 1998, 91–94).

It was the 1976 reform and 1979 constitution that largely standardized the present-day local government structure in Nigeria and enshrined local government councils as a third tier of the federal government (Galadima 2009, 245). The 1976 reforms were therefore a "watershed in the history of the evolution of the local government system in Nigeria" in that, "[a]lthough the states retained power to enact laws for local government administration, they were compelled to adhere to uniform guidelines ... set by the federal military government" (Galadima 2009, 240). Two key components of the reforms were central for empowering local government councils: first, new provisions for financial and administrative functions granted local governments a level of autonomy from the state governments. Second, the reforms prescribed democratic, fixed-term

---

[8] As Ndam (2001, 15) notes, the Nigerian local government administration was formalized under the "Local Government Ordinance ... enacted by the Colonial Administration in 1950 which was patterned after the English system of Local Government." Mamdani (1996, 104) also observes that while the same reforms were adopted for the whole of Nigeria, the agenda "set a different pace for the north than for the south, so that while the electoral principle was introduced in the entire country, elected representatives were confined to a minority in the north but were allowed a majority in the south."

[9] Note that during this period, the designation "native authority" was dropped, as it was considered pejorative (see Oyediran and Gboyega 1979).

elections for seats on the local government councils.[10] These reforms constituted a significant break with the colonial system of Indirect Rule and the authority traditional rulers had continued to exercise over local councils following independence. Ukiwo (2006, 8–9) describes the series of changes the reforms ushered in noting,

> The reforms were revolutionary in the sense that it was the first time a uniform local government was being initiated for the entire country. The reforms were also revolutionary in the sense that by one stroke, local governments were equipped with political, administrative and fiscal capacities ... Revenue was guaranteed because federal and state government were statutorily mandated to devote a specific percentage of revenue to the local government. Traditional rulers could only serve the councils in advisory capacities. Local government service boards or commissions were constituted at the state level for the recruitment, promotion and discipline of staff. Above all, the 301 local government areas were listed in the 1979 Constitution to guarantee their perpetual existence. In creating these local government areas, the military government emphasised the need for viability and administrative efficiency. The minimum population for an area to qualify for local government was 150,000 while the maximum was 800,000.

Up until this point, local councils did not have independent authority over decision-making, serving instead as administrative wings subject to the whim of state government officials or traditional authorities. The reforms now introduced a nation-wide, constitutionally mandated system for local autonomy, authority, development, and popular participation (Suberu 2001, 34–35).

Under the Babangida military administration, the government instituted further reforms intent on strengthening local governments. Decree No. 15, which came into force in 1989, further defined the balance of power in the executive and legislative functions of local governments. As Mead (1996, 163) notes, "LGAs were structured following the lines of the presidential system in the United States, complete with a separation of powers and legislative impeachment and removal of the elected executive." This is the model of the present-day local government system, with a mix of elected and appointed officials constituting local government councils. The chairman, deputy chairman, and councilor or legislative assembly seats are elected posts. The number of councilors in an individual local council generally corresponds to the number of wards in that area, as residents of the wards elect a councilor to represent them in the

---

[10] As Mamdani (1996, 106) explains, "When the military handed power back to civilians in 1979, local government was for the first time constitutionally entrenched in the Nigerian political system."

local government assembly. In terms of appointed positions, the elected chairman appoints the secretary – the third most important seat of the local government – along with a handful of special advisors and a supervisory committee whose members oversee projects or departments on public works, education, social services, and agriculture, for example. Finally, although traditional authorities or chiefs no longer wield formal government power, due to their highly respected status, they continue to be influential in communal life and in the negotiation of local conflicts or issues as they arise. Chiefs or traditional leaders – particularly the Paramount Chief who presides over all the chiefs of the various ethno-tribal groups in any local government area – therefore may work closely with their local government councils or serve as district heads. Since the number of tribal groups living in an area may vary, the number of chiefs too may vary. In some places in the country, disputes over whether or not to grant "chieftancy" rights to a tribal group have erupted in violence.

In general, the 1970s reforms were a watershed moment in the establishment and democratization of local government authority and representation, especially across northern Nigeria where, in contrast to the southern region, popular representation had not been widely implemented or respected up to this point. Due to the new authority vested in local government councils, however, local politics emerged as an important arena for ethno-tribal political competition. In any one LGA, an ethno-tribal group's representation in local executive office could grant their leaders considerable influence over the local distribution of national revenue allocated to their area.

### THE REALITY AND OUTCOME OF THE 1970S REFORMS

Ultimately, the democratizing potential of these reforms has been hamstrung or unsettled over the past few decades. The new power vested in local government councils and the enshrinement of popular representation naturally heightened the political importance of local government councils. Consequently, reforms created incentives for political manipulation of the councils, cracking the door open for new abuses of power.

#### State-level Interference

The relationship between local government councils and their state governments is one level at which the independence of local governance has been compromised. State governors seeking to increase their own political power and wealth, for example, may attempt to wield influence over local positions for the purpose of patronage, accumulation, and vote-seeking (Ukiwo 2006; Mead 1996). Also, although the decentralization reforms stipulated that a percentage of federal funds must go to local governments, confusion over states' roles in the distribution of those funds created the opportunity for abuse and misuse of these funds. State leaders, for example, have at various times siphoned off, blocked, or delayed funds earmarked for local councils until those councils have complied with nefarious conditions imposed by their state government counterparts (Ukiwo 2006, 9). Consequently, one Nigerian report criticizes the 1999 constitution as, once again, subjecting local governments to the whims of state governments or consigning them to the status of mere appendages, since local government councils are dependent on the states for "their establishment, structure, composition, finances and functions" (Ndam 2001, 17). Since funds coming from the *national* coffers are still distributed through the *state* governments, this raises opportunities for the peddling of funds for influence, ultimately reducing the autonomy of local governments. The meddling of states is symptomatic of the national government's efforts to reduce state power and the states' efforts to reassert themselves. Osaghae (1998, 118) notes that the creation of local governments served as a "major source of conflict" between the states and federal government, since the federal government "actively supported local government autonomy which it saw as weakening the states, and the states which took local government subjugation as part of the process of reclaiming ground lost under military rule." As one local expert on Nigerian federalism bemoaned,

> Most of the time, the resources meant for governance are cornered by the governors and a token is given to pay salaries at the local government level, and you find it difficult for projects to take place. There is no salaries delivery at that level of government, no accountability at that level, and that breeds a lot of conflicts, because most of the time people don't have access to ... education, people don't have access to agricultural support facilities, they don't have access to basic needs, they don't have access to income generating activities ...[11]

Despite the supposed independence of local government councils, therefore, their capacity for governance can be severely hampered by state leadership.

---

[11] Anonymous(C), interview by Laura Thaut Vinson, Jos, Plateau State, September 14, 2011. See also Mead 1996.

## National-level Interference

Local government politics is also not insulated from events and political wrangling occurring at the national level or between states and the central government, therefore. Before the return to civilian rule in 1999, for example, the electoral process was occasionally compromised by delayed local elections or the substitution of local councils with "caretaker committees" or "sole administrators" appointed by military regimes. Periods of unstable national rule, therefore, have given state governors or national military rulers influence over the local election process and, in some cases, the power to remove local government chairman of whom they disapprove (Mamdani 1996, 105–106).[12] For example, during the rule of Alhaji Shehu Shagari from 1979 to 1983, local elections were suspended and local council leadership replaced by stooges of the state governments who conveniently commandeered local revenue in the process (Galadima 2009, 240). From 1983 to 1987 during the brief military regime of General Muhammadu Buhari and subsequently under General Ibrahim Babangida, the Nigerian military government administered local governments and appointed management committees and sole administrators, sapping the local government system of its electoral democratic function. Although General Babangida ordered the renewal of local elections in 1987, in 1993, General Abacha then disbanded local government leadership and replaced chairmen with military appointees (Mead 1996, 162; Galadima 2009).[13] Due to the interference of heavy-handed military regimes, confusion over reforms at the state level, and lack of oversight,

---

[12] Interference in the local electoral process is not simply a military-era problem. In 2011, a legal dispute arose over just such an abuse of power by Governor Jonah Jang of Plateau state who attempted to remove the recently elected chairman of Kanam local government from office because the chairman changed political parties, abandoning the governor's PDP party.

[13] Galadima (2009, 260) highlights the inconsistency in local elections taking place in some fashion in 1976, 1987, 1996, 1998, 2001, 2004, and 2007. Elected councils' tenures have been cut short due to delays in elections, the appointment of caretaker committees filling-in between election cycles (or at the whim of governors abusing their authority), or with the appointment of sole administrators by military regimes. Presently, LGA elections also do not always occur at the same time or in the same year depending on local tensions. Mukoro (2003, 175) observes that during military rule, "the little democratic elements left in the local governments [had] taken flight. The management of local governments now became based strictly on appointments by the state governments and the viability of local governments began to deteriorate alarmingly in the country which led qualified personnel abandoning the place for mediocres to handle ... local government more or less became agents of the central government."

the democratization of local government in Nigeria has been tumultuous to say the least.

Nevertheless, despite these disruptions to the democratization and democratic processes of local government administration, decentralization did reduce the power of traditional rulers to a more advisory function and elevated the "middle strata" in a constitutionally enshrined third tier of local government. Traditional leaders remain respected and important leaders in their communities with some degree of social and political legitimacy – advising local leaders and helping maintain communal harmony – but they no longer hold primary political authority and veto power (Mead 1996, 166–167; Galadima 2009, 245). The reforms and iterations of the constitution since the mid-1970s enshrined elected civilian representation, a significant political departure for communities in the north where the Hausa-Fulani Muslims had historically dominated.

The obstructions to the local government electoral processes or lack of independence might nevertheless suggest that local politics has actually declined in importance and there is little interest in contestation for local council seats. As the following section explains, however, the opposite has occurred. Despite, or rather, *because* national and state politics stunts the ability of local government leaders to effectively devote resources to a wide range of local development projects, local control over scarce resources is all the *more* important, not less.

## LOCAL GOVERNMENT CONTESTATION AND COMPETITION

The initiation of a more representative third tier of government in northern Nigeria in the 1970s and the influence of local councils over communal life elevated the significance of these bodies among the citizenry. If anything, outside meddling has rendered competition for local control all the fiercer. In pluralistic communities, therefore, lack of inclusive political representation can enflame local disputes, and, in concert with religious identity politics, create the conditions for inter-religious violence.

The nature of resource allocation and dependence is one of the main reasons competition for local government leadership continues to be a major issue. Local government councils are dependent primarily on revenue allocations from national coffers, supplying about 70–80 percent of funding for LGA councils (Suberu 2001). These allocations are central not merely for the functioning of the local council, but because the funds go to support various development projects in an LGA related to agriculture, education, and social services. While the purse strings can be subject to the whims of state administrations, the resources that do make their way to the local level are critical in shaping what development projects are implemented and who benefits. Since resources are limited, therefore, the issue of which ethnic groups control – through representation in key local council seats – the resources allotted to the LGAs is critical. Hence, the politics of inclusion and exclusion in local councils and competition for those seats has fed, in some cases, perceptions of ethnic conflict and inter-religious strife.

The politics of local governments creation over the years is perhaps most indicative of this competition for national resources. The number of LGAs ballooned following decentralization, as ethno-tribal groups in various states clamored for the right to self-governance. In 1976, there were 301 LGAs, by 1981 there were 781, a reduction to 301 in 1984 in an attempt to reverse the proliferation, followed by a steady increase to 774 LGAs by 1999 – the number of LGAs now enshrined in the current constitution (Ukiwo 2006, 1, 11; Galadima 2009, 240; Suberu 2001; Akpasubi 1990, 1-A2).[14] General Babangida's administration also enabled the establishment of intra-LGA "development areas" to calm ethnic groups' agitation for more LGAs (Mead 1996, 164). In light of this proliferation, at the end of the 1970s and beginning of the 1980s, actors debated what body had the right to sanction LGA creation – the state governments or the national government – with the national government claiming that prerogative and occasionally dissolving unsanctioned LGA creation. Ultimately, the waves and reverse waves or nullifications of new LGAs transformed the ethno-tribal balance in many communities, creating new tensions between the presumed indigenous and non-indigenous majorities and minorities in some cases. The chiseling out of new states and LGAs sometimes

---

[14] Mukoro (2003, 175) notes that in 1984 the Buhari regime sought to cut back the number of LGAs to the original 301, but the intended reforms never came to fruition due to the 1985 coup that brought General Babangida to power. According to Suberu (2001, 106), there were 301 LGAs in 1976, this number rose to nearly 1000 by 1979, retracted again to 301 in 1984, expanded to 450 in 1989, 589 in 1991, and 774 in 1997. In 1996, the "Mbanefo committee on states creation ... received eighty-five requests for new states and 3,000 for new local governments" (Osaghae 1998, 294). Suberu (2001, 108) goes on to observe, "If the imbroglio over local government reorganizations convey a lesson for Nigeria, it is that the pressures for new localities in the country are bound to remain insatiable and intractable as long as they are linked to the communal struggle for access to an expanded share of central resources, opportunities, and representation rather than to the quest for local self-governance and self-reliance."

exacerbated the politics of indigeneity in the north, since, as Alubo (2009, 7) explains:

> whenever new states are created, some who were hitherto indigenes of the previous states cease to enjoy that status. In this way, the creation of states, ipso facto, redraws the borders and also reconstructs identities. From past experiences, people who lorded it over others as fellow indigenes became bitter enemies. State and local council creations construct and re-construct identities because indegeneity is based on claims to having an ethnic territory within a state.

Contestation for local political leadership and the degree of representativeness, therefore, is a central issue for local ethno-tribal groups (see Suberu 2001, 43). As Osaghae (1998, 94) notes, the powers granted to state and local governments with the post-1976 reforms, "also gave state and local government administrators an instrument for excluding non-indigenes of their states from property relations, thus defeating one of the very purposes for which it was enacted," and thereby inducing the "unintended consequence of strengthening regionalism and statism." Due to limited resources, representation in a key seat of local government leadership can shape which ethno-tribal groups obtain the benefit of revenue allocations (or corruption), such as development and education funds. Also, because of the relatively small geographical size of LGAs, people are not far removed from these issues of who benefits and how resources are invested. As one interviewee noted, "most indigenes know the entire Area Council," and they "can see, touch and feel the effects of any development programme first hand."[15] Hence, local government positions may be hotly contested between local ethno-tribal leaders seeking the advantages and largess associated with leadership (Galadima 2009). Patronage and clientilism become obstacles to communal peace, since council leadership becomes a position from which to provide advantages to friends and family members or one's ethnic group. As one local scholar observes,

> Local government councils have become a center of conflict. In many cases, the local governments, depending on where the chairman comes from – which ethnicity or which group the chairman comes from – favors his ethnic group and his community to the disadvantage of other people. And in many cases, the local government chairman favors his friends from his communities, not the entire community. And so, that's why there's fierce competition over who becomes the local government chairman, because the local government

---

[15] Anonymous(C), interview by Laura Thaut Vinson, Jos, Plateau State, September 14, 2011.

chairman will obviously not take everyone aboard, but will prefer to favor his cronies at the local level.[16]

In this context, mechanisms or institutions that can help local governments better navigate the competition over rights and representation in ethnically pluralistic communities and provide a more representative system of local government are critical to communal peace.

## CONCLUSION

The discussion of ethnic conflict in Nigeria cannot be disassociated from that of Nigeria's federal character. Due to strong regional differences and centers of power on the eve of independence, ethno-regional divisions characterized federal politics – rather than a strong, unified central government – and the competition between powerful ethnic majorities ultimately led to a devastating civil war within the first decade of independence that nearly fractured the country. Nonetheless, the federal character principle has been the mainstay of Nigerian politics despite reflections on its inadequacies in stemming corruption, election manipulation, clientilistic politics, and inter-group conflict or violence (Agbaje 1998; Ayoade 1998; Suberu 2013; Lewis 2011; Paden 2005; 2012; Osaghae 2015). During the debate about the appropriate post-colonial political structure in the 1950s, federalism was seemingly the only viable institutional model that Nigeria's powerful ethnic blocs and minorities could agree to subject themselves to. As Fashagba (2015, 94) observes, "Historically, although subnational autonomy has been abridged on different occasions, especially under various military administrations, decentralization of institutions, powers, and structure of government has always characterized the operation of the Nigerian state, especially since 1954 when federalism was embraced."

An understanding of Nigeria's federal structure and character is important for making sense of the shifts in the nature of political contestation and conflict. It helps us understand why ethnic identity has become a central cleavage in political conflict and competition, and how the

[16] Anonymous(C), interview by Laura Thaut Vinson, Jos, Plateau State, September 14, 2011. See also Galadima (2009, 254) in which he highlights the extensive problems, noting, "There are numerous cases of financial mismanagement, misappropriation, recklessness, bloated contracts, invisible projects, violation of budgetary provisions, claims for nonexistent journeys, and massive fraud. Other forms of the mismanagement of council funds include over-invoicing for contracts, payment for jobs not executed at all, and raising multiple payment vouchers for jobs already paid for, among many others."

changes to the federal structure with both greater political centralization and decentralization after the 1960s affected the calculus and locus of ethnic politics and contestation. It helps us understand the tensions and tug-of-war over political influence and autonomy between the tiers of government – between the central government and states and between the states and local governments. And, finally, it helps us understand why political parties have coalesced around certain ethnic cleavages and political identities.

Focus on the adoption of power-sharing mechanisms at the national level, however, is not sufficient to explain the subnational variation and uptick in communal inter-religious violence in the latter part of the 1980s. The analysis must go deeper, as this chapter argues, to examine the ramification of decentralization for contestation at the local government level. For this reason, the chapter emphasizes the importance of local government reforms and decentralization – an attempt to create administration that more effectively meets the socio-economic and development needs of local populations and provides greater local representation and democratic participation. Local government representation after 1976, therefore, took on new meaning in Nigeria. Traditional authorities in the north could no longer preside unquestionably over local communities, and the population could now vote for the local government leaders they desired. The emergence, dysfunction, and, yet, centrality of local government in northern Nigeria highlights its importance as a potential site for communal conflict. It is at this local government level that representation and its disparities are most felt by communal ethnic groups, since local governments are intended as the sphere of government more attuned to the basic needs of their communities. Yet, as Suberu (2001, 131) observes, "there have been relatively few discussions of the application of federal character, or the diversity principle, at the state and local levels" where the "constitutional guidelines on its application are more nebulous" and "tended to be even more contentious."

This arena of local-level politics and ethnic cleavages and contestation goes overlooked in power-sharing studies, as scholars have focused on the formal institutional variant at the national level. The lack of attention to local implementation or adoption of the federal principle or forms of power-sharing is a significant oversight, as local governments are a site of significant contention and, in recent years, inter-religious and ethno-tribal communal conflict. With the expansion of access to local representation, *who* has power now matters a great deal more for the local ethno-tribal groups. Representation means control over local resource

## Conclusion

distribution and development. Even with the federal and state governments' interference in resource allocation, control over the key seats of representation has become a focus of contestation and competition.

Evidence presented in the following chapters argues that local government power-sharing institutions have been key in warding off divisive ethnic politics and religious violence in LGAs in Kaduna state and Plateau state. Informal power-sharing institutions not only exist at the local government level, but they can be critical for mitigating perceptions of exclusion and ethno-religious favoritism, which have fueled the communal violence in northern Nigeria since the 1980s.

# PART II

# MAKING THE CASE FOR POWER-SHARING: THE EMPIRICAL EVIDENCE

# 4

# A Theory of Local Government Power-Sharing

For the past few decades, international observers and scholars have affirmed and been active in promoting power-sharing or consociationalism as a tool to end violent intra-state conflict or civil war and to create a stable peace. Power-sharing, its proponents argue, offers representatives of the conflicting parties in post-civil war states or unstable democracies a stake in the national pie and decision-making process, thereby conferring greater legitimacy on the state and reducing the incentives for insurgent groups to re-mobilize. In Chad, Ethiopia, Rwanda, Angola, Zimbabwe, Benin, South Africa, Sri-Lanka, Lebanon, and the Philippines, as well as a number of other countries, leaders have negotiated some manner of formal power-sharing arrangement.

In the case of Nigeria, official or formal power-sharing takes the form of ethno-federalism. Nigeria's power-sharing or consociational features derived from its commitment to a federal character include a zoning mechanism that incorporates representatives in the National Assembly from all of Nigeria's states or senatorial zones, the informal adoption of a rotational presidency (between the north and south) since 1995,[1] the

---

[1] In presidential election seasons, for example, political parties will select their nominees to compete in party primaries in keeping with the rotational principle of the presidency. The decision by Goodluck Jonathan to run in the 2011 election was the subject of much debate (and, in some quarters, opposition), since he took over Yar'Adua's presidency for about two years; Yar'Adua was sick and being treated abroad while in office and then died in mid-2010. Hence, the question was whether Jonathan should run for the presidency in 2011, in light of the informal rule that the presidency should regularly rotate by region and geographical zone. As Lewis (2011) notes, "His decision not to step aside for a Muslim northerner, while constitutional, went against the informal power-sharing arrangement

split representation of the north and south in the positions of president and vice president, the requirement that two-thirds of Nigeria's states be represented in party leadership, and that presidential and governorship candidates win "a quarter of the votes in two-thirds of the states or localities, respectively" (Suberu 2013, 89–90; see also Paden 2008, 19–21, 89; 2012). Such power-sharing mechanisms derive from a strategy to reduce ethnic competition at the center by being broadly inclusive, and informal efforts are made to observe this principle in other branches of state power. As highlighted in the previous chapter, the adoption of federalism in 1954 – further enshrined in subsequent constitutions – aimed to balance the competing interests of Nigeria's main ethnic groups and to construct a cohesive state out of an otherwise ethnically and politically fragmented society following colonial rule.

Yet, despite its prominence among international actors and peace negotiators as a solution to intra-state conflict, power-sharing's track record in Nigeria and many other countries leaves much to be desired. Why is this? What explains the failure of national power-sharing institutions to prevent the re-emergence of conflict in the longterm? Can power-sharing be salvaged as a prescription for ending communal conflict in which the state is not one of the warring parties?

This chapter takes up these questions, laying out a theory of why local power-sharing institutions are not necessarily prone to the same weaknesses as those at the national level. The central argument of this book is that to make sense of communal or ethnic conflict, broadly speaking, it is necessary to examine how local political institutions shape representation in pluralistic communities. While national level institutional analysis cannot explain the regional and sub-state variation in inter-religious violence (Varshney 2002, 38), the degree of group representation in local government institutions may better explain the likelihood of intergroup violence. It is not necessary, therefore, to throw out an institutional theory altogether. As the tier of government most proximate to the people in many states, local government institutions directly affect which group interests are represented, whose rights are respected or favored, and how resources are distributed. Because local government representation shapes perceptions of inter-group inequality – whether "everyone is being carried along" – the presence or absence of power-sharing at this level shapes incentives for local actors to mobilize or participate in communal ethnic

---

that had stabilized elite politics for more than a decade." See also Paden (2012) for further detailed discussion.

# The National Power-Sharing Ideal and Limitations

violence. As I will later show, tribally and religiously diverse communities in Kaduna state and Plateau state that adopted inter-tribal power-sharing arrangements following 1976 local government reforms introduced an institutional mechanism that subsequently helped to prevent the inter-religious conflicts that increasingly characterized many Middle Belt communities. Although ethno-religious cleavages were not as politicized or pronounced in the 1970s, the construction of these agreements in pluralistic LGAs along *tribal* lines created a *religiously* neutral system of representation as well, offering a political bulwark against the subsequent politicization of religion in Nigerian national politics. Overall, this book makes the case that the puzzle of Middle Belt Nigeria – why it is that inter-religious violence breaks out in some pluralistic communities and not others – can be explained by the presence or absence of local government power-sharing, and international and domestic actors concerned about instability and communal violence should focus attention on sub-national, not only national, political rights and representation.

To distinguish this local government theory of power-sharing from the national-level variant, the first and second sections of this chapter address the main critiques leveled against national power-sharing arrangements and make the case for why local power-sharing can better foster inter-group peace. The third section of this chapter discusses the importance of local institutions as a locus of contestation, and the function and logic of four main forms of local government power-sharing identified in Kaduna state and Plateau state LGAs.[2]

## THE NATIONAL POWER-SHARING IDEAL AND LIMITATIONS

In Lijphart's 1977 seminal work on power-sharing in divided societies, he makes the case that regimes characterized by formal power-sharing or consociational institutions are more likely to achieve successful democratization and avert ethnic conflict. Power-sharing, in Lijphart's (2002, 39) classic formulation, takes the form of executive power-sharing, mutual veto, proportionality, and group autonomy,

---

[2] These two states are the focus of this study, since they show considerable variation in Muslim–Christian violence, encompassing pluralistic LGAs well-known for inter-religious violence since the 1980s, and other similar LGAs where religion is not a major source of violence. Hence, they present an important context in which to study the relative importance of local government dynamics in shaping patterns of communal violence or peace.

giving warring parties a joint stake and role in the decision-making power of the state. While, as Rothchild and Roeder (2005, 29–50) note, power-sharing may take different forms or comprise different combinations of mechanisms, the essence of power-sharing is political inclusion "accomplished through fixed political processes, such as coalition governments formed through elections" and "consociationalism, which entails a combination of specific institutional arrangements under unusual conditions" (LeVan 2011, 33).[3]

The concept, therefore, largely refers to a political or electoral strategy to reinforce government legitimacy across group cleavages and thereby construct a stable national government in an unstable or post-conflict society. Otherwise, without a stake in the decision-making process, aggrieved groups will reject the regime in power, further entrenching conflict and perhaps (re)creating the conditions for ethnic violence instead of long-term democracy and peace (Spears 2002; Hartzell and Hoddie 2003; Norris 2008). All of the following are cited as possible benefits of power-sharing arrangements: elites have the incentive to bargain or collaborate, to accept the rules of the game, and to moderate demands, thereby maximizing the number of stakeholders, dampening the effect of ethnic intolerance, increasing the perception that the rules of the game are fair and legitimate, convincing leaders of different blocs that they have a say or their constituents' interests are represented, and enhancing consensus-building in post-conflict situations (Norris 2008, 24–25; Gates and Strøm 2007, 3–5).

Despite the value attributed to the power-sharing model, recent scholarship finds little ground for optimism. To the contrary, the problems of power-sharing highlighted in the literature form an impressive list: it concentrates power in a few critical decision-making arenas, it can be used as a mutual veto weapon, conciliatory policy commitment diminishes over time, it creates government

---

[3] As Rothchild and Roeder (2005, 29–50) note, power-sharing make take the form of an "inclusive decisionmaking" approach which aims for representation of all major ethnic groups in a central decision-making body (e.g. the legislature), or a "partitioned decisionmaking" model that accords ethnic groups their own communal agencies or bodies to administer policies for their members and give voice to their ethnic group's interests." Additionally, Gates and Strøm (2007, 4) observe that the power-sharing components identified by Lijphart "can in many contexts exist independently of one another" and that "these features do not fully specify or exhaust the world of possible power-sharing arrangements." See also Spears (2002, 133).

rigidity, it is difficult to enforce the rules because of opportunistic leaders, it merely postpones rather than resolves conflict, it leads to incumbent manipulation, it is subject to the whims of self-interested and power-hungry politicians unwilling to accommodate rivals, the personality differences of actors hinders effectiveness, the incumbency advantage makes inroads difficult, it can be used as a political tool for one group to accumulate more power, it assumes static rather than fluid political interests, it leads to changes in government without new elections, and it emphasizes rather than diminishes ethnic differences (Spears 2000; 2002; LeVan 2011; Cheeseman and Tendi 2010; Oyugi 2006; Rothchild and Roeder 2005; Tull and Mehler 2005; Jarstad 2008; Sisk 1996). Hardly cause for optimism. Or, as Cheeseman (2015, 205) argues in his discussion of democracy in African states and the principle of inclusion, there can be *too much* power-sharing when it "stifles political competition ... [e]xcessive inclusion is therefore just as bad for democracy as excessive competition."

Exploring specific power-sharing cases, Rothchild and Roeder (2005, 41) cite 11 out of 16 power-sharing experiments that were not sustainable – Burma, Chad, Cyprus, Ethiopia, Guyana, Iraq, Lebanon, Nigeria, the Philippines, Sri-Lanka, and Sudan. Other questionable experiments include Bosnia and Herzegovina and Czechoslovakia (Norris 2008, 39). In the case of Ethiopia, Spears notes that parties were unable to sustain a power-sharing arrangement that allocated seats between the Ethiopian People's Revolutionary Front and a number of other ethnically based parties after the overthrow of the Dergue regime in 1991. The arrangement collapsed after a year. Similarly in Angola, parties to a 1991 peace agreement did not consider power-sharing a viable option. In 1994, they were "finally induced to sign a power-sharing agreement," but it "became severely strained" and fell apart with renewed war in 1998 (Spears 2000, 106). In the case of Burundi, power-sharing institutions successfully helped to end war, but the agreement did not institutionalize democratic institutions, with the country instead reverting to authoritarian style politics and violence (Vandeginste 2009, 81; Cheeseman 2015, 207–211, 215).[4] So too in

---

[4] Although Lemarchand (2006) highlights Burundi as something of a carefully crafted success case for consociationalism that has managed to keep the peace (for the time being), he ultimately questions whether power-sharing is to thank or the societal conditions or context that enable the relative success of power-sharing. Lemarchand (2006, 20) notes that a "power-sharing solution to the Burundi crisis proved utterly unworkable in 1994 but reasonably promising in 2005."

Rwanda, power-sharing failed due to the lack of all of the following: a committed leadership, a concept of a shared destiny, and the desire among elites to accommodate one another (Traniello 2008). Ultimately, as Mehler (2009, 472) notes in his discussion of recent power-sharing agreements, generally overlooked are important questions regarding who represents the parties at the negotiating table and how or whether these agreements address the management or generation of local security and conflict.

In the end, despite the international community's penchant for advocating power-sharing as a solution to ethnic conflict or civil war, a number of recent studies find that power-sharing limits democracy, can lead to a renewal of conflict, and, ultimately, is not the solution to long-term instability as policy practitioners had hoped (Tull and Mehler 2005; Lemarchand 2006; LeVan 2011; Oyugi 2006; Cheeseman 2015; Cheeseman and Tendi 2010; Spears 2000; 2002; Rothchild and Roeder 2005; Trianello 2008; Vandeginste 2009). In practice, therefore, the goals that power-sharing attempts to accomplish seem to be the conditions necessary for its success. For power-sharing to succeed, studies emphasize the need for a political culture of accommodation, economic prosperity, equality, demographic stability, strong government institutions or a strong state, stable hierarchical relations, a supportive international environment, elite dominance/enforceability, and a constructive relationship with the international community – all of which are unlikely to be present after severe conflict or in unstable democracies (Rothchild and Roeder 2005, 41–47; Horowitz 2002, 20; Lemarchand 2006; Spears 2002; Gates and Strøm 2007; Jarstad 2009).[5] In short, as Cheeseman's (2015) analysis of democracy in African states makes clear, power-sharing is not a simple panacea for divided societies, and it is not one-size-fits-all.

---

[5] "Much of the [African] continent," Lemarchand (2006, 2) observes, "has become a graveyard of consociational experiments ... a point on which most observers would agree." As Spears (2000, 106) concludes, "[W]hile power-sharing or inclusion has been cited as a necessary direction which African leaders should follow, it remains relatively unproven as a means of conflict resolution. There are, in fact, relatively few examples of successful, formalised power-sharing in Africa which warrant its advocacy. Even those developing world examples cited by power-sharing's main proponent, Arend Lijphart, tend to be relatively few and, with the exception of South Africa, none of them has been initiated in the past 25 years."

## THE CASE FOR INFORMAL, LOCAL POWER-SHARING

Clearly, significant critiques have been leveled against power-sharing. While the verdict on power-sharing is strongly tilted toward the negative, the level of analysis may be misplaced and the breadth of study thereby stunted. This section lays out why a new theory of informal local power-sharing can nonetheless hold despite these empirical criticisms of power-sharing. I make the case that local government power-sharing is not necessarily prone to the same weaknesses. This emphasis on the importance of informal- and local-level institutions is not merely abstract theorizing. Recent scholarship confirms the importance of local-level communal politics and institutions in shaping incentives for or the patterns of conflict, on the one hand, or mitigating identity cleavages, on the other hand (MacLean 2004, 590; see also Boone 2003, 375–376). In postcolonial African states struggling to establish a stable form of democracy, informal relationships and institutions continue to play a role in structuring communal life and linking local and national politics. As Boone (2003, 369–370) notes, "political society at the local level is structured by informal institutions that define community hierarchy, cohesion, and control over access to local resources and to the state," and, she continues, "[i]n much of rural Africa, access to some key economic resources, adjudication of ordinary civil disputes, and brokering relations with national-level politicians and state agents remains in the hands of local notables" (see also Baldwin 2015). A top-down model of power-sharing, even in the form of ethno-federalism or provisions for cultural autonomy, does not have the capacity to address the subnational variation in socio-economic grievances, representation, or political cleavages and their construction as identity issues. Although international and state actors focus on the implementation of power-sharing agreements at the national level, informal power-sharing institutions at the district or local level can be key in ameliorating the group cleavages that spawn ethnic conflict. There are four primary reasons why informal power-sharing institutions at the local government level can effectively shape inter-ethnic relationships and reduce motivations for violence.

### The Logic

In its underlying logic, informal power-sharing can strengthen the intended democratic purpose of formal institutions. In Azari and Smith's (2012, 42) language, it can act as a "parallel" arrangement in which informal institutions "operate parallel to formal institutions, exerting joint but separable effects on behavior in a given domain" such that "behavior is governed simultaneously by formal and informal precepts." Like formal or regulated national power-sharing arrangements, the informal institution essentially attaches a condition to electoral arrangements to ensure more representative local government. Since electoral rules could de facto exclude significant ethnic blocs from local representation and create divisions, power-sharing fosters broader representation for ethno-tribal groups while offering political incentives for majority ethno-tribal groups to comply with the arrangement. In this sense, informal power-sharing also plays a "coordinating" role, "creating stable expectations where there would otherwise be conflict or uncertainty" and functioning as the "unwritten rules by which political actors resolve, or at any rate contain, inter-institutional tensions and conflicts" (Azari and Smith 2012, 42).[6] Not only may they fit a strategic logic, but such informal institutions may also comply with a communal normative logic – not by cancelling out the formal institutional arrangement, but by reconstructing its outcomes to comply with a normatively, as well as strategically, acceptable goal.

Paralleling formal institutions, there are a number of reasons to theorize local and informal power-sharing's greater effectiveness in mitigating ethnic cleavages than the formal national arrangements. First, local power-sharing is more effective in dispelling communal violence that can arise between minority groups due to its proximity to the groups and communities that local councils govern. In contrast to the national level variant, local council leadership is embedded in their communities, and the actors and political leaders are well-known by their constituents. In this sense, power-sharing through the inclusion of the predominant local tribal groups in the most important seats of a local government can help address one of the main weaknesses of decentralization highlighted in the previous chapter – the shifting of the locus of conflict from

---

[6] In Helmky and Levitsky (2004, 729) language, informal power-sharing institutions could be referred to as "accommodating" institutions, as they "create incentives [for actors] to behave in ways that alter the substantive effects of formal rules, but without directly violating them; they contradict the spirit, but not the letter, of the formal rules" and help to "reconcile these actors' interests with the existing formal institutional arrangements." The informal institutions can either be complementary or competing with formal institutions, as well as accommodating and substitutive. These are also what Tsai (2006, 117–118) refers to as "adaptive" informal institutions that "represent creative responses to formal institutional environments that actors find too constraining."

competition over control of the central government to competition over control of its subnational units. If power-sharing institutions are in place at this *subnational* level, governance will more effectively and comprehensively reflect the principle and purpose of federalism, addressing not merely the representation of the majority ethnic groups through power-sharing mechanisms at the national level, but, critically, at the subnational level through inclusion of minority groups in the key institution of governance where they predominate. Absent mechanisms of local council power-sharing, even informal ones, it is no wonder that federalism and decentralization have not been the panacea to conflict in ethnically pluralistic societies. There is little reason to expect that federalism or other power-sharing mechanisms at the national level can effectively eliminate the potential for devastating and destabilizing communal violence if groups perceive a sense of exclusion from the institutions that they interact with and local government policies they feel the effects of on a daily basis.

Also, local political leaders can more effectively observe the direct effects of power-sharing whether in local resource allocation, in communal relationships, or in other informal offshoots of the power-sharing arrangement. While one may also be able to observe the adherence to national-level power-sharing, the arrangement itself is not likely to have a direct or traceable effect on localized conflicts, grievances, relationships, or representation among ethnic groups in the state's highly pluralistic locales. In contrast, the link between local power-sharing institutions and the possible benefits for a local community are more easily observed, whether in the granting of indigenous certificates, the building of new schools, efforts to prevent discrimination in employment or education, the location of new public works, the more equitable allocation of administrative posts, and so on. In this sense, beyond being able to observe, as at the national level, whether or not leaders are abiding by a power-sharing arrangement, the *ramifications* of local power-sharing can be more easily observed. An important corollary is that if the benefits of power-sharing can be more easily observed, then the same is true of defection from the arrangement. That is, ethnic groups can mobilize in opposition to and vote against leaders if they attempt to defect from the arrangement. In contrast, due to the scale of the system, there is less direct agency or a less direct line of accountability from local groups to the national power-sharing stage. Each voice – in particular, each ethnic group's voice – matters more in their local government area. Unlike a national power-sharing institution, the spatial proximity of local government power-sharing to the groups concerned empowers the local populations to hold leaders accountable to the power-sharing mechanism (or to punish defection from power-sharing arrangements by voting a leader out of office). At a national level, the incentives for accountability (as opposed to mere monitoring) are ambiguous when the connection between leaders' decisions and the local interests of their constituents and the country's various minority groups is unlikely direct or explicit.[7]

Second, following on the above logic, local power-sharing represents the groups and issues specific to a locale. In highly heterogeneous countries like Nigeria, with approximately 250 ethnic groups, a national power-sharing arrangement cannot take into account or address all the local variations of political or socio-economic competition or grievances. The day-to-day issues of poverty and economic and political inequality break down along different ethnic lines. Although individual states elect representatives from Senatorial Zones to the National Assembly, the local government councils make important decisions in how the national revenue allotted for LGAs is allocated to economic, agricultural, social, and educational projects. Since significant rights, resources, and representation are shaped by who controls local government councils, a power-sharing institution that more broadly represents the pluralism of a district will concretely affect people's daily lives and perceptions of ethnic relationships. In contrast, at the national level, the benefits of power-sharing for an ethnically diverse population are more difficult to discern, the mechanisms of accountability more ambiguous, and, hence, leaders' incentives to sustain such arrangements more tenuous.

Third, power-sharing may also be more sustainable at the local level, since, for the above reasons, it can foster greater institutional legitimacy. As interview subjects in Chikun LGA in Kaduna state emphasized, the fact that they can see that "everybody is being carried along" reinforces their support for the power-sharing arrangement.[8] Leaders risk a direct electoral backlash if they defect from the arrangement, and the moderating influence and legitimacy of power-sharing incentivizes parties to only run ethnically mixed tickets. As one local chief from the area of Kanam noted

---

[7] As Sisk (1996, 33) observes, the issue of political engineering in divided societies goes to the question of "how can the incentive system be structured to reward and reinforce political leaders who moderate on divisive ethnic themes and to persuade citizens to support moderation, bargaining, and reciprocity among ethnic groups?"

[8] Anonymous(A), interviewed by Laura Thaut Vinson, Chikun, Kaduna State, November 10, 2011.

regarding the power-sharing precedent in the LGA, "Whoever does not give us mixed, we will not go with him."[9]

This type of legitimacy is more difficult to foster with national power-sharing arrangements for the reasons noted above. The local variant militates directly against incentives to employ mutual veto tactics or threaten defection, a central critique made of national power-sharing agreements (see Rothchild and Roeder 2005, 37; Jarstad 2008; Gates and Strøm 2007). Indeed, perceived responsibility to one's local ethnic kin, among other incentives, may make leaders *more* wary of risking defection from power-sharing, particularly when their ethnic group may not otherwise have the political clout to ensure significant representation in an "every man for himself" political contest.[10] Local government power-sharing, then, may achieve the type of legitimacy originally envisioned by power-sharing proponents, setting a precedent for representation that is more difficult for elites to renege on and providing a basis for inter-ethnic negotiation and more equitable distribution of resources.[11] Indeed, power-sharing arrangements in LGAs such as Chikun go back to their founding over a decade ago, or, in the cases of Kanam and Bassa, as far back as the end of the 1970s and beginning of the 1980s.

Fourth, in response to criticisms that power-sharing can rigidify or "freeze" ethnic conflict lines (Jarstad 2008, 125; Norris 2008, 28), indeed, local power-sharing may not reduce the saliency of religion or kinship. For the reasons noted above, however, local power-sharing may help to reduce these identities' saliency as *conflict* cleavages – the primary goal. For example, where the chairman and the deputy chairman of the local government must run on the *same* electoral ticket but cannot be from the same ethno-tribal group, a candidate who politicizes his/her particular

---

[9] Anonymous(B), interview by Laura Thaut Vinson, Jos, Plateau State, October 13, 2011.

[10] As Horowitz (2002, 25) notes, "politicians who benefit from electoral incentives to moderation have continuing reason to try to reap those rewards, whatever their beliefs and whatever their inclination to toleration and statesmanship. Politicians who are merely exhorted to behave moderately may be left with mere exhortations." There can also be historical incentives for leaders to form power-sharing institutions; in Kanam, for example, those involved in the power-sharing decision saw it as a strategy to avoid continued rule by the Hausa-Fulani, their former colonial proxy rulers who dominated local politics before decentralization in the 1970s.

[11] These dynamics, then, also suggest that local government power-sharing is less prone to the "second-generation problem" for which national power-sharing institutions are critiqued, wherein the incentives that held at one point in time may not hold in the future under new leaders. Rather, the sustainability of local power-sharing is a topic for further empirical research and not an innate feature of power-sharing at all levels (Rothchild and Roeder 2005, 38).

tribal or religious identity may significantly hinder their likelihood of (re)election. Because local power-sharing shifts disputes away from identity-based cleavages through broader local representation, this helps to negate claims that one group is not being fairly represented due to their *religious* identity. In Nigeria's sacralized political environment, Muslim and Christian identities are powerful religio-political categories around which actors at the national and local levels can mobilize and demonize one another. By mitigating perceptions that religiousidentity is a divisive local issue or is the basis of discrimination, power-sharing, therefore, presents a stumbling block to political or religious actors who might otherwise map religious cleavages onto local political disputes. Since power-sharing promotes broader ethno-tribal representation than might otherwise exist in a religiously pluralistic LGA, it is also more difficult to legitimately claim that one ethno-religious group is dominating local political office to the detriment of the other. For this reason, power-sharing LGAs are more resistant to inter-religious violence. Hence, local power-sharing helps to avoid politicization of ethnic cleavages or the perception that local socio-economic or political challenges are due to ethno-religious competition.

Fifth, additional critiques associated with national power-sharing arrangements are not necessarily applicable to a local power-sharing model. These critiques include arguments that power-sharing institutions create greater government inefficiency with more government bureaucracy and agencies, that they create government rigidity by not being amenable to changes in social conditions following conflict, and that there are inadequate enforcement mechanisms to protect against defection (Rothchild and Roeder 2005, 39–41; Jarstad 2009, 42–43). Regarding the first critique, power-sharing arrangements do not inherently create more bureaucracy; mechanisms of greater representation can be instituted within or supplementary to *existing* institutions or democratic arrangements. The stipulation in cases of local council power-sharing in Kaduna and Plateau states – that candidates from different ethno-tribal groups run for office together – does not create a new bureaucracy; rather, it redefines the premise of electoral competition and renders it more normatively acceptable to pluralistic LGAs. Regarding the second critique that power-sharing creates government rigidity, the *informal* nature of local power-sharing discussed in this book suggests that governance is *more* flexible in the face of socio-demographic changes. Its informal nature means that that there is room for possible renegotiation, not of power-sharing itself, but of its particular form. Quite simply, at a local government level, the socio-political and institutional dynamics and their scale are quite different, and so assumptions about the weaknesses or strength of power-sharing must be assessed separately. Further empirical studies could explore the conditions under which forms of local council power-sharing are sustainable and effective in different countries in the face of new socio-demographic changes or conflict dynamics. Considering the last critique noted above – the need for formal enforcement mechanisms – the lack of regulation simply does not imply the doom of local government power-sharing, as this study will further elucidate. As already highlighted, incentive structures at the local level and their re-enforcing mechanisms may sustain agreements. Defection from local power-sharing is not cost-free.

Sixth, a critical function of local power-sharing is its self-reproducing or re-enforcing potential. As the case studies show, power-sharing provides a foundation for subsidiary peacebuilding – greater coordination and collaboration among Muslim and Christian elite to prevent or resolve local tensions. For example, in the case of Chikun, local council leaders have used their purview to create "local development areas," designating development funds to bolster the autonomy and representation of minorities in a particular area of the LGA. These are minorities who do not otherwise form a large enough ethno-tribal bloc to gain an executive position on the council. In another outgrowth of the power-sharing arrangement in Chikun, Muslim and Christian traditional leaders have instituted an early warning system to work together to stem violent reactions among their youth when inter-religious violence flares up elsewhere. In Bassa LGA, the power-sharing arrangement spawned the creation of integrated Muslim–Christian vigilante groups to patrol communities at night to ensure peace. By patrolling neighborhoods together, they help to silence claims that one side is against the other, and, if any incident were to occur, they can dispel accusations of religious partisanship. In contrast, these offshoot informal peace-keeping institutions could hardly be imagined in Jos North, an LGA that lacks a power-sharing institution and is far more prone to inter-religious conflict.

Finally, although critiques of power-sharing note the risk of negating the competitive nature of democratic contestation, this is not necessarily the case. The goal of power-sharing is to foster ethnic harmony where manipulation of political office and policies of exclusion propagated by a predominant ethnic group in a locale might otherwise produce imbalance and inspire ethnic conflict. In the context of weak states, "democracy" is not always synonymous with "representative," and in such cases power-sharing can actually help to equalize the political contest.[12] Power-sharing in this form does not, however, obviate the value of fair and free elections or imply coercion. In the cases of local government power-sharing in Nigeria discussed in this book, the population is not required to vote for a particular representative, even if it is "the turn" of one particular ethno-tribal group to hold the chairmanship. Parties can run various candidates or chairman-deputy combinations from the designated ethnic groups. In this sense, the candidate who wins the election is not necessarily pre-determined by the power-sharing arrangement (although it may be subject to other manipulation outside of the power-sharing arrangement, as noted in the previous chapter). Competition and voter choice is still involved. Informal power-sharing can thus be accommodating to the democratic ideal, compensating for claims of marginalization and helping to create peace and stability in ethnically pluralistic communities. Although such institutions "violate the spirit of the formal rules, they may generate outcomes (democratic stability) that are viewed as broadly beneficial" (Helmke and Levitsky 2004, 730).[13]

~

Note that the argument here is not that power-sharing eliminates clientilistic politics, manipulation of power, misuse of resources, and ethnic favoritism characteristic of politics in weak states such as

---

[12] As Rothchild and Roeder (2005, 31) observe, while "power-sharing arrangements are seldom fully inclusive because the dominant political elite typically leaves the leaders of small groups – who lack bargaining leverage – out of the decisionmaking process," the main objective, rather, "is to include all groups that can threaten political stability if kept outside the arrangements." See also Gates and Strøm (2007).

[13] This point also responds to an important critique of power-sharing – that it is not truly democratic or that it suffers from transaction costs or agency costs, such as the moral hazards problem (Rothchild and Roeder 2005, 36–37; Gates and Strøm 2007, 6–9). This argument assumes, however, that politicians who are democratically elected in the absence of a power-sharing institution will *not* use their positions to exploit resources to the advantage of their own ethno-tribal community, friends, and family members. Yet, democratic elections do not *necessarily* inspire democratic politics and discourage misuse of resources or patronage politics once a politician is elected into office. While power-sharing is not a solution to corruption in office, a power-sharing model that rotates ethno-tribal representation in the executive seats of local government leadership can help to avoid the tendency toward exploitative control by the majority ethnic group and potentially encourage greater accountability. Furthermore, it is not clear from Gates and Strøm's (2007) discussion why transaction costs or agency costs are *particularly* associated with power-sharing institutions and not democracy in general. See Jarstad (2008) and Lemarchand (2006) for discussion of critiques of power-sharing that incorporate (i.e., reward) leaders of rebel or an armed insurgency group.

Nigeria. Nor is the argument that local leaders under an informal power-sharing arrangement will suddenly ensure accountability to the voter or interests of all constituents (e.g., in the distribution of resources or policy choices). Rather, ethnic groups are better able to hold their leaders accountable to the power-sharing arrangement at the local than at a national level, and representation is more directly observable. The consequences of defection from the arrangement are more likely to be noticed (and elicit response or opposition) at the local level. Further, even though this argument asserts no expectation about the elimination of ethnic favoritism or clientlistic politics, the nature of local power-sharing arrangements and their proximity to the constituent population can provide leaders with incentives to better represent the interests of their ethnically mixed population. The particular incentives and forms this takes may vary depending on the type of power-sharing arrangement. On the one hand, the chairman of an LGA may simply favor his/her group when in office, such that group favoritism occurs, essentially, on a rotating basis and does not produce major incentives for communal violence. On the other hand, there are grounds to argue that a power-sharing arrangement that rotates the ethnic representation of the chairmanship gives the elected leaders incentive to govern more inclusively for two reasons. First, favoritism of one's kin group could backfire by inspiring the subsequent leader to then favor his/her ethnic group; this is not necessarily appealing to political actors and their constituents. Second, as I note in subsequent discussion, since the power-sharing arrangement requires a chairman and deputy-chairman to run for office on the same ticket, they must jointly appeal to the broader community, working to obtain votes beyond their own constituencies. (Note that this is also the logic of parties' adherence to the informal principle of having a northerner and southerner from different zones of Nigeria run on the same ticket in presidential elections.) This places pressure on candidates to obtain the votes of a wider swath of the local population and to more broadly represent the population to maintain broader support and local legitimacy once in office.

Of course, an important corollary of the local power-sharing theory is that there must be a stable expectation of regular and recurring elections. Where there is uncertainty regarding the time horizon (e.g., due to outside meddling in the election cycle or a system that only weakly adheres to democratic rules), the incentive structure for leaders to abide by a power-sharing arrangement is more tenuous.[14] For example, if the main ethno-tribal groups in an LGA rotate control of the chairmanship from one election cycle to the next, the guarantee of regular election cycles is critical to avoid uncertainty and to keep leaders and ethnic groups on board with the agreement. In short, assuming a stable time horizon, the incentives for accountability to local constituents in the administration of the local government can work in various ways, and, as discussed in the following section, the type of local power-sharing arrangement – e.g., static seats or rotating seats, rotation among local government zones – can affect the political incentives as well.

## LOCAL GOVERNMENT POWER-SHARING IN NIGERIA

Having discussed the *logic* of a theory of local and informal power-sharing, what *form* does power-sharing take at this level? Must it take one particular form in order to quell politicization of identity and representation? Data and case study evidence gathered at the local government level in Nigeria's Kaduna state and Plateau state revealed different forms of informal local government power-sharing institutions. As discussed in chapter seven, the conditions shaping elites' incentives to establish power-sharing have varied from one LGA to another, but the institution is informal in the sense that it is not mandated by the national government. Instead, local power-sharing institutions identified in this study are "organically" grown from local socio-political dynamics. As informal institutions, they are "socially shared rules, usually unwritten, that are created, communicated, and enforced outside of officially sanctioned channels" (Helmke and Levitsky 2004, 727).[15] These local government power-sharing institutions emerged following the decentralization of Nigerian politics in 1976 (or upon the subsequent formation

---

[14] For example, the Plateau state government excluded Jos North LGA from the 2014 LGA elections, claiming security concerns if the election went ahead. Although Jos North is not a case of power-sharing, this type of uncertainty surrounding the election cycle only further compounds fears of ethnic exclusion, insecurity, and further reduces incentives for leaders to agree to a power-sharing arrangement if there is no certainty of subsequent rotations in power.

[15] Note that Rothchild and Roeder (2005, 19–20) observe that power-sharing can also refer to informal compromises, but that "[i]n the interest of precision," they "invoke the narrow list of more formal arrangements," such as "federalism, collective executives, communal legislative chambers, reserved seats in legislatures, the list system of proportional representation with a low threshold, and formal rules mandating proportional presidencies ... and schemes of nonterritorial federalism."

of a new local government area), creating a three-tiered federal structure for the governance of the country.[16] In some cases, power-sharing is an explicit agreement between ethno-tribal elite, and in other cases, it is implicit in a zoning arrangement that rotates representation among the wards of a pluralistic LGA. It could not always be ascertained from the information and data gathered from LGAs which type of power-sharing characterizes each LGA, but the power-sharing agreements take two overarching forms – rotational or static representation – which I will expound upon here.

Under what I will call "rotational power-sharing," the main ethnic groups agree to rotate the executive of the local council from one election to the next. This system characterizes local councils such as Bassa and Kanam in Plateau state. The basic idea of this form of power-sharing is to rotate the top two or three positions of local government leadership – the chairman, deputy chairman, and secretary – to more fairly or broadly represent the major ethno-tribal groups in the LGA. The rotation of ethno-tribal and religious representation can be of two different subtypes – by seat or by zones/wards – although the adoption of either makes no difference in the empirical analysis. Either a seat or a ward rotation principle results in the same outcome: local councils that more broadly represent the main groups in that area.

In *rotating seat-based* power-sharing, leadership of the local government council rotates on the basis of ethno-tribal identity such that consecutive chairmen of a local government council do not come from the same tribal group. In this scenario, contesting political parties will, based on the informal institution, only put forward a candidate for chairman from the ethno-tribal bloc whose turn it is to lead the council, and he/she will run on a mixed ticket with a deputy chairman candidate of another ethnic affiliation. If, in the case of Bassa, the chairman of the local government council was a Rukuba in one administration, then it should rotate either to the Pangana or Irigwe in the next. In explicit power-sharing districts such as Bassa and Kanam in Plateau state and Sanga[17] in Kaduna state, the particular order of rotation may not always be

---

[16] Note that there have been periods of expansion and contraction in the number of local government areas in Nigeria over time.
[17] A local official reported that recently the appointment of the secretary's position changed; whereas in the past, it was allocated by the chairman, the common practice, it is now allocated by the state. It is unclear what prompted this change and whether it is the same across LGAs in Kaduna state.

126  A Theory of Local Government Power-Sharing

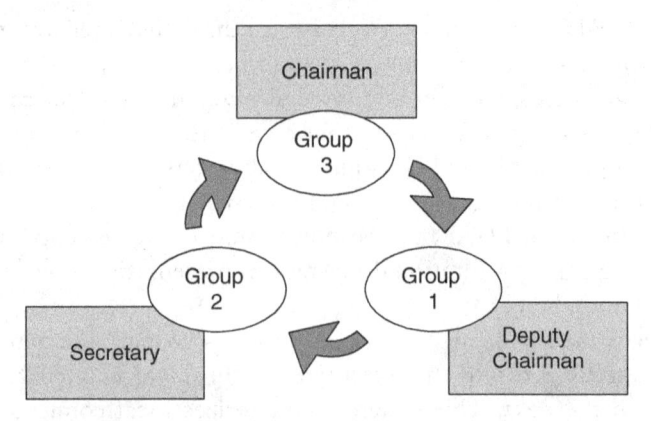

FIGURE 4.1 Rotating seat-based power-sharing model

consistent, but it *generally* follows this pattern such that no single ethnic/religious group is always accorded the chairmanship (Figure 4.1).

In *rotating zone-* or *ward-based* power-sharing, the same rotation is reflected, but on the basis of a different principle: the rotation of local government leadership among the wards or zones (with zones constituted by a set of wards). That is, if one set of wards held the chairmanship in the previous election, then a different set of wards will hold the chairmanship in the subsequent election. The system is implicitly power-sharing since the pluralism among the wards means that the candidates generally rotate ethno-religious group representation. This is a power-sharing arrangement in principle and practice, even if based on a different logic of executive rotation, providing broader representation of ethnic groups in these primary seats of local government power.

In what I refer to as "static power-sharing" arrangements – the second type of power-sharing system identified in Plateau state and Kaduna state – ethnic groups agree to share the main seats of local government leadership, but the positions represented by each ethnic group are static over time. The institutional arrangement can also take one of two forms – seat- and zone/ward-based.

Chikun district in Kaduna state is an example of the *static seat-based* version. The agreement stipulates that the Gbagyi, because they constitute the majority ethno-tribal group in the district, should always hold the chairmanship, but, because the Hausa-Fulani are also indigenous and a major ethno-tribal group in the area, they should hold the important deputy chairmanship. The Kabilu, the next major group in the LGA, is a mix of non-indigenous ethno-tribal groups from other parts of Kaduna

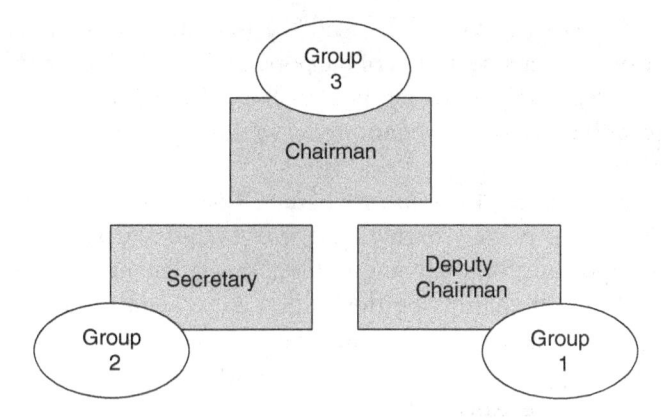

FIGURE 4.2 Static seat-based power-sharing model

state who are then appointed to the secretary post to recognize their significant presence in the area. In this static power-sharing scenario, the candidates for chairman and deputy chairman of different ethno-tribal groups will also run on the same ticket (Figure 4.2).

In a static zone- or ward-based arrangement, power-sharing may also rotate representation of wards or zones with the idea being that, even if the same ethnic groups generally occupy certain government council positions, the candidates are drawn from a different set of wards to broader represent the populations as well. Kajuru LGA is the closest example of this type of power-sharing. Although fieldwork did not confirm an explicit power-sharing arrangement, local leaders do abide by a zoning arrangement that implicitly serves a power-sharing function, particularly along ethno-religious lines. While the Kadara make up the majority of the population (around 70 percent, according to local estimates) and are predominantly Christian, the data suggest that some portion of the Kadara are also adherents of Islam, along with the Hausa-Fulani, who compose about 30 percent of the population. Kajuru's zoning arrangement, therefore, has resulted in both Christian *and* Muslim Kadara representatives in local government leadership since 1997, and Muslim Hausa-Fulani have also been appointed to important posts in the local government, even if not the top elected positions.[18] Although the data for the

---

[18] For example, the available data show that a Muslim Hausa-Fulani has chaired a caretaker committee twice, served twice as a vice chairman on two other caretaker committees, and Hausa Muslims have also been chosen to serve as secretaries in two elected administrations under Kadara leadership.

elected councils since 1997 could not be obtained for some elections, this rotation and representation of the population in the local government suggests a regular pattern of power-sharing that renders the LGA less susceptible to the instigation or spillover of Muslim–Christian violence.

It is important to note that this study does not categorize a local government as a power-sharing case if it excludes from the arrangement an important minority and politically significant ethnic group in the LGA. How might this be the case? Zango-Kataf and Jema'a, for example, report that they have an ethnic power-sharing arrangement of either an explicit or implicit (zone-based) nature, but the electoral data gathered revealed that their "power-sharing" nonetheless excludes a) a historically and politically important minority (i.e., Muslim Hausa-Fulani) in the LGA, which compromises the principle of power-sharing as an "inclusive" institutional mechanism, and b) also does not reflect mixed *religious* representation. This second level of assessment confirms the importance of the supplementary electoral data and deeper case study work into the history of communal relationships – to assess whether supposed power-sharing is reflected in the electoral pattern over time and truly represents the most prominent minorities in a district.[19] Whatever the precise arrangement, the main objective and mark of a power-sharing arrangement is that it "include all groups that can threaten political stability if kept outside the arrangements," and, in light of the context of inter-religious violence in Nigeria, the representation of Muslims and Christians is key (Rothchild and Roeder 2005, 31).

## CONCLUSION

One of the main weaknesses noted in the discussion of decentralization in the previous chapter was the shifting of conflict away from the

---

[19] Furthermore, further study revealed that the selection of candidates for the chairmanship has been compromised by outside interference, creating significant consternation and tensions between local ethnic groups. Locals complain that their candidates have to be approved (and, hence, selected) by the Hausa-Fulani Muslim emirate leadership, a holdover authority arrangement from colonial days. This lack of independence compromises the system of local representation and the original intention of decentralization. This dispute over the continued interference by the historically powerful Jema'a emirate in local politics, therefore, further supports the decision not to code Jema'a and Zango-Kataf as power-sharing cases.

center. While national-level power-sharing and ethno-federalism may reduce competition for control of the state, power-sharing can hardly be considered a success if it merely redirects competition and violent conflict to the subnational or communal level. Without addressing ethnic cleavages at this level, states risk the intensification and spillover of identity politics and grievances, which, as the case of Nigeria exemplifies, can destabilize the state, deplete resources, and incur devastating costs to human life and property. Hence, power-sharing at the local government level may facilitate successful conflict management under conditions of ethnic diversity and rampant politicization of identity.

There are a number of reasons why I expect the goals of power-sharing pursued through representative institutions at this level may be more effective and attainable. As the preceding discussion highlighted, for example, local level political institutions are by nature closer to the direct concerns, fears, and needs of the people, and are more likely to impact group relationships. In Nigerian society, access to resources and socioeconomic rights (or lack thereof) are influenced in important ways by group representation in local political institutions. Furthermore, in ethnically heterogeneous countries, the ethnic cleavages vary not just from state to state, but from community to community – cleavages that a broad-based national power-sharing arrangement will be unable to mollify. More inclusive *local* governments may therefore succeed in reducing perceptions that inequalities and grievances are a product of ethnic competition, thereby mitigating incentives for violence. While the particular conditions shaping the incentives for (or against) power-sharing can vary depending on the LGA, which I address in the subsequent chapter, power-sharing can help ensure broader representation and communal peace in states like Nigeria, where ethnic and religious politics, in particular, have become divisive and violent.

In this sense, the limitations or apparent failures of power-sharing identified by scholars are not due not to its mechanisms of inclusion, but rather its level of application – national, as opposed to (or in addition to) local. Yet, the potential value of local power-sharing institutions in creating conditions for peace or conflict is only recognized in passing in the literature (Spears 2000, 115). Thus, focus merely on the success or failure of national-level power-sharing arrangements not only misses important subnational variation in ethnic communal violence, but also overlooks the presence of power-sharing arrangements at the subnational level and their capacity to promote communal peace and cooperation in the face of divisive religious narratives.[20] For this reason, studies of the effectiveness of local power-sharing in stemming communal violence should be disaggregated or studied separately from the relationship between conflict resolution and national power-sharing.[21]

Finally, a national-level theory of power-sharing and ethno-federalism cannot adequately explain the pattern of inter-religious violence in Nigeria. In the Nigerian context, religious identity is a highly politicized category that can easily be mapped onto inter-ethnic conflicts regarding

---

[20] Power-sharing, as this discussion highlights, is not merely applicable to states emerging from civil war. Nigeria is not generally treated as a post-civil war case in the power-sharing scholarship, since the Biafran civil war ended in 1970 and the most prevalent form of violence is now communal rather than insurgencies against the state. LeVan's (2011) research extends the study of power-sharing to unstable democracies (i.e., Kenya and Zimbabwe) that have experienced ethnic violence in response to a flawed or contentious election. In this sense, despite the prevalence of communal violence in the post–Cold War world, the relevance of power-sharing to these subnational disputes is overlooked.

[21] Note that the scholarship also often appears confused in its level of analysis when assessing the empirical evidence for power-sharing success and failure, often treating post-civil war, unstable, and "ethnic conflict" states interchangeably in the analysis and policy inferences (e.g., Rothchild and Roeder 2005, 21). Lack of a clear rational for the inclusion of these different types of states in the assessments of power-sharing renders the unit of analysis and the generalizability of the findings unclear (see Saideman et al. 2002). Recent work by Cheeseman and Tendi (2010) and LeVan (2011), for example, assesses power-sharing in unstable or uncertain political environments. In this sense, the scope of the cases themselves is unclear across the scholarship. Ethnic conflict states are not necessarily interchangeable with civil war states in the analyses, as the former may include inter-ethnic *communal* violence while the latter generally refers to insurgents versus the state. Additionally, as Jarstad (2009) and Gates and Strøm (2007, 5–6) note, some scholars refer to power-sharing as a means to end civil war, while others see it as a means to develop democratic governance in plural societies or both. These analyses potentially require very different research designs and assumptions about what serves as effective power-sharing, yet they are rarely kept distinct by scholars who study power-sharing. While Jarsted (2006, 4) argues that "we know very little about which type of power sharing works to accommodate conflict and why," we know very little about which type of power-sharing works to ameliorate which *type* of conflict and why. Also, the comparative case study designs often fall into the trap of selection bias, as Gates and Strøm (2007, 1, 6–7) observe, excluding from the analysis cases not characterized by conflict, despite sharing similar societal characteristics as those that have descended into conflict. Additionally, as Gates and Strøm (2007, 7) note, studies that find that power-sharing is effective at prompting peace and good governance – such as Hartzell and Hoddie (2003), Binningsbo (2005), and Reynal-Querol (2002) – tend to "suffer from sample bias and possible endogeneity problems. Case studies are notorious for selecting on the dependent variable, and case studies of power-sharing may have had a tendency to concentrate on the more durable and successful cases."

group inequalities or rights. Why is it, then, that only some pluralistic communities in the Middle Belt – in particular in Kaduna and Plateau state – are prone to Muslim–Christian violence? Where local government power-sharing is absent, I argue, communal conflicts or grievances are more likely to become sacralized and spiral into inter-religious violence. In contrast, where local government power-sharing is present, this institutional foundation can not only help to mitigate the sacralization of local communal politics, but also inspire inter-religious cooperation and collaboration. The evidence for this theory I take up in the following chapter.

# 5

## Power-Sharing Data and Findings

In 1987 in the small town of Kafanchan in southern Kaduna state, the image of inter-religious peace in northern Nigeria suddenly shifted. The scene of the crisis was the Kafanchan College of Education during a week of Christian events and festivities on campus called "Mission 87." Christian students held sessions for prayer, testimonies, films and other events. While such religious events on the college campus were common, a banner over the entrance gate to the school with the words "Welcome to 'Mission '87' in Jesus Campus" caused some consternation among the Muslims students, and the school authorities removed it when students complained (Falola 1998, 180). Tensions were already high; the Muslim Student Society (MSS) on campus held their own religious program the week prior (Boer 2003, 51). It was the meeting of Christian students on Friday, March 6, that set in motion the tide of violence that snowballed and soon engulfed the town itself.

Although both sides dispute who threw the first punch, the accounts of the event are fairly consistent. Reverend Abubakar Bako, a former Muslim convert to Christianity, was invited that evening to speak to a group of Christian students to give his testimony of conversion. A Muslim girl sitting nearby in the library overheard his conversation with the students, and, claiming that Reverend Bako defamed the Prophet Mohammed and the Qur'an, she ran out onto the campus shouting of his defamation to fellow Muslim students. A close friend of Reverend Bako's, who was deeply involved in work with students in northern Nigeria universities at the time, notes that Bako "was not the kind of ... Christian fundamentalist that went up and down causing trouble," but when the girl heard him say the name of the Prophet, "she simply went out and started shouting and screaming 'They are blaspheming Mohammed's name! They are calling Mohammed's name in a Christian gathering meeting!'"[1] Muslim students then rushed to the scene, and, although the leaders appealed for calm, a violent brawl ensued that engulfed the campus and spilled over into the town the next morning and resulted in at least 11 deaths and 16 injuries at the end of three days. Three mosques, a church, and many buildings and vehicles were also damaged (Adeyi-Adikwu 1987a; 1987b; Boer 2003, 51). "The Muslims went off to tear apart a nearby church, and the Christians set the school mosque and its Qur'ans on fire," and the town was "thrown into mass confusion" as students began mobilizing more support (Falola 1998, 181).

The violence in Kafanchan did not end there, however. As calm returned to Kafanchan, Falola (1998, 183) notes:

Muslims were busy organizing mobilizations against Christians elsewhere. Muslims who heard that Rev. Bako had denigrated the Qur'an in Kafanchan decided that it was time for war, not for reconciliation ... to those among them who saw the Kafanchan riots as a victory for the Christians, it was time for revenge. Indeed, the Federal Radio Corporation of Nigeria, a well-established pro-Islam radio station, broadcast exaggeratedly that many Muslims had been killed in Kafanchan, and that their houses and mosques were burned. This broadcast fueled a raging fire.

Subsequently, clashes between Muslims and Christians ensued in a number of towns, including Kaduna, Zaria, Samaru, Wusasa, Kankia, Malufanchi, Katsina, and Funtua in Kaduna state, as well as Kano in Kano State. The violence continued for ten days, and, although accounts of the level of destruction vary, rioters destroyed anywhere from 113 to upwards of 200 churches (Adeyi-Adikwu 1987a; Falola 1998, 183; International Crisis Group 2010, 34). Markets closed, officials suspended university classes, food prices shot up, people lost billions of naira in property, and security forces were mobilized to try to restore calm. This violence marks what scholars of Nigerian conflict generally refer to as the beginning of devastating inter-religious violence in northern Nigeria (Falola 1998, 179; Boer 2003; Osaghae and Suberu 2005), and illustrates how destructive subnational conflict can be.

Beyond the Kafanchan violence, there have been many cases of subnational conflict over the past three or four decades. Some cases have been strongly characterized by a religious dimension; other incidents, however, are characterized more by clashes between tribal or communal groups

---

[1] Anonymous(H), interview by Laura Thaut Vinson, Jos, Plateau State, June 3, 2011.

over important sources of economic sustainability, such as land or cattle. This chapter will explore these cases of violence in northern Nigeria, investigating how the types differ in number and in character. First, I briefly review the scope and quality of existing datasets that contain information on communal violence in northern Nigeria, emphasizing the need for original data collection. Second, I describe original newspaper data collection undertaken for this project, explaining how the new data were gathered in order to explore the puzzle. Third, I discuss data collection on power-sharing arrangements notably and specifically with regard to two selected states in Middle Belt Nigeria. Finally, I summarize initial findings, nuances, and caveats, all of which prepares for material in the subsequent chapters regarding the power-sharing mechanism itself.

## REVIEW OF EXISTING CONFLICT DATASETS

Exploring the puzzle of subnational violence in northern Nigeria requires closer attention to existing data on its scale. Specifically, what datasets exist that contain information on ethnic identities and communal violence in Nigeria? Obtaining or constructing data on cases of ethnic and communal violence, much less indicators of their pattern, with sufficient detail to test the relationship between identity and conflict is no simple task, requiring a finely grained dataset with geographic and characteristic information reflecting incidents over time. Nevertheless, exploration of existing datasets reveals that a few research programs have begun to produce datasets of intra- and non-state conflict that can capture small-scale communal violence. These include the Social Conflict in Africa Dataset (SCAD), the Armed Conflict Location and Event Dataset (ACLED), and the UCDP Non-State Conflict Dataset. Analysis of these datasets shows they are not suitable for the purpose here, however. While the SCAD, ACLED, and Non-State Conflict datasets represent an impressive effort to capture cases of intra- and non-state conflict globally and may considerably advance the study of intrastate conflict, they are less reliable or useful for honing in on the particular dimensions and dynamics of ethno-religious and ethno-tribal communal violence in specific countries. These three primary datasets will be briefly reviewed in turn.

First, the SCAD dataset is perhaps the most comprehensive in its coding methodology, containing nearly 700 cases of conflict in Nigeria from 1990–2011 ranging from riots and strikes to violent conflict. Yet, when filtered for cases of Muslim–Christian communal violence that occurred in the north of Nigeria, there are a total of only 89 cases. A review of northern Nigeria's history over the last several decades suggests this number is too low, perhaps extremely low. Additionally, a close look at the sources for the data suggests that the number of cases pitting religious actors against one another and that were characterized in some respect by religious issues might be far higher if the dataset relied more on local news sources rather than the stated *Associated Press* and *Agence France Presse* newswires; that is, this dataset seems to primarily capture those incidents that make international news, which presumably would severely limit the overall number of cases. With such a low number of recorded cases, disaggregation of the data in any meaningful way becomes highly problematic, if not impossible.

Second, in the ACLED dataset, there are 4,140 coded event days for Nigeria from 1997–2011. These data are even more difficult to disaggregate than the SCAD data, however, since cases are not coded by unique event; that is, violence between communal actors that took place continually over several days receives a separate row for each day of the conflict. A basic attempt to disaggregate the data by *distinct* event (i.e., going through each individual case/row and removing "duplicated" events), by location in northern Nigeria, and by cases in which Muslim and Christian actors are on *one or both* sides of the conflict quickly whittles down the total to 124 cases. There were also cases coded twice from reports of the same event that were simply published on different dates. Additionally, these data do not offer a finer grain of detail on the issues or precipitating factors surrounding instances of violence, nor is it possible to decipher anything concrete about the religious or other ethnic dimensions of the cases. Further, no local Nigerian new sources are listed in the ACLED dataset for the cases reviewed, meaning the ACLED dataset falls prey to the same criticism leveled at the SCAD data – reliance on international news sources, which likely miss many incidents of inter-religious communal violence relevant for the question here.

Third, the Non-State Conflict dataset only includes cases of 25 deaths or more, yielding just over 60 total cases for *all* of Nigeria from 1998 to 2011. Only thirty-four of these cases – in which *both* religious and other ethnic/tribal actors are identified – took place in northern Nigeria. This is an even greater underreporting of cases, and excludes cases with lower levels of mortality that might otherwise be highly significant. A series of incidents each with fewer than 25 deaths would not be reflected in the Non-State Conflict dataset, much less incidents of violence with *no* deaths that otherwise involve destroyed property, injuries, displacement of people, interrupted commerce, and so on. Such "lower level" events have in fact occurred in northern Nigeria, and are important to include in analysis in order to understand overall patterns of violence.[2] The Non-State Conflict dataset is therefore insufficiently detailed for use here. Further, like the ACLED dataset, conflict issues or triggers are not coded, and hence nothing can be derived in this respect from the data, even if the 25-deaths threshold were not applied.[3]

None of this means that these datasets do not have value. Rather, they are simply insufficient for the question posed here. The three datasets referenced are, in fact, considerable advancements in scholars' ability to track *global* intra-state conflict, and the critiques above should not detract from this; it would be nearly impossible to code every case of intra-state conflict for every country in the world from local news sources (to ensure the highest level of event capture). More recently initiated data collection projects greatly contribute to the study of conflict in Nigeria. The Nigeria Social Violence Project based at Johns Hopkins University and directed by Peter Lewis collects data on incidents of social violence, including communal violence, and is based on domestic as well as international sources. For the purposes of this study, the data are not sufficient, however, since the data collection only extends back as far as 1998. Additionally, the Nigeria Security Tracker data collection, associated with the Council on Foreign Relations, surveys both domestic and international sources for incidents of violence, but it only captures cases of violence since 2011. For purposes here, then, a new source of data is required, one that codes cases from local sources that can reveal something more specific about the micro-dynamics and identity dimensions of ethnic communal violence.

---

[2] For example, a case that appears in my dataset, but does not appear in any of the datasets discussed here, is a 2009 clash in Bauchi state in its capital city of Bauchi. Two *Guardian* articles from February 27 and 28 note that there were four days of inter-religious rioting and clashes in Bauchi city from around February 21 to 25, apparently sparked by the burning of two mosques overnight following recent attacks on mutual places of worship. Although the articles did not report that more than 25 people were killed, it cites the following devastation: 11 dead, 100 hospitalized, 4,500 displaced, 200 houses destroyed, 6 churches destroyed, and 3 mosques burned to the ground. Whatever the total reported death count, clearly this was a significant inter-religious clash on many levels and devastating to Christian–Muslim relations in Bauchi city.

[3] For further discussion of key differences in these datasets, see UCDP's comparison (ACLED "Dataset Comparison 2"). See also Kristine Eck, 2012, "In Data We Trust? A Comparison of GED and ACLED Conflict Events Datasets," *Cooperation and Conflict*, 47(1): 121–141.

## CONSTRUCTING A NEW DATASET

To explore the subnational variation and pattern of ethnic violence in northern Nigeria, therefore, I constructed an original dataset of communal violence. Like Varshney's (2002) and Wilkinson's (2004) work on communal violence in India, I code local newspaper reports of clashes involving different ethnic groups, work undertaken primarily during fieldwork from February to December 2011. The resulting dataset covers the years 1979 to 2011[4] or 13,759 daily editions of *The Guardian*, a major Nigerian newspaper.[5] While this method of data collection does not ensure the capture of every case of communal violence, the results of the data collection provide the best available picture of the subnational concentration and dynamics of the last 40 years of ethnic violence in northern Nigeria. In total, the number of cases of ethno-religious and ethno-tribal violence since 1979 amount to well over four-hundred[6] (see Figure 5.1).

"Ethno-religious" violence here refers to those cases in which the actors involved on both sides of the conflict are reported as religious (e.g., Muslim versus Christian) even if their tribal or communal affiliations are also noted (e.g., indigenous Christians versus indigenous Muslims, Berom

---

[4] Inter-religious violence did not become a major headline until 1987; rather, intra-Muslim violence was a bigger issue in the early 1980s. I use 1979 as the start date for the collection of cases to capture any events perhaps overlooked by scholars or commentators prior to 1987.

[5] The analysis of daily editions of the *Guardian* amount to around 90 percent of all possible editions from 1983 to 2011. The choice of the *Guardian* stemmed from discussion with local scholars and librarians, who recommended it due to its coverage of Nigeria's northern region, the fact that it is not owned by the government, and its strong journalism. Research assistants were trained to help identify cases of inter-group violence in daily editions of the *Guardian*, but I conducted all coding. Note that the *Guardian* did not begin publication until 1983, and, hence, I substituted two other newspapers – the *New Nigerian* and the *Nigeria Standard* – substituted for case-collection for the years 1979–1983. Both newspapers were used, since the former is thought to have a Muslim/northern bias while the latter a more Christian/southern bias. Nonetheless, both papers meet the criteria noted above, as well, and are headquartered in the north. These two papers were also referred to for coverage of a few months out of the total 32 years when no *Guardian* issues were available.

[6] The number of cases of *ethno-religious* violence shown in Figure 5.1 would be nearly double if cases of *intra*-religious violence or any case of conflict involving a reported religious group were included in the analysis, such as a terrorist group targeting a police station (see Appendix F). The focus here, however, is on cases of *inter-group* ethnic conflict in order to assess the effect of power-sharing on the propensity for inter-group ethnic conflict in pluralistic LGAs. Therefore, intra-group incidents are not included in these counts.

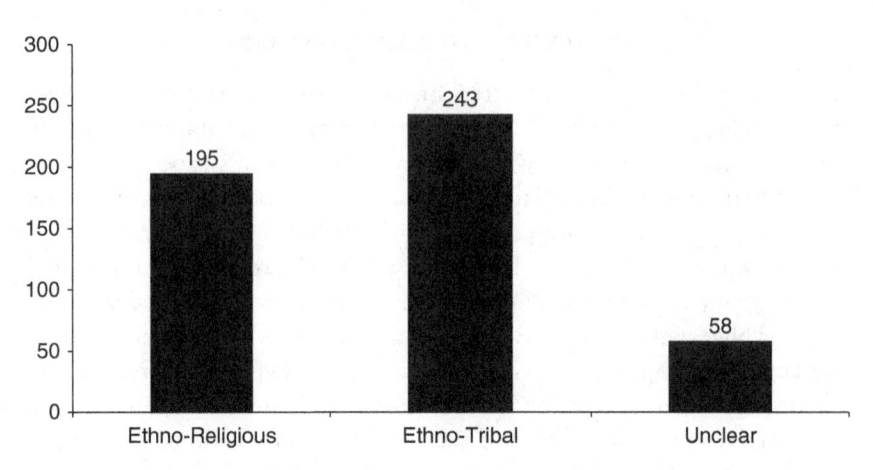

FIGURE 5.1 Cases of ethno-religious and ethno-tribal violence, 1979–2011

Christians versus Hausa-Fulani Muslims).[7] Cases designated in the dataset as ethno-tribal violence, in contrast, are cases that report *only* the tribal or communal identities of the opposing groups and no religious identities (e.g., Tiv and Jukun, farmers versus cattle-herders). This may seem to give preference to categorizing cases as "religious" rather than "tribal," but the goal in creating these categories was to identify those conflicts that have a religious dimension, and to distinguish them from those that do not.

The reported identity of the groups alone – used to categorize a case as either ethno-religious or ethno-tribal – does not, of course, make an event a case of religious or non-religious conflict, or say anything about how identity plays a role. The distinction is supported in the analysis of the precipitating events associated with the reported types of violence, however (see Appendices G and H). Cases were tested to see whether ethno-religious and ethno-tribal cases are equally likely to be associated, for example, with a religious precipitating event. The observed difference is stark and highly statistically significant ($p$ = .000): 88 percent of cases of ethno-religious violence cite a religious precipitating event compared to 1 percent of ethno-tribal cases (see Appendix I). Examples of a religious precipitating event might be a Christian walking through a Muslim prayer ground, or the burning of a Bible or a Qur'an. Importantly, religious

---

[7] The identities of the groups involved in each case of violence are coded according to the identity referred to in the newspaper. That is, if the report notes the religious identities of the participants in the violence (e.g., Muslim and Christian), or both a religious and tribal identity, then the case is coded as ethno-religious.

precipitating events are often symbolically weighted in this fashion. Ethno-tribal precipitating events, on the other hand, are often related to historic tribal conflicts or land disputes, such as who owns a particular field or bean tree, and can thus be classified as tribal or economic.

Of course, it could be argued that journalists may merely be looking for a precipitating event that produces a narrative – they identify a religious dynamic and therefore conclude the violence is religious. Admittedly, without possessing god-like knowledge of what is truly fundamental to the actors' decision-making processes, and lacking the ability to transport oneself back in time to "truthfully" and objectively observe all instances of communal violence to deduce the religious-ness of any events, issues of reporter bias may indeed affect the findings; this is an admitted shortcoming of *any* dataset that relies on news reports. This limitation, however, while important to note, does not sound a death knell for the approach; in this dataset, the coherence of the findings support the veracity of the argument that religious and tribal identities are associated with different conflict triggers embedded in particular identity understandings and politics. From a coherence theory standpoint, if it is indeed the case that ethnic identity conflicts have different logics of mobilization, then one should observe in the data that the precipitating events are *predominantly* of religious symbolic significance when associated with opposing Muslim and Christian groups. In other words, there should be narrative cohesion between religious precipitants and a supposedly religious clash, and one should not observe this pattern in other cases. If the identity dimension is not salient, the cases of "ethno-religious" violence and "ethno-tribal" violence should more closely mirror one another or be associated with a range of political, economic, and social disputes or grievances. The coherence of the data stands out. Further, the adamant skeptic has to conclude that every reporter who writes about the violence is biased and inserts his or her own narrative into every case of "religious" violence. Such an assumption is also problematic. Additionally, there are too many cases of communal violence that cannot be explained if religious sympathies do not play any role. Inter-religious communal violence frequently spreads from one place to another very rapidly where the conflicting groups are otherwise distinct in their identities *except* for religious affiliation. When, for example, the defamation of the Prophet Mohammed, the destruction of a Qur'an, the burning of a church or mosque, and other symbolic religious offenses trigger violence in a community that then spreads to other communities – with quite different tribal affiliations and socio-economic contexts – and splits communal actors along

Muslim and Christian religious lines (even of the same tribal group), it is difficult to conclude from this pattern of events that the particularly symbolic religious dimensions and narratives did not affect the instigation and subsequent pattern of violence. Did the economic conditions and the political balance of power of all of the communities suddenly change? The pattern of ethnic violence and conflict triggers cannot be explained merely by structural, institutional, and political conditions in northern Nigeria; identities and their socio-political symbolisms have concrete analytical and empirical significance.

Admittedly, there are other potential biases and problems with a method of data gathering that relies on coding newspaper reports. Some of these criticisms arise in Davenport and Ball's (2002) analysis of how different sources – newspapers, NGOs, and individual witnesses – report violations in Guatemala. The set of critiques leveled against newspapers center on the finding that they tend to give a distorted picture of events, focusing more on the following types of incidents: urban cases as opposed to rural ones, events in which the violence is larger or more bizarre, and events in closer proximity to the news agency. Also, information that comes to the news source may come through any number of channels and may not report all of the details or angles of the event (Davenport and Ball 2002, 430). In particular, one of the main criticisms of news sources is that they will be less likely to report on state agents involved as perpetrators in a violation, or state actors may unduly influence the reporting.

These are all important critiques, but they are more or less relevant depending on the method of newspaper selection, the type of incident being reported, and the weight placed on different findings from the data. In general, these critiques appear to be less serious in this dataset of communal violence, although challenges to reliability and validity cannot be fully resolved. First, I selected the newspaper source itself based on three main criteria: it is non-government owned, it has good coverage of the northern states, and it tends to emphasize news events as opposed to magazine-style commentary. Second, cases of violence in the dataset occurred in urban areas only around 23 percent of the time (i.e., cities with at least 50,000 people).[8] Third, while there is greater newspaper coverage of events with higher deaths, one would expect greater coverage of more deadly ethnic clashes. Approximately 52 percent of reports cover cases with more than 25 deaths, averaging 6.4 stories per case and

---

[8] Population data from Johnson (2007).

compared to an average of 1.9 articles per incident of violence with 25 or fewer deaths.[9] Fourth, the most significant critique leveled against newspaper data – potential bias due to the sensitivity of reporting state repression and the desire to avoid censorship – seems less applicable to this particular dataset, as the focus is not on cases of *state* repression, but rather on *communal* violence between non-state actors.

One more potential critique of the data needs to be addressed. Are cases of ethno-religious violence more *sensationalized* than ethno-tribal violence in the newspaper source? It is conceivable that newspaper reports could sensationalize religious sentiments. If so, this may indicate a problem with source bias that compromises the dataset to some degree. One way of testing this possibility is looking at whether religious incidents tend to be more prominently featured in the newspaper. However, analysis shows no clear bias; religious violence is about 14 percent more likely to be featured on the front page, both types of communal violence are generally equally likely to be reported on the subsequent three pages of the paper, and ethno-tribal cases are around 14 percent more likely to be covered on the back page of the newspaper.

While one might argue that this indicates that ethno-religious stories are perhaps more sensationalized – appearing more often on the front page – such a conclusion is problematic. First, top featured political news stories often appear on the *back* page of the *Guardian* as well, balancing out the difference to some degree. Second, even if the front page is more prominent, cases of inter-religious violence have been (a) increasing over time in Nigeria since the end of the 1980s and (b) have seen high death tolls in individual incidents in recent years. It would make sense, therefore, that a somewhat higher proportion of cases of ethno-religious violence appear on the front page of the newspaper source. Ultimately, this analysis cannot conclusively support a claim of press bias. To the contrary, the findings suggest that ethno-religious and ethno-tribal cases receive fairly equal treatment.

In any event, it is hard to conceive a more reliable dataset than one based on news sources of some kind, the alternative being first-hand

---

[9] In some cases, the number of deaths had to be estimated. This is because a news story sometimes covers a series of incidents across multiple locations, typically as part of a whole set of violent events. In such cases, discrete locations might not include a specific number of deaths, with only an overall death toll being reported. In these cases, the number of deaths was averaged across the cases. This actually works in the argument's favor, as any error introduced by such estimation would typically increase the number of "25+ deaths" incidents.

observation (whether in person or through technological means). This constructed dataset, then, follows the standard approach to building a dataset of violent events, but it is more comprehensive and fine-grained, allowing careful analysis of patterns of violence in northern Nigeria. The dataset includes additional variables regarding scale of the violence (including property destruction and injuries), duration, precipitating events, actors, and so on, such that patterns of communal violence can be readily identified.

### THE PATTERN OF THE PUZZLE

With this new dataset, then, we can return to the puzzle. With data on the concentration and pattern of inter-group violence at the LGA level over the past few decades, it becomes possible to analyze the relationship between communal violence and local government power-sharing. However, because data on *power-sharing* at the local level did not exist prior to this study (at least in a collected, accessible format), a new dataset on power-sharing was also developed. Given that the only way to collect these types of data was in-person, however, the dataset was of necessity limited to two select states, chosen based on the states' histories as well as the patterns of violence observed in the communal violence dataset. This section presents how, using histories and the newspaper dataset, two states were selected for power-sharing data collection. Note that these two states were *not* selected based on power-sharing arrangements – which were unknown at the time of selection – but rather for the variation observed on the dependent variable (interreligious violence at the LGA level) and their comparative value in controlling for other potential competing theories.

### Selecting Plateau and Kaduna States

The states selected for power-sharing analysis (and consequently power-sharing data collection) were Plateau state and Kaduna state (see Figure 5.2). These states are ideal sites for comparative analysis; Their LGAs share a similar colonial history, have a mixed ethnic makeup, and some areas were more integrated while others less integrated and assimilated into Hausa-Fulani Muslim colonial rule. In Plateau state, where Jos North is located, the overall population is now majority Christian (around 70 percent) due to the rapid growth of Christianity over the last five decades. Similarly, although Kaduna state is majority Muslim, the

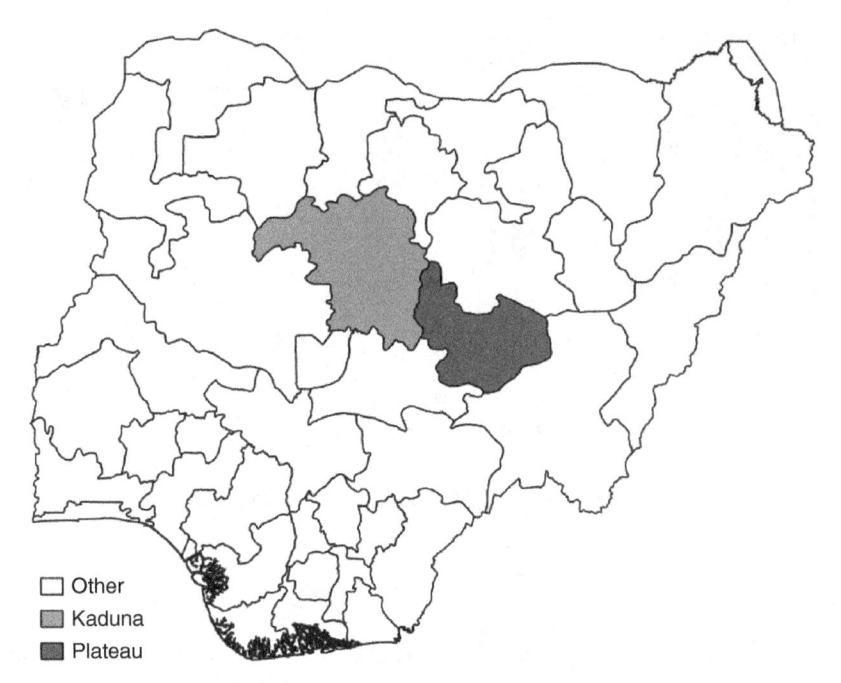

FIGURE 5.2 Outline of Nigerian States, Kaduna state and Plateau state emphasized

southern part of the state experienced a similar rapid growth of Christianity with the conversion of non-Muslims to Christianity, rendering it close to a 50/50 religious demographic. In southern Kaduna, therefore, Islam is the minority religion.

Also, critical for the comparative analysis is the variation in the incidence of ethnic violence at the local level, as observed in the data. Some pluralistic LGAs in Plateau state and Kaduna state have experienced intense inter-religious violence over the past three to four decades, but others have remained relatively peaceful despite the Muslim–Christian violence ripping apart communities in neighboring areas. Inter-religious violence is not the bane of *all* pluralistic communities or LGAs in these two states. Further, while the levels of ethno-religious and ethno-tribal violence for these two states are higher than some others, the frequency of ethnic violence cannot be reduced to mere population levels. As Figure 5.3 shows, Plateau state has a population that is smaller than or similar to a number of other northern states, but it has the highest reported incidence of Muslim–Christian violence and the second highest ethno-tribal violence. Furthermore, as Paden (2012, 95) notes, "Plateau State is in the

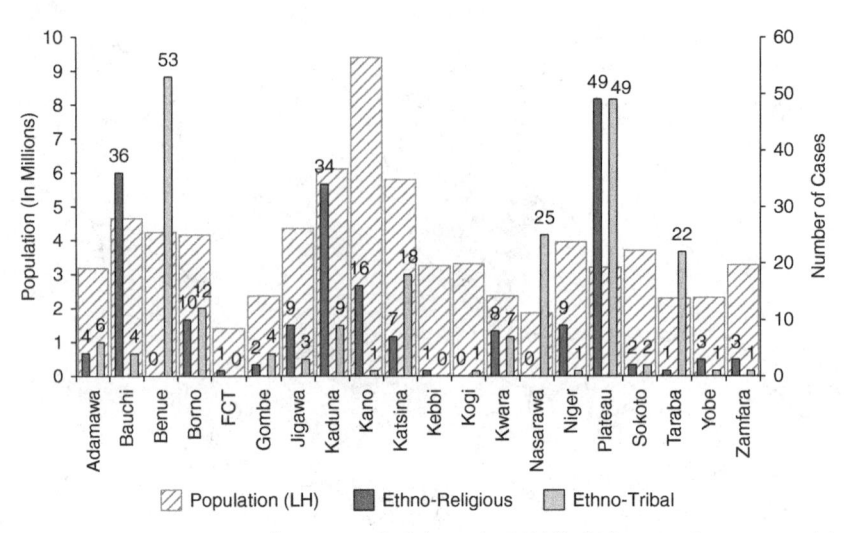

FIGURE 5.3 Frequency of communal violence in Middle Belt states (1979–2011)*

center of the country, where the plate tectonic of ethnicity and religion interact, and where the symbolism of Muslim Christian cooperation or conflict have enormous implications for the whole country." The same could be said of Kaduna state. For these reasons, these two states are ideal candidates for investigating the puzzle.

## Collecting Power-Sharing Data in Kaduna and Plateau States

The power-sharing data are based on the collection of as many of the election/appointment records as available for local councils in Plateau state and Kaduna state. My research assistants and I interviewed respondents in most of the LGAs, inquiring generally about the structure of local government and issues of peace or conflict.[10] In order to gain a more holistic picture and confirm the nature and extent of power-sharing arrangements, it was necessary to not only gather data on local council election results

---

* Population data obtained from the National Population Commission's 2006 census data. See Appendix J for total numbers. Note that ethno-tribal cases that were cross-border (involving a tribal/communal group from one state clashing with a group in a neighboring state) are not included in an individual state's count of cases.

[10] In most cases, during these interviews, it was not necessary to initiate a question about whether formal or informal power-sharing arrangements exist among the ethno-tribal groups, as this often came up naturally in the course of conversation.

over the years, but also the ethnic identities of individuals who served in local government. The driving question behind this data gathering project was: in pluralistic LGAs where respondents claimed to function under a power-sharing arrangement, is this reflected in their election results and/or political appointments? Also, in LGAs characterized by communal violence, do their election and appointment outcomes show lopsided political control considering the major ethno-tribal groups in the LGA? This analysis is the main indicator of variation in power-sharing.

Gathering this data represented a major hurdle; records of local government elected/appointed officials are generally nonexistent in Nigeria apart from locally maintained lists of past chairmen or the previous one or two local government councils. The National Electoral Commission, the state government offices, and LGA headquarters do not have consistent records. To gather the electoral/appointment data on the 17 LGAs of Plateau state and the majority of Kaduna state's 23 LGAs, therefore, research assistants and I spent time in each of the local governments, coordinating with them to compile the names of the officials and their ethnic identities for past administrations. This effort often involved speaking directly with former chairmen, deputy chairman, secretaries, information officers, and councilors who were able to assist in the reconstruction of information on the various administration officials. Where possible, the data were cross-checked through verification by multiple officials who served in a single council or from other sources, such as a complete national list of local government officials published in one election cycle. Although it was not possible to obtain comprehensive records for some local governments, the result of this data collection effort is a compilation of the most comprehensive data on local government officials and their ethnic identities in Plateau state local councils and for the majority of Kaduna state local councils.

Finally, a further note on the data and its interpretation is necessary. Local government elections or leadership changes do not occur at consistent intervals. This is due to factors such as the national regime in power – which in the past has been known to suspend local government elections (e.g., during military rule) and appoint Sole Administrators[11] – or due to

---

[11] In this appointment scenario, the officials are not necessarily appointed from the local government itself. They may come from a different local government or even another state. These dynamics have varied over time during different civilian and military regimes. For this reason, weight should not be placed on sole administrators or outside appointments when examining the pattern of power-sharing.

inefficient state governments or state election commissions in charge of the administration and organization of local government elections. In other cases, contested results have delayed the implementation of a newly elected local government council, extending the administrative period of transition committees or caretaker committees. The data reflect these "inconsistencies," but it is still possible to observe the overall *pattern* of local government power-sharing or lack thereof in terms of the ethno-tribal and -religious groups who are represented in the primary seats of local government councils from one leadership change to the next.

As noted in the previous chapter, the particular pattern of power-sharing may vary. In some cases, local councils abide by a *rotating seat-based* or *ward/zone-based* power-sharing agreement whereby the executive positions – chairman, deputy chairman, and secretary – rotate among the major ethnic groups in the local government from one local election to the next. In other cases, councils follow a *static seat-based* or *ward/zone-based* power-sharing arrangement, according the major ethnic groups a position of local council leadership, but a representative of the same ethnic group generally is allotted the same position. Among the three major ethnic groups in Chikun LGA in Kaduna state, for example, one group holds the chairmanship, another the deputy-chairmanship, and a third the secretary position. There is mixed ethnic representation in council leadership, but elections function by an implicit or informal rule that the ethnic groups do not rotate through the top three positions (as in a *rotating* power-sharing agreement).

The main point here is that there is not necessarily one *type* of power-sharing arrangement that can accomplish the principle of shared representation. For the purpose of this analysis, the key issue of interest is whether the ethnic groups in a pluralistic LGA abide by *any* type of informal power-sharing arrangement. Hence, the data collected on power-sharing in Kaduna and Plateau LGAs make it possible to test the theory that ethnically pluralistic areas with a power-sharing arrangement are less likely to experience inter-religious violence. Of course, in local governments that are homogenous – largely populated by one ethno-tribal group of a single religious identity – I expect a power-sharing arrangement to be both less likely and less politically relevant. The following section presents the analysis of both the inter-group violence and power-sharing data, confirming the importance of informal power-sharing institutions in sustaining inter-religious peace in pluralistic LGAs.

# FINDINGS AND DATA ANALYSIS: PLATEAU STATE

## (Non)Violence and Power-Sharing

Although the problem of inter-religious violence came later to Plateau state than Kaduna state and other surrounding areas, Plateau has been one of the hardest hit in terms of number of incidents of Muslim–Christian clashes (as highlighted previously in Figure 5.3), particularly since the beginning of the 2000s. Paden (2012, 79) also observes, "Without question, Plateau State has had the largest number of violent deaths from conflict of any state in Nigeria: many thousands have died since 1999." However, analysis of the power-sharing data reveals that, in Plateau state's pluralistic LGAs, those with a power-sharing arrangement have been far less likely to experience ethnic clashes. Table 5.1 provides a summary of the overall pattern, contrasting pluralistic Plateau state LGAs by a) whether they have a power-sharing arrangement and b) whether they experience relative inter-religious communal peace or violence. I also contrast in these tables the LGAs that lack a power-sharing arrangement but are largely *homogenous* in their ethno-tribal composition (bottom-left cases).[12]

As illustrated above and supporting the theory, pluralistic Plateau state LGAs with a power-sharing arrangement have been less prone to inter-religious violence since the 1980s. Based on analysis of the data, these are the LGAs where the top-tier positions of the local government – chairman, deputy chairman, and secretary – are generally shared by the primary ethno-tribal groups in the LGA, and, due to their implicit

TABLE 5.1 *Pattern of Power-Sharing and Violence, Plateau State*

|  | Low/No Violence | High Violence |
|---|---|---|
| Power-sharing | Pankshin, Mangu<br>Bassa, Mikang<br>Kanam, Bokkos |  |
| No power-sharing | (homogeneous)<br>Riyom, Kanke,<br>Jos East, Langtang North<br>Langtang South, Barkin-Ladi | Jos North, Jos South*<br>Qua'an Pan, Wase<br>Shendam |

\* Jos South's degree of pluralism is difficult to state conclusively, as discussed here, but seems to best fall into the pluralistic category based on research and interviews regarding its level of pluralism prior to major violence in the first part of the 2000s. Also note that Pankshin and Mikang are predominantly Christian LGAs, but they have considerable tribal pluralism.

[12] Note that best estimates of homogeneity are derived from interviews with locals as well as academic studies or reports. There are no official statistics, as ethnic identity data were barred from census collection after 1963.

religious pluralism, also reflect mixed Muslim and Christian representation.

The map of Plateau state LGAs also represents the correlation between power-sharing and communal inter-religious violence. The darkest-shaded local governments are those that lack a power-sharing arrangement and are also more prone to Muslim–Christian violence. The gray-shaded LGAs are those that possess power-sharing arrangements and are free of or less prone to the inter-religious clashes occurring in neighboring areas. The non-shaded LGAs are largely homogenous and hence outside the framework of this analysis for obvious reasons; in LGAs essentially homogenous in their ethno-tribal and ethno-religious dimensions, power-sharing among *ethno-tribal* groups would make little sense (Figure 5.4).

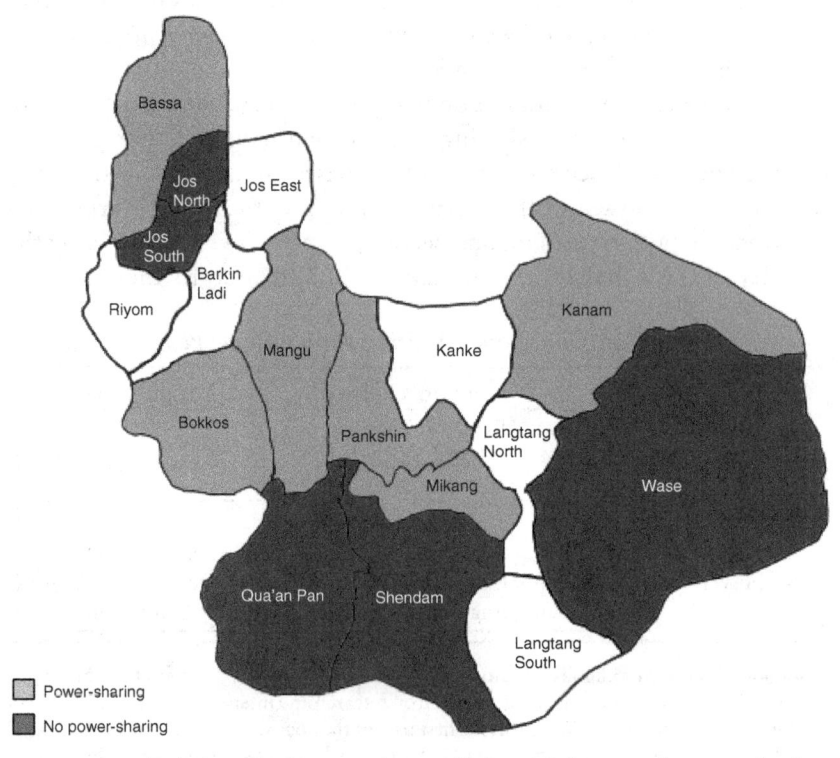

FIGURE 5.4 Relationship between inter-religious violence and power-sharing, Plateau state

## Interpreting the Data

Table 5.2 on the following page presents the number of ethno-tribal and ethno-religious clashes by each LGA, and indicates whether they have a power-sharing arrangement, are largely homogeneous, or have no power-sharing arrangement despite the ethno-tribal heterogeneity of the population. At first glance, the relationship between the incidence of violence and the presence of power-sharing is not entirely clear cut. That is, LGAs such as Jos South appear to go against the theory, as a number of inter-religious clashes have been recorded in Jos South despite its present-day predominantly indigenous Christian population. What explains this? Similarly, a number of inter-religious clashes have occurred in Langtang North and Kanam in the eastern part of Plateau state. If Kanam is a case of power-sharing, as the data confirm, and if Langtang North is a largely homogenous Christian indigenous population, then these LGAs should not be sites of recurring inter-religious clashes.

These apparent discrepancies can be addressed by examining the *nature* of the clashes more closely. To understand the data and what they signify, the following distinctions need to be made: whether or not a case is an *intra*-LGA incident of violence, involves Fulani cattle-herders, or occurs in a location that involves parties fighting across the borders of two LGAs (indicated in the columns to the right of "Total Cases").

### *Intra-LGA vs. Cross-LGA and Cross-state Cases*

First, while there are a number of cases of inter-religious or ethno-tribal violence involving Langtang North and Kanam, it is important to note that almost all of these cases are clashes between a group in one LGA with a group in the other. Seven out of eight cases recorded for Kanam and 15 out of 18 cases involving Langtang North were cross-LGA border clashes (e.g., clashes between Christian Taroh from Langtang North and Muslim Bogghom from Kanam local government). These cross-border disputes stem from two factors: a) long-standing disputes on the border area between the two ethno-tribal groups that also fit a Muslim–Christian dimension, and b) the heightened tension due to inter-religious violence occurring elsewhere in the southern part of Plateau state at the time (i.e., Shendam and Wase).[13] A number of cases of ethno-tribal and ethno-

---

[13] During the early 2000s, major inter-religious violence occurred in Shendam LGA that soon spread to Wase and polarized groups as far north as Langtang North and Kanam LGAs. Because ethnic groups took sides based on religious identity, the spillover was widespread. Hence, it is no surprise that the predominantly Christian Langtang North

TABLE 5.2 *Plateau State LGAs: Power-Sharing and Count of Ethno-Religious and Ethno-Tribal Violence*

| | Ethno-Religious Violence | Ethno-Tribal Violence | Unclear | Total | Spillover | Cross-LGA | Cross-State | Fulani Herders |
|---|---|---|---|---|---|---|---|---|
| **Power-sharing** | | | | | | | | |
| Bassa | | 3 | 1 | 4 | | | | 3 |
| Bokkos | 1 | 3 | | 4 | 1 | 1 | | |
| Kanam | | 3 | 5 | 8 | 4 | 7 | | |
| Mangu | 1 | 3 | | 4 | 1 | | | |
| Mikang | | | | 0 | | | | |
| Pankshin | 1 | | | 1 | 1 | | | |
| **No power-sharing** | | | | | | | | |
| Jos North | 15 | 3 | 4 | 22 | 5 | | | 3 |
| Qua'an Pan | 1 | 5 | 1 | 7 | 1 | | 3 | 3 |
| Shendam | 5 | 4 | 3 | 12 | 5 | | 2 | 1 |
| Wase | 10 | 4 | | 14 | 10 | 7 | | 1 |
| **Religious homogeneity** | | | | | | | | |
| Barkin Ladi | 3 | 8 | 4 | 15 | 4 | | | 10 |
| Jos East | | | | 0 | | | | |
| Jos South | 10 | 6 | 3 | 19 | 9 | | | 8 |
| Kanke | | | | 0 | | | | |
| Langtang North | 6 | 7 | 5 | 18 | 10 | 15 | | |
| Langtang South | | 2 | 1 | 3 | | 2 | | |
| Riyom | 1 | 4 | | 5 | | | 1 | 3 |

* Note that the total number of ethno-religious and ethno-tribal cases of violence may total more than 49 each, since a case that is cross-border between two Plateau state LGAs is counted as a case for both LGAs (as groups from both LGAs were involved). Also, regarding the analysis of Qua'an Pan, a zoning arrangement between wards in Qua'an Pan LGA results in rotation of leadership. The data and limited information on Qua'an Pan make assessment difficult, but it appears that the conflict in the LGA in the mid-2000s over the creation of a new development area was primarily a dispute with an ethno-tribal group not reflected in the rotation, thus its designation as a "no power-sharing" case. For Wase, the LGA did not provide sufficient data for a complete assessment, but interviews and secondary sources suggest that the struggles between the Taroh and the Hausa-Fulani are symptomatic of a lack of power-sharing.

religious violence involving Wase groups are also cross-LGA (7 out of 14 total cases), but Wase differs from Langtang North and Kanam in that it has also been prone to clashes between the majority Hausa Muslims and the minority Christian Taroh due to division over political authority or representation and control of land (e.g., lack of power-sharing).

Apart from these cross-border clashes, the communal groups *within* these two local governments of Langtang North and Kanam are largely peaceful – Kanam with its power-sharing arrangement and Langtang North with its largely homogenous ethnic population. Most important for this analysis of the effects of power-sharing institutions, therefore, is the incidence of ethnic violence between groups *within* the same LGA. That is, if power-sharing is providing effective representation to the main groups in a pluralistic local government, then the likelihood of inter-ethnic clashes within that LGA should be lower. No claim is made here about the relationship between local power-sharing institutions and the likelihood of cross-border or cross-state[14] ethnic violence.

## Fulani Cattle-herders vs. Farmers

Another common type of ethno-tribal communal clash in northern Nigeria is violence stemming from conflict between cattle-herders and local farmers. As previously noted, the precipitating events associated with ethno-tribal violence tend to be of an economic nature, such as disputes over land rights or cattle grazing on farmland, whereas ethno-religious violence is commonly associated with precipitating events of symbolic religious significance. Nomadic Fulani herdsman and farmers have increasingly come into conflict over competing land claims (Ofuoku and Isife 2009; Abbass 2014; Human Rights Watch 2014). The tensions are the product of a few converging pressures, including heightened

---

and the predominantly Muslim Kanam LGAs had a few cross-border inter-religious clashes, as the communal groups identified with the warring parties in the Shendam and Wase violence, and the surrounding LGAs were also major recipients of those fleeing the southern Plateau state violence.

[14] I distinguish cases of communal violence that are *cross-state*, between, for example, groups on either side of the border of Plateau state and Benue state. Indeed, there have been long-standing border disputes between some of the groups in these areas, dating back to the time when Plateau and Benue were a single state. Hence, cases of cross-state ethno-tribal clashes have occurred between groups in Qua'an Pan, Riyom, and Shendam LGAs with groups in a state bordering Plateau.

resource competition due to incursions of farmers into cattle grazing areas (and vice versa), new population pressures, and the decline in grazing land for cattle as a result of drought and climate change. Consequently, one of the striking differences between the cases of inter-religious and ethno-tribal violence in Plateau state is that many of the cases of ethno-tribal violence in some LGAs are disputes between nomadic Fulani herdsmen (informally settled in an LGA) and members of the local community. For example, all of the reported clashes between ethno-tribal groups in Barkin Ladi are clashes between Fulani herdsman and a local farming community. Barkin Ladi is otherwise home to a largely homogeneous ethnic population and less prone to inter-group violence. The same distinction can be applied to other LGAs such as Riyom that are less prone to inter-religious violence (largely homogenous population), but have occasional clashes between nomadic Fulani herdsman and farmers; three of the four reported ethno-tribal clashes here involved Fulani herdsman and farmers. Those cases of violence between Fulani herdsman and indigenous farming communities, indicated in Table 5.2, must be distinguished from the main focus of this study – communal violence occurring between the local ethno-tribal groups resident in an LGA.

### *City-merged LGAs: Jos South and Jos North*

A final note regarding the interpretation of the data for LGAs where they comprise a city center, such as Jos North and Jos South, as well as Kaduna North and Kaduna South; although Jos South is more homogenous, primarily home to a Christian indigenous population, it is characterized by a high number of cases of ethnic violence similar to Jos North. This would seem to go against the argument about relative peace where the population is basically homogeneous. Jos South must be understood differently for two reasons, however. First, both Jos North and Jos South comprise the Jos metropolis and its environs. Hence, there is no clear dividing line between the two LGAs. An incident occurring in one neighborhood of Jos, therefore, can easily spill over into either Jos North or Jos South depending on where Muslim and Christian youth mobilize. Consequently, six out of the ten cases of ethno-religious violence recorded for Jos South spilled over from Jos North clashes. Note that "spillover" cases are those in which the violence occurred in response to violence that recently occurred elsewhere or is ongoing (i.e., a nearby neighborhood or in another town, LGA, or state).

Second, and perhaps most important, it is only in *recent* years that Jos South has become largely homogenous, due to the inter-religious violence that has encouraged (or forced) Muslims to leave their former homes to move to majority Muslim Hausa areas in Jos North LGA. Estimates of the Muslim population in Jos South prior to 2001 can vary drastically, as high as 30–40 percent Muslim or as low as 5 percent, depending on one's interlocutor. There are no official statistics, and population numbers are highly sensitive in the Jos area, in particular, since population size can be used to buttress claims to indigenous status, land ownership, and rights to political power. Hence, when asked about the pluralism of the Jos South community prior to 2001 compared to the present, members of different ethnic groups are likely to cite far different population numbers, or refuse to make any assertion due to the question's sensitivity. Whatever the exact numbers, it is clear that Jos South was more heterogenous and mixed prior to 2001, and there are only small concentrations of Hausa-Fulani Muslims in Jos South today, as many migrated either to Jos North or to other parts of the north following the communal clashes in the Jos area from 2001 to 2010. It is no surprise, therefore, that conflagrations of Muslim–Christian violence in the general Jos metropolis or Jos North have also spilled over into Jos South or have been enflamed by communal differences there as well.

In sum, these cases which may appear as discrepancies at first glance can be explained within the framework of the power-sharing theory. Pluralistic LGAs with a power-sharing arrangement among their ethno-tribal groups – such as Bassa, Mangu, and Kanam – have lower incidence of inter-religious violence. In contrast, local councils without power-sharing are more prone to inter-religious violence as well as spillover violence. In LGAs where representation is already unequal, mere identification with co-religionists embroiled in conflict elsewhere can serve as a rallying cry for groups unhappy with their own perceived political marginalization. The prevalence of the us-versus-them narrative of religious conflict in Nigeria means the religious narrative can easily be mapped onto violence between Muslim Hausa-Fulani and indigenous Christian groups in Middle Belt Nigeria. Inter-religious violence is *trans*-tribal in Nigeria, salient beyond or not constricted by tribal boundaries.

FINDINGS AND DATA ANALYSIS: KADUNA STATE

## Power-Sharing and (Non)Violence

The power-sharing pattern also holds for the Kaduna state LGAs for which sufficient data could be obtained – 20 of 23 local councils (see Table 5.3 and Figure 5.5). Those LGAs that have been most prone to Muslim–Christian violence since the 1980s, according to the collected data and interviews, are also ones that lack a power-sharing arrangement between the main ethno-tribal groups. Although adequate data could not be obtained for some local councils due to the hesitancy of officials to provide the information (in some cases due to worries about its political sensitivity), it is clear that the mere presence of Muslims and Christians living together in pluralistic communities does not inherently inspire violence. Indeed, in Chikun, Birnin-Gwari, and other areas where the ethno-tribal and religious mix of the population might suggest a greater likelihood of violence – if nothing else due to affinity with Muslims and Christians clashing in proximate areas – towns in these LGAs remain peaceful compared to other offending LGAs such as Kaduna North, Kaduna South, Zangon-Kataf, and Jema'a. As the data reveal, these peaceful areas also happen to be where a rotational system of representation or power-sharing structures local political life and incorporates both Christian and Muslim leaders in the top-tier council leadership on a fairly regular basis.

TABLE 5.3 *Pattern of Power-Sharing and Violence, Kaduna State\**

|  | Low/No Violence | High Violence |
|---|---|---|
| Power-sharing | Kachia, Chikun<br>Kajuru, Kaura<br>Birnin-Gwari, Sanga |  |
| No power-sharing | (homogeneous)<br>Jaba, Kubau, Makarfi<br>Sabon-Gari, Ikara, Kudan<br>Igabi, Soba, Giwa | Kaduna South<br>Kaduna North, Zangon-Kataf<br>Jema'a, Zaria |

\* Insufficient data to determine the status of Kagarko, Kauru, and Lere. Although not verified in interviews with local officials, data obtained for Kachia reflect and are highly suggestive of a power-sharing arrangement. Also, data for Kajuru indicate zone-based, rotational power-sharing.

FIGURE 5.5 Relationship between inter-religious violence and power-sharing, Kaduna state

## Interpretation of the Data

As with Plateau state, the data for Kaduna requires careful interpretation (see Table 5.4). Qualitative fieldwork is an important component of this research, therefore, as it not only augments the research by painting a fuller picture and offering thicker description, but it also provides important context for *understanding* the data where they might otherwise appear messy or contradictory. Interpreting the pattern of power-sharing and violence for Kaduna LGAs requires attention to the following: the demography in its historical context, the inclusiveness of power-sharing, and the spillover effect upon LGAs that merge in major metropolitan areas.

### Demographics and Their History
First, due to its history and geography, the ethno-religious demography of Kaduna state very much reflects the diversity of the Middle Belt. The far

northern Kaduna LGAs are virtually exclusively Muslim, while the LGAs spanning the center of the state are home to a mix of Muslims and Christians of various ethno-tribal groups, and the LGAs in the southern half of Kaduna are majority Christian.[15] In southern Kaduna, the minority communities of Hausa-Fulani Muslims are extremely important in the analysis. Although these LGAs are predominantly home to indigenous Christian groups, the historical rule and religio-political domination of the Hausa-Fulani Muslim emirs and chiefs in this region of Kaduna state renders the relationship between the local Christian ethno-tribal groups and the small enclaves of Muslim Hausa-Fulani politically important and, in some cases, tense.

This dynamic is particularly evident in LGAs such as Zangon-Kataf, Jema'a, and Kajuru. In Zangon-Kataf, Hausa-Fulani are predominant in the town of Zango, in Jema'a they are the majority in the town of Kafanchan, and the Hausa-Fulani in Kajuru are concentrated in the ancient cities of Kasuwan Magani and Kajuru (the headquarters of the LGA). Hence, despite their minority status, issues of Muslim Hausa-Fulani control and the absence of power-sharing continue to be important issues due to the historical pattern of settlement, power relations, and changes over time.

### *Power-Sharing by Zone-based Rotation*

Second, although an informal agreement to rotate local government leadership positions by zone or ward can serve as *de facto* power-sharing, the particular *nature* of the zoning arrangement must be parsed to determine whether it indeed facilitates power-sharing. While the rotation of representation by zones functions as an effective power-sharing arrangement in some areas (e.g., Kajuru), it does not represent a true power-sharing arrangement in others (e.g., Zango-Kataf and Jema'a), or it is irrelevant to this analysis in some cases as the population is largely homogenous in its tribal and religious demographics (e.g., Kudan, Makarfi, Ikara).

In the case of Kajuru, although an explicit power-sharing arrangement could not be confirmed, local leaders have adopted a zoning arrangement that implicitly serves a power-sharing function, particularly along ethno-

---

[15] Note that there are no recent national census data available to document the ethno-tribal and ethno-religious composition of the LGAs. Hence, discussion of the population dynamics are based on general local knowledge, information provided in interviews with local officials to some degree, scholarly sources, and population dynamics reflected in the electoral data.

TABLE 5.4 *Kaduna State LGAs: Power-Sharing and Count of Ethno-Religious and Ethno-Tribal Violence*

| | Ethno-Religious Violence | Ethno-Tribal Violence | Unclear | Total | Spillover | Cross-LGA | Cross-State | Fulani Herders |
|---|---|---|---|---|---|---|---|---|
| **Power-sharing** | | | | | | | | |
| Birnin-Gwari | 0 | 1 | 0 | 1 | | | | 1 |
| Chikun | 2 | | 1 | 3 | 2 | | | |
| Kachia | | | 2 | 2 | 2 | | | |
| Kajuru | | 1 | | 1 | | | | |
| Kaura | | | | 0 | | | | |
| Sanga | | 2 | | 2 | | | | |
| **No power-sharing** | | | | | | | | |
| Jema'a | 3 | 2 | 1 | 6 | | | | |
| Kaduna North | 6 | | 10 | 16 | 3 | | | |
| Kaduna South | 7 | | 12 | 19 | 6 | | | |
| Zango-Kataf | 3 | 1 | | 4 | | | | |
| Zaria | 6 | | 3 | 9 | 3 | | | |
| **Religious homogeneity** | | | | | | | | |
| Giwa | 2 | | | 2 | 2 | | | |
| Igabi* | 4 | | 2 | 6 | 5 | | | |
| Ikara | 1 | | | 1 | 1 | | | |
| Jaba | | | | 0 | | | | |
| Kudan | | | | 0 | | | | |
| Kubau | | | | 0 | | | | |
| Makarfi | 1 | | | 1 | | | | |
| Sabon Gari | 1 | | | 1 | 1 | | | |
| Soba | | | | 0 | | | | |
| **Unclear** | | | | | | | | |
| Kagarko | | | | 0 | | | | |
| Kauru | 1 | | 1 | 2 | 1 | | | 1 |
| Lere | | 1 | | 1 | | | | |

* Note that all but one of the Igabi LGA cases were reported as occurring in the Rigasa neighborhood of Kaduna city.

157

religious lines. While the Kadara make up the majority (around 70 percent, according to local estimates) and are predominantly Christian, the data suggest that some portion of the Kadara are also adherents of Islam, along with the Hausa-Fulani Muslims who comprise about 30 percent of the population. Unlike Zangon-Kataf and Jema'a, Kajuru's zoning arrangement, therefore, has resulted in both Christian *and* Muslim Kadara representatives in local government leadership since 1997, and, interestingly, Muslim Hausa-Fulani have also held important posts in the local government, even if not the top elected positions. For example, the available data show that a Muslim Hausa-Fulani has chaired a caretaker committee twice, served twice as a vice chairman on two other caretaker committees, and Hausa Muslims have also served as secretaries in two elected administrations under Kadara leadership. Although the data for the elected councils since 1997 could not be obtained for some elections, this rotation and representation of the population in the local government suggests a regular pattern of power-sharing that renders the population less susceptible to the instigation or spillover of Muslim–Christian violence.

Similarly, in the pluralistic Kachia LGA, an explicit power-sharing institution was not confirmed, but power-sharing is implicit in the data, as it reflects a regular rotation of council leadership between the Adara, Jaba, Hausa, and others, resulting in both Muslim and Christian community members serving in the top leadership posts. From 1980 to 1983, an Adara Muslim held the chairmanship, and the seat was then won by a Hausa Muslim in 1983, for example. Although records for many of the vice chairmen and secretaries for a number of administrations could not be obtained, a Muslim (Hausa or Adara) served as a vice chairman or secretary in three of the other elected administrations since the 1980s, apart from occasional leadership in non-elected administrations (e.g., caretaker or sole administrator appointees). This power-sharing dynamic suggests a more equitable system of representation in the local government, reinforcing greater inter-religious stability in Kachia despite violence in surrounding areas. With the prevalence and rampant narrative of Muslim–Christian violence in Nigeria since the late 1980s, a system of local government leadership incorporating both Muslims and Christians is an important barrier to the pernicious spread of inter-religious violence.

Jema'a and Zangon-Kataf present an important contrast. In theory, because these two local councils also report a zoning arranging – leadership rotating among the zones of the LGA – leadership should more equitably reflect the ethnic groups in the LGA. Yet, not every system of zone-based representation is also power-sharing in nature. In these two

LGAs, the particular political context and nature of the zoning arrangements do not lend themselves to inter-religious harmony. Jema'a, home to a number of different local ethno-tribal groups – including the Kagoma, Bajju, Ninzo, Kanikon, and Hausa – reflects an impressive system of seat-based leadership rotation over the years. The chairmanship rotates among the various ethno-tribal groups and, whichever tribal group holds the chairmanship, the deputy and secretary must then come from different tribal groups. This dynamic was reported by local officials and is also reflected in the collected data. However, unlike Kajuru, the data appear to suggest that, unless appointed (likely from the outside) to lead as a sole administrator or caretaker, the Hausa-Fulani are infrequently represented in the main leadership of the local government. More importantly, the history of political struggles matters here. As will be discussed in Chapter 8, the history of the relationship between the local Christian tribal groups and the Hausa-Fulani Muslims renders the politics of identity far more volatile, helping to explain why religion has served as a major cleavage and source of tension and occasional violence in Jema'a.

Similarly, although Zangon-Kataf has a zoning arrangement and reportedly adopted a power-sharing arrangement in 2008, a history of struggle over local political control has fueled conflict. Local Christian ethno-tribal groups have sought for some time to obtain autonomy from, in their view, the old Zaria emirate system's stranglehold on LGA politics. Hence, although the local *Christian* ethno-tribal groups rotate local council leadership, rotation of religious representation is foiled by the long-standing and unresolved history of political tensions and perceived "outside" Hausa-Fulani domination. True decentralized political control – local autonomy from control of the Muslim emir – has been a major point of contention between the local Christian ethno-tribal groups and Muslims, enflaming local politics and leading to a deterioration of inter-religious relationships. In this context, various political issues are able to spark identity disputes, resulting in a socio-political environment more prone to Muslim–Christian violence. While this dynamic in both Jema'a and Zangon-Kataf and its historical underpinnings will be discussed in greater detail, this brief discussion highlights the importance of power-sharing in practice – between the main politically influential ethnic groups in an LGA – and not in name only.

### *City-merged LGAs: Kaduna North, Kaduna South, and Igabi*
Finally, as with the cases of Jos North and Jos South LGAs in Plateau state, the meeting of LGA borders in a major metropolis makes it more difficult

to prevent the spillover of inter-religious violence from one neighborhood/ LGA to another neighborhood/LGA that mutually constitute the city. Hence, the frequency of inter-religious violence in Kaduna city, the capital of Kaduna state, is the bane of Kaduna South, Kaduna North, and Igabi LGAs. There is no clear geographical demarcation between these areas; Kaduna North and South are chiseled out of different sections of the metropolis, and some neighborhoods of the city are technically within the borders of Igabi. This dynamic renders the politics and tensions within these areas difficult to disentangle. With such a densely populated urban area of more than one million people, the oddly demarcated LGAs (parts of Kaduna South LGA reach into the northern part of the city and vice versa) means that violence in neighborhoods in either Kaduna North or South can easily spill over into the other. This dynamic helps to explain the high number of incidents of inter-religious violence for Kaduna North and Kaduna South – at least 16 and 19 cases, respectively, when one includes the cases that are "Unclear" or unspecific about whether it occurred in Kaduna North or South (see Table 5.4). And while Igabi *appears* more susceptible to inter-religious violence (six cases recorded), the violence is concentrated in Rigasa neighborhood, part of the Kaduna metropolis. The violence, in this sense, does not stem from political disputes within Igabi LGA, which is a largely homogenous Muslim Hausa population. The politics of Kaduna North and South is far more contentious with its minority Christian population. In Kaduna South, for example, there is some suggestion in the data and from local officials that elected Hausa leaders in this majority Hausa Muslim LGA sometimes select a Christian (Bajju) to serve as a deputy chairman. This does not appear consistently over time in the data, however, and Hausa Muslims have generally led the many caretaker committees. Furthermore, the ethno-tribal populations of the local government have shifted over time, creating new geographical concentrations of Muslims and Christians, which seems to have further accentuated the division and heightened fears of violence.

~

In short, as with Plateau state, the pattern that emerges in the data is that pluralistic LGAs are less prone to inter-religious violence where power-sharing arrangements truly reflect the tribal *and* religious diversity of the area. This discussion does not, of course, explain why ethno-tribal leaders in only some LGAs and not others adopted power-sharing. Why, for example, did leaders in very pluralistic Chikun opt for a static seat-based power-sharing arrangement and its neighbors did not?

The exploration of the strategic interests and incentives requires attention to the historical and contemporary developments in the politics of these LGAs, which the following case study chapters will explore. In general, however, the data confirm that pluralistic LGAs that have adopted informal power-sharing institutions are far less susceptible to Muslim–Christian political tensions and recurring inter-religious violence.

## DISCUSSION

### Similarity of Pattern between Ethno-Religious and Ethno-Tribal Violence

An important question that arises from the data presented in the preceding sections is why, within a given LGA, the level of ethno-tribal versus ethno-religious violence varies. The data presented in Tables 5.2 and 5.4 show that LGAs' levels of ethno-religious and ethno-tribal violence do not in fact generally mirror one another, contrary to what one might expect. That is, areas such as Kaduna North, Kaduna South, Zaria, Jos North, Wase, and others that lack power-sharing and are more prone to ethno-religious violence, do *not* also have high levels of ethno-tribal violence. In Jos North, while 15 cases of ethnic violence fall into the category of ethno-religious, there are three cases of ethno-tribal violence reported. There are less than half as many cases of ethno-tribal violence in Wase as there are inter-religious violence. Also, LGAs with high levels of ethno-tribal violence are not necessarily prone to ethno-religious violence. In Kaduna state, violence with a reportedly religious dimension is a far more frequent phenomenon than ethno-tribal clashes.

This may at first seem counterintuitive. Since leaders of ethno-tribal groups adopted power-sharing with the goal to more broadly represent the tribal groups in an LGA, one would expect that this would reduce or similarly affect the likelihood of inter-tribal violence. Indeed, because religious and tribal identities often overlap, one would expect the pattern of ethno-tribal and ethno-religious violence to be generally consistent. While local councils without power-sharing are indeed more prone to *intra*-LGA ethnic conflict, there are a few reasons why the number of cases designated religious or tribal may not necessarily be equivalent.

First, many cases of ethno-tribal violence occur across LGA borders, involving groups from two different LGAs. As previously discussed, therefore, a power-sharing agreement may be effective in reducing the likelihood of inter-tribal violence within the borders of the LGA, but not between groups on either side of an LGA border. It may appear, therefore, that a power-sharing local council has a higher level of inter-tribal violence within the LGA than it actually does; this is why cases of cross-LGA or cross-state violence are distinguished in Tables 5.2 and 5.4.

Second, cases of ethno-tribal and ethno-religious violence tend to be sparked by very different events. Religious events are most frequently precipitated by news of prior violence occurring elsewhere between Muslims and Christians,[16] but also by a host of other events that can raise the ire of religious actors, such as religious defamation, disruption of religious observance, attack on a religious place of worship, and disputes over implementation of Sharia, to name a few. In contrast, ethno-tribal violence tends to be precipitated by clashes over disputed land, or cattle grazing rights on land claimed by farmers, as well as sparked by previous violence between tribal groups (see Appendix K). Where power-sharing is absent, therefore, the frequency of one type of ethnic violence or another will be shaped by how often these types of precipitating events occur.

Third, since religion is not simply a proxy for tribe, the pattern of ethno-tribal and ethno-religious violence may also vary. In cases of inter-religious violence in Shendam and other LGAs in Plateau state in 2004, for example, the Muslim–Christian violence pitted members of the same tribal group and even the same families against one another. Religious identity can serve as a defining cleavage and basis for mobilization apart from or in order to span other ethnic markers of identity like tribe. This helps to explain why ethno-religious violence can spread to other LGAs and states even though the groups share no ethno-tribal affinity with the groups where the violence originated; major instances of inter-religious violence in some areas in the north have been sparked merely by the spread of news that Muslims and Christians had come to blows in another LGA or state. Or, in a number of cases, international events with religious symbolism – such as the U.S. invasion of Afghanistan in 2001, the

---

[16] Wase LGA became a major arena for inter-religious violence in the spillover of violence from neighboring Shendam LGA. This dynamic is largely due to the disputes between the Hausa-Fulani Muslim majority and the large population of indigenous Taroh Christians in the southern part of Wase LGA. When the violence broke out in the Shendam LGA between 2001 and 2004, the Taroh's identification with the oppression of Christian indigenous groups, as well as the Taroh's grievances over lack of representation in Wase LGA, lit the fuse. Ethno-religious identity became a major rallying point or interpretive lens through which not only the local Wase ethnic groups mobilized, but also groups in surrounding LGAs.

Miss World Pageant debacle in 2002, and the Danish Cartoon Crisis in 2006 – have sparked major Muslim–Christian violence in northern Nigeria, events which hold no symbolic meaning for specific tribal groups. In short, where power-sharing institutions are not in place to militate against perceptions of religious or tribal inequality, these narratives of religious conflict and events imbued with perceived religious symbolism can more easily map onto local grievances and mobilize Muslim–Christian violence. This is one reason why levels of ethno-tribal and ethno-religious violence do not mirror one another even in LGAs that lack informal power-sharing institutions.

The main point of this preceding discussion is to recognize that the symbolic mobilizing power or saliency of religious identity and tribal identity differ in northern Nigeria. It is important to remember, however, that LGAs that do have power-sharing institutions tend to be more peaceful *overall* than those without power-sharing.

## Demographic Pattern?

Although the causal story behind this relationship will be explored further in subsequent chapters, it is worth noting here that the ethno-tribal balance of the population does not predict which LGAs are most likely to adopt power-sharing. As noted in the opening chapter, one could make an argument for why areas with more or less ethnic pluralism might be more likely to negotiate power-sharing. On the one hand, in LGAs where one group is predominant, there seems little incentive to share power with minority tribal groups. On the other hand, where the population balance is more evenly split, one might argue that in *this* case, there is less incentive for power-sharing, since leaders would appeal to and exacerbate tribal cleavages in order to win votes. Why agree to a power-sharing arrangement in this situation? In other words, a demographic theory could be articulated either way.

The data for Plateau state and Kaduna state also show that a demographic structural theory cannot explain the pattern of power-sharing in these two states; something else must be driving leaders' decisions to pursue or reject power-sharing. Jos North, an LGA strongly affected by ethno-religious violence, is home to about an equal proportion of Muslims and Christians based on best estimates by locals. While Jos North may be the LGA closest to a 50/50 split, other LGAs such as Chikun and Kanam with a slight Christian majority and Muslim majority, respectively, have adopted power-sharing. Further, there are LGAs with strong

Christian or Muslim majorities that have and have not adopted power-sharing. In short, a demographic argument provides little purchase in explaining this pattern.

## Statistical Support for Power-Sharing Theory

Although these data show a general pattern or relationship between inter-religious violence and power-sharing in Plateau state and Kaduna state LGAs, the data raise a number of questions about the causal relationship between violence and power-sharing. Perhaps there is some other underlying association that explains why some pluralistic LGAs are more prone to Muslim–Christian violence. It may be the case that some pluralistic LGAs have lower levels of inter-religious violence because they have lower levels of economic inequality or poverty, and elites are less likely to manipulate ethnic cleavages for their own political gain. In contrast, this institutional power-sharing theory posits that LGAs with power-sharing will be less prone to clashes that might otherwise arise from economic grievances or disputes. This is because the power-sharing system gives leaders fewer incentives to mobilize inter-religious violence. For example, when chairmen and deputy-chairmen of different ethno-tribal groups run together on the same electoral ticket, exploiting differences in ethnic affiliation will be self-defeating.

To test the competing theories, Bunte and Vinson (2016) compiled further LGA-level data on the combativeness of elite rhetoric, perceptions of communal competition, as well as individuals' levels of wealth. The analysis also controlled for individuals' perceptions of economic hardship, opportunity, and causes of poverty. In short, controlling for these and a number of other factors, we found that LGAs with power-sharing were significantly less likely to experience inter-religious violence than those without a power-sharing institution. Further, we found that the rhetoric of elites is significantly more cooperative and conciliatory in LGAs with power-sharing than without. Regarding the population's perceptions, individuals' perceptions of insecurity are lower and they are less likely to cite "too much competition" as the cause of poverty in areas with power-sharing. In short, whether using my original dataset of communal violence or ACLED and GDELT data, this further analysis reveals a strong statistically significant effect of power-sharing on lowering the likelihood of inter-religious violence in Kaduna state and Plateau state LGAs.

## CONCLUSION

Inter-religious violence, as should now be quite clear, is by no means inevitable. Rather, the data presented in this chapter paint the picture of the relationship between local representation and the likelihood of inter-religious violence. Areas with power-sharing arrangements tend to be less prone to Muslim–Christian and ethno-tribal violence. These findings also militate against claims that ethnic groups in conflict societies must segregate into separate, homogenous political units, as is sometimes argued in the ethnic conflict and civil war literature (see Kaufmann 1996, Sambanis 2000, Fearon 2004, Chapman and Roeder 2007, Carter 2008, Sambanis and Schulhofer-Wohl 2009). Homogenous societies or political units are not a prerequisite for peace; rather, representative political institutions are essential to inter-ethnic peace, as they militate against perceptions that poverty, inequality, and marginalization are a product of the political domination of one group over another.

What these data cannot specify, however, is the underlying processes or mechanisms whereby power-sharing in these communities is associated with inter-religious peace. The data indicate a correlation or association. How does power-sharing actually discourage inter-religious discord and reduce incentives for youth to mobilize in the streets? Further, why did elites adopt power-sharing arrangements in the first place? The next two chapters take up these important questions, focusing on the actual mechanisms of power-sharing and power-sharing's origins through in-depth case studies of select LGAs. The case studies verify the significance of the relationship between power-sharing and inter-religious peace by delving into the history of power-sharing in the LGAs, the peace-inducing impact on communal relationships in the face of inter-religious tensions and violence elsewhere, and their sustainability over time. As this analysis will show, the history and nature of local level ethno-tribal relationships and the presence or absence of power-sharing institutions since the 1976 decentralization reforms are key for explaining the likelihood of communal violence in pluralistic areas of northern Nigeria.

# 6

# Case Studies and the Power-Sharing Mechanism

How are informal local government power-sharing institutions effective in defusing inter-religious tensions? Building on the findings presented in the previous chapter – which showed that pre-existing power-sharing between ethno-tribal groups in Plateau state and Kaduna state LGAs is associated with a lower frequency of communal violence – this chapter focuses on the causal mechanisms through which power-sharing serves as a basis of greater cooperation and peace. Specifically, this chapter examines the mechanism of power-sharing in creating conditions for sustainable inter-religious peace through careful case study analysis, using a series of paired comparisons: Jos North and Chikun, Kanam and Shendam, and Bassa and Zango-Kataf. Each pair comprises a case of communal violence and case of peace, while varying in other relevant respects important for testing competing theories.[1]

---

[1] In Jos, where I lived during the fieldwork year, my research involved 37 individual interviews in which I spoke with a broad range of religious and political figures (Christian and Muslim), NGO peace activists, and scholars. Apart from interviews, key insights also came from attending approximately 20 peace meetings and religious events during the year. These organized gatherings were particularly insightful; a number of local leaders presented their divergent perspectives and popular sentiments on the driving forces of inter-religious communal violence in Jos, Plateau state, and northern Nigeria as a whole. This does not count the dozens of conversations with local Nigerians in daily interactions, as well as with missionaries long resident in Jos and the north who have stayed put during the various episodes of violence. In Chikun, I carried out eight interviews with religious and political leaders, in addition to a focus group style meeting with approximately 30 youth leaders, peace organizers, and local political representatives who spoke to the conflicts in Kaduna state (or more broadly) and reflected on the reasons for the relative peace in Chikun LGA. In Kanam, I interviewed a mix of eight religious and political leaders (including former chairmen of the local government), as well as the current elected

In the first part of the chapter, I discuss the logic of the paired comparisons themselves, and explain the nature of the power-sharing arrangement in each of the three power-sharing cases. Then, drawing on examples from the power-sharing cases, the chapter turns to the avenues through which power-sharing exerts a pacifying effect on the politics of religion and group relations. I then contrast this with the non–power-sharing cases, highlighting the ways in which the risks of identity politics and religious conflict are heightened where power-sharing is absent.

## CASES AND LOGIC OF COMPARISONS

The diverse sample of LGAs in Plateau and Kaduna present a rich field of study for exploring why inter-religious violence is more common in some otherwise similar communities and not others. While no two LGAs are identical in every minute respect, the paired cases reflect a number of important similarities, allowing one to explore why some are more prone to inter-religious violence than others (case studies indicated in Figure 6.1). These six case studies were selected because they, in some measure, are heterogeneous in their tribal/religious composition, but have either a) experienced recurrent bouts of inter-religious violence or b) remained relatively peaceful. The logic in selecting the paired comparisons follows Mill's method of agreement; they share many important similarities, but they nonetheless differ significantly on the variable to be explained (violence vs. peace).[2] This section lays out a more detailed explanation of each paired comparison.

---

chairman of the local government and a group of Muslim and Christian political representatives. Due to the availability of secondary sources and reports on the conflict in Southern Plateau state and southern Kaduna state, I relied on these sources to construct the analysis of Shendam LGA. I did, however, conduct approximately ten interviews with political leaders, traditional rulers (in a meeting at the Emir's palace), and peace activists from neighboring Wase, an LGA also caught up in the violence that spilled over from the Shendam crises. Similarly, with the secondary sources and reports available on violence in Zango-Kataf and Jema'a LGAs, I relied on such studies to analyze these cases. In Bassa, I conducted eight interviews with political officials, traditional leaders or chiefs, and local peace activists.

[2] Note that the case study work and power-sharing data collection occurred in tandem, and so these particular case studies were selected solely on the basis of their status as a known case of inter-religious violence or peace.

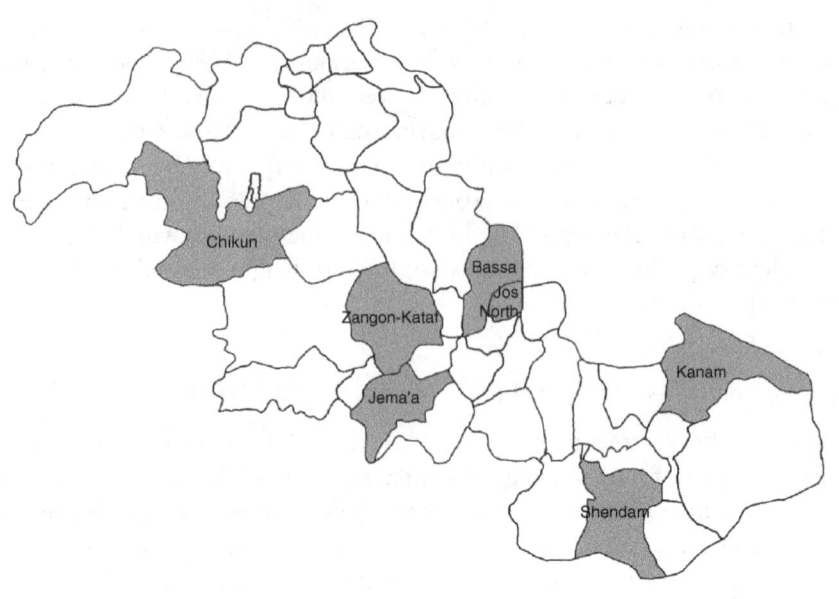

FIGURE 6.1 LGAs included in comparative case studies, Plateau state and Kaduna state*

## Jos North and Chikun

In demographic terms, Jos North and Chikun hold many similarities. Both LGAs have populations around 400,000–500,000 and a mix of both Muslims and Christians (indigenous and non-indigenous).[3] Jos North comprises the urban center of Jos city, the capital of Plateau state, and one of the largest cities in northern Nigeria. Chikun is the fourth most populated of the 23 LGAs in Kaduna state. Chikun merges with the thriving Kaduna city metropolis – also one of the largest cities in Nigeria with around 1.3 million inhabitants.[4] Although Chikun is much larger than Jos North, encompassing a vast rural stretch in north-central Kaduna state, the southern part of Kaduna city stretches into Chikun's northeast corner. Consequently, both Jos North and Chikun comprise urban centers or metropolises that are hubs for commerce, business, and industry.

---

* Note that Jema'a local government is included in the discussion of Zangon-Kataf.
[3] See Tables 6.4 and 6.5 in Appendix L for population figures based on the 2006 census.
[4] Note that Kaduna metropolis is constituted by Kaduna North, Kaduna South, and parts of Chikun and Igabi LGAs.

In both cases, the Christian ethno-tribal groups are the majority. Best estimates are that the Hausa-Fulani constitute up to half of the Jos North population (though they are a minority in the larger urban Jos metropolis, which extends into Jos South), and the Hausa-Fulani constitute around 30 percent of Chikun's population. In the Jos area, the Christian population is made up primarily of the Anaguta, Afizere, Berom, and other small ethno-tribal groups, while the Muslim Hausa-Fulani population is the significant minority. In Chikun, there are three major local ethno-tribal blocs; the majority Christian Gbagyi, followed by an indigenous Hausa Muslim population, and the Christian Kabilu.

These LGAs have both been significantly shaped by the migration of people for commerce and employment. Jos became more populated in the 1900s during colonial rule when the area was discovered as a source of tin. Subsequently, a tin mining industry grew up around the 1920s and attracted laborers, particularly Hausa Muslims, from other areas of northern Nigeria (Samuel et al. 2011, 184). Chikun is also a melting pot in its own right, as laborers were attracted to this business and industry center of the state around the capital city.[5] As residents of Chikun and a local traditional ruler noted, the local government has so many different tribes as a result of migration that it is a "mini Kaduna state."[6]

With the rise of inter-religious violence in northern Nigeria since the 1980s, both LGAs have also been surrounded by "bad neighbors" and received many displaced people fleeing the violence elsewhere (before Jos became a generator of displacement itself). As a close neighbor to the violence in southern Kaduna state, as well as Bauchi state, Jos was known as a safe haven for people fleeing instability and violence. Similarly, Chikun is also proximate to the epicenters of major Muslim–Christian clashes in the state, including the recurring bouts of inter-religious violence in Kaduna city (formed of Kaduna North and Kaduna South LGAs).

---

[5] As Okpanachi (2012) notes, "Kaduna received a large number of immigrants relative to the indigenous population after the federal reorganization in 1976 ... also spurred by its urbanization in the late 1970s. A significant number of immigrants from other northern and middle-belt states moved to Kaduna as part of labor migration. This process of urbanization included young laborers temporarily moving from rural villages and towns during the dry season and eventually permanently settling in Kaduna after finding work in the heavy manufacturing industry. Over time, this large migration led to nearly indistinguishable lines between 'settlers' and 'the smaller indigenous' communities. Also, considerable inter-marriage between the two communities fostered new kinship ties across ethnic and religious lines."

[6] Anonymous, interviews by Laura Thaut Vinson, Chikun, Kaduna State, November 10, 2011.

TABLE 6.1 *Similarities between Chikun and Jos*

| | |
|---|---|
| Tribal and religious pluralism | Urban and commercial centers |
| Areas that have attracted migrants | Similar population size |
| Integrated populations (before violence) | Within heterogeneous states |
| Similar colonial history | "Safe havens" for the displaced |
| Exacerbated religious cleavages | "Bad" LGA and state neighbors |
| Rapid Christian growth | Lacked prior major violence |

Muslims and Christians of different ethno-tribal groups have also settled in Chikun after fleeing inter-religious violence in southern Kaduna state, in LGAs such as Zangon-Kataf and Jema'a. Even with the flurry of conflict in the region since the end of the 1980s, Muslims and Christians of various tribal identities have lived side by side in integrated communities, inter-marrying and participating in one another's religious holidays and other festivals in both Chikun and Jos (before about 2001) (Table 6.1).

Despite these similarities, the LGAs of Chikun and Jos North are very different in their experience of religious and tribal cleavages. Since a small skirmish in 1994, there have been four major inter-religious clashes in Jos – in 2001, 2002, 2008, and 2010 – in which upwards of 3,000 people have been killed (Human Rights Watch 2010). This does not include a number of "smaller" cases of deadly ethnic or inter-religious violence that continue to fuel tensions and solidify the acrimonious nature of religious identity in Jos and other parts of Plateau state. Yet, Chikun has largely avoided this degree of inter-religious tension, despite its convergence with the large urban metropolis of Kaduna city, a city hit hard by recurrent inter-religious clashes. The case of Chikun is all the more impressive since clashes among co-religionists in other LGAs are one of the most common precipitators of subsequent inter-religious violence in the north. Indeed, the absence of inter-religious crises emanating from or spilling over into Chikun was a point of pride that a number of local government officials and community leaders emphasized during field research.

## Kanam and Shendam

The second paired case study comparison is that of Kanam and Shendam in southern and eastern Plateau state. Kanam, established in 1976 and forged out of neighboring Pankshin LGA, is home to nearly 180,000 people and has two predominant ethno-tribal groups – the Boggham and the Jahr – though there are subdivisions within them (Plateau state, "Local Government Areas"). Unlike many other LGAs in Plateau state, Kanam local government has a larger Muslim than Christian population – somewhere in the neighborhood of 50–75 percent Muslim according to local estimates.[7]

Shendam, created in 1976, emphasizes its status as the breadbasket of Plateau state in its local government flyers and is home to approximately 210,000 inhabitants (Hoomlong 2008, 25). The two primary ethnic groups are the Muslim Jarawa (the Hausa) and the Goemai (Christian and Muslim), and a diverse set of smaller ethno-tribal groups such as the Taroh and Montol from surrounding LGAs who also settled in Shendam.

Both Kanam and Shendam are home to a religiously and tribally pluralistic population. Both LGAs have large Christian ethno-tribal groups and long-resident Muslim Hausa-Fulani. Perhaps most important for this analysis, there is religious pluralism *within* their respective local ethno-tribal groups such that religion and tribe do not map neatly onto one another in these two cases; some portion of the Bogghom in Kanam and of the Goemai in Shendam are Christian and others Muslim, and there is inter-marriage between Muslims and Christians. This pluralism makes it possible to examine whether religious identity is really just a proxy for tribal identity in northern Nigeria. That is, if there is truly a "religious" dimension to the conflicts that is not in reality driven by the underlying tribal disputes and cleavages, then the clashes should pit members even of the same ethno-tribal group against one another on the basis of religious affiliation.

While Shendam and Kanam are similar in a number of respects, they diverge in their experience of ethno-religious conflict or violence. Since the 1990s, violent clashes between communal groups have rendered Shendam one of the more volatile LGAs and reconstituted the ethnic settlement pattern. While occasional skirmishes between farmers and cattle-herders have resulted in the deaths of perhaps a handful of people, the cases of inter-religious violence (or cases that morphed into a religious conflict) led to the deaths of hundreds and sparked retaliations and clashes in

---

[7] Estimates were based on interview information, since no official census figures exist. The 75 percent estimate was noted by one of Kanam's former chairmen during an interview in Kanam LGA. A scholar of local government politics at Jos University estimated that the religious balance is close to 50/50.

TABLE 6.2 *Similarities between Kanam and Shendam*

| Identities | Geographic |
|---|---|
| Tribal and religious pluralism | Similar population size |
| Intra-tribal religious heterogeneity | LGAs both within Plateau state |
| Similar history of religious change | "Bad" LGA neighbors |
| History of Hausa-Fulani rule | Not major urban centers |

surrounding LGAs of Plateau state. Major rounds of Muslim–Christian violence in 2004 led to hundreds of deaths and massive destruction of property. Kanam LGA, however, remained relatively peaceful despite its proximity to the clashes, the influx of refugees, and the ethno-tribal and -religious affinity between groups in Kanam and some of the perpetrators and victims in the neighboring flashpoints (Table 6.2).

## Bassa and Zangon-Kataf/Jema'a

The third paired cases are Bassa and Zangon-Kataf located in Plateau state and Kaduna state, respectively. Zangon-Kataf, founded in 1989, is home to a Christian majority and is located in southern Kaduna state. According to the 2006 census, it is home to a population of 318,991.[8] Bassa, like many of the other LGAs in Plateau and Kaduna state, was founded in 1976 during the decentralization reforms that reshaped local government representation in Nigeria. Bassa is home to a population of around 190,000 and sits on the border with Kaduna state, as well as neighbors Jos North and Jos South.

Again, these are LGAs both religiously and tribally pluralistic, but the Christian population in these cases is the vast majority. Although Bassa and Zango-Kataf are both predominantly Christian, the minority Hausa-Fulani Muslims are by no means an unimportant political voice and group in either LGA, particularly as they tend to be concentrated in certain towns or districts. In Bassa, the main local or indigenous ethno-tribal groups (i.e., major chiefdoms) are the Rukuba, the Pengana, and the Irigwe, along with a significant minority population of Hausa-Fulani Muslims. While the three main local ethno-tribal groups are largely Christian, there are areas of the local government where Muslims are more concentrated, including in Jengre, which is one of the most ethnically diverse and more populated of the towns in Bassa.

[8] See Appendix A.

TABLE 6.3 *Similarities between Bassa and Zangon-Kataf*

| Identities | Geographic |
|---|---|
| Tribal and religious pluralism | Proximate areas of the Middle Belt |
| Majority Christian/Minority Muslim | "Bad" LGA neighbors |
| History of Christian religious change | Not major urban centers |
| History of Hausa-Fulani rule | |

Like Bassa, Zango-Kataf is pluralistic and home to a majority Christian indigenous population as well as a significant minority Hausa-Fulani Muslim population. The main ethno-tribal groups are the Atyap (also known as the Kataf), Bajju, and Ikulu, as well as other smaller Christian minorities. The exact ratio of Christians to Muslims is difficult to estimate, however, since this information is excluded from the census. In Zango town, the locus of much of the conflict between the Kataf and Hausa-Fulani in the LGA (and where the Hausa population had historically settled in greater number), violence has also affected the population dynamics. Many locals fled the area, and neighborhoods segregated along Muslim–Christian and ethno-tribal lines in response to inter-religious clashes (Ololade 2011) (Table 6.3).

This inter-religious violence in Zangon-Kataf between the local Christians and the "settler" Hausa Muslims has been intermittent since the end of the 1980s. In contrast, Bassa has avoided major Muslim–Christian religious violence despite its pluralism and proximity to Jos North conflagrations and the violence in neighboring Kaduna state. While there has been an occasional flare-up of violence in the Miango district of Bassa, this is the product of localized and longstanding land disputes between nomadic Fulani cattle herders and local farmers. The inter-religious violence of the type that has occurred in Jos, Kaduna, Kano, Bauchi and other areas of the Middle Belt is absent.

~

In short, these paired cases are illustrative of the general puzzle – LGAs similar in many critical respects, but with divergent patterns of inter-religious violence. Why has religious identity galvanized the population in some LGAs and not the others where one would otherwise expect a similar propensity for mobilization? It is remarkable, for example, that inter-religious violence does not follow the displaced to Chikun or Kanam, or that politicians in some of these LGAs do not exploit ethno-religious cleavages for political ends. The next sections therefore delve into these case study pairs, investigating first the power-sharing cases and then the non–power-sharing cases in order to better elucidate how power-sharing works.

## THE POWER-SHARING CASES

The adherence to an informal power-sharing arrangement clearly emerged in fieldwork and interviews conducted in Chikun, Kanam, and Bassa LGAs. In each case, however, the power-sharing dynamic was somewhat different. Each LGA's power-sharing arrangement is therefore first briefly described in this section, followed by a more general discussion regarding commonalities observed across all three in the ways the power-sharing mechanism functions to maintain peace.

### *Chikun*

In Chikun, the executive local government seats are allocated to the Gbagyi, the Hausa, and the Kabilu. As a former chairman of Chikun explained, if the Gbagyi is the chairman, then the Hausa will represent the deputy chairman position, and the Kabilu the secretary. Another local official went on to explain,

> So in any zoning arrangement for positions, maybe the Gbagyi, we'll say, 'Okay, he's the son of the soil so he's taking the chairmanship.' You cannot go to Zango or Jos and contest for chairmanship there. So we understand with him and say, 'Okay, first born of the family, take that spot,' and then we the Kabilu and the Hausa-Fulani will now come and sit down in our kitchen cabinet and decide who [will] take number two. That is the vice-chairman[ship]. We can either give the spot to the Hausa-Fulani – perhaps they are more in number – or whatever arrangement ... we can give them that. And then we say, 'Okay ... now, the Kabilu, now we ... take the secretariat,' so that we do all the right thing and include all ... So that is the arrangement that has been helping us include."[9]

This is a static seat-based power-sharing arrangement. The structure of the power-sharing agreement also appears to incorporate a zoning principle so that representatives are not drawn from the same wards every election, and the three executive leaders represent different wards. Interestingly, many, if not all, of the subjects from Chikun that I interviewed about this arrangement arrived at the same observation when probed about the underlying factors sustaining peace in Chikun; the answer is this power-sharing arrangement. Indeed, my guide, a long-time political figure in Chikun and Kaduna state politics, appeared to grow weary with my research method of asking subjects the same questions and getting the same responses, because as he noted, "See, they're going to keep telling you the same thing I did – power-sharing."[10]

---

[9] Anonymous(J), interview by Laura Thaut Vinson, Chikun, Kaduna State, November 9, 2011.
[10] Anonymous(I), interview by Laura Thaut Vinson, Chikun, Kaduna State, November 9, 2011.

## Kanam

In the case of Kanam, the power-sharing arrangement follows a seat-based rotational power-sharing arrangement, rotating the leadership of the local government council between the two majority ethno-tribal groups from one election to the next. As a former chairman of Kanam local government explained, if the last local government chairman was Bogghom, then a Jahr man will be the subsequent chairman.[11] "If any party files a candidate who is not a Jahr, it is going to be difficult for him to win an election," he went on to note. As with Chikun, the power-sharing arrangement also follows a zoning rule. A traditional leader and political figure describes the nature of the power-sharing arrangement as follows:

> Kanam is one of the most democratic in power-sharing. Power is shared between the two ethnic groups. If the chairman is from one ethnic group, then the deputy is from the others. It is the same with other positions. They believe in rotational/zoning – if today the person comes from one side, the next is from the other side ... There is no village that is not given an opportunity to present one or other for position. There are six zones for chairmen to come from, for example. Three for each tribal group. If the chairman comes from one zone of one ethnic group, for example, it changes to another the next time. That group/zone that represented the previous time will not even attempt to put up a candidate the next time around. It even goes this way with political appointments – it switches from one side to the other. It is practiced in the localities too – at even the village level.[12]

The informal arrangement, not codified in any legal sense, has persisted since the 1970s. "It wasn't an established rule ... it is a concept that we buil[t] within ourselves, and everybody is respecting it," a former chairmen explained, going on to note that the power-sharing arrangement is so ingrained in the political and communal consciousness of the people that even the political parties will present a candidate to reflect the rotational power-sharing arrangement.[13] Describing the informal nature of the agreement, the chief explains, "Yes, it was an unwritten understanding/agreement. An MOU. This aspect is very strong and has kept the peace. Everybody abides by the power-sharing arrangement, even councilors."[14]

## Bassa

In Bassa, a rotational power-sharing institution has characterized its system of local level representation since the LGA's inception in 1976. As with Kanam, Bassa follows a seat-based rotational power-sharing

---

[11] Anonymous(K), interview by Laura Thaut Vinson, Kanam, Plateau State, October 18, 2011.
[12] Ibid., Anonymous(B), interview.   [13] Ibid., Anonymous(K), interview.
[14] Ibid., Anonymous(B), interview.

model. If one of the three major chiefdoms – the Rukuba, the Pengana, or the Irigwe – enjoys leadership of the local government one election cycle, then the chairmanship will go to another chiefdom in the subsequent election. Although the power-sharing arrangement is not a formal, codified agreement between the local ethno-tribal leaders, one community leader notes, "you discover that even in the different political parties that we have, they will only fill in candidates from that chiefdom [whose turn it is] for that office."[15] The tradition of power-sharing has so infused the local government that political parties only run candidates as the institutional arrangement dictates. Consequently, according to this arrangement, the elected chairman is only able to serve one term so that the office may rotate to a representative of one of the other chiefdoms. As one community youth leader explained,

for the position of local government chairman, usually it is rotated to the chiefdoms. Like presently, Rukuba chiefdom was supposed to be occupying [the chairmanship], but unfortunately the man ... passed away some time last year in a motor accident, and his deputy who is from Pengana chiefdom assumed the responsibility of local government chairman. So, the late chairman's wife from Rukuba [chiefdom] was made ... the deputy chairman, while the secretary of the local government is from Irigwe chiefdom. So, that is how you have the spread. And truly they have respected [the agreement] very well over the years ... So you discover that even in the different political parties that we have, they will only fill in candidates from that chiefdom for that office.[16]

Regarding its effectiveness, he continues, it is an "unwritten agreement, it has worked perfectly."[17]

## The Mechanisms of Power-Sharing

There are myriad ways in which the mechanism of power-sharing at the local government level has helped to reinforce peace and keep inter-religious violence at bay in these LGAs. In particular, power-sharing helps to constrain the politicization of ethnicity, dispel fears of unfair play, encourage representation of minority ethno-tribal groups, promote other forms of inter-tribal and inter-religious collaboration and cooperation, and ultimately defuse the narrative of inter-religious competition or conflict.

---

[15] Anonymous(M), interview by Laura Thaut Vinson, Bassa LGA, Plateau State, October 27, 2011.
[16] Anonymous(N), interview by Laura Thaut Vinson, Jos, Plateau State, October 10, 2011.
[17] Ibid.

### Constrains Politicization of Ethnicity

As a political mechanism for inclusion, power-sharing provides incentives for local leaders to appeal to the broader ethnic community during elections. In LGAs such as Chikun, leaders must appeal across the spectrum and not merely to their own ethnic contingency to increase their likelihood of being voted into local office. Since the candidates for chairman and deputy of the local government run on the same ticket and must come from different tribal blocs, exacerbating tensions between their respective tribal or religious groups would be counterproductive. In other local government areas that also have power-sharing arrangements, the political parties themselves select candidates from the appropriate ethnic group. Hence, the informal arrangement feeds into the formal contestation over local representation, shaping the broader "ethnic choice" for voters, but still leaving the choice of individual representatives open to the people. In this form, power-sharing requires leaders to work together to achieve their aims, building trust through various forms of collaboration in the administration of the LGA.

### Dispels Fears of Unfair Play

Power-sharing is also key in shaping the perceptions of the local populations by helping to dispel fears of an unfair political advantage between groups. As interviews highlighted, when the leadership represents the tribal and religious diversity of an LGA, it decreases perceptions that one group is monopolizing local resources to the disadvantage of others. For example, in a gathering of about 30 local leaders in Chikun – representative youth leaders, councilors, activists, and other local officials – they described the power-sharing arrangement as central to peaceful relationships among the Muslim and Christian ethno-tribal groups in the local government. As one local community leader explained,

> Sometimes crises arise where there is no fair play ... [I]n the local government, if the chairman is from this area, then the deputy and secretary [are] from the other area. Then they spread the positions in such a situation [so that] everybody is being carried along. And when people are being carried along, there will be nothing like suspicion or crisis. So in Chikun ... the structure has been around and everyone has been carried along, even though not everybody has been satisfied at the same time. But it has been like this for over 10 years, and I think we are okay. We are okay. Things are going on well, politically we are moving forward.[18]

---

[18] Anonymous(A), interview by Laura Thaut Vinson, Chikun, Kaduna State, November 10, 2011.

One local government administrator further noted that the arrangement reflects a principle of inclusion, "so that everyone will feel a sense of belonging," and, as a result, he continues "that has really helped us to stop lies, our crisis politically, for example."[19]

Further analysis and data collection from Kaduna and Plateau LGAs substantiated the relationship between power-sharing and inter-group perceptions. Bunte and Vinson (2016) found that the population in LGAs with power-sharing are less likely to cite inter-religious competition as a primary cause of poverty or insecurity than the population in LGAs without power-sharing. That is, by mitigating perceptions of inter-religious competition as the cause of economic hardship or insecurity, power-sharing reduces incentives for inter-religious conflict.

*Better Represents Minorities*
A third function of power-sharing in helping to reduce incentives for violence is that it may better represent minorities who otherwise would not necessarily have the political clout to advance their interests. In Kanam, power-sharing not only ensures representation among the two prominent ethno-tribal groups, it also enables smaller ethno-tribal groups in various wards to have a stake in local government affairs. This function reduces incentives for violent mobilization. In Bassa, although the power-sharing arrangement for the core leadership of the local government council is largely coordinated between the three major indigenous ethno-tribal groups in the LGA – the Pengana, Irigwe, and the Rukuba – interviews and collected data revealed that the power-sharing principle can promote broader political inclusiveness.

In Jengre, the area of Bassa where Hausa-Fulani Muslims are the majority, a local chief explained that, while the three major chiefdoms rotate the chairmanship of the local government council (as well as the deputy chairman and secretary seats as well), some Fulani Muslims have also held the position of deputy chairman. While non-indigenous representation in the executive positions of the local government council is less common, it is not unheard of. In this sense, the rotation is not exclusive to the three main, largely Christian, ethno-tribal groups.[20]

Further, as members of the Mista-Ali community in Bassa noted, non-indigenous persons are also elected as councilors. For example, in two

---

[19] Ibid., Anonymous(J), interview.
[20] Anonymous(P), interview by Laura Thaut Vinson, Bassa LGA, Plateau State, October 27, 2011.

previous election cycles, councilors have been elected from the minority Jere, Amo, Lemoro, Buji, and Hausa tribal groups. Of course, since councilors are elected at the ward level, the group that most populates a particular ward is most likely to win councilorship representation. Nonetheless, in combination with the broader inclusiveness of the LGA, the assurances of power-sharing among the larger tribal groups promotes greater inter-tribal and inter-religious peace. Locals also emphasized that the ethno-religious identity of representatives is taken into account, noting that a Muslim is currently leading the local government council despite the Christian majority composition of the LGA.[21] In short, by representing the main ethno-tribal groups in the LGA, there is less incentive for inter-group political competition and marginalization, which helps to dispel religious tensions.

*Spawns Broader Cooperation and Informal Peacebuilding*
The effectiveness of power-sharing is not merely restricted to the creation of a more representative local government council. Rather, it serves as a foundation for broader inclusiveness at other levels of political and communal life. In Chikun, for example, power-sharing appears to infuse all of local government administration; it extends to which groups represent the top three council positions, which zones are represented when, and how political parties select their leadership. In the case of political parties, one interviewee noted that with the party structure, "it is the same thing; if the Gbagyi, say they are taking the executive seat, okay, we say, 'Hausa-Fulani you take the chairmanship of a party.'"[22] As quoted previously, one traditional leader and political figure in Kanam noted that the power-sharing principle extends even to non-elected political appointments and is "practiced in the localities too – at even the village level."[23]

The creation of "local development areas" in LGAs such as Chikun is another way in which power-sharing branches off into subsidiary political structures. Interviewees in Chikun noted that, based on the principle of power-sharing, the political leadership has designated local development areas where minority ethno-tribal groups are concentrated. This provides these groups with greater representation and autonomy in meeting their local development goals, giving them more say in the allocation of funds to development projects in their neighborhoods.

---

[21] Anonymous(Q), interview by Laura Thaut Vinson, Bassa LGA, Plateau State, October 27, 2011; Anonymous (N).
[22] Ibid., Anonymous(J).   [23] Ibid., Anonymous(B).

Additionally, regarding the election of councilors from the various wards in Chikun, one leader explained that while a ward will likely elect a Hausa man if the Hausa dominate that particular ward, even these wards may still elect a Christian councilor. The reason for this, he explained, is that the leaders advise the population in their wards to also try to share leadership at the councillorship level.[24]

Beyond party structures, local development areas, and power-sharing at the councillorship level, another example of power-sharing suffusing communal life beyond the political and electoral arena is found at the level of traditional rule or the chieftancy system. Although political institutions wield formal political power, chiefs still play an important role as respected local leaders of ethno-tribal groups. While chieftaincy disputes and appointments can be a source of conflict, unlike other parts of southern Kaduna, each of the ethno-tribal groups in Chikun has their own chief who serves as a district or ward head.[25] Other smaller tribes within a ward are further allowed their own chief who is under the local district head. In this sense, small ethno-tribal groups still maintain their traditional titles and have a voice in local affairs. In Bassa, even the position of Paramount Chief follows a power-sharing rotation among the Rukuba, Pengana, and Irigwe. The Paramount Chief is the most distinguished traditional leader in the community, presiding over the chiefs of all of the other local ethno-tribal groups. During an unannounced visit to one local chief, Muslims and Christians of various ethno-tribal groups were observed calling on the chief. In attendance was a chief from a neighboring Muslim Hausa community who, while the host was absent from the room, described their friendly relationship and noted that their religious differences had never been a barrier to them working together.[26]

In addition to the foundation of trust that power-sharing has fostered among the local religious, traditional, and political leaders, the power-sharing arrangement has also spawned new local initiatives to maintain inter-religious peace. As a local youth leader and peace activist in Bassa explained, after local leaders worked together to quell fears of a potential clash between displaced Christians and Muslims in 2010, they decided to take a more activist approach to prevent inter-religious violence. The Muslim and Christian religious, tribal, and political elders in Bassa

---

[24] Ibid., Anonymous(I).
[25] The Paramount Chief, the Sagbagyi, presides over the other chiefs.
[26] Anonymous(R), interview by Laura Thaut Vinson, Bassa, Plateau State, October 27, 2011.

met to brainstorm ways to prevent inter-religious violence from sprouting in their communities. One solution they agreed to with the local vigilante leaders was the formation of integrated Muslim–Christian vigilante teams (similar to a neighborhood watch system) to protect neighborhoods at night from potential trouble-makers. "So the vigilante group are always keeping watch over the community," he notes, "10 o'clock every night they begin ... and if you are seen after that time, you will have to give a concrete reason as to why you are going around at that time."[27] Initially, when local leaders and community members were discussing the formation of the vigilante groups, they proposed separate Muslim and Christian vigilante groups for their neighborhoods. The peace activist explained, however, that local leaders quickly realized that, based on the power-sharing precedent, integrated vigilante groups could serve a far more effective symbolic and unifying purpose, dispelling perceptions that one or the other religious group is at fault if trouble occurs. This integrated approach to neighborhood self-policing, as local leaders observed, has been an effective mechanism in helping to maintain local peace.

As highlighted in this discussion, it is not an anomaly for Muslim and Christian religious leaders to coordinate peacebuilding activities in power-sharing LGAs. For example, in a meeting with leaders of the local Muslim and Christian religious communities in Chikun, they showed a great deal of camaraderie and knew each other well. Remarking on the 2000 crisis in Kaduna, one member of the Jama'atu Nasril Islam (JNI) Muslim organization pointed to the good political leadership present in Chikun, enabling religious leaders from the local wards to form a joint committee of five Muslim and five Christian religious leaders to work together to bring quick resolution to any inter-religious crises. As further example of their cooperation, they noted that there are zonal meetings in which the 37 Christian Association of Nigeria (CAN) representatives in the LGA meet with Muslim leaders to resolve problems.[28] Thus, in coordination with religious leaders and traditional rulers who know their youth and area well, the local government leadership is also able to effectively identify troublemakers.

---

[27] Ibid., Anonymous(N).
[28] Anonymous(S), interview by Laura Thaut Vinson, Chikun, Kaduna State, November 10, 2011.

## *Defuses the Narrative of Religious Conflict*

As the examples above indicate, it is also more difficult in a power-sharing context for religious identity to become (or be politicized as) a major cleavage. In these pluralistic power-sharing LGAs, both Muslims and Christians are invariably elected or appointed to local government positions even if the power-sharing arrangement is not specifically organized to rotate leadership on the basis of religious identity. In Kanam, the Bogghom are majority Christian, but there are also Christians among the Jahr population as well. Describing his period of tenure, a former chairman explained,

> [T]he issue of religious difference [is] not all that prominent in our politics or in the living. That's why, like myself when you look at it, when I was elected as a chairman, I was elected along with a deputy who is a Christian. So even the council members of mine ... because we have 10 councilors, I think about three or two of them [were] Christians. And one of my councilors [was] a pastor ... Yeah, three. So that is how we operated.[29]

Reflecting on this pattern of representation, a local chief also observed that "before now, there is no way you would have a chairman being a Muslim where the deputy was not a Christian," and he also noted that sometimes the supervisory council would also be represented equally between Christians and Muslims. Although most of the wards are Muslim majority, he noted that in some of the wards, the religious split is around 40/60 Christian/Muslim respectively, but locals have "equally elected Christians" as councilors to the local government council from those wards. "In all those wards," he explained, "there have been cases where Christians are the representatives" and elected by a Muslim majority. He continued, "people will elect persons from either side (regardless of their ethno-religious identity). So people don't look at the candidates on religious grounds. Religion hasn't been an issue in this place."[30] During a meeting at the local government headquarters with Dr. Saleh Galadima Kanam, the elected chairman of the LGA in 2011, and a dozen or so local government officials, a question regarding the religious balance of the local government council raised a chuckle. Going around the room, he began introducing the Christian officials present.[31] His point was that religious differences obviously neither dissuaded him, as a Muslim, from

---

[29] Ibid., Anonymous(K).  [30] Ibid., Anonymous(B).
[31] Dr. Saleh Galadima Kanam, interview by Laura Thaut Vinson, Dengi, Kanam LGA, Plateau State, October 19, 2011.

appointing Christians to his administration nor prevented Muslims from voting for Christians.

~

As illustrated in these many examples above, the power-sharing model creates a representative foundation for local ethno-tribal groups, enabling local leaders – whether Muslim or Christian – to form alliances with one another to combat inter-religious tensions and thwart the potential for violence. In LGAs like Bassa, Kanam, and Chikun, inclusiveness at the level of local government councils has spawned other informal institutional arrangements that help to promote peace and cooperation across ethno-tribal and ethno-religious divisions, as well as reinforce power-sharing itself. Where power-sharing institutions are not in place, politics and disputes are more likely to be interpreted through a Muslim-versus-Christian lens, rendering broad-based inter-religious cooperation and understanding far more difficult to achieve.

## CONSEQUENCES: POWER-SHARING'S ABSENCE

Lacking this informal institutional mechanism, what are the consequences? Study of Shendam, Zango-Kataf, and Jos shows three main characteristics that blight local governments without power-sharing. Seemingly minor offenses or sparks can trigger inter-religious clashes, disputes more easily take on a religious dimension, and violence spreads more easily across ethno-tribal boundaries. In each of the LGAs, religious difference itself is not the *cause* of conflict, but perceptions of marginalization and unequal representation set the stage for competing interests to mutate beyond political division and feed a narrative of religious conflict. In Jos, the creation of the new local government council of Jos North in 1991 and subsequent disputes over political control exacerbated local tensions. In Shendam, the absence of inclusive local government created conditions ripe for disputes over political rights and the economic interests of the community as a whole. Similarly, in Zangon-Kataf, the persistence of colonial-era outside political interference in local politics contributed to the deepening of local political grievances and perceptions of marginalization that thwarted the development of power-sharing institutions. Unmitigated by local government power-sharing, competition and mistrust cultivated an environment ripe for inter-religious tensions to flare, even from the smallest spark.

## Sparks That Trigger Fires: Devastation

Although the inter-religious violence experienced in Jos since 2001 goes deeper than simply religious differences, it has not always taken much to trigger inter-religious clashes. In 1994, rioting over a local political appointment led to small-scale violence, but it was merely the harbinger of more intense violence that followed in the 2000s. In 2001, the Jos population was embroiled in a political dispute over the appointment of one Mallam Muktar Usman Mohammed, a Jasawa (Hausa-Fulani) man, to the position of Coordinator and Chairman of the Monitoring Committee of the National Poverty Eradication Program. The local ethno-tribal elite strongly opposed the appointment, but it was a scuffle at a local mosque that lit the fuse when a Christian woman reportedly ignored a warning not to walk through an area outside a mosque where Muslims were holding prayers. Whatever the exact details, the event led to the death of as many as 1000 people. In other cases, perceptions of election foul play, reconstruction of property (destroyed in previous violence) in a disputed area, and Muslims symbolically praying at an abandoned mosque in a predominantly Christian neighborhood have sparked violence. Apart from smaller incidents of violence in tit-for-tat scenarios, major clashes occurred in 2001, 2002, 2008, and 2010, killing hundreds, if not thousands, and generating thousands of displaced, many injuries, and billions of naira in damage.

Similarly, violence in Shendam in 2002 and 2004 started from a seemingly minor inter-communal dispute. It ultimately morphed into a larger dispute that pitted Muslims and Christians against one another not only in Shendam, but also in other vulnerable LGAs. In June 2002, at least six people were killed in Yelwa when a Christian girl was assaulted after she rejected warnings from her kinsmen against courting a Muslim boy. Violence intensified, however, when Muslims carried out an attack mainly on local Christians in the town of Yelwa in response. This sparked subsequent reprisal attacks in nearby villages and, as victims fled, violence flared in the surrounding LGAs of Wase, Langtang North, and Langtang South. In addition to those killed, many people were injured, and rioters vandalized or burned several worship centers, fuel stations, and vehicles (Best 2011, 33; Human Rights Watch 2005).

It was the Feb 2004 violence, however, that sent shockwaves throughout Plateau state and other states in northern Nigeria. While accounts of the precipitating events vary, on February 24 of that year, Christians who took refuge in a COCIN church in Yelwa were hacked and burned alive after fleeing to the church for safety in response to a report that armed Muslims were coming to attack the residents in the town. Around 78 people were killed in the church or as they tried to escape (Human Rights Watch 2005, 15). Following this event, Human Rights Watch (2005, 20–21) notes that up to 22 different attacks of Christians against Muslims or Muslims against Christians occurred between February and May in 17 different locations, killing around 82 people. From May 2 to 4, the Christian majority Goemai population, along with other minority Christian ethno-tribal groups, carried out a massive retaliation against the Muslims in Yelwa. According to Human Rights Watch, the attack was well-coordinated and pre-planned; well-armed groups of men who surrounded Yelwa began systematically eliminating any Muslims. In the end, after two days of attacks when soldiers finally came in to quell the violence and mass burials began, they found 660 to 700 Muslims slaughtered.

Crises in Zangon-Kataf have occurred intermittently over the last three decades. When trouble does break out between the Christian Kataf (or Atyap) and the Muslim Hausa-Fulani, the violence is usually large in scale and often spreads to other vulnerable LGAs in Kaduna state that lack power-sharing institutions. Perhaps the most well-known are the two major clashes that occurred in 1992 – one in February in which about 60 people were killed and one in May in which at least 400 were killed. The violence in February followed a contested decision by new local government leadership to move the main Zango marketplace from a Muslim part of town to a new marketplace in a Christian part of town, a move for which the Kataf advocated (Falola 1998, 213; see also Gwamna 2010, 80; Boer 2003, 56–63). The Hausa saw this as an attempt by the Kataf to deprive them of their economic livelihoods, but the Kataf claimed that the new area was more "neutral," and they would then be able to sell pork and alcohol, which was prohibited in the former location. In combination with an incident on some farmland – both sides claiming to be the victims – Hausa and Kataf people took to the streets in harrowing bloody clashes that quickly spread to other towns in Kaduna.[32] Summarizing the outcome of the three days of fighting, after the police finally intervened, Falola (1998, 217) notes,

Over four hundred corpses littered the streets, and most of the houses were burned to the ground. Many of the dead had been killed by massive dagger and machete

---

[32] Falola (1998, 215) describes the 1992 clash between Hausa Muslims and Kataf Christians in the LGA as "so bitter and so destructive that the 1987 Zaria crisis paled in comparison" (see also Ololade 2011).

wounds; some were shot through with poisoned arrows and bows. In a few cases, people had been shot with guns, and others had been burned in their cars or homes. All the major churches and mosques were destroyed. Many were injured, many had fled, and many more were to die later in hospitals or at home from their injuries.[33]

As these examples highlight, the danger for LGAs that lack representative local government councils is the increased risk of inter-group violence. Without inclusive local representation, trust in political leadership suffers, giving rise to fears of partisanship in adjudicating concerns central to the livelihoods of the various ethno-tribal groups. In this context, local disagreements or disputes over various matters – large or small – can be sufficient to spark inter-religious violence as groups try to correct the perceived wrongs or injustices incurred at the hands of their neighbors.

### Religious Dimension

Due to the rise in inter-religious violence in Nigeria since the 1980s, not to mention the increasing intensity and frequency of terrorist attacks in the north with the rise of the radical Islamic group Boko Haram (and its splinter groups), part of the volatility of the communal violence in the pluralistic Middle Belt is the ease with which it may take on the garb of religious conflict. This is the danger that Middle Belt LGAs such as Jos, Shendam, and Zango-Kataf face in attempting to balance competing interests without the necessary inclusive political institutions present in power-sharing LGAs.

#### Jos

In the case of Jos North, although the communal violence is rooted in the political exacerbation of disagreements over local government representation, a religious dimension or a "religious coloration" has increasingly characterized and fueled the violence, seemingly making it more intractable. For example, as one participant at a peace meeting of high-level officials and community leaders in Jos emphasized, part of the danger of recognizing the religious dimension of the conflict is that it may make the conflict intractable. "Be careful not to paint it as a religious crisis," he urged. "If it's ethnic, it can be resolved ... but when it becomes religious, we cannot go anywhere ... religious crisis will break the country."[34]

---

[33] Regarding the events, see also Ladan (1999, 105).
[34] Recorded notes by Laura Thaut Vinson, Plateau State, Nigeria, 2011.

Despite the broader and varied dimensions of the conflict and debates about whether local violence is religious, tribal, political, or economic, there is plenty of evidence that the religious dimension has increasingly fueled conflict since the 1990s. Religious events or perceived offenses are now sufficient to spark devastating violence mobilized along Muslim–Christian lines. Indeed, as highlighted in the previous chapter, religious events or violence between co-religionists elsewhere more frequently precipitate inter-religious violence than political or economic events such as elections or land disputes.

A number of cases of communal violence in Jos have evidenced this new reality of sacralized communal violence. In a Human Rights Watch (2001, 9) report of the communal violence in 2001, it recounts,

[Both sides] set up roadblocks all over the town, allowing people to pass if they were of their own faith and stopping and attacking those of the opposite faith. People were targeted clearly on the basis of their religion or ethnicity. A Christian man who was stopped at a Muslim roadblock told how Muslim youths were encouraging each other to pick out as many Christians as possible, as if it were a kind of competition to see who could kill the most Christians. A Muslim leader was stopped by about eighteen Christian youths armed with sticks and machetes who were shouting "Useless Muslim!" and "Useless Hausa man!" at another Muslim ahead of him. In some areas, Christians and Muslims set up joint patrols in a bid to limit the spread of violence, but it became difficult to maintain these once the fighting had escalated.

During this time, even members of small ethno-tribal groups from southern states who lived in Jos, but were not involved in the political dispute between the indigenous and settlers, were targeted on the basis of religion. One report notes that although Christian Igbos were not initial targets, they too were engulfed in the violence, since "Hausas regarded them same as unbelievers like the indigenous" (Abdulsalami 2001, 7). In the end, Human Rights Watch (2001, 10) and other reports recorded approximately 1000 deaths, dozens or hundreds injured, 50,000 displaced in 16 camps, and billions of naira in property destroyed, including a number of places of worship (see also Abdulsalami 2001, 7; Human Rights Watch 2010, 7).

In the large-scale violence in 2008 and 2010, the disputes once again took on a religious coloration with churches and mosques targeted and burned to the ground. Remarking on the 2008 violence in an interview with *The Guardian*, Alhaji Alhassan Shaibu, the Secretary General of Jamatu Nasri Islam (JNI), observed, "The cause of the crisis to me is political. But when it took off, it metamorphosed into a religious dimension" (Abdulsalami 2008, 8). In one account, the major 2010 inter-religious violence was sparked by the refusal of Christians to allow a Muslim man to rebuild his home (destroyed in previous communal violence) in an area now dominated by Christians. Another account is that the mobilization of violence occurred after a Muslim man attacked a church full of Christian worshipers in Jos. Either way, the perception of a Muslim versus Christian conflict was clear. Both the 2008 and 2010 inter-religious violence resulted in hundreds of deaths and injuries, further creating the perception of an insurmountable religious cleavage in Jos.

Other smaller incidents have also propelled the narrative of a religious battle. In 2010, "hoodlums" reportedly attacked members of the Christian Association of Nigeria while they were leaving a meeting in Jos. On August 30th, 2011, a church was destroyed and more than two-dozen Christians and Muslims were killed following a confrontation when Muslims went to pray at an abandoned mosque in a now predominantly Christian area of the city. In March 2012, suspected Boko Haram extremists bombed the COCIN church and headquarters in the city, which led to at least ten retaliatory killings as Christian youth took revenge by killing innocent Muslim motorcycle transport drivers stopped at makeshift roadblocks.

### *Shendam*

The pattern is similar in Shendam LGA. Whatever the original political dimensions of the violence, by the time of the Christian attack on the Muslims of Yelwa in 2004, the violence had taken on broader ethnic dimensions, attracting Christians from neighboring LGAs to join their co-religionists in the attack.[35] The victims were targeted on the basis of their religious identity. As Human Rights Watch (2005, 21–22) notes, "The victims were also from many different tribes, with only their religion in common: almost all of them were Muslim." Facilitating the attack and perceiving the religious dimension the violence had taken, "almost all Christians moved out of Yelwa, and the town became a no-go zone for Christians" (Human Rights Watch 2005, 44).[36]

---

[35] Human Rights Watch (2005, 21) notes, "As in the case of some of the earlier attacks by Christians, the perpetrators were initially described as Tarok [or Taroh] by the media and others; in reality, it was not only the Tarok but many different groups who participated in this attack. Eye-witnesses mentioned a wide range of tribes among the attackers, including the Tarok, Gamai, Montol, Angas, Kwalla, Birom, Sayaway, and Jukun." See also Act!ionaid (2008, 142–143).

[36] Human Rights Watch (2005, 44) goes on to note that "After the May 2004 attack, the number of displaced was even higher: tens of thousands of Muslims moved out of their

The conflict in Shendam LGA had clearly spiraled beyond its original political dimensions, fitting neatly into the us-versus-them politics of religion in Nigeria. Religion emerged as the primary ascriptive and mobilizing narrative. Despite their shared ethno-tribal identity, even the Muslims who were Goemai were not safe from the violence unleashed by Christian Goemai. Ethno-tribal groups who had no association with the conflict other than their religious affinity were drawn into the violence to defend their co-religionists.

*Broader Plateau State*

As these Plateau state cases emphasize, whatever the underlying political dimensions of the local disputes, the violence is often triggered by an event of some religious significance or it quickly takes on the garb of a religious conflict as Muslims and Christians mobilize to confront one another. A sentiment often echoed in interviews, peace meetings, or informal conversation in Jos is that Christians fear the perceived "jihadist" religio-political agenda of northern Muslims and blame the conflicts on these ulterior motives. As a local professor of religion explains, there is a very strong fear among Christians that Muslims are intent on "taking over the whole of Plateau State and making it an Islamic state ... everybody becoming a Muslim by force," and ultimately pushing south to take over the whole of Nigeria. Although rather an extreme view, he emphasized that it is a "very strong fear."[37] This fear was reflected on a number of occasions in meetings or interviews with locals and religious leaders who believe that Muslims and Christians are in a state of religious war and peace is no longer conceivable.

*Zango-Kataf*

Although issues of political control and local government representation are at the root of the tensions in Zango-Kataf and Jema'a in Kaduna state, the religious dimension of the violence between Hausa-Fulani Muslims and Kataf Christian has helped to fuel broader violence. In reaction to the

---

homes in Yelwa and the surrounding area. Of a population of around 32,000, only around 1,000 people were left in the town of Yelwa following the May 2004 massacre. It was an indication of the extent of Muslims' fears that most of them felt safer fleeing to neighboring Nasarawa and Bauchi states, rather than to other parts of Plateau State ... By June 2004, an estimated 40,000 to 60,000 people from Plateau State were internally displaced, either within the state or in neighboring states."

[37] Anonymous(G), interview by Laura Thaut Vinson, Jos, Plateau State, Nigeria, April 4, 2011.

massive killings in Zangon-Kataf in 1992, Muslims mobilized in retaliation in Kaduna, Zaria, Zonkwa, and Kagoro, to name a few places. In Kaduna city, the Hausa, "believing that the Kataf had killed their people, launched a massive attack on Kaduna residents of southern Zarian origins" (Falola 1998, 218). Religious preachers in Kaduna city and Zaria invoked a religious jihad or, along with rioters, attacked those who failed to "identify their religion and ethnicity by reciting verses of the Qur'an or by speaking Hausa with an identifiable accent" (Falola 1998, 218–219). Churches filled with worshipers also became easy targets for retaliation. The Christian population too fought back in self-defense, but the overall reaction was so intense that the violence in Kaduna reportedly killed more than the initial Zangon-Kataf violence, resulting in more than 1000 deaths, many injured people, extensive property damage (including churches and mosques), and thousands were displaced overnight.

Driving through Zangon-Kataf during fieldwork in 2011, the evidence of communal violence still marked the LGA. In the center of Zango town, buildings are still scarred black by fire or sit as idle empty shells, grasses growing up and around their crumbling forms. Zango town is not the only area of Zangon-Kataf marred by inter-religious violence in recent years, however. Zonkwa, the headquarters of the LGA, was one of the worst hit areas in the April 2011 post-election violence. Although the violence was a reaction to the presidential election results, it took the form of Muslim–Christian conflict. The riots and bloodshed began in the run up and following the announcement of the win of southern Christian candidate Goodluck Jonathan over the northern Muslim candidate Muhammadu Buhari, easily fitting into the narrative of a Muslim–Christian conflict and reflected in the mobilization of the attacks. Reports of hundreds killed and thousands displaced in the LGA began circulating along with other cases of Muslim–Christian/political violence in the north (BBC News 2011; Lewis 2011, 70). According to Human Rights Watch (2011), more than 800 were killed in 12 northern states during three days of rioting, and rioters destroyed more than 350 churches. In a report by the National Emergency Management Agency on family reunification efforts, the Nigerian *Guardian* newspaper noted that an estimated 75,000 people were displaced by the violence in Kaduna state overall (Obayuwana and Njadvara 2011, 7). In Zonkwa in particular, Human Rights Watch (2011) found that Muslims were the primary victims.[38]

---

[38] According to Human Rights Watch (2011), "Men from the predominately-Christian Bajju ethnic group in the town of Zonkwa burned six of the town's mosques, as well as

Following the post-election violence, Zonkwa was once more the scene of trouble after a gunman attacked a church in the town on November 3, 2011, killing two and injuring 14 people. Travelers were again instructed not to drive through the southern part of Kaduna due to the uncertainty about potential retaliation. The BBC News (2011) report noted that youth attacked a mosque in revenge and, "[f]ollowing the attack on the church, the state governor was forced to abandon his attempt to visit the town after Christian youths blocked the roads with burning tyres."

### Evidence from Broader Kaduna Spillover

The violence in other communities – such as Kafanchan in neighboring Jema'a LGA – has also taken a "religious turn." In the September 1996 violence, the clash between Muslims and Christians was due to the abduction of a Christian preacher, Mr. Monday Yakonat, for apparently blaspheming the Prophet Mohammed during a sermon. While he was later released, the abduction nonetheless instigated violence between the ethno-religious communities, violence which then spread to Kaduna city, where radicalized Muslims were protesting the detention of their leader, El-Zak Zaky (Akhaine 1996).

The May 1999 violence in Kaduna state also highlights the ascriptive power of Muslim–Christian religious identity. While the 1999 violence in Kafanchan resulted in the deaths of perhaps a dozen people, the violence quickly spread to other towns and took on greater proportions. Christians were targeted in retaliation in places such as Kaduna, Zaria, Samaru, Wusasa, Kankia, Malufanshi, Katsina, and Funtua in Kaduna state (Falola 1998, 183). Rioters burned more than 100 churches, and the events convinced Christians that violence was a valid form of self-defense. As Falola (1998, 185) notes, "they now began to speak of the law of Moses – an eye for an eye," since the "rioters sent a loud and clear message to Christians: northerners could not openly profess Christianity and escape unharmed." In response, Falola continues, the reaction of Christians was to "strengthen their faith, seeking stronger ways to

---

homes, shops, and vehicles of Muslim residents. Witnesses said the violence began late in the afternoon of April 18 and continued throughout the night. By mid-morning on the following day, the Bajju men had killed or displaced nearly all of the town's Hausa-Fulani residents ... 311 Muslims, nearly all of them men, were buried in a mass grave in Zonkwa later that week, while the remains of 24 others, many of their corpses charred beyond recognition, were buried in one of the town's wells. Christian leaders in Zonkwa told Human Rights Watch that 10 Christians had also been killed in the town and surrounding communities. No churches were destroyed."

confront the Muslims the next time." Adding fuel to the fire, CAN asserted that the violence was an attack against the Christian faith, and "Christian leaders began to call for a great Christian revival to surmount what they called the devil represented by Islam" (Falola 1998, 186).

~

These are only a handful of cases of communal violence in non–power-sharing LGAs that highlight the symbolic significance that religion has assumed in local disputes over representation and rights, seemingly dwarfing the original underlying political causes of the disputes. The ascriptive power of religious identity in these cases of violence emphasizes the importance of religious change and the politicization of ethno-religious identity in the post-colonial period. As in Plateau state, cities and towns are also increasingly divided along ethno-religious lines as a result of the recurrent violence; once-integrated neighborhoods divide like oil and water with Muslims primarily congregating in certain neighborhoods and Christians in others. As an International Crisis Group (2010, 35) report notes concerning the capital of Kaduna state,

> In Kaduna city, particularly, these conflicts have redrawn the ethno-religious demography. A climate of fear has forced Muslims, mostly the Hausa-Fulani who resided in Narayi, Sabon-Tasha, Barnawa, Ungwar Pama, Ungwar Romi and other Christian-dominated areas to move to the predominantly Muslim Tudun-Wada area. Similarly, Christians in Muslim-dominated areas, including up to 10,000 Igbo entrepreneurs, have largely moved to the southern part of the city, which they dubbed "New Jerusalem". Many who fled the state during the Sharia crisis have returned, but they are also massed in the southern parts of the city. Others would like to return to where they lived before 2000 but sold their properties. Ten years after the Sharia riots, the segregated settlement remains largely unchanged.

In sum, pluralistic LGAs that have failed to adopt power-sharing arrangements to better balance the competing political interests of ethno-tribal groups are at greater risk of the politicization of identity, particularly religious identity. This politicization can, in turn, take the form of or morph into inter-religious violence. Whether or not the triggering event is locally generated, inter-religious violence is not restricted by ethno-tribal boundaries. Muslim–Christian violence has flared in non-power-sharing LGAs in reaction to inter-religious violence elsewhere even when the ethno-tribal groups are distinct and have no connection to the original incident.

The absence of power-sharing in some pluralistic LGAs, however, does not mean that *everyone* in those LGAs is advocating violence and that no peacebuilding efforts are taking place or they are futile. To the contrary, there are a plethora of moderate religious leaders and activists – Muslim and Christian – who are aghast at any violence interpreted as a religious duty, and they actively organize their people to stand for peace and to restore the relationship between Muslims and Christians. The Sultan of Sokoto himself has repeatedly called for the violence to end, and admonishes Muslims to follow the commands of Islam to live in peace. At a peace meeting in 2008 in Jos with political and religious leaders (including the CAN president), the Sultan of Sokoto appealed to adherents stating,

When the Almighty God created us in different places and into different religions so that all of us can become one and we are all equal in the eyes of the Almighty ... therefore, we cannot fathom how individuals will just get up one night and tear apart all that Almighty God declared holy and sacrosanct, claiming people's lives in the name of religion or in the name of ethnic background or whatsoever, destroying people's property in the name of religion, in the name of ethnic background. This madness must stop. (Abdulsalami and Okoronkwo 2008, 2)

Similarly, one Anglican Bishop beseeched fellow religious leaders and pastors at a peace meeting:

War will beget war, peace will give birth to peace ... the peace brought by the Prince of Peace is all-embracing, it does not discriminate. When Christ gives the peace it is for everyone ... Peace is difficult, but that is what is expected as people of God ... If we are still living today, it means that God expects better things. Call them [Muslim] friends, give a text to them. If we expunge a whole people from the community, do you think peace will be there for us?[39]

Jos itself is home to numerous organizations attempting to restore inter-religious and inter-tribal relationships in the community. Peace activities, meetings, and seminars coordinated by various organizations at both the grassroots and government level seemingly took place every week in Jos, if not multiple times a week, during this period of fieldwork. The challenge for these LGAs, however, is that without a political structure or framework for broader representation, peace activists and organizations face a steep uphill battle.

## CONCLUSION

The case study evidence discussed in this chapter illuminates how power-sharing can mitigate the likelihood of inter-religious violence. By reducing

---

[39] Notes recorded by Laura Thaut Vinson, Plateau State, 2011.

perceptions of inter-ethnic marginalization and competition, the power-sharing mechanism provides a foundation and incentives for local leaders across the tribal, religious, and political spectrum to cooperate and build stronger inter-ethnic ties. Consequently, the forms of cooperation deriving from the political institution also help to reinforce the legitimacy of power-sharing, which explains its sustainability over time despite the increase in inter-religious conflagrations in the Middle Belt.

Where power-sharing at the local government level is absent, however, LGAs are more susceptible to the coloration of political disputes as religious, as the cases of Jos, Zangon-Kataf, and Shendam illustrate. The politicization of religious identity – and the fact that it is a strongly salient category of belonging shared by many in northern Nigeria whatever their tribal affiliation – means that intra-LGA tensions can easily take on a religious dimension and spark violence in other LGAs equally weakened by lack of power-sharing.

Of course, this discussion of mechanisms assumes the general expectation of regular local government election cycles. This is not always the case; occasionally, depending on the LGA in question or particular circumstances, elections may be delayed, with caretaker governments instituted in such cases. Caretaker governments generally take two forms – either the appointment of a sole administrator generally from outside the community (common during military rule), or some sort of committee of local leaders appointed to fill the gap until an election is held. The reasons for delayed elections can vary – lack of organization on the part of the state electoral commission, concerns over the possibility of election-related violence in an unstable community (i.e., Jos North local government), the meddling of state leaders/party officials in the case of an unexpected local government loss or the defection of a chairman from the party after winning the election (e.g., Kanam local government), the death of a chairman while in office, and so on. Or perhaps more commonly, caretaker committees are also referred to as "transition" committees – local government leadership that serves only for a brief period of time while the old local government transitions out and the new administrations comes in. Consequently, the circumstances surrounding the appointment of a caretaker committee can vary vastly in their political sensitivity. Generally, as observed in the data collected on local government administrations in this study, caretaker committees are short-lived, serving anywhere from a few months to a year, or perhaps two years depending on the circumstances (in this sense, Jos North is an exception from the norm). While the theory and mechanisms of power-sharing in this study do not explicitly apply to caretaker committees due to their transitory nature, communities with a tradition of informal power-sharing also tend to reflect this dynamic – mixed representation from local ethno-tribal groups – in their caretaker committees when the leaders are drawn from the community.

Overall, the case studies further demonstrate that the key difference shaping the propensity for inter-religious violence is the presence or absence of local government power-sharing. Considering the importance of local government power-sharing, the following chapter takes up the question of why some LGAs adopted power-sharing while others did not. Further analysis of the paired comparison case studies shows that there is no one specific set of factors or institutions that determined adoption of power-sharing. Rather, incentives for power-sharing were shaped by how particular social, political, and economic changes affected LGAs in the Middle Belt.

# 7

# Case Studies and the Origins of Power-Sharing

Having explored the significance of the power-sharing mechanism and its relationship to communal peace, an important question remains; if power-sharing is indeed the key to greater local inter-religious stability in pluralistic Middle Belt LGAs, as the previous chapter argued, why is not power-sharing the preferred political institution of LGAs everywhere? Why did political leaders in LGAs such as Jos, Zangon-Kataf, and Shendam not adopt power-sharing institutions to promote greater communal peace and inter-religious understanding? Or, conversely, given that these power-sharing institutions are informal – no national regulation prescribes the institution – and that African politics is generally noted for the pervasiveness of clientism and patronage centered around ethnic ties,[1] why did any leaders opt for cooperation? Simply, what are the origins of these power-sharing institutions?

It should be stated at the outset that I find no evidence that power-sharing was merely adopted by leaders where groups were more peaceful prior to the 1980s. Further, colonial-era ethnic cleavages did *not* pre-determine the likelihood of inter-religious violence some forty years later. In fact, the main finding is this; the research and case studies show that there is no one path to power-sharing, no one set of factors that determined where power-sharing would and would not appear attractive or take root. Rather, the strategic incentives for power-sharing varied according to the effect of particular exogenous

---

[1] See Diamond 2008; Van de Walle 2009; Arriola 2009; Bratton and Van de Walle 1997; Lemarchand 1972.

post-colonial political, social, and religious changes on individual LGAs. To the extent that these changes pushed groups toward greater assimilation and political integration, the elites of such LGAs were more primed for power-sharing agreements after the 1976 decentralization reforms.

This chapter therefore argues that power-sharing was ultimately less likely to emerge where existing ethno-tribal cleavages or tensions were exacerbated by post-colonial political changes. That is, the history of assimilation and integration (or lack thereof) among the local populations offers important insight into the constitution of ethnic groups and identity in a particular area, but other factors specific to LGAs were central in shaping the power-sharing calculations, including patterns of migration, exogenous political interventions, state creation, and the degree of religious change, to name a few factors. This chapter explores the support for this argument, drawing on the evidence from the paired comparison case studies of Chikun and Jos, Kanam and Shendam, and Bassa and Zango-Kataf, as well as referencing the experiences of other LGAs such as Jama'a in Kaduna state.

## GENERAL HISTORICAL FRAMEWORK

As already stated, what became clear from the case studies was that the specific incentives for power-sharing varied depending on the community in question. This does not mean, however, that nothing can be said about general observable patterns or principles, simply that each LGA's local context and particular history must be considered in order to fully understand how a power-sharing arrangement (or its absence) came into existence. In advance of exploring each case study pair in detail, then, this section presents a framework for understanding the general conditions under which local leaders saw power-sharing as an attractive political decision.[2]

---

[2] While I aim to identify some of the strategic reasons that elites did or did not form power-sharing arrangements, as well as the conditions under which power-sharing is sustainable, I do not claim to provide an exhaustive study of the motivations for power-sharing in *every* context. Rather, this section presents a mere framework for understanding the conditions under which local leaders saw power-sharing as an attractive political decision. That is, the framework must be considered as exactly that, a *framework*, with nuance and caveats provided by the case study details.

## Cultural Assimilation and Political Integration

As part of the general framework, two elements are important to highlight: the effect of post-colonial changes on the cultural assimilation and political integration of ethno-tribal and ethno-religious groups. By "cultural assimilation," I am referring to minorities' adoption of or incorporation into the Hausa-Fulani way of life in the north, including but not limited to the Hausa language and Islamic religion and rules. "Political integration" refers to minorities' adherence to the traditional political rule of Hausa-Fulani Muslim emirs and elites who dominated the northern Nigerian political establishment prior to colonialism and subsequently under the auspices of the British crown. In particular, the strategic incentives for power-sharing were more conducive in LGAs where the post-colonial events and changes pushed groups toward greater cultural assimilation and political integration by the time decentralization reforms were implemented in the mid-1970s. Hence, local ethno-tribal groups were less likely to perceive power-sharing as an affront or major political concession where

a there was greater cultural assimilation and political integration[3] during colonial rule (or where the Hausa-Fulani made up a small proportion of the local population),

b *and* post-colonial changes and political events did not exacerbate or create new local ethno-tribal cleavages.

Where post-colonial political changes and events did nothing to ameliorate these prior cleavages, there was less incentive for local elites to negotiate an informal power-sharing arrangement. Power-sharing would be perceived as a major concession to former colonial rulers. Further, it would waste the opportunity for greater self-rule created by decentralization, compromising the implicit purpose of the 1976 reforms: to rewrite or democratize the pattern of local rule and

---

[3] Note that the assimilation and integration may have been characterized by voluntary conversion in some cases and by forceful imposition/coercion in others. Affecting the degree of assimilation and integration during the pre-colonial period, some areas were further from the center of Hausa-Fulani rule or on the fringes of the conquered territory, making them more difficult to pacify through religion and force of arms. These areas were, thereby, more likely to put up resistance to any incursions and maintain their own African traditional religions. Subsequently, during colonial rule, these areas were, in general, also more resistant to the British-backed imposition of Hausa-Fulani religio-political rule. Other factors, such as variation in colonial policy and patterns of immigration, also played into the degree of assimilation and integration in some cases.

representation. Thus, power-sharing was less likely where the reverse conditions applied:

a  pluralistic ethno-tribal communities were less culturally assimilated and politically integrated under colonial-era Hausa-Fulani Muslim rule,
b  *and* subsequent post-colonial socio-political and religious changes reinforced these cleavages.[4]

Regarding political incentives for power-sharing, therefore, the perceived costs and benefits varied from one LGA to another depending on how inter-group relationships evolved with post-colonial changes. For some groups, aligning with their local counterpoints (even Hausa-Fulani) through power-sharing served as a better means of achieving self-representation. Also, minorities in some communities were motivated to adopt power-sharing since they might not otherwise gain seats in local government leadership. Additionally, in areas where demographics of the population were likely to shift over time (such as LGAs with a large urban area), leaders with a long-term focus had incentive to establish strong institutional representation through power-sharing. The barriers to negotiating such an arrangement were, in short, lower for such LGAs.

Figure 7.1 lays out the general framework of this argument with the caveat that the specific changes or events that shaped the degree of cultural and political ties or relationships for any one community can and have varied a great deal. As the Figure illustrates, therefore, pluralistic ethno-tribal and ethno-religious communities that were less assimilated and integrated were less likely to pursue power-sharing at the time of local government reforms if post-colonial changes had not altered the perceived ethno-tribal cleavages and inequality (Cell D).

In contrast, communities where the Hausa-Fulani Muslims were more assimilated and integrated with the local ethno-tribal populations *and* this relationship was maintained in the post-colonial period, the issue of power-sharing was less contentious in the first place since the relationship between the ethno-tribal groups was more seamless (Cell A). In some

---

[4] In the Middle Belt region or fringe areas of the north, as previously noted, it was more difficult for the Hausa-Fulani to impose their British-backed rule, and, in some cases, the emirs allowed limited political and religious autonomy, or the British were forced to intervene to quell resistance by force (resistance that had been present even prior to the British conquest of northern Nigeria). Consequently, ethno-tribal cleavages were different in nature in these areas where Hausa-Fulani Muslim culture/religion and attendant forms of political rule were not broadly accepted (or enforced).

|  | High Post-colonial Integration | Low Post-colonial Integration |
|---|---|---|
| High Colonial-Era Integration/Assimilation | (A) Higher likelihood of Power-Sharing | (B) (indeterminate) |
| Low Colonial-Era Integration/Assimilation | (C) (less contentious) | (D) Lower likelihood of Power-Sharing |

FIGURE 7.1 Pattern of power-sharing adoption in the pluralistic Middle Belt

pluralistic LGAs of this type where the Hausa-Fulani Muslims have a small presence, however, they may not rotate into the top positions of the local government, as these posts are more likely to be divvied up between the major ethno-tribal groups.

In the scenario of greater resistance to Hausa-Fulani Muslim rule during the colonial era (low degree of assimilation/integration), sociopolitical events and religious changes – such as migration patterns or demographic changes and the spread of Islam – promoted greater political integration even if not full cultural assimilation, and power-sharing was a less contentious alternative among local elites (Cell C). In this scenario, the colonial-era legacy does not necessarily rule out power-sharing, as subsequent changes can alter the inter-group relationships and incentive structure for power-sharing.

In contrast, in an LGA where communities were largely assimilated and integrated during the colonial era, but experienced greater differentiation due to events and changes in the post-colonial era or exogenous shocks, power-sharing is more difficult to either negotiate or to maintain (Cell B). This cell better represents those LGAs that face new pressures on inter-religious cohesion due to the acrid Muslim–Christian political relationship prominent in contemporary Nigerian politics and due to the inter-religious violence in surrounding LGAs. Some pluralistic LGAs in Niger state, for example, may fit this bill.[5]

~

[5] In Niger state – formerly part of Sokoto state, the site of the Islamic Caliphate – Muslim elite and emirs dominated the political sphere without the resistance widespread in other non-Muslim areas of the Middle Belt. With the stronger political foothold in Niger state, cultural assimilation (adoption of Islam and the Hausa-Fulani culture) was also stronger

In sum, and to be clear, the relevant events or changes that lowered the incentive for power-sharing have not been the same across power-sharing LGAs; their colonial experiences, pattern of ethnic group settlement, degree of pluralism, and post-colonial religious, social, and political changes have varied. Hence, the adoption of power-sharing institutions cannot simply be reduced to prior peace or violence between ethnic groups, their demographic or electoral balance, or the history of colonialism in northern Nigeria. The adoption of power-sharing must be understood in broad brush strokes, rather, with the particular incentives specific to the political relationship and changes in any one LGA. What can be derived from the case study and interviews with local leaders, however, is that decisions for power-sharing following decentralization in 1976 were less likely in local government areas where assimilation and integration were low (exacerbated by events and changes over time) between the majority and minority groups. Power-sharing, in those contexts, possessed greater representational costs to the local ethno-tribal groups seeking a "new era" of post-colonial self-autonomy and representation.[6] In other cases, leaders of some communities in the Middle Belt region acted quickly (and successfully) at this transition point in Nigeria's federal structure to create power-sharing arrangements that would protect their groups' rights where they had previously been marginalized.

than other parts of the northern fringe. Inter-marriage, for example, is a normal part of communal life even though Christianity grew strongly in the post-colonial period. In the last 5–10 years, however, pressure for self-representation among the Christian population appears to be growing, and the state government has sought to keep inter-religious violence at bay in the face of a handful of small incidents. One of the reasons cited by interviewees for this shift is the increasing education among the Christian population, which is bringing "enlightenment" or political self-awareness and increasing their involvement in and contestation for political office and influence. With the unsettling of the local political *status quo* in the current religio-political environment in northern Nigeria, this scenario may create challenges for the formation of power-sharing arrangements. The history and long-standing cultural assimilation may, however, offer incentives for a power-sharing solution to potential tensions.

[6] This is not to say that power-sharing arrangements do not exist in other communities, such as more religiously homogeneous communities with a mix of ethno-tribal groups. They do, but they are less likely, of course, in religiously homogenous communities where one major ethno-tribal group predominates. Again, some sort of zoning rotational system may be in place, but not as a power-sharing arrangement between disparate ethno-tribal groups. Power-sharing in these contexts is targeted more at the geographical representation of the local government. However, my focus is on pluralistic communities where one finds both an ethno-religious and ethno-tribal mix and where one would expect the tension between Muslims and Christians to be most volatile.

Power-sharing, therefore, was the product of strategic action to achieve self-governance where it had not been possible before.

While the origins of the power-sharing institutions cannot be reduced to any one factor or characteristic common to all such power-sharing communities, the purpose of this discussion is to provide a general framework for understanding how the incentive structure might vary across the LGAs. With this in mind, the following two sections examine power-sharing and non–power-sharing cases through this lens.

## PATHS TO POWER-SHARING

This preceding framework helps to make sense of why leaders of some communities were more likely to opt for a power-sharing approach to local governance while leaders of other similar pluralistic communities did not. Based on research and interviews in the LGAs, this section presents the decision-making and strategic incentives for power-sharing among leaders in Chikun, Kanam, and Bassa, highlighting that there was no one path to power-sharing. As noted above, the logic of power-sharing depended on how various post-colonial changes affected the degree of political integration and cultural assimilation among ethno-tribal groups in specific LGAs.

### Chikun

In Chikun, the informal local government power-sharing arrangement between the three main ethno-tribal blocs – the Gbagyi, Hausa-Fulani, and Kabilu – offers broader guarantees among the major ethnic groups to the rights, resources, and representation associated with local government leadership. As noted in the previous chapter, the benefits are more broadly felt in the community, as power-sharing has spawned greater coordination and collaboration among tribal elders, political elite, and religious leaders across ethnic divides, particularly during times of tension or crises in the vicinity.

Power-sharing in Chikun was not predetermined, however, considering that the history of southern Kaduna is one of tension between indigenous groups and Hausa-Fulani. Unlike Jos, however, Chikun did not experience the same "exogenous shock" or sudden reorganization of local government power – a product of national government policy in 1991 – that introduced new inter-group pressures. Instead, the explanation for Chikun's adoption of power-sharing can be fairly simply told. The strategic factors relevant in the formation of power-sharing in Chikun LGA can be traced to the settlement and migration pattern of the area, its geographic convergence with Kaduna metropolis, and expected demographic changes.

In the first place, any successful power-sharing in Chikun necessitated inclusion of the Hausa-Fulani Muslims, since they too are considered indigenous to the area. For the indigenous Christian Gbagyi population, the majority in the LGA, it was clear that a power-sharing arrangement would only be effective if it recognized the historical roots and claims of the other ethnic groups. Although the Kabilu non-indigenous Christian population are not considered "sons of the soil" in the LGA, they too form part of the power-sharing arrangement. According to a former chairman and recent member of the state legislature, power-sharing was a strategic reaction to the dynamics of the settlement of the LGA and its prospects for growth due to convergence with Kaduna city.

Because of this ethno-tribal makeup of the population, the incentives to work out an agreement with the Hausa-Fulani Muslims were two-fold. Due to the ethno-tribal balance of the LGA, although the Gbagyi are the majority group, political leadership or influence would not necessarily be guaranteed if the other large minorities formed a political alliance, especially if the demographic balance of the population changed over time. A political arrangement in which the dominance of the Gbagyi in the LGA is recognized – by allotting the Gbagyi the chairmanship of the LGA – recognizes their majority status. Also, an informal arrangement for the Hausa-Fulani and the Kabilu to sit on the executive of the local government council also provides their groups with a sense of political security, as electoral politics could also work against them depending on how local political alliances fell. In short, local government power-sharing was a way for all three ethno-tribal blocs to protect their future political influence in the LGA.

These groups had good reason to consider how the future might affect the local political balance. Considering the geography of Chikun, power-sharing was also a strategic option for the Gbagyi. Local leaders explained that the Gbagyi agreed to the power-sharing institution because they saw that, although they were in the majority, different tribes would eventually populate the area as people migrated to the LGA for trade and business. Hence, the Gbagyi aimed to ensure that their role in local representation would not be compromised by population changes.[7]

In this sense, the particular historical and geographic context of the LGA made power-sharing a strategic option even though not mandated by the Nigerian state. In the context of recurring and intensifying religio-political disputes and inter-religious violence since the 1980s, the power-sharing institution – incorporating both Muslim and Christian ethno-religious groups – has ultimately helped to maintain inter-religious peace and cooperation. As discussed in the previous chapter, power-sharing has also been self-reinforcing, as it has provided a foundation for other forms of inter-tribal and inter-religious collaboration and cooperation to flourish, thereby reinforcing favorable attitudes toward the institution.

## Kanam

With its seat-based rotational power-sharing arrangement, Kanam's power-sharing arrangement allocates the main seats of local government leadership to the two main ethno-tribal groups in the LGA – the Bogghom and the Jahr. The Hausa people also have an important history and presence in the local government although they constitute a smaller ethno-tribal bloc. Recounting the history of the area, a former chairman of the local government noted that the Hausa people came to the northern part of the local government not through conquest or war, but through migration from Kano and settlement in Kanam.[8] During the colonial period, when the colonial authorities set up their system of Native Authority or Indirect Rule, it was the Hausa, the dominant political power in the north, which came to rule over the people of what is now Kanam LGA. In this case, the largely peaceful migration and settlement of the Hausa-Fulani facilitated greater cultural assimilation and more peaceful political integration (recall that Kanam is a majority Muslim LGA).

In an interview with another former chairman in Dengi, the province headquarters of Kanam LGA, he reflected on the emergence of the power-sharing arrangement in the local government between the Boggham and the Jahr people. He explained that the elders or leaders of the two tribal groups "sat down and agreed to the arrangement based on the

---

[7] Anonymous(I), interview by Laura Thaut Vinson, Chikun, Kaduna State, November 9, 2011.
[8] Anonymous(L), interview by Laura Thaut Vinson, Kanam LGA, Plateau State, October 18, 2011.

understanding that the national cake should be shared equally."[9] Pressing these former local government officials on where the power-sharing agreement came from or why local elite of the different ethnic groups agreed to it, one former chairman observed, "It was just a concept that we built within ourselves," which he noted the people have continued to respect.[10] Out of what historical context did the power-sharing arrangement emerge, however? What incentives did the elites have to agree to rotate power, and why or how does the informal institution persist? While the pattern of colonial assimilation and integration tells us something about the ethno-tribal cleavages or cohesion in Kanam at the time of independence, the emergence of the power-sharing arrangement is rooted in postcolonial political and religious changes in the communal life of the LGA.

The nature of colonial rule in Kanam area highlights the significance of the 1970s reforms in the LGA and the strategic incentives for the two major local ethno-tribal groups to form a power-sharing arrangement. As a former chairman noted, during the colonial period, the British reinforced the Hausa-Fulani emirate system, rendering the local ethno-tribal groups subject to this powerful emirate rule.[11] The chief of the Hausa people "became the paramount chief of all of us, and also the leader of the Native Authority," another former chairman observed.[12] At the same time, however, he noted that the Hausa ruled by the "collective will of the people," since the manner in which the Hausa people first arrived in the area was not through conquest, but rather, migration. For this reason, the relationship between the Hausa and the local indigenous groups in Kanam has been less combative than in other areas of Plateau state or Kaduna state where the non-Muslim local ethno-tribal groups were engaged in organized resistance against the Hausa-Fulani Caliphate even prior to colonial rule. With the arrival of Hausa Muslims in the Kanam area, the population became more Islamized with the conversion of local Jahr and Bogghom to Islam, and, hence, the people were more loyal to their Hausa rulers upon the establishment of a major emirate in Kanam.[13]

In this sense, the local ethno-tribal groups in the Kanam area were more politically integrated and culturally assimilated with the Hausa than were ethno-tribal groups in other areas of Plateau state, as well as Kaduna state.

---

[9] Anonymous (O), interview by Laura Thaut Vinson, Kanam LGA, Plateau State, October 18, 2011.
[10] Anonymous(K), interview by Laura Thaut Vinson, Kanam LGA, Plateau State, October 18, 2011.
[11] Ibid.   [12] Ibid., Anonymous(L), interview.   [13] Ibid.

Even today, Kanam is one of two remaining emirates in the state. Between the 1940s and the 1960s, all political authority remained under the emirate, and members of the ruling family always received the emir-ship and served as both traditional leaders and administrative heads.

In 1976, however, the politics of rule in Kanam LGA underwent a major shift with decentralization reforms. Although the indigenous ethno-tribal groups (non-Hausa) were more integrated and assimilated into the religio-political system of colonial rule, their lack of opportunity for self-representation, combined with the realization that the reforms would now accord them a say in the election of local government officials, created incentives for indigenous leaders to assert their political influence in the form of a power-sharing arrangement. With the establishment of local level elections and the diffusion of power away from traditional rulers to the people, it became possible for the local ethno-tribal groups to elect their own people to the local government council. They "still had respect for the emirate traditional rule," one non-Hausa chief observed, "but the local man had a say now."[14] Although a Hausa man was the first elected government chairman in 1976, in 1979, the chairmanship for the first time went to an indigenous leader, rather than the ruling emirate family. "This time around," a former chairman observed, "they found it difficult to go to impose their people to these wards ... we had about 14 wards. So, each member came from the indigenous of that place and not the Hausa people again."[15] "Because of elections," he continued, "[the Hausa rulers] found it difficult ... to go and impose their people there."

Although, as one former chairman noted, the royal family saw the developments as "a strange thing" that they did not desire, they had to "accept the voice of democracy."[16] Since the ruling Hausa formed a smaller ethno-tribal bloc among the population compared to the Bogghom and the Jahr, decentralization of local government authority naturally shifted the balance of power to the indigenous ethno-tribal groups that made up the majority in the various wards. Subsequently, the Bogghom and Jahr gained a number of political appointments and, since the 1980s, have dominated the local government leadership.

Democratization of local government rule, therefore, was a turning point for the indigenous Bogghom and Jahr population. Their local leaders acted on the opportunity to achieve greater representation by combining their political weight as a voting bloc. Considering the strategic

---

[14] Anonymous(B), interview by Laura Thaut Vinson, Jos, Plateau State, October 13, 2011.
[15] Ibid., Anonymous(L), interview. [16] Ibid.

advantages, they instituted an informal power-sharing arrangement. It no longer made sense to the local ethno-tribal elite in the new political environment (nor was electorally feasible) for the Hausa-Fulani to dominate politically, since the Bogghom and the Jahr constituted the vast majority of the LGA's population. Thus, to avoid Hausa political elite splitting the indigenous vote, Bogghom and Jahr leaders found it advantageous to agree to share the executive seats of local government authority in exchange for support for one anothers' candidates. Hausa representatives, meanwhile, would still be able to participate and gain representation as legislative councilors or through local government appointed positions.

It was not simply this watershed moment in Nigerian national politics that suddenly rendered a power-sharing arrangement an attractive political option for local elite. Nor can the decision of the Muslim/Christian Bogghom and Jahr elite and the peace with the Hausa Muslims simply be ascribed solely to the colonial legacy of stronger cultural assimilation and political integration. The religious change initiated with the end of colonialism explains the formation of a distinct Bogghom and Jahr political identity. In particular, the spread of Christianity and missionary work affected not only the ethno-religious composition of Kanam, but brought western education to the local population. This change shaped the political self-awareness of the Bogghom and the Jahr. Although the British limited the incursion of Christian missionaries in the north so as to protect their relationship with the Hausa Muslim proxy rulers, some exceptions were allowed in areas of the Middle Belt such as Kanam. Consequently, the subsequent post-colonial religio-political changes that occurred in Kanam as a result of Christian missionary work and education reshaped the political self-awareness of the population. This was extremely important for the local indigenous groups, as they were the most disadvantaged educationally during colonial rule (see Turaki 1993; Falola and Heaton 2008).

The consequences of these changes were emphasized in interviews with former and present local leaders in Kanam. As more than one interviewee noted, with mission schools, the now "more enlightened indigenous groups" began to organize themselves politically to contest the oligarchy of the emirate system. Indeed, as a former chairman explained, western education shaped their political awareness and the decision to pursue a power-sharing arrangement: "So, in fact, most especially the Bogghom and Jahr [gathered] themselves to say that 'why should we be ruled by the Hausa man, imposing people on us?' So, we grouped ourselves to say that we should elect *our* people, not that they should impose their people on us."[17] The expansion of missionary education produced a new generation of political leaders and demands for political rights and autonomy from the emirate system. A local chief observed that, with the "advent of western education, the children of the ruled came back to challenge the oligarchy of the emirate system."[18] A power-sharing arrangement, they concluded, was the most effective political strategy for ensuring the local ethno-tribal majority did not lose out to a Hausa alliance in the new era of decentralized and democratized local electoral politics.

In sum, unlike LGAs such as Jos North, the creation of Kanam and the implementation of local government democratic reforms in the 1970s were not seen as political concessions to former colonial rulers. Just the opposite, the reforms opened up space for local Bogghom and Jahr, the majority ethno-tribal groups in the LGA, to achieve representation. Religious change with Christianity's expansion in the post-colonial period and its introduction of western education helped to create the political awareness and activism for self-representation. While the Bogghom and Jahr's prior political integration with Hausa emirate rule and religio-cultural assimilation rendered relations between the local ethno-tribal groups and their colonial rulers less hostile, the post-colonial changes in the local government were the primary determinants of the politics of power-sharing. Power-sharing in Kanam was a strategic and viable option for local leaders and continues to be a salient foundation for negotiation of inter-religious tensions.

## Bassa

Like in Chikun and Kanam, the seat-based rotational power-sharing agreement in Bassa between the Rukubu, Pengana, and Irigwe helps to quell claims of political marginalization both along ethno-tribal and religious lines. While there are a number of important similarities between Bassa and Zango-Kataf – its counterpart in the paired comparisons – power-sharing was a more viable political negotiation in Bassa, as it has not been subject to perceived outside political interference in the right to local self-governance. In contrast to Zangon-Kataf, power-sharing in Bassa, even with its religious pluralism and colonial history, reinforced rather than jeopardized significant self-representation in the era of decentralized rule.

---

[17] Ibid., Anonymous(L), interview.   [18] Ibid., Anonymous(B), interview.

As in Kanam, initial accounts of power-sharing's origin tended to emphasize its seemingly obvious logic. A prominent local chief described how the power-sharing institution originated when three of the leaders – one from each of the major chiefdoms – sat down and formed the agreement.[19] While the younger generations in the local government are not necessarily sure how the power-sharing arrangement originated, one local teacher and peace activist echoed the chief's account, commenting that some elders simply sat down together and saw the need for it. Their purpose was to avoid marginalization of any one of the groups, since each of them constitutes a significant portion of the local population and is considered indigenous to the area.[20]

This assessment may not be far off the mark. In a conversation with a long-time Fulani traditional ruler and member of the Islamic Jama'atu Nasril Islam (JNI), he recalls a pattern of power-sharing dating back to the colonial period when local leaders would meet with colonial authorities in neighboring Jos to arrive at coordinated decisions or solutions to disputes.[21] It is unclear how frequently this occurred, but it suggests that the groups in present-day Bassa LGA may have had historical precedent for power-sharing, facilitated by the mediation of colonial authorities. This was the only LGA that noted the role of colonial authorities in helping local ethno-tribal groups arrive at mutually acceptable decisions.

The colonial legacy and history of cooperation was not sufficient, however, to guarantee peace between the indigenous ethno-tribal groups themselves and with the minority ethno-tribal groups upon the establishment of the LGA in 1975. Rather, the particular ethno-tribal composition of the LGA and consideration of the political tradeoffs after 1976 shaped the political calculation. That is, power-sharing emerged as the optimal political arrangement to guarantee the indigenous majority ethnic groups stable representation. The alternative was the possibility that the political competition introduced by the 1976 reforms could enable minorities in the LGA to employ a divide-and-conquer electoral strategy to prevent any one of the Pengana, Rukuba, or Irigwe tribes from achieving meaningful leadership in local government. In this sense, it was in the interest of the majority ethno-tribal blocs to come to an informal power-sharing

---

[19] Anonymous(T), interview by Laura Thaut Vinson, Bassa, Plateau State, October 27, 2011.
[20] Anonymous(U), interviewee by Laura Thaut Vinson, Bassa, Plateau State, October 27, 2011.
[21] Ibid., Anonymous(T), interview.

agreement. Thus, to whatever extent the leaders of the major local ethno-tribal groups were able to draw on the historical precedent to their advantage, a power-sharing agreement ensured that each had a key stake in local representation.

While power-sharing might have been in the interest of the majority indigenous tribes, what were the incentives for the minorities to tolerate the arrangement? LGAs like Bassa do not avoid inter-religious violence because the minorities are simply *too small* to mobilize. This is hardly the case. LGAs in southern Kaduna state, such as Zangon-Kataf and Jema'a, with Christian indigenous majorities and only a small Muslim Hausa-Fulani population, have been deeply affected by Muslim–Christian violence over the years. The history and (continued) power of the emirate system to intervene in the local politics of these LGAs despite their supposed right to self-governance makes these cases, and the power-sharing calculation, distinct from Bassa. Rather, as discussed in the previous chapter, the minority ethno-tribal groups in Bassa had incentives not to contest the power-sharing arrangement, since, depending on how the electoral chips fell, the minorities might otherwise fail to achieve any electoral representation in the local government. Further, due to the stability of the arrangement over the years, its flexibility has provided room for even non-indigenous Muslims to serve in important local government posts, helping to defuse claims of religious marginalization or fears of Muslim–Christian violence. In general, as local interview subjects noted and the data reflect, the religious identity of representatives is taken into account to better represent the religious pluralism of the LGA.

An alternative explanation for the calm in Bassa and for why local elders found a power-sharing solution feasible in Bassa might be the presence of the major Nigerian military barracks located near its headquarters. This argument is difficult to substantiate, however, since Jos is still prone to recurrent inter-religious violence despite the deployment of 16,000 extra troops to the area at the beginning of 2011 and despite its close proximity (perhaps 10 minutes) to the military barracks as well. Furthermore, the base's location in one particular area of Bassa does not explain why the local government as a *whole* is relatively calm, particularly in Jengre where the Muslim population is larger.

The case of Bassa, therefore, reinforces the argument that power-sharing at the local level and on an informal basis can be both a politically strategic and effective means of promoting ethno-tribal *and* inter-religious peace. As a local chief noted, there is peaceful co-existence among the Muslim and Christian communities in his area of Jengre, despite the majority Muslim population. This is due to their commitment to treating people fairly, he explained. The Fulani are given land in Bassa and are not rejected as strangers. To treat people otherwise, he notes, "will definitely lead to failure in the community."[22]

~

In general, the informal power-sharing institutions in these three LGAs offer two important insights. First, one has to look beyond the colonial experience and legacy to understand the stability of ethno-tribal relationships since the late 1970s. The demarcation of the boundaries of the LGAs themselves in the *post-colonial* period shaped which ethno-tribal groups would form the majority, as well as local leaders' political incentives to form power-sharing arrangements.

Second, these cases demonstrate the persistence of an *informal* power-sharing arrangement, which, based on the spoken promise of a few elites or community leaders, can entrench itself in the communal blueprint and political life of a community. As detailed in the previous chapter, the power-sharing mechanism provides a foundation for other forms of communal cooperation to prevent the spillover of violence from neighboring LGAs or states, reinforcing political stability in a time when the relationship between identity and politics is particularly volatile in the Middle Belt and north.

## MISSING/LOSING THE POWER-SHARING PATH

In the cases above, the incentives for leaders of the ethno-tribal groups in an LGA to agree to a power-sharing arrangement were shaped by a range of factors specific to the history and post-colonial developments in those LGAs. There was no one path to power-sharing. Similarly, the cases of Jos North, Zangon-Kataf, and Shendam make it clear that there was nothing inevitable about their failure to form more inclusive local government councils. The following discussion explores these three cases, examining the exogenous and endogenous factors that shaped post-colonial ethno-tribal relationships in these communities and led them down the path of ethnic tensions and greater susceptibility to inter-religious violence.

---

[22] Anonymous(P), interview by Laura Thaut Vinson, Bassa, Plateau State, October 27, 2011.

## Jos North

Since the early 2000s, the city of Jos has experienced a handful of major inter-religious clashes killing and displacing hundreds or thousands, along with intermittent smaller but deadly communal clashes. These conflicts have pitted the indigenous Christian ethno-tribal groups – the Afizere, Anaguta, and Berom – against the non-indigenous Hausa-Fulani Muslims (although the designation "non-indigenous" is part of the local debate). The failure of local ethno-tribal leaders to form a power-sharing agreement created an environment in which political changes and new disagreements could escalate. Jos was not doomed by its colonial legacy and history of ethnic politics to a cycle of intermittent violence, however. Indeed, the case of Jos is particularly interesting because it was for some time considered a bastion of peace while inter-religious violence raged elsewhere in the Middle Belt and north. In this particular case, exogenous political events steered ethno-tribal groups in Jos away from political integration and created *dis*incentives for power-sharing.

The post-colonial politics of state creation and LGA formation had a deleterious effect on communal relationships in Jos. The main event that shifted the tide and created new disharmony was the national government's decision to create the new Jos North LGA in 1991, chiseling it out of the single Jos LGA. Without warning, this event significantly and unexpectedly re-drew the boundaries of local political control and representation. This is not to say that disputes between the local ethnic groups did not exist prior; rather, this decision by the national government destabilized local ethno-tribal politics as it never had been before. To the local predominantly Christian ethno-tribal groups, the designation of Jos North and its particular boundaries appeared to re-channel the political authority held by local ethno-tribal groups to the "non-indigenous" Hausa-Fulani Muslims, playing easily into a disruptive narrative of political concession to former colonial rulers. Consequently, it shifted the political calculus away from any sort of power-sharing détente.

Some background is necessary to understand the significance of this event for local politics. The first signs that ethnic bonds might deteriorate into violent conflict emerged in the early 1990s, but the fundamental dispute over rights and representation between the significant Hausa-Fulani minority and the majority local ethno-tribal groups had long been present. On the one side, the Hausa-Fulani Muslim elite contended that they had been historically under-represented in the former Jos LGA due to their supposed "settler" status. They argued that they were denied the political and socio-economic rights of their ethnic counterparts despite having originally settled in the area in the 19th century and despite their central role in local administrative and economic development.[23] One of the primary disputes between the Hausa-Fulani and the local Anaguta, Berom, and Afizere bloc has been over the "ownership" of Jos – the capital of Plateau state and its major metropolis. The Hausa-Fulani elite assert that they are the original founders of Jos and have resided in the area for generations (Hausa-Fulani Elders' Forum 2009, 72–73).[24] Responding to two newspaper Op-Ed pieces written in 1981 on claims to ownership of Jos, Umaru Sani (1981, 8–9, 12), articulating the side of the Hausa-Fulani community, argues:

'Berom intellectuals' claim that Hausa-Fulani never ruled Jos, they were only made 'sarkin Hausawa' [community leaders] in places like Narkuta, Dilimi, Jos etc ... [T]he Hausa/Fulani founded and ruled [Jos] from about 1880 to late 1940s ... Since both groups of writers admitted that the settlers did not settle as a result of conquest, it stands to reason that the lands (Narkuta, Jos etc. areas) were virgin lands at the time they arrived. The Anguta were settled around the hills and the Beroms were unquestionably far South of Jos.

Contending that the Hausa-Fulani were the founders of Jos and actively developed the area as colonial administrators up until 1950, Sani (1981, 7) goes on to note,

It could be seen that the Hausa/Fulani were not only the forefounders of Jos but had also played a leading role in developing the area and its people. If there is anybody who deserves honour, respect and the claim of ownership of the town [the Hausa-Fulani] should be at the forefront. The exploitation argument of the

---

[23] Indigenous status, as opposed to settler or non-indigenous status, can confer employment, education access, political representation, and other rights to which the non-indigenous do not necessarily have access. As the Human Rights Watch (2005, 8) report aptly summarizes, "Throughout Nigeria, groups considered 'indigenes', or the original inhabitants of an area, are granted certain privileges, including access to government employment, scholarships for state schools, lower school fees, and political positions. To secure access to these privileges, they have to produce an 'indigene certificate' which is granted by the local authorities. 'Non-indigenes' or 'settlers' are denied these certificates and the accompanying privileges. Different groups are considered 'indigenes' or 'settlers' in different areas. The definition of the term 'indigene' is commonly understood to be based on a person's place of origin, but many people born and brought up in a particular area are not accorded that status, even though they may never have lived in any other part of Nigeria. No official document or legislation defines these categories precisely or sets out clear criteria as to how a person's 'indigeneship' is determined. The Nigerian constitution refers to the concept of 'indigene' but fails to define it."

[24] Also based on Anonymous(E), interview by Laura Thaut Vinson, Jos, Plateau State, September 7, 2011.

Plateau tribes is untenable. If their grand-parents were intensively exploited through the then local chiefs ... it was purely an accident of history. The British adopted a uniform system of indirect rule for the administration of its domain not only in Jos but all over Nigeria and indeed throughout its West African colonies. Again the exploitation was not limited to the Plateau tribes, the settlers [Hausa/Fulani] felt the pinch more; they formed over 90 per cent of the labour force in the mines, paid heavy taxes and were forced to license their bicycles and pay for various permits for social functions ... The Hausa/Fulani in Jos Township have suffered enough. It's high time they were politically integrated for peace, tranquility and good government of Plateau State. They are now, like other groups, requesting for a local government of their own. It's only fair if they are given. They are not asking for the Jos traditional chief-dom, nor are they asking for political appointments; what they want is fair treatment, just like all the other groups.

Local ethno-tribal groups dismiss these claims as historically false (Ostein 2009). In a rejoinder to these assertions, historians M. Y. Mangvwat and Charles Gonyok, speaking from the perspective of the local ethno-tribal groups, challenged Sani's evidence. Among other issues, they note that the Hausa-Fulani unsuccessfully attempted a military invasion in the 19th century from the Bauchi area and that the Hausa/Fulani – along with the Yoruba, Kanuri, and Igbos – did not establish a significant presence in the Jos area until 1915 during the British tin mining era (when a Hausa leader was brought in from Bauchi by the colonial authorities to preside over the Hausa mining settlements). Instead, Gonyok and Mangvwat (1981, 6) argue that colonial direct rule presided in the area of Jos township, "pending the indigenous chiefdoms would evolve larger and acceptable form of administration." Upon the effective local organization of the indigenous chiefdoms, they note, "the colonial government did the only logical thing, namely the incorporation of the former so called 'Hausawa Areas' into the various polities and chiefdoms of their habitants," and this "naturally raised the dissatisfaction from the 'Sarkin Hausawa areas' and their clique."

While the administration of the Jos Native Authority area following the 1950s was a rocky one and subject to the competing interests of the indigenous and settler tribes in the area, these historians argue that the Hausa-Fulani claims of exploitation cannot be substantiated. Along these lines, the local ethno-tribal groups assert their historical ancestry in the area and, hence, their ownership of the contested area of Jos. As one local leader proclaimed during a program intended to promote peace and reconciliation,

The Plateau people should be left to rule their own land. [The indigenous of Plateau] can't go to Katsina and take land! Plateau has been too hospitable; the visitor in her home wants to overthrow her from her seat in her own father's home. Whoever does not know his roots should go and find his roots. Settlers want to take over the state, and this is not possible.[25]

As this brief account highlights, the dispute over rights, representation, and ownership of Jos has been long-standing.[26]

Yet, despite the competing claims and clashing historical accounts, major violence did not erupt between the ethnic groups in Jos prior to 2000. Certainly the case of Jos demonstrates that the competing indigenous-versus-non-indigenous disagreements did not and do not inherently spell ethnic violence. Indeed, it was not until General Babangida, the military leader of Nigeria, made an executive political decision in 1991 to simply create a new local government to "resolve" the Jos issue that the tensions morphed into something more threatening and violent. With the demarcation of new local government councils across Nigeria, the former Jos LGA (in which the Christian indigenous tribal groups were the dominant majority) was carved up into Jos North and Jos South (and later Jos East). Due to the way in which the boundaries of the local government were newly delineated, the Hausa-Fulani achieved one of their central demands – their own local government in the form of Jos North, since, as Ostein (2009, 8) notes,

[w]ithin the new Jos North, in particular, the local peoples were no longer so predominant, most of them living with less admixture of other ethnic groups in Jos South; in elections to city-wide offices in Jos North, therefore, other groups, like the Hausas, might now expect to win. This in fact is believed by the Plateau indigenes to have been the exact purpose [for] which Jos North was created: to give the Hausa community of Jos an LGA they could control.

In reality, the new Jos North LGA was not entirely populated by Hausa-Fulani, but they were now on par in population size with the Anaguta (or perhaps even a majority; this is part of the debate). Whatever the exact ratio, this political event led to a new more volatile politics of indigenous versus non-indigenous identity and, ultimately, religious identity politics and violence. To the local Christian ethno-tribal groups, this move was seen as an affront, an attempt to appease the local Hausa Muslim population that was presumably advocating for more political power than acceptable. Angered by the concessions, the move decreased the space for compromise

---

[25] Community event, notes recorded by Laura Thaut Vinson, Jos, Plateau State, 2011.
[26] For more on the issue of indigenes versus settlers, see Ostein (2009).

in a period when the sacralization of politics, religious cleavages, and violence in surrounding states was on the rise. For the first time, no longer a political minority, the Hausa-Fulani could potentially control a local government area that included in its boundaries Jos metropolis – the state capital, and an area the local ethno-tribal groups long considered their own.

The results of this political sea-change became quickly evident. Following the creation of Jos North in 1991, the subsequent election for the chairmanship of the LGA went to a Hausa Muslim or "Jasawa" man by the name of Sama'ila Mohammed, much to the chagrin of the indigenous in the area. The chairman's subsequent liberality in dispersing indigenous certificates to Jasawa, as well as their domination of important local government positions, raised the specter of an exclusivist approach to governance (Ostein 2009, 11). While no violent clashes occurred during Samai'ila Mohammed's leadership, subsequent events created the impression that the Hausa-Fulani Muslims would once again rule the local ethno-tribal groups.

The political cleavage became starker with new political developments. When the Nigerian state reverted to military rule under General Abacha in 1993, the state nullified local government councils, instituting "caretaker committees" selected by the military regime. Consequently, when Alhaji Sanusi Mato, a Hausa Muslim, was appointed to the Jos North Management Committee in 1994, this raised a firestorm. Not only was the management committee perceived as dominated by Hausa Muslims, but the appointed governor of Plateau state was also a Muslim. These actions were "interpreted by both indigenes and settlers alike as a deliberate removal of Plateau natives (arna) away so as to pave way for the Hausa-Fulani settlers to take absolute control of Jos, the capital city of the State," and "[a]s expected, the Hausa-Fulani settlers jubilated while the indigenes greeted it with anger, anguish, protest and petitions" (Mangvwat 2011, 14). Members of the local indigenes mobilized in protest, marching to the Jos North Local Government Secretariat to prevent the swearing in of Mato in 1994. When Governor Mato succumbed to the pressure, the Hausa Muslims counter-protested and clashed with police and those opposed to the appointment. In the subsequent violence, markets, parks, and other public places were destroyed, and four people were killed and others injured.[27]

---

[27] For a discussion of the grievances and debate, see also Ostein (2009, 12), Dung Pam Sha (2005, 56), Hart and Oladimeji (1994, 1), and Hart (1994, 13). These sources note that, as a result of the dispute, Mato was asked not to assume office. This action then led to the

This crisis was the first of what would become endemic violence in Jos over the next two decades. The dispute over political control of Jos North continues and is exacerbated by the recent *indigenous* domination of leadership in the local government council, giving rise to accusations by the Hausa-Fulani that elections are rigged and fraudulent. Indeed, at the time of writing and since 1994, a Hausa Muslim has not served as the chairman of the local government council despite their significant presence in Jos North. One local scholar observed that the fact that both the chairman and deputy seats went to a Christian in the last Jos North election in 2008 was clearly "not realistic, fair, or just."[28] As a result, Hausa-Fulani elite argue,

> It is a government-promoted injustice, targeting total systematic marginalization and exclusion of our people from any benefit connected with state resources, despite our physical presence, contributions to the development of Jos and its environs. The most disturbing aspect of our persecution is the actual steps being taken by the indigenesi and their government to annihilate our people from Jos North Local Government. (Hausa-Fulani Elders' Forum 2009, 72)

In contrast, judicial committees and leaders of the local ethno-tribal community continue to refer to their indigenous status and dismiss the "rights" of the Hausa Muslims to rule what does not belong to them.

The roots of the tensions could also be traced to the broader post-colonial trend of demarcating new states. Describing the evolution of these events, one local historian explains that the post-colonial creation of more states over time in Nigeria reorganized the colonial pattern of communal relationships. When the national government carved Plateau state out of the former Plateau-Benue state and implemented the 1976 decentralization reforms, the Hausa population in Plateau state became a minority among the Berom, Afizere, and Anaguta people in an area where they had previously been a political majority. He notes,

> [W]hen the Benue-Plateau state was created, [the Muslims] had no cause to fear ... [b]ecause in that state you had pockets of Muslim emirates in the Middle Belt state to whom they related ... So the fear that they [were] being dominated ... was

---

demonstration by Mato's mainly Muslim supporters who clashed with police and indigenes opposed to the appointment. Muslim youth converged at the Islamic Primary School and marched to town chanting slogans in support of Mato, and they forced passersby/motorists to repeat the slogans. The police presence was minimal and overwhelmed by stone throwers. The rioters went on to destroy markets, parks and other public places, and demonstrators and indigenes clashed at Gada Biu junction.

[28] Anonymous (AB), interview with local scholar by Laura Thaut Vinson, Jos, Plateau State, July 28, 2016.

less ... Then Benue-Plateau state was severed and a Plateau State was created. Now, in the old Plateau state, again, they had no cause to fear because the emirates in Nasarawa, in Keffi, in Lafia, in Wase, in Kanam were still there ... Wase and Kanam were, you know, and are still acknowledged emirates, created during the Jihad ... Now, with the creation of the new state and now local government ... when you now merge with that of the natives, the Hausa are about to become a minority. And this is what has happened. And that is why the only local government that they control was now about to be taken over by the, you know, an alliance of the natives and these other Christian groups from the south. Now, it was with the realization of that that President Ibrahim Babangida then split Jos into Jos North, Jos East, and Jos South, by which he had hoped that Jos North would belong exclusively to the Hausa-Fulani.[29]

Subsequent political moves to resolve the dispute reinforced the divisions and made a power-sharing solution all the more untenable.

Under these conditions, a divisive religious othering and a narrative of Muslim–Christian conflict, already rampant in Nigerian national politics and in communal violence in areas surrounding Plateau state, found fertile ground in Jos. In a short space of time, following the creation of Jos North, Jos went from being a peaceful vacation destination and home to displaced fleeing inter-religious violence to one of the hotbeds of recurrent Muslim–Christian clashes, generating thousands of displaced people of its own. A small-scale violent clash in 1994 over the political appointment of a Hausa Muslim portended more violence to come, violence that would take on a strongly religious dimension and render Jos one of the perceived no-go zones of northern Nigeria. The city itself is now segregated along Muslim–Christian lines, and many Christians fear entering Muslim neighborhoods and vice versa. Bouts of violence occasionally flare and are unpredictable, killing anywhere from relatively few to a few hundred.

Yet, the conflict was not inevitable. While the relationship between the local ethno-tribal groups and the Hausa-Fulani was clearly shaped by the colonial legacy – lack of assimilation and political integration – it was subsequent political events and changes *particular* to this area of Plateau state that tipped the balance toward conflict rather than compromise. The creation of Jos North established a political impasse, removing incentives for any sort of power-sharing solution. In this context and despite having lived peacefully together for generations, trust and collaboration between the leaders of the local ethnic groups became unsustainable. Religious rhetoric and religious events have become powerful triggers for communal conflict as a result.

---

[29] Ibid., Anonymous(E), interview.

## Shendam

Along with Jos, the case of Shendam contrasts starkly with Chikun, Kanam, and Bassa. Similar to other areas where colonialism imposed Hausa-Fulani rule, the pre-colonial area of Shendam was largely non-Muslim and not culturally assimilated or politically integrated with the Hausa-Fulani political empire. This historical context did not condemn the ethno-tribal groups in present-day Shendam to a future of religio-political impasses and inter-religious violence. Violence was not inevitable; indeed, as in Jos, despite disagreements, groups had lived together peacefully for generations. The two primary ethnic groups are the Muslim Jarawa (the Hausa) and the Goemai (Christian and Muslim), and a diverse set of smaller ethno-tribal groups such as the Taroh and Montol from surrounding LGAs who also settled in Shendam. However, post-colonial changes and the expansion of Christianity in this area did nothing to shore up relationships between the Hausa-Fulani minority and the local ethno-tribal groups of present-day Shendam. In this case, it was not one major event that negated incentives for power-sharing. Instead, a combination of events – political disputes over traditional leadership roles and rights, the threat of political re-engineering with the politicization of religious identity, the actual re-engineering of districts, and the underlying tension between Muslim and Christian religious leaders over local predominance (particularly with the rapid growth of Christianity among the non-Muslim population in the post-colonial period) – created a power-sharing impasse between the Christian Goemai and the Muslim Jarawa/Hausa. Consequently, the eruption of inter-religious violence in Jos North, Bauchi, Kaduna, and Kano in 2001 provided a framing narrative for local tensions in Shendam. The decades-long failure to resolve long-standing political and economic disputes culminated during a period of intense Muslim–Christian violence in other areas of Plateau state and the Middle Belt. The lack of a power-sharing institution to ameliorate tensions and defuse perceptions of socio-economic and political marginalization meant that Shendam was more prone to inter-religious violence. This section briefly traces how ethno-tribal relationships unfolded in Shendam.

One of the central cleavages between the local ethno-tribal groups in Shendam – the predominant Goemai population and the large Jarawa Muslim minority – was a long-standing debate over ownership of the town of Yelwa, a town central to the socio-economic life of the LGA. Yelwa was at the heart of the conflict and inter-religious violence, since the town is both an important metropolis and market town in the southern senatorial zone of the state, and, prior to the violence, settled by a large number of Muslims as well as Christians. As in Jos North LGA, the Muslim "non-indigenous" claim to be indigenes of the area dating back some 200 years to their migration from Dass in Bauchi state (Hoomlong 2008). Thus, both the Jarawa and the Goemai have presented various arguments and documents to substantiate their story and claims to indigeneity (Hoomlong 2008, 29–33; Gonshit and Kums 2007, 235; Plateau State of Nigeria 2004, 26, 38). As in Jos, this dispute did not automatically spell violence and impasse. Instead, secondary source material highlights a series of events and changes in the communities that, lacking any outside political mediator, emphasized their cleavages and created a context within which religion could become the basis for violent mobilization in June 2002, February 2004, and May 2004. Hoomlong's qualitative on-site research highlights some of these post-colonial political events and religious changes that affected communal relationships.

First, the lack of cultural assimilation led to a fundamental disagreement about the right of the Hausa-Fulani Muslims to choose their own traditional ruler. In particular, the inability of the Muslim Yelwa residents to elect their own traditional leader after his death in 1992 created a debacle. The Long Goemai, the traditional leader of the local Goemai people, appointed a new Muslim traditional leader based on the premise that it is within the Long Goemai's traditional authority to appoint chiefs. This move was not viewed by Yelwa Muslims as the Goemai's legitimate right, however, and they "decried the absence of their own leader, a leader of their choice and culture [to] whom they could owe allegiance" (Hoomlong 2008, 35). The Jarawa leader appointed by the Goemai was ultimately removed in the face of these protests. This event did little to promote understanding between the ethno-tribal groups.

Second, the 2002 election of the Ward Chairmanship of the People's Democratic Party (PDP) became contentious when the Muslim and Christian contenders mobilized PDP's otherwise mixed constituency along religious lines in order to guarantee the electoral outcome. Without a power-sharing arrangement, local politicians could exploit religious identity to their own ends. Claims of vote manipulation and fraud on both sides created the increasing perception that religion was the basis of political exclusion (Hoomlong 2008, 34–5).

Third, reminiscent of the political havoc associated with the creation of Jos North, the local government accepted requests for the creation of new districts in Yelwa not long after the debacle of the PDP ward elections. The expectations of the Muslim community were sorely disappointed when the new districts were announced in May 2002 (Hoomlong 2008, 36). Not only were wards that the Jarawa/Hausa Muslims thought belonged to them included in the Nshar non-Muslim area, but leaders also added insult to injury by changing the Hausa names of communities to the Goemai form.[30] Essentially, this political redistricting was seen as a "gerrymandering" move, an attempt to curb the political rights and autonomy of the Muslim population by reducing their ability to gain councilorship seats. Since councilors are selected at the ward level, any change in the ethnic balance of a ward can make it far more difficult for a minority ethno-tribal group to gain representation in the local government legislative assembly. Consequently, while the data on election and appointment results for Shendam could not be completed for many administrations, the data that were collected show that Christian Goemai have dominated not only the positions of local government leadership, but also the legislative/councillorship positions that derive from ward elections. Even in the wards or districts where smaller ethno-tribal groups are more likely to gain legislative representation, Goemai Christians dominate. It was no wonder, therefore, that the establishment of new districts aggravated the relationship between the ethno-tribal groups.

Finally, the religious changes in the local government in the post-colonial period as the non-Muslim population overwhelmingly converted to Christianity also reshaped socio-religious relationships. As Chapter 2 highlighted, Plateau state, along with a number of other Middle Belt states, experienced a rapid conversion of its non-Muslim population to Christianity following the end of colonial rule with the removal of the barrier to missionary evangelism, and subsequently with the Pentecostal-charismatic revival that began to sweep the Middle Belt in the 1970s. Thus, while tensions were mounting in political relationships, the same was true among religious leaders. For example, local Christian religious leaders instigated a new effort to keep a tight rein on their youth (with the support of some Muslim religious leaders) by banning relationships between Christian girls and Muslim boys. Religious leaders were so serious about this order that they set up "a vigilante patrol team ... to

---

[30] Hoomlong (2008, 36) recounts the ordeal, observing, "[D]uring the confirmation of the districts ... the composition of the districts was read out and to the anger of the Yelwa community, their request was turned down and places the Muslims had thought belong to Yelwa community were given to Nshar community ... Also, wards in Nshar which had formerly been named Angwan Madaki were renamed Angwan Kangtun (the names which used to be Hausa were changed to names in the Gamai dialect)."

enforce the separation," and "[g]irls caught relating with Muslim boys were to be punished" (Hoomlong 2008, 37).

Contributing to this religious cleavage was a dispute between Muslims and Christians over the possibility of two new mosques opening in the market area of Yelwa. Generating significant opposition among Christians, they called for the local government council to prevent the mosques from opening. When the Long Goemai attempted to visit the market to investigate the matter and Muslims "retaliated by stoning his entourage and calling him the Chief of Infidels," Hoomlong (2008, 38) notes that this "insult led to the banning of the unholy yoke [between Muslim men and Christian women] and the Muslim community responded by also banning their people from eating at restaurants owned by Christians or buying meat slaughtered by Christian butchers." The first major incident of communal violence occurred two days later. Although the two communities dispute the details of the events or incidents leading up to the violence, in a context of foggy rumors and random threats, Muslims men ultimately attacked a church in which dozens of Christians were hiding, killing 78 people (Hoomlong 2008, 39–41).

The notion that Shendam has historically been characterized by violence between its ethno-tribal communities and that this explains its susceptibility to inter-religious violence is insufficient. To the contrary, this claim would not explain why the violence only erupted (on a grand scale) in 2002 and not earlier, or why it took on a starkly religious dimension. Ultimately, a series of political, economic, and cultural or religious changes and events gradually exacerbated socio-political relationships. In contrast to LGAs that also have an ethnic pluralism but balance competing claims through a power-sharing arrangement, elites adopted no such institution in Shendam. In this case, there were fewer incentives for power-sharing, and the general lack of anything bordering on a power-sharing arrangement rendered one political issue after another a potential trigger for communal violence – everything from relationships between Christian girls and Muslim boys, the opening of a new market in Nshar district, and cultural festivities, to cattle-grazing disputes became points of conflict and justifications for violence (Hoomlong 2008). No institutional mechanism was in place to mediate or resolve conflict among the competing ethno-tribal groups. Issues of economic poverty and political marginalization were, therefore, interpreted as problems rooted in *inter-group* competition and inequality (Human Rights Watch 2005, 48).

This analysis does not mean that it was impossible for the ethno-tribal leaders to come to a power-sharing solution and avoid inter-religious violence. If nothing else, in light of the success of power-sharing in promoting ethno-tribal cooperation in nearby LGAs, the case of Shendam highlights the need for state or national level efforts to encourage power-sharing institutions where local initiatives have not been attempted. The alternative – the potential for heightened conflict and violence as the case of Shendam highlights – leaves much to be desired.

### Zango-Kataf/Jema'a

As with other LGAs on the fringes of Hausa-Fulani rule during the colonial period, communal violence in Zangon-Kataf during the 1980s and in subsequent years was not inevitable. Rather, the lack of reforms to local governance as envisioned with decentralization, religious change with the expansion of Christianity among non-Muslims, and the organization of local elite around demands from the Muslim emirs for reforms and self-governance all combined to create a volatile situation in Zangon-Kataf that has precluded power-sharing. The acrimonious politics of religion in Nigeria during the 1970s and 1980s only increased the potential for religion to become the basis for conflict and violent mobilization over local grievances.

The nature of rule during the colonial era is an important, even if not sufficient, background for understanding contemporary ethno-tribal and ethno-religious relationships and politics in LGAs such as Zangon-Kataf and Jema'a. These areas of present-day southern Kaduna state (known as Southern Zaria in colonial times) strongly resisted Hausa-Fulani Muslim rule in pre-colonial as well colonial times. Indeed, when the British appointed the Hausa-Fulani as indirect rulers, it was the British colonial forces that imposed a cessation to conflict between the Hausa-Fulani Muslims and the southern Zaria non-Muslim population (Turaki 1993).

Subsequently, like other areas on the fringes of the former Hausa-Fulani empire, the subjugation of local ethno-tribal groups to the Hausa-Fulani system under British Indirect Rule was not welcomed. Indigenous non-Muslim groups reticently came under the Zaria and Jema'a emirates under threat of colonial force (Falola 1998, 214). Instead of being ruled by an autonomous local chiefdom as in some of the other non-Muslim areas, the Emir of Zaria controlled the administration of the region and appointed the ruling chiefs. Continued adherence to African Traditional Religion and the desire to be ruled by indigenous traditional chiefs was not lessened under emirate rule, as "Hausa administrators treated the ethnic Atyap [Kataf] population with contempt and brutality throughout much of the colonial period" (Human Rights Watch 2006, 51). As Osinubi and Osinubi (2006, 9) summarize, "the history of Southern Kaduna is essentially a history of resistance and struggle by the various ethnic groups to the emirate system, which was imposed on the area by the British colonial indirect rule system." Cultural assimilation and political integration, needless to say, never took root between the local ethno-tribal groups and the Hausa-Fulani in Zangon-Kataf and Jema'a.[31]

Prior treatment under colonial indirect rule did not, however, render inter-religious violence inevitable decades later. If so, Muslim–Christian conflict should be the bane of all pluralistic LGAs in southern Kaduna state and Plateau state. Rather, local politics in Zangon-Kataf were significantly shaped by the subsequent social, religious, and political changes in the post-colonial period. One development that had a significant impact on the Zangon-Kataf community was the rapid conversion of the non-Muslim indigenous groups to Christianity. From the 1960s onward, when the north opened up to Christian evangelization and mission efforts, Christianity made deep inroads among the non-Muslim groups that had rejected Islam. Christianity became the predominant religious identity among the non-Muslim groups, accounting today for approximately 35 percent of Kaduna's population (Johnson 2007). The Kataf, having rejected Islam, took to Christianity en masse. In Zangon-Kataf, as Falola (1998, 215) notes, Islam and Christianity "thus became well-established in the areas: Islam among the Hausa, and Christianity among the Kataf. Religion combined with ethnicity to polarize the town."

While religious change considerably shaped local identities, this change alone was not sufficient to create a power-sharing impasse, as the case of Kanam showed. Rather, unlike areas of Plateau state and other LGAs, post-colonial reforms had a more limited impact on Zangon-Kataf, failing to provide broader self-representation for indigenous Christian ethno-tribal groups. This exacerbated inter-group relations and provided little

---

[31] As Falola (1998, 214) notes, "The Kataf regarded the Islamic emirate, established in the nineteenth century, as an enemy, along with the pro-emirate colonial and postindependence governments." Toward the end of the colonial period, local elites began to assert demands for self-rule through nascent forms of political organization – such as in the movement for a Middle Belt Zone – that would make them independent of the northern region and Hausa-Fulani Muslim political elite.

incentive for power-sharing, rendering religion a source of cleavage and, ultimately, violence.

The contentious politics of the area and its significance are clear in the historical accounts of the region. Despite some reforms in the 1960s, for example, one point of contention was the right of indigenous ethno-tribal groups to appoint their own village and district heads. In the Kataf view, the appointment of local leaders would provide them with at least *some* say in matters like the allocation of land, particularly land dominated by the Hausa-Fulani, in an environment of increasing land pressures. A relaxation in representation among the various ethno-tribal groups was not immediately forthcoming, however. Zangon-Kataf reflects Kalu's (2009, 77–79) observation that "when Nigeria secured her independence in 1960 and the exit of the British, the prevailing colonial institutions still held sway as the dominant orthodoxy." Although some groups were allowed the right to appoint local heads, the appointments still had to be endorsed by the emir. This was deemed unacceptable to the Kataf, infringing on their right to local self-representation. The Kataf rejected the legitimacy of even Kataf Christian appointments, since, "[i]n the Kataf view, the emir approved only the appointment of puppets" (Falola 1998, 215). The organization of political power changed little, as the Kataf were "lumped together with the rest of Zaria province and subjected to the overlordship of the emir, who appointed village heads to govern them" (Falola 1998, 215).

The 1976 decentralization reforms should have ameliorated some of this concern over self-representation. The reforms were intended to strengthen local government representation, shifting the locus of power away from the emir or chiefs to elected local government councils. As Mamdani (1996, 104–105) notes, up until the period of local government reforms, governance was chief-in-council instead of chief-and-council, which means that the chiefs or traditional authorities could make decisions whether or not the local governing council agreed with the decisions or not. Hence, the local ethno-tribal groups viewed the local government reforms of the 1970s and 1980s as an opportunity to achieve broader say in local representation. Indeed, with the 1976 reforms and the official designation of Zangon-Kataf LGA (carved out of Kachia LGA), the Kataf were the dominant majority in the LGA.

The reforms did not take effect in Zangon-kataf as hoped, however. The emirate clung on to religio-political control. A paper presented by Abdul Raufu Mustapha (2003) at a United Nations Working Group on

Minorities explained the deadlock following local government reforms as follows:

> However, in their [the Kataf] view, this development did not address their problem as the elected local government chairmen were incorporated into the Zaria Emirate Council as subordinates of the Emir. Furthermore, all District and Village Heads, though employees of, and paid by, the local government, continued to be appointed by, and reported directly to, the Emir of Zaria. Though Kataf men were now both Local Government Chairman and District Head, Kataf disaffection continued to simmer, fuelled by what they regard as their continued subordination to Zaria, and the alleged nepotistic appointment of the minority, but now 'allegedly indigenous', Hausa/Fulani elements from the southern Kaduna area to political and other offices in the State and Federal governments as 'representatives' of the people of the area.

Expectations of autonomy and self-representation were far from realized, thwarted by a political regime that refused to implement or respect the full meaning of the decentralization reforms.

These events prevented a more equitable, inclusive form of local representation from emerging between the Christian indigenous groups and the Hausa-Fulani. The notion of a power-sharing arrangement could have little traction when Kataf indigenous saw the structure of local political leadership and representation as something of a farce in the first place. The consequences for inter-group relations in Zangon-Kataf were toxic. Reminiscent of conditions in Jos North between the local ethno-tribal groups and the Hausa-Fulani Muslims, perceptions of intractable differences flourished in this setting, as

> The Kataf believed that the Hausa minority marginalized them at all times, abusing their power to take land, dominate resources, and exploit the Kataf as slaves ... The Kataf blamed the crisis on the emir for denying them the right to appoint their own chief, a right their neighbors were given. The emir, the Kataf alleged, usually resolved chieftaincy and land disputes in favor of the Hausa (Falolo 1998, 214).

The post-colonial political events and religious changes, therefore, merely built upon colonial era (and prior) grievances. A Human Rights Watch (2006, 51–52) account reflects this narrative:

> The Atyap have struggled, successfully, for a greater degree of local autonomy since independence but have never forgotten the historical wrongs their community suffered under Emirate rule. As is increasingly true throughout Nigeria, having been able to secure recognition as the true indigenes of their community, many Atyap feel it only appropriate that all the benefits flowing to their local government should go to them alone. Atyap rejection of their Hausa neighbors' claims to

indigene status is also fueled by a belief that the Hausa have an inherent predilection for the domination of others and seek indigene status only in order to subjugate and marginalize the Atyap. That belief, common in political discourse throughout southern Nigeria and the Middle Belt, is fueled by the intemperate rhetoric of political and community leaders throughout southern Kaduna.

In contrast, the Hausa-Fulani of Zango-Kataf claim that, although they have resided in the area for at least 200 years, the Kataf have marginalized them. From this perspective,

> The Hausa saw the Kataf as uncivilized, constantly complaining 'pagans.' They believed that the facts of history and conquest gave them both control of the land, saying the Hausa could not be called outsiders, since their ancestors had been living there for hundreds of years.[32] The Hausa viewed the Kataf as hostile, accusing them of bow-and-arrow attacks on innocent Hausa farmers. (Falola 1998, 214)

While violence was not preordained, contemporary politics helped to embed these local narratives and grievances in this particular LGA.[33] By the 1990s, combined with religious change and sacralization of national politics, the stage was set for various offenses or local disputes to trigger violence and feed on a narrative of inter-religious difference.[34]

---

[32] The question of who settled the area first is a constant refrain between the ethno-tribal groups. "The Atyap and the Hausa have long been embroiled in a bitter and seemingly interminable debate about which group settled the area first," notes Human Rights Watch (2006, 50), "a disagreement that has proven impossible to resolve empirically because both groups have inhabited the area since at least the mid-18th century and possibly as far back as 1650."

[33] The story is similar for Kafanchan, the headquarters of neighboring Jema'a emirate. Protest against the Jema'a emirate system and demands for its dissolution continued in the post-independence period among the indigenous Christian population. While their demands for autonomy achieved little, the death of the tenth emir in 1998 presented an opportunity for change, particularly in the representation of indigenous groups in the chieftaincy system. One of the demands submitted by the indigenous was that the "change should be far-reaching enough to include representatives of our various communities in the council of kingmakers and expand the ruling houses to include us" (Idunwo 1999, 6–7). When their demands for self-determination went unheeded and it appeared a new emir would be installed, indigenous members of the local government council continued to work for a solution with representatives of the ruling emirate. Elders reached a new agreement that an indigenous chiefdom should be installed on the same day as the new emir. Yet, when the day came, the installation of the new chiefdom ceremony was not announced with that of the new emir, leading the local ethno-tribal population to conclude that the agreement would not be respected. Rioters then mobilized, blocking the ceremony from occurring in Kafanchan. Violence soon broke out, evolving into a Muslim–Christian conflict that sent shockwaves throughout the north (Idunwo 1999, 6–7).

[34] As Falola (1998, 216) notes, "in the 1990s, fresh struggles emerged over control of the new local government and market and over questions about allegiance to the emir of

Had the 1976 local government reforms been respected or enforced, the story of Zango-Kataf may have been much different. Since the 1992 violence, some changes have taken place in the communities of Zangon-Kataf. Egwu (1998, 115) notes that the "recent [1996] creation of independent chiefdoms in Southern Kaduna for the Kataf, Bajju and other minorities in Zangon-Kataf who were previously administered under Zaria emirate provides a good starting point in addressing the grievances of ethnic minorities" (See also Mustapha 2003). He goes on to observe, "Although it is far from providing an enduring solution to the problem, it has considerably whittled down tension in the area" or "calmed nerves" (Egwu 1998, 115).

While relations are more peaceful, the disputes over land and representation that culminated in the 1992 violence and demonization of ethno-tribal and religious groups does not auger well for a grassroots-led power-sharing arrangement and a stable peace. Hausa displaced by the 1990 violence complain that their land has not been returned to them despite their appeal to the local government. In interviews with Hausa leaders in Zangon-Kataf, Human Rights Watch (2006, 52) was told, "If we want anything we have to go through the local government ... But those people, they hate us and will do nothing for us." They go on to note,

> Several other individuals confirmed this impression, alleging that they were denied the right to compete for jobs and other opportunities made available through the local government administration. One man complained that "[t]hey will call all of the people from the LGA for interviews, saying that they want to recruit one person [for a job]. When we send our boys there the LGA sends them home." Members of the community also complained that despite repeated government promises, much of the land that had been seized from them by their Atyap neighbors after the 1992 violence had yet to be returned. (Human Rights Watch 2006, 52)

Thus, the violence in 1992 heightened misgivings on both sides and further entrenched stereotypes and a politics of exclusion among the majority Kataf and the minority Hausa who returned to the Zangon-Kataf after the 1990s violence. The LGA continues to be known as one of the more volatile in terms of ethno-tribal and Muslim–Christian relations. Conflict was not a foregone conclusion, but the stranglehold of colonial-era forms of political power particular to this area of Kaduna state, as well as the politics of

---

Zaria. The Kataf felt that they and not the emir, should appoint the head of their local government. Kataf nationalists said there would be no peace until the power of the emirate was completely removed from their town and the Kataf were given charge over their own community."

religious change and disappointed expectations of the 1970s reforms, exacerbated identity cleavages in Zangon-Kataf and created little incentive or opening for a power-sharing alternative.

~

Power-sharing in Kanam, Chikun, and Bassa, as the discussion thus far highlights, is an arrangement that grew out of the historical realities and changes specific to these local governments. Despite the informal nature of the institution, it manages to persist, reinforcing and legitimizing itself through the representation of the major ethno-tribal groups in the LGA. As one local leader in Kanam observed, "Whoever does not give us mixed [representation], we will not go with him."[35] Claims of religious marginalization, in the context of power-sharing, are far more difficult to politicize.

Where post-colonial changes exacerbated ethno-tribal relationships and raised fears of a zero-sum game over local rights, representation, and resources, power-sharing was less likely to appear feasible at the time of decentralization. In Jos, an exogenous shock – General Babangida's decision to create Jos North LGA – heightened political conflict to an unprecedented degree, increased ethno-tribal competition, and reduced political incentives for power-sharing or compromise. The impact of post-colonial reforms, the spread of Christianity, patterns of migration, land pressures, outside political interventions, and the nature of competing institutions are among a number of factors that played out differently in communities of the north. Thus, unlike other LGAs, power-sharing between indigenous Christian ethno-tribal groups and minority Hausa-Fulani held little strategic interest in Zangon-Kataf or Shendam. Among other factors, the precedent of indirect rule established by the British did not change significantly in the post-colonial period, and local government reforms did not alter the equation sufficiently to prevent new pressures and local disputes from spiraling into inter-religious violence.

## CONCLUSION

As this chapter makes clear, the institutional legacies of colonial politics cannot simply be dismissed as unimportant, but these legacies are not sufficient to explain subsequent ethno-tribal communal relationships and politics. On the one hand, one could argue that the pattern of colonial-era

---

[35] Ibid., Anonymous(B), interview.

repression or control was so much more severe or institutionalized in LGAs such as Zangon-Kataf and Jema'a under the Zaria and Jema'a emirates that they were predestined for a future of inter-religious violence. In the case of Shendam, the Goemai and Hausa-Fulani Muslims' lack of integration during the colonial period may have created insurmountable cleavages. In contrast, the peaceful manner of Hausa-Fulani migration to the area of present-day Kanam may have ensured the cultural assimilation and political integration necessary for future political stability. In this sense, one could argue that the colonial-era political and social differentiation or grievances engendered between groups may have set areas of southern Kaduna state on a path toward recurrent and inevitable conflict.

On the other hand, however, an argument based entirely on the colonial precedent is too simplistic. First, such an argument does not explain why LGAs such as Chikun and others in present-day southern Kaduna state – areas that were also under the same colonial system of rule and have similar pluralism – experience greater harmony. It is true that Zangon-Kataf and Jema'a diverge from other cases (such as Bassa, Chikun, and Kanam) in that, while they experienced similar rapid growth of Christianity among the non-Muslim ethno-tribal groups, the emirate system persisted in its efforts to influence and thwart the political independence of local politics. Yet, if colonial politics predetermined this kind of interference by religio-political elite and were sufficient to explain power-sharing decisions, we should see power-sharing precluded in far more LGAs in both Kaduna and Plateau state.

Also, while it is indeed true that the levels of integration and cultural assimilation diverged in these areas of Shendam and Kanam dating back to the colonial period, to overlook the contemporary political and social changes and reactions to these events would truncate the story. Colonial-era politics cannot, in this sense, explain the *temporal* variation in inter-religious violence – why violence broke out when it did and not earlier. The thesis also cannot explain the clear religious dimensions of the violence that pitted not only Goemai against Hausa-Fulani, but also Goemai Muslims against Goemai Christians. As noted in prior discussion, redistricting politics, the death of a traditional ruler (and subsequent dispute over a new appointment), and religious changes that imposed new strict standards on social relationships were precursor events that hindered the development of a more collaborative system of local governance. Clearly, the religious dimensions of the conflict challenge the story that the violence was merely a product of a long-standing history of Hausa-Fulani versus Goemai ethno-tribal political discrimination and inequality.

Finally, the most important observation is that there is no one colonial institutional arrangement that can be pointed to as a sufficient condition for the adoption of power-sharing institutions decades after independence. After all, colonial institutions did not "determine" the advent and rapid spread of Pentecostal-charismatic Christianity in Nigeria and the attendant politicization of religion. Many non-Muslim or animist ethno-tribal groups largely converted to Christianity after independence when the barriers to evangelization fell, and Pentecostal-charismatic Christianity has rapidly penetrated the Middle Belt since the 1970s. Nor did colonialism determine the 1976 policy decision to create a system of local government and further democratize and decentralize political power. Also, as noted in Chapter 1, there were seemingly many colonial-era parallels in the region of the Middle Belt, but only some of the present-day LGAs adopted power-sharing.

Ultimately, there is no clear relationship between one colonial institution or precedent and present-day inter-religious or ethno-tribal violence. Colonial institutions were not sufficient to predispose some groups toward more cooperative post-colonial political ties, and such an argument glosses over far more variegation in the story of and relationship between ethno-tribal groups in this region of Nigeria. The legacies of history can linger, but the *strength* of those lingering effects depends on their interaction with subsequent events and changes experienced by LGAs. As this chapter contends, factors beyond colonial-era politics – or the ghosts of its institutions – and specific to the LGA in question explain the variation across cases following the 1976 decentralization. Individuals and groups do not make decisions and act in a straightjacket of history. With decentralization in the 1970s, communities that made the strategic choice to adopt power-sharing put in place an institutional precedent that would subsequently prove better able to withstand the communal tensions and the politicization of religious identity characteristic of contemporary Nigerian politics.

Having made the case that there was no single historical precedent that shaped incentives for power-sharing, however, this discussion has not exhausted the potential counter-arguments or competing theories for the pattern of power-sharing observed in the data and case studies. Is it the case, perhaps, that there is some other characteristic common to present-day power-sharing LGAs that explains the variation? The following chapter considers this possibility, exploring other competing explanations.

# 8

# Considering Competing Hypotheses

In challenge to the preceding chapters, is power-sharing really the best explanation for the observed patterns of peace and violence, or is there a better explanation? What if some LGAs were just more peaceful historically than others, and this predicts power-sharing? Or is it the case that perhaps power-sharing depends on the population balance between ethno-tribal or religious groups? That is, considering the hypothesized relationship between a lower likelihood of inter-religious violence and power-sharing institutions, are power-sharing institutions endogenous to some other unspecified factor or variable common to local councils with power-sharing? If so, then the emphasis on power-sharing as the primary explanation for the variation in communal violence is misplaced, as some other factor is providing the foundation for power-sharing. Further, considering the argument for the importance of local government power-sharing, is the claim here that LGAs with power-sharing are now impervious to the politicization of religion? Or conversely, are LGAs that presently lack a power-sharing institution doomed to recurring violence and political impasses?

This chapter considers these questions, primarily exploring alternative hypotheses or variables that may perhaps better explain the pattern of inter-religious violence or peace since the mid-1980s. The chapter also reflects on the durability of the power-sharing arrangements, suggesting that, while local power-sharing is certainly not invincible, it has endured significant pressures and been an important stabilizer of inter-group relations. And while the present politico-religious cleavages in Nigerian politics suggest that achieving a consensus around power-sharing in LGAs that have experienced major inter-religious violence will be a significant uphill battle, the argument is certainly not that there is no path forward. This chapter, then, seeks to assess counter-arguments and refine the argument.

ALTERNATIVE EXPLANATIONS

Is it power-sharing that is doing the heavy-lifting of peacebuilding and peace maintenance in the LGAs identified in this study, or is there some other fundamental characteristic providing a mantle of inter-religious peace and the conditions for power-sharing? It is important to consider some of these alternative explanations in order to be sure that the proper inferences are being made from the data and case studies regarding the relationship between the pattern of power-sharing and likelihood of religious violence. This section gives careful consideration to important competing arguments.

Comparable Cases?

One possible challenge to the causal claims regarding the mechanism of power-sharing is that the paired case comparisons, despite the similarities described in the previous chapters, are not really comparable since the ethno-tribal groups in each LGA are not identical. The local indigenous groups – apart from Hausa-Fulani – are different in each LGA. In Jos North, the Afizere and the Hausa are the majority, but in the broader Jos area (e.g., the confluence of Jos metropolis with Jos South and Jos East LGAs), the Christian indigenous Afizere, Anaguta, and Berom ethno-tribal groups compose the majority. Chikun is also home to a mix of ethnic groups, the three major ethno-tribal groups being the Gbagyi, Hausa-Fulani, and the Kabilu. Zangon-Kataf is home to the Christian Kataf or Atyap, along with a minority Hausa-Fulani Muslim population concentrated in certain areas. Similarly, in Bassa, the Christian ethno-tribal groups – the Pangana, Irigwe, and Rukuba – are the majority population and the Hausa-Fulani are a minority.[1] In Kanam, the two main ethnic groups are the Bogghom (Muslim and Christian) and the

---

[1] Although highlighting the predominant majority and minority groups in the LGAs, this does not mean that there are absolutely *no* members of other ethno-tribal groups residing in these areas. For example, there are very small groupings of six or seven additional ethno-tribal groups in Bassa LGA; the purpose here though is to highlight those whose population sizes render them the most politically salient groups.

Jahr (predominantly Muslim), and, in neighboring Wase, the Hausa Muslims and Taroh Christians are the major groups.

While one might argue that the analysis is compromised in not comparing apples to apples – LGAs with identical ethno-tribal compositions – there are two problems with this claim. First, one would be hard-pressed to find two LGAs in Plateau state or Kaduna state with an identical set and proportion of ethnic groups. Indeed, the national government or local groups generally sought to construct the parameters of LGAs in accordance with the settlement pattern of various ethno-tribal groups. As a result, the LGAs – conflict-prone and otherwise – tend to reflect different ethnic majorities and minorities. The specific tribal groups and their proportion in an LGA do not, therefore, explain the pattern or likelihood of communal violence

Also, the goal of this study is not to explain *particular* ethno-tribal cleavages and communal violence, but to understand why some LGAs with *various* ethno-tribal compositions are prone to inter-religious violence while others are not. As I discovered in the course of fieldwork, many instances of inter-religious violence that spread from one place to another occurred between ethno-tribal groups *distinct* from those involved in the original clashes. The Muslim–Christian divide is the common denominator. If the communal violence were simply reducible to particular ethno-tribal cleavages, one would expect to only see spillover violence in those areas where the ethno-tribal groups are identical. In essence, there is nothing particular or primordial about Nigerian ethno-tribal groups that makes them prone to communal violence.

The findings regarding the politics of identity and conflict, therefore, have broader implications for other countries with pluralistic communities and contentious ethnic politics. The overarching question is, in pluralistic communities that have undergone rapid religious change and are prone to widespread politicization of religious identity, under what conditions does religious identity become a salient cleavage associated with communal violence? In this sense, holding ethno-tribal identity constant is neither feasible nor relevant for the broader theoretical and empirical goals of this study. As one of the most ethno-tribally diverse countries in the world, with over 250 ethno-tribal groups, Nigeria is ideal for subnational comparative study on this topic.

## Religion Just a Proxy for Tribe?

The argument above also touches on another possible critique – that religion is really just a proxy for tribe in these cases. That is, these are conflicts between tribal groups that also happen to have different religious identities. Religious identity, then, is not really the central cleavage or salient dimension of the violence. As noted above, if this is the case, then we should find three patterns. First, none of the cases of violence should, on the basis of religious identity, pit members of the same ethno-tribal groups against one another in incidents of communal violence. Second, we should not see violence spread from one LGA to another unless the ethno-tribal affiliation of the groups is the same; that is, they are only inspired by the offense against members of their same tribal groups. Third, there should be no difference in the pattern of precipitating events associated with ethno-religious and ethno-tribal violence. They should be just as likely to be triggered by religious offenses as land disputes, for example. None of these stipulations hold.

Regarding the first stipulation, the communal violence in southern Plateau state in 2002 and 2004 pitted members of the same ethno-tribal groups and even families against one another. In Mikang LGA, Dinshak (2008, 88) notes that the violence "metamorph[iz]ed into waves of violence by 2004, when the prominence of religion had become quite evident by the way and manner in which they were carried out: members of the same ethnic identity in the same community and even families turned against one another under the banner of their religions."[2]

Regarding the second stipulation, reprisal attacks have clearly occurred (in non-power-sharing LGAs in particular) where the tribal affiliations of the groups are distinct from those involved in the original incident except for religious identity. Drawing on the example of the Yelwa violence in 2004, Hoomlong (2008, 44) notes, that the reverberations were felt widely, beyond Shendam as news trickled out. A Human Rights Watch (2005, 1) report notes,

One week later, on May 11 and 12, Muslims in the northern city of Kano – several hundred kilometers away from Plateau State – took revenge for the Yelwa attack and turned against Christian residents of Kano, killing more than two hundred. A once localized dispute in a specific part of Plateau State had escalated into a religious conflict of national dimensions.

---

[2] While one could argue that the prevalence of inter-marriage, in particular, may help to explain the lack of inter-religious violence in some areas, this hypothesis lacks empirical basis as highlighted here. As other experiences of communal violence demonstrate (e.g., Rwanda and Indonesia), inter-marriage is not a necessary or sufficient condition for ethnic peace.

The violence only spread to other LGAs and states because of identification with co-religionists, since the violence was interpreted as a Muslim–Christian conflict. This trend has repeated itself in many cases, emphasizing the importance of not simply treating religion as a proxy for tribe.

Finally, little needs to be said regarding the third stipulation. As Chapter 5 discussed in some detail, there is a clear and statistically significant difference in the pattern of precipitating events between cases of ethno-religious and ethno-tribal violence. Cases reported as ethno-religious are far more likely to be precipitated by offenses or disputes with an explicitly religious dimension, whereas ethno-tribal clashes are more likely to stem from disputes over economic issues such as land and cattle grazing rights.

## Prior Peace?

Another possible explanation for the adoption of power-sharing mentioned in passing elsewhere may simply be that areas with a history of peaceful relationships between ethnic groups had fewer barriers to power-sharing. A precedent of cooperative relationships and peaceful coexistence may have laid the groundwork for power-sharing. This potential issue of reverse causality – peace begetting power-sharing and not the other way around – is challenged by the case study evidence and data, however.

First, the history of cases such as Jos North in Plateau state presents a foil. If prior peace or violence explained the pattern, then one would expect Jos to have had higher levels of violence before the formation of local governments in the 1970s, rendering it less likely to adopt power-sharing. The evidence does not fit this argument, however. In fact, prior to 2001, Jos was considered a bastion of peace and stability in the Middle Belt, even a vacation destination, boasting an integrated communal and religious life. Indeed, Jos was no more characterized by inter-religious conflict than Chikun through the end of the 1990s. In this particular case, an exogenous political event – the national proliferation and restructuring of LGAs – reshaped local government boundaries and group relationships in Jos, exacerbating local identity politics and reducing incentives for power-sharing. Ethnic or religious violence had not, however, been a defining historical feature of Jos communal politics. In this sense, there was no one historical factor or primordial dimension that pre-determined the transition from inter-religious peace to violence. Rather, a particular set of political events and contemporary changes converged, heightening the perceived political stakes and reducing incentives for strategic collaboration between the predominant local indigenous groups and the Hausa-Fulani.

Second, evidence from pre-colonial or colonial periods also does not support an argument that prior ethnic violence or peace predetermined the likelihood of power-sharing. In fact, the ethnic minorities of present-day southern Kaduna state and Plateau state (encompassing both power-sharing and non-power-sharing districts) had a similar tumultuous relationship with the British-backed Hausa-Fulani Muslim rulers during the colonial period – one of general opposition. Local leaders organized resistance and advocated for independence from the political and cultural domination of the Hausa-Fulani Muslims, even pushing for the establishment of a separately governed Middle Belt region in the 1950s. During and following the colonial era, the adoption of Christianity by the non-Muslim population in this "fringe" Middle Belt region was indicative of the resistance to Hausa-Fulani Muslim political dominance (Okpanachi 2012). Yet, some of these areas with a mixed Hausa-Fulani Muslim and Christian population nonetheless developed power-sharing, while others did not. Consequently, the peace in LGAs such as Chikun in Kaduna state cannot be attributed to having a less tumultuous ethno-political history than the Jos area. As Okpanachi (2012) observes, "Kaduna has long been polarized violently along converging ethnoreligious, regional, socioeconomic, and political fault lines," and this has "pitted the state's Muslim Hausa-Fulani political-economic power group, which is based mainly in the northern portions of the state, against a constellation of non-Muslim southern Kaduna minority tribes." This historical dynamic did not foreordain the breakdown in communal relationships.

Finally, further addressing the potential of reverse causality, Bunte and Vinson (2016) examined data on violence from 1955 to 1985 contained in the Social, Political, and Economic Event Database (SPEED) to examine whether LGAs without power-sharing today historically had higher levels of violence, and vice versa. The dataset contains events of "politically motivated attacks," including attacks involving ethnic or cultural groups, as well as events of threatening political speech. We found that districts without power-sharing were no more likely to have a history of attacks or records of threatening political speech. Prior experience of ethnic violence is, therefore, not a significant predictor of the absence of power-sharing (Bunte and Vinson 2016, 15).

## Demographics and Electoral Incentives?

Another important hypothesis for why leaders in some LGAs pursued power-sharing may simply be the ethno-tribal demographic balance in the LGA (Posner 2004; Wilkinson 2004). That is, in LGAs where one ethno-tribal group forms a strong majority, one would expect decreased incentives for power-sharing, since electoral dominance could be achieved without appealing to minority ethnic groups for political support. In this scenario, tensions and conflict might develop between the majority and minority ethnic groups excluded from political leadership. In contrast, in LGAs where the ethnic composition is more evenly split, a power-sharing arrangement might appear more attractive, so that neither ethnic group risks being excluded from council leadership. Similarly, in an LGA with greater pluralism where one group may be more prevalent but smaller ethno-tribal groups form the majority, one might also expect a power-sharing arrangement, since the most prevalent ethnic group would need to form alliances with one or more of the smaller ethno-tribal groups in order to ensure local council executive representation.

The demographic argument, however, does not explain the variation in local power-sharing institutions in Kaduna and Plateau state. In fact, power-sharing institutions exist in LGAs that vary in their ethnic composition. The case of Bassa, for example, would seem to most closely fit the demographic-votes thesis. Three Christian indigenous groups predominate in the LGA, and a number of other minority ethno-tribal groups constitute the rest of the population, including the Hausa-Fulani Muslims who are strongly represented in a particular area of Bassa. In light of this diversity in the LGA, it might not be surprising that elites of the three main ethno-tribal blocs formed a rotational power-sharing arrangement in the 1970s that persists to this day; in this way, they ensure more equitable and stable representation on the council.

Yet, power-sharing between these particular ethno-tribal groups was not inevitable. A different power-sharing composition could also have made strategic sense in light of the LGA's pluralism. Additionally, the thesis does not explain why the relationship with the minority Hausa-Fulani Muslims has not been a powder keg for violence, as it has been in Christian-majority LGAs such as Zango-Kataf and Jema'a in southern Kaduna state. In other words, there is more to the story, and the story of this particular expression of power-sharing is rooted in the history and politics of the Bassa area.

## Alternative Explanations 239

In the case of Kanam in eastern Plateau state, the power-sharing institution between the Bogghom and Jahr might also seem to hold an obvious strategic electoral logic. Together the indigenous Bogghom and Jahr ethnic groups constitute the majority of the population, perhaps as high as 70 percent, according to local officials. However, the demographic composition alone did not pre-determine the power-sharing outcome. Indeed, in light of the largely peaceful relationship with the non-indigenous Hausa-Fulani Muslims in the area dating back to colonial times, it was not outside the realm of strategic sense for the Hausa-Fulani Muslims and their Muslim Jahr counterparts to form a power-sharing arrangement to the exclusion of the religiously mixed Bogghom. Or, in another scenario, all three ethno-tribal groups might have formed a power-sharing agreement, since members of the Bogghom are also Muslim. Again, what was perceived as "strategic sense" must be explored and understood in its larger historical context.

Two other cases that seem to go directly against the strategic logic are also worth mentioning briefly. First, based on the demographic-votes thesis, one would expect that the elites in Jos North – split between the Hausa-Fulani Muslims and indigenous Christians – would have formed a power-sharing agreement. The difficulty of gaining a majority should moderate identity politics and incentivize power-sharing. To the contrary, for various reasons specific to the Jos area, groups did not form a power-sharing arrangement, and this has allowed religious cleavages to take on central importance in multiple instances of communal violence.

Second, the case of Chikun in Kaduna state also goes directly against a demographic-votes hypothesis. In this case, the Gbagyi Christian ethnic group forms the majority in the LGA, but there are two main minority groups – the Hausa-Fulani Muslims and the Kabilu (members of ethnic groups from southern Kaduna state who are largely Christian and migrated at some point to Chikun). Yet, instead of outright domination, the Gbagyi formed a power-sharing arrangement with the other two ethnic groups. For a number of reasons, including the tensions between Hausa-Fulani Muslims and indigenous Christians that are a part of the history of southern Kaduna state, power-sharing seemingly goes against strategic political logic. Indeed, the Gbagyi could have simply formed a power-sharing agreement with *only* the Kabilu who are also predominantly Christian and include many who have fled violence with Hausa-Fulani Muslims in the southern part of the state. Yet, leaders formed a static power-sharing arrangement between all three ethnic blocs, which has also spawned broader cooperation between ethnic and religious groups in Chikun.

In another formulation, perhaps LGAs in which the population is more evenly split between Muslims and Christians are more prone to divisive identity politics. To control for this possibility, I selected Jos North and Chikun for comparison, since their populations are the closest to a 50/50 split of the population, and they were formed during a time when religion was becoming increasingly politicized and inter-religious violence more frequent in the north. Yet, one adopted power-sharing while the other did not; a simple religio-demographic argument cannot explain this dynamic.

Further, there are a number of LGAs with either small Christian minorities or small Muslim minorities that fall into either the power-sharing and non-power-sharing categories. For example, in Bassa LGA, the Hausa-Fulani Muslim population is a minority group, but the LGA is largely peaceful despite being next door to the volatile Jos North. Shendam LGA has an ethno-religious balance similar to Bassa, but it has experienced intense inter-religious violence. In Bauchi state to the north of Plateau State, Christians are a minority, but there have been many cases of inter-religious violence in some of its LGAs.

As these brief accounts emphasize, there is no one demographic balance that determines the adoption or non-adoption of power-sharing; it either goes against expectations in some cases, or the particular ethnic form it takes seems counterintuitive or at least not strategically obvious. The general argument here, then, is that the strategic incentives and disincentives for power-sharing cannot be reduced to a simple demographic calculation. In fact, power-sharing institutions exist in LGAs that vary in their ethnic composition. Rather, as emphasized in the previous chapter, only by taking into account the social, political, and religious changes or exogenous events that have shaped specific group relationships can we derive the various incentives for particular forms of power-sharing between groups in some LGAs and not others. What does emerge clearly, however, is that power-sharing – whatever the particular convergence of incentives – shapes whether religious identity in present day Plateau and Kaduna state is likely to become the basis for political competition and violence, irrespective of the ethnic population balance.

### Rapidness of Religious Change?

The rate of religious change among the population in an LGA might be an important variable explaining vulnerability to inter-religious violence. For example, perhaps LGAs like Jos, Zangon-Kataf, and Shendam experienced more rapid and destabilizing religious change than Chikun, Bassa, and Kanam. In the case of Jos, perhaps it experienced such a rapid religious change that the perceived threat to the Muslim population was so destabilizing that it triggered the rise of inter-religious tensions and violence in the community.

The impact of religious change on the Middle Belt and Nigeria as a whole has indeed been profound. In post-colonial Nigeria, the removal of restrictions on Christian missionary activity in the north, along with the Pentecostal-charismatic revival of the 1970s and 1980s, opened a space for the politicization of religious identity in national and local politics. This religious change involved not merely growth in the number of adherents, but also the emergence of a more educated and politically influential Christian political class in the north, as well as a doctrinal about-face among denominations toward active political engagement. The Christian Association of Nigeria (CAN) was established to advocate for Christian interests, and a radical and violent strand of Islam also emerged with devastating consequences by the beginning of the 1980s. A series of religio-political disputes since the 1970s – including disputes over Nigeria's membership in the OIC and the implementation of Sharia in northern states – also reified political identities along ethno-religious lines, as Chapter 2 discussed in detail.

While it is true that the spread of Christianity, in particular the evangelical-charismatic type, is strongly evident in Jos, and the adoption of Christianity by the non-Muslim groups in southern Kaduna state was associated with resistance to the religio-cultural assimilation of Hausa-Fulani rule, the phenomenon of religious change has not been unique to those LGAs. Rather, the expansion of Christianity has swept across the whole of the Middle Belt, making a significant impact on the development of political awareness among the indigenous tribes of more peaceful LGAs like Kanam, as well. A factor common to all of these LGAs cannot, therefore, explain the variation in peace or violence. Further, if the rapid religious change and the politicization of religion alone were sufficient to spark conflict, one would expect inter-religious clashes to be far more prevalent, particularly in pluralistic local government areas in the Middle Belt such as Chikun. While religious change helps to explain the politicization of Muslim and Christian identities in Nigeria and its salience as a communal cleavage, it does not explain why some LGAs are more prone to inter-religious violence than others.

### Prior Civic Integration or Associationalism?

It could be the case that the different trajectories of LGAs can be explained by the strength of their inter-ethnic networks and/or degree of civic associationalism. Greater interaction, integration, and information shared about and among ethnic groups may be key to maintaining cooperative relations or peace-promoting institutions and averting violence-inducing "exogenous shocks" (e.g., Fearon and Laitin 1996; Varshney 2002). This argument implies that groups that live in integrated communities and that have long interacted, intermingled, and even intermarried are not conflict-prone.

To the contrary, there are a number of cases in northern Nigeria where ethnic groups have lived in integrated communities for decades or even generations, but the bonds of community broke down along some ethnic cleavage in a short span of time. The violent clashes in 2002 and 2004 in southern Plateau state in which inter-religious violence turned even members of the same family and tribe against one another are particularly illustrative (Hoomlong 2008).

Furthermore, as previously noted, Muslim–Christian violence was largely unheard of in Jos before 2001, and Jos showed strong levels of integration in civic associations – such as in the mining union in the 1960s. Prior to violence in the 2000s, Muslims and Christians engaged in everyday interaction, living and socializing together in mixed neighborhoods and buying/selling together in the market. This is a common observation among Jos residents when they reflect on life in Jos prior to 2001. Muslims and Christians celebrated holidays with one another. Religion was not a defining cleavage any more than it is a defining cleavage in Bassa. Communities "largely coexisted peacefully" (Samuel et al. 2011, 184). At a peace meeting in early 2011, one religious leader recalled

> Long before now we had enjoyed so much peace... [we could] go into the house of a Muslim and visit freely. Until trouble started in 1994. Because of the experience we are going through here, everyone has become an enemy... Trust for each other is right now very low. Is there any hope for a return to those days? ... I remember that in 1975 I was living in Bauchi Street and the people living next to us were Muslims, but today, that's not the case – everyone to his tent (religious, ethnic, tribal). So a very old battle line is drawn; whether it's real or imagined, it exists.[3]

The issue was not ultimately one of integration or lack of prior civic associationalism, but, rather, a lack of power-sharing at the local level

---

[3] Notes recorded by Laura Thaut Vinson, Plateau State, March 23, 2011.

in the context of the new Jos North LGA creation, opening the space for religious identity politics and violence to flare. A theory of civic associations does not explain Jos' dramatic shift from one of the most peaceful areas of northern Nigeria to one of the most violence-prone.

### Effects of Displacement?

The effects of violence and displacement can be destabilizing not only for the areas affected by the violence, but also for areas receiving displaced populations. Does this dynamic explain why some areas have been more prone to inter-religious violence over time in the Middle Belt?

The paired comparison of Jos and Chikun addresses this possibility. Perhaps Jos was destabilized due to the arrival of displaced people from other conflict areas, causing greater strain on local resources and sparking conflict over access to local resources and rights. If this is the case to some degree – although never mentioned by interview subjects – it does not explain why Chikun, an area to which both Christians and Muslims from southern Kaduna have fled to escape recurring ethnic violence, is not a major center or generator of ethnic violence. The Kabilu – members from a hodgepodge of ethnic groups who have fled the violence in southern Kaduna state and migrated to Chikun – are the fastest-growing group in Chikun LGA. If flows of displaced people and population changes were the key explanatory variable and destabilizing factor, Chikun should have followed the same trajectory as Jos. It has not.

### Economic Inequality?

An argument largely unaddressed up to this point is the possibility that LGAs with higher levels of economic inequality were more likely to experience inter-group tensions, rendering adoption of power-sharing less likely. For example, it is clear that access to and control over the market in Yelwa – the center of commerce in Shendam – was a considerable source of tension between the local ethno-tribal groups. Inequality may increase competition for scarce resources and grievances or perceptions of marginalization, making groups less willing to cooperate at the political level. Here, economic inequality would be doing the explanatory work, not lack of power-sharing.

Both qualitative and quantitative evidence challenge this argument, however. While economic inequality and perceptions of economic discrimination may be part of the explanation for tensions in an LGA, this only further highlights the importance of political representation. That is, the more fundamental question is: what conditions shape the local distribution of resources or determine who gets what? While the purse strings can be subject to the whims of the state government administration, the resources that do make their way to the LGAs are critical in shaping what development projects are implemented and who benefits. Due to the limitation on resource distribution at the local level, representation in a key seat of local government leadership can be an important determinant of whether an ethno-tribal group obtains the benefit of allocations (or patronage), such as development and education funds or indigenous rights/certificates. This is why, as one local scholar and expert, noted,

> Local government councils have become a center of conflict. In many cases, the local governments, depending on where the chairman comes from – which ethnicity or which group the chairman comes from – favors his ethnic group and his community to the disadvantage of other people. And in many cases, the local government chairman favors his friends from his communities, not the entire community. And so, that's why there's fierce competition over who becomes the local government chairman, because the local government chairman will obviously not take everyone aboard, but will prefer to favor his cronies at the local level.[4]

Hence, a power-sharing arrangement increases the likelihood of broader equality in the distribution of local resources. Whoever controls the reins of the local council wields control over whose grievances are heard and addressed and which ethno-tribal groups are favored in decisions about the demarcation of districts and the location of markets. Where a more representative system of local government leadership is absent, the patronage and clientilism associated with control over LGA revenue and resources can intensify local competition and economic inequalities. An economic grievance and inequality argument, therefore, is difficult to separate analytically from the key issue of local government representation.

Second, using data from Nigeria's Core Welfare Indicators Survey Bunte and Vinson (2016) were able to control for economic grievances or perceptions of inequality in looking at the relationship between inter-religious violence and power-sharing. The analysis shows that individuals in districts with power-sharing were far less likely to cite competition as a primary reason for poverty. This supports the argument above. LGAs

---

[4] Anonymous(C), interview by Laura Thaut Vinson, Jos, Plateau State, September 14, 2011.

without more inclusive local government leadership are more prone to conflict associated with economic grievances or inequality.

## Context of Sharia Rule in Kaduna?

A possible critique of the comparative case study approach employed in this study is that the cases of Plateau state and Kaduna state are not comparable, since one key difference between these two states is that Kaduna adopted Sharia, while Plateau state did not. The tensions and violence associated with the adoption of Sharia in northern Nigeria around 1999 were intense.

This factor does not, however, make a significant difference for the analysis. First, although the implementation of Sharia in 12 northern states following the move of Zamfara in 1999 led to riots and violence in a number of northern states, the violence occurred in *both* Kaduna state and Plateau state. The outcry and political concern among the Christian population was widespread. Second, the implementation of Sharia in Kaduna state has been far less contentious since that time. "It has followed a more benign trajectory," Suberu (2009, 552) notes, with Kaduna state adopting a "legally pluralistic, compromise version of Sharia implementation that eased tensions between its majority Muslim and minority Christian communities," such that the "'Sharia bomb' was more or less defused by the … country's evolving federal democratic structure" (see also Paden 2008, 59–60).[5] Third, if anything, the Sharia issue only further emphasizes the puzzle; one would expect that peaceful pluralistic LGAs in Kaduna state, such as Chikun LGA, would be the site of major riots and violence, not Jos in Plateau state, particularly since Chikun is on the doorstep of Kaduna North and South, the epicenter of much of Kaduna state's inter-religious violence.

---

[5] As Suberu (2009, 553) notes, "Sharia-implementing states have sought to respect the constitutional prohibition of a state religion by preserving the liberal democratic political and judicial institutions in the states and by substantially excluding their non-Muslim residents from the application of Islamic law." Okpanachi (2012) also observes that the violence following Sharia implementation led administrators to realize the need for "dexterity by crafting out frameworks that assuaged the fears of the non-Muslim groups," such as through the creation of "Sharia-free zones" in Kaduna, particularly in the southern part of the state where the non-Muslim population is concentrated, so that these populations are "largely exempted from the implementation of Sharia."

## Political Parties and "Godfathers?"

Before concluding this discussion of alternative hypotheses, it is worth discussing the role of political parties. Considering the dominance of political parties and party leaders or "godfathers" in Nigerian politics, one could argue that this theory overlooks their potential interventions and control of local government politics. Indeed, the propensity for political competition among and within states to coalesce around political parties is another dimension of the political arena affected by the nature of Nigeria's federal system and the localization of conflict. This has important implications for the nature of political competition at the state level for a number of reasons briefly discussed here, but I argue that it does compromise the argument.

First, regarding the influence of party politics, because electoral politics is identified with certain regional and ethnic interests, states and their local councils generally fall under the sway of a dominant political party. Hence, as one local scholar of Nigerian politics explained, the party in power at the state level is generally in power in all of the local government councils as well, working to ensure that the local council chairmen are from a state's ruling party. Further, since the state electoral body is appointed by a state's governor, they are "expected to deliver the party of the ruling governor" to prominence in state elections, including at the local council level.[6] This advantages the incumbent party and governor in a state, making it difficult for opposition parties to gain power. For example, in Plateau state, the People's Democratic Party (PDP) has dominated the state since 1999 up until the most recent election in 2014, when the All Progressive Congress (APC) won the governorship. When local government elections are next conducted, it is likely that the party in control of the state's local councils will also change over to the APC.

Second, the primary party in power within a state tends to dominate because state governors or "godfathers" protect their own and limit the viability of political opposition. As Fashagba (2015, 106) explains, "in states with a dominant political gladiator or godfather ... [s]uch political godfathers usually have the final say on the choice of candidate for governorship election and others." As head of the incumbent political party, the governor then wields considerable power over who the party nominates to run as state legislators, and, indeed, helps to fund and ensure

---

[6] Anonymous(AA), interview with local scholar by Laura Thaut Vinson, Jos, Plateau State, June 28, 2016.

candidates' victory (Fashagba 2015, 109; Baba 2015, 127).[7] As another prominent local scholar also noted, "The governor of a state has enormous power," and can propagate his party's control both because he, in practice, is the party leader, and because he also controls state resources.[8] The governor and dominant party in the state legislative assemblies can exert considerable influence in how revenue is allocated at the state level (Baba 2015, 123; Paden 2012, 52). It is no wonder then that a single political party in each state generally dominates its political apparatus from one election to the next (Baba 2015, 127).

Third, the system can propagate itself through ties between the states and the regime in power at the national level; power and patronage from the national party or the executive can reinforce the candidacy of party members in state political contests. At the same time, Nigeria's federal structure can also produce tensions between the party in power at the national level and state governments or legislative assemblies dominated by a competing party (Fashagba 2015). Indeed, Suberu's critique of the federal system's impact on the character of political parties and ethnic politics is damning. While promoting the formation of multiethnic governing coalitions," Suberu (2013, 90) argues,

The federal character rules have fuelled communal contention for patronage within parties, undermined the ideological and organization coherence of the parties, reduced them to weak, faction-ridden, personality-driven institutions, and detracted from their potential roles as genuine instruments of national integration, as distinct from mechanisms for organizing an ethnic spoils system" and failed to avoid "the development of ethnically based opposition parties at the periphery of the federal system.

Finally, although Nigeria successfully made the transition to civilian democratic rule in 1999, the weaknesses of its institutions heighten the risks of election violence and electoral manipulation and fraud by political parties and politicians. Onlookers celebrated the orderliness of the 2015 presidential election compared to the widespread post-election violence in 2011. In the 2007 election, massive manipulation, vote-rigging, and violence occurred (Paden 2008, 34–25; Lewis 2011, 63–64). Hence, as the second successful turnover in party power, the 2015 presidential

---

[7] As Baba (2015, 128) notes regarding state legislatures dominated by a single party, "most of the candidates in the dominant parties are selected for elections at the party level only with the support of the governors, and their elections nearly funded wholly by the governors."

[8] Anonymous(AB), interview with local scholar by Laura Thaut Vinson, Jos, Plateau State, June 28, 2016.

election was heralded as a sign of the deepening of competitive, freer, and fairer democracy in Nigeria.

While ethnic cleavages can be exacerbated by party politics, what should be clear from this analysis is that the key factor is not necessarily what party is in power at the local level, but whether party politics are consistent with power-sharing arrangements. That is, does the PDP, for example, run candidates on its ticket who represent the pluralism of the local government in accordance with a power-sharing arrangement? Whatever party dominates local council elections in a state, the more important question is the ethnic inclusiveness of representation. Party identity in Nigeria is porous; ethnicity is not. As a local scholar explained, people have a "party of the stomach" mentality – party loyalty can be set aside, since you "go where you get your pay." The argument, therefore, is not about the manner of rotation of party leadership at the local government level, but, rather, that there is power-sharing in the *ethnic* composition of local governments, whether or not a single party generally dominates local governments across a state. As one Kanam LGA interlocutor explained, if a party does not run a ticket that reflects the ethnic pluralism of the LGA, they will not receive the votes. The ethnic identity of the candidates, rather than the individual him or herself and their ties to the party, is what is critical for dispelling fears of ethnic favoritism or exclusion.

### IMPERVIOUS TO VIOLENCE?

The differences in the pattern of violence experienced by LGAs with and without power-sharing raises a final question. Since LGAs with power-sharing institutions are less prone to inter-religious violence, does that mean the power-sharing "shield" renders these LGAs impervious to inter-religious tensions and violence? An affirmative answer would be too simplistic and short-sighted. While I find that power-sharing LGAs are *less likely* to experience inter-religious violence, there are still dangers that their leaders must be attentive to, as the Kanam, Chikun, and Bassa cases emphasize.

### Kanam

While Kanam has been a relatively peaceful LGA without internally generated communal violence, some former local government leaders acknowledged that recent inter-religious violence in surrounding LGAs and Jos

North has occasionally threatened these peaceful relations. For example, during the 2004 inter-religious violence in Shendam LGA to the south, the violence soon spread to neighboring LGAs, including Wase, Langtang North, and Langtang South – all of which border Kanam. Fellow Christians in Langtang North, identifying with their co-religionists in Shendam and Wase, mobilized to defend Christian Taroh in southern Wase who were fighting against the Hausa Muslims. In response to these events, one local Christian religious leader noted that many Christians in Kanam fled Dengi, the headquarters of the LGA, to other areas "just in case" or out of fear of retaliation, since Kanam is home to some of the ethno-tribal groups involved in the conflict in the neighboring local governments.[9] Similarly, it was perhaps no surprise that Christians who were living along the border area with Langtang North, a Christian majority LGA, migrated to Langtang. Indeed, the religious leader recounted how one Christian man was killed in Dengi during this time.

While this crisis was not conceived in Kanam, it did create tensions that put pressure on communal relationships in the local government, raising the question of whether power-sharing can ameliorate or survive this type of exogenous shock – the incidence of Muslim–Christian violence and its symbolic significance in present-day Nigerian politics. According to the religious leader cited above, non-indigenous Christians, in particular, felt most threatened. Kanam local leaders, therefore, face the question of how power-sharing can accommodate the concerns of non-indigenous ethno-tribal groups. Additionally, in the last few years, in light of the religious tensions prevalent in the state, one politician observed that the few local government positions that have gone to the indigenous Christians are now threatened, and Christians are now perhaps less likely to take Muslims as running mates.

It remains to be seen, however, whether a new pattern of local politics will challenge the power-sharing status quo in response to these exogenous shocks. As with General Babangida's political intervention in the Jos ownership debates of the 1990s, outside politicians can disrupt local politics in potentially destabilizing ways. The intervention in the outcome of the Kanam electoral results in 2011 by Governor Jonah Jang, the Plateau state governor, raises these very concerns. Disgruntled with the elected Kanam Chairman for abandoning the Governor's political party after being elected, Governor Jang decided to dissolve the local

---

[9] Anonymous(V), interview by Laura Thaut Vinson, Kanam LGA, Plateau State, October 18, 2011.

government council and appoint an administrator of his own choosing. Refusing to accept this interference, the elected Chairman obtained two high court orders to reverse the Governor's decision and reinstate the elected council, although the Governor still refused to recognize the council. More significantly, highlighting the potential for the politics of Kanam to be influenced by the narrative of religious conflict, the elected Chairman noted in the *Daily Trust*, a national Nigerian newspaper, that political interests in opposition to him had

> created a negative impression that I do not like the Christians in the local government which is not the case because that has never been an issue before we were forced out of office. Again there has been negative propaganda about lack of peace in Kanam, which is not also the case because no local government in Plateau is as peaceful as ours. So our priority is to restore confidence in our people and correct some of these negative impressions. (Agbese 2011)

In other words, such "exogenous shocks" or outside political interference has at least the *potential* to create instability in local political relationships, requiring more concerted efforts on the part of local elite to maintain the power-sharing status quo and to defuse rumors.

Despite these potential challenges, my data reveal that a Christian fills at least one of the three top local government positions from one election or administration to the next. In general, the strength of the ethno-tribal power-sharing arrangement is that it does not discriminate on the basis of religious identity, but, rather, is designed so that both the Bogghom and Jahr rotate leadership and are represented in the leadership of any administration. The task ahead, for the Bogghom and Jahr elite, therefore, will be to ensure that religious discrimination does not influence candidate selection and political appointments. It is more difficult to make the case, in this context, that groups are being marginalized politically due to their ethnoreligious identity. At the time of this research in 2011, one local political figure brushed aside the notion that religious identity is a cleavage issue, pointing out that the secretary is a Christian, three of the councilors are Christians, and the Advisor on Education to the chairman is a Christian.[10]

## Chikun

While the power-sharing arrangement between ethnic groups in Chikun helps to provide a foundation for cooperative inter-religious

[10] Anonymous(W), interview by Laura Thaut Vinson, Kanam, Plateau State, October 19, 2011.

relationships, it too is not impervious. For example, with the population growth of the Kabilu over the last few years, they have clamored for adjustment to the power-sharing arrangement. Having overtaken the Hausa-Fulani community in demographic terms, the Kubilu are advocating for an "upgrade" that would allow them to preside in the local government council as deputy chairmen rather than only as secretaries, the third position in the hierarchy. This situation has reportedly produced some tension between the Kabilu and the indigenous Hausa-Fulani community. The "formula may reach a stage where it can't work," noted one insider.[11]

The Gbagyi population and leadership might also face some pressure. With the increase in the Kabilu population, as well as an increase in the Hausa population, the Kabilu and the Hausa-Fulani elite may be tempted to form an alliance to demand a change in the power-sharing arrangement. This situation, a former chairman notes, could be a potential problem. In the meantime, however, there are other factors that go into the strategic calculations. The violence that occasionally flares up in the southern part of the state, for example, prevents an alliance between the Hausa-Fulani and the Kabilu; it was observed that they are not on particularly good terms due to the Kafanchan violence. Much of the growth in the Kabilu population in Chikun is a product of displaced people arriving from areas where communal violence has occurred between their kin and the Hausa-Fulani Muslims in the southern zone of Kaduna state. Muslims and Christians in some areas of Chikun have felt pressure to uproot their families and segregate out of fear for their future safety living in pluralistic communities.

Nonetheless, in a forum discussion with local community leaders, this very question of how the power-sharing arrangement would survive changes in the composition of the local government was a topic of discussion. "The question I want to ask," one organizer initiated, "with this proper arrangement which has been in existence for years and with the present influx of people, the Kabilus ... do you think this arrangement can still hold?" One local political figure, referring to the knowledge accumulated as changes have come to the LGA, argued in response,

Yes, this arrangement can still hold. There is nothing that is going to change the arrangement. Only an understanding [will work]. When we sit down and we

[11] Ibid., Anonymous(I), interview.

understand ourselves – because we know that society is getting more and more complex ... as they come in, so always we are growing in our knowledge. When we sit down and discuss, we can solve our problems by ourselves.[12]

Another respondent continued:

Let me just add. I think the recent development, the political scenario, has given us [a] better channel for addressing such a problem when it arises in the future. For instance, this area is dominated by Kabilu, the [] development area, so the leadership of Chikun will always insist that the leader of this area should be Kabilu. So you see the community has within itself general adjustments that will fit the dynamics that may occur later. So I don't see anything affecting it per se.[13]

So too another community member equated the power-sharing arrangement with the Biblical demand to "Give to Caesar what is Caesar's," arguing in a lengthy speech that is worth recounting in whole,

You see, any community that does not develop the issue of give to Caesar what belongs to Caesar, then in that community there's that tendency of having crisis, and that is what is happening in Jos. Monopoly. You want to monopolize everything. Whether it is your own or not your own or it is your own [expressions of agreement around the room].

So that is the problem. And we are trying to see here in our own local government how we can continue to maintain that platform of give to Caesar what is Caesar's. Even if it is done wrongly, let us try to uphold this virtue because that is the only thing that will help us live in peace ... Even if the Kabilus are so many here, and within the Kabilus there is the idea that there is so many, okay, give them. Give them the head, and others will follow. That is why during our own time, when the issue of this development came, we said, give the Hausa their own development area. Give the Kabilu their own development area. Give the [Gbagyi] their own development area so we can live peacefully with one another [further expressions of agreement around the room].

Let everyone now control his own development area. If there are problem with the youths in the local government area ... Okay, go to your administrator and say there is a problem here. He will go and see what, find out what is the problem. They will now sit down and see what we can do. When it comes to the local government as a whole where the chairman is there and he has his ... councilors, these councilors come from all these areas [wards] ... everybody will now table his own problem based on a presentation to the chairman, then we now decide how do we share these allocation, what will go to the Hausa people, what will go to the Kabilu people, what will go to the [Gbagyi] people ... so we share these based on

---

[12] Anonymous(J), interview by Laura Thaut Vinson, Chikun, Kaduna State, November 10, 2011.
[13] Anonymous(X), interview by Laura Thaut Vinson, Chikun, Kaduna State, November 10, 2011.

the allocation so that everybody will now have something to tell his people, "I'm representing you, this is what I have brought for you. And that is how we have been moving thus far.

But I'm not saying there are no problems or certain issues that will crop up and may give us the opportunity to think on how to go about it. The problem here is that the moment there is crisis in Zaria or there is crisis in Kafanchan, the problem is the Chikun local government is the melting point, because that is where we get the wahala [trouble] because every tribe is here. And every time there is this problem, the vengeance is taken up from here. So that is one thing we have been having problems here now. But we thank God that after first crisis – even because of this political crisis that came this time around – I don't think we'll be having any problem, we'll be living peacefully with one another, and we'll continue to think on ways to solve any problems that may come, because we are getting more people day by day. We don't even know where they come from. Day by day Chikun local government is getting visitors day by day. People are ... we don't even know where it's coming from, what was he doing, what is his nature, what has been his trade. Even from Jos people are coming from Jos ... So that is that.[14]

What this says is that, while leaders in the LGA recognize the potential threats to inter-religious peace, the informal power-sharing arrangement serves not only as a principle for political harmony, but also reinforces their commitment to the institution itself and to the application of the principle to other levels of communal life and administration. In this sense, the power-sharing mechanisms and organization of development areas and wards in Chikun provides the flexibility to adjust to societal changes in the ethnic composition of the LGA.

Whether the optimism of some of the leaders in the local government will prove warranted remains to be seen. While the power-sharing formula has worked well in the past, changes in the LGA may require more flexibility in the power-sharing arrangement, something the informal nature of the institution could allow. Meanwhile, however, the institution is self-enforcing through the representational gains and assurances it provides to local ethno-tribal groups, as well as through the organization of development areas and in the autonomy of smaller ethno-tribal groups to appoint their tribal chiefs. All of these factors have thus far reinforced the power-sharing institution in the face of potential strife, providing political, tribal, and religious leaders a foundation upon which to promote and protect peace in Chikun.

---

[14] Anonymous(Y), interview by Laura Thaut Vinson, Chikun, Kaduna State, November 10, 2011.

### Bassa

While Bassa has avoided the inter-religious violence that occasionally flares up in neighboring areas, the LGA is also not necessarily immune to inter-religious tensions. As one peace activist noted, religious tensions in Bassa have arisen on several occasions due to the inter-religious violence taking place elsewhere in Plateau state or neighboring states. "Where one's brother is being attacked elsewhere, there is pressure to retaliate against the religious other in one's own community," he explained.[15] Indeed, events in Jos have threatened to spill over into Bassa on several occasions.

The local government power-sharing institution – and the other forms of cooperation and peacebuilding it has engendered – has helped to sustain peace in Bassa in the face of these tensions, however. For example, as one peace activist recounted, during violence in Jos in 2010, a number of Muslims from the city started fleeing to Bassa. Tensions in the area began to rise as a rumor spread that the Muslim displaced people were armed and intended to attack Christians in Bassa late in the night. Violence was ultimately averted, however, when local leaders and peace activists, in conjunction with the local government chairman, organized a spur of the moment meeting with Muslim, Christian, and tribal leaders from the area to appeal to their youth for calm as they sorted out the situation. After putting the rumors to rest and clarifying events, peace was restored.[16] Bassa's foundational power-sharing institution has been key for inter-tribal and inter-religious trust and coordination of peace activities, keeping major conflict in the LGA at bay. Bassa is "not as turbulent as Jos," argued one peace activist, because of the many measures community leaders take to keep the calm. They "always preach peace" and there is a forum for them to come together and discuss any potential alarm or hints of trouble.[17] Thus, while tensions are not non-existent in Bassa, they are less common and more likely to be solved through the structure of leadership and authority established among the local leaders and peace activists.

~

In sum, the preceding discussion of power-sharing's institutional dynamics does not mean that communities in the LGA are unaffected by

---

[15] Anonymous(U), interview by Laura Thaut Vinson, Bassa LGA, Plateau State, October 27, 2011.
[16] Anonymous(N), interview by Laura Thaut Vinson, Jos, Plateau State, October 10, 2011.
[17] Ibid., Anonymous(U), interview.

the inter-religious clashes occurring nearby or in other states. In reality, local leaders have had to act quickly on a number of occasions to quell tensions that have threatened the peace of Chikun following major violence in other areas. Due to the heightened sensitivity to divisive religious rhetoric and Muslim–Christian clashes, tensions and the impetus for Muslim and Christian youth to mobilize are not entirely absent in these areas of Nigeria. Nonetheless, these cases highlight how a system of local power-sharing reinforces peace, enabling ethno-tribal and religious leaders to better respond to and nip potential crises in the bud before they erupt.

## CONCLUSION

As this chapter emphasizes, alternative hypotheses for the pattern of peace or violence or alternative explanations for the relationship between peace and power-sharing fall short. It is important to emphasize though that this argument also does not presume that power-sharing is impervious to, in Grief and Laitin's (2004) language, exogenous shocks and endogenous parameter shifts.[18] Indeed, there are pressures threatening the sustainability of these power-sharing institutions in the cases analyzed. Depending on the institution and its ability to subsume or adapt to new conditions or pressures, it will be more or less likely to survive. These self-reinforcing or -undermining factors are important when examining not only the formation of informal power-sharing institutions in Nigeria, but also their sustainability over time. As with formal institutions, Helmke and Levitsky (2004, 732) note that "informal institutions may also change as the status quo conditions that sustain them change." The potential gains for groups to go outside the institutional rules and framework places pressure on power-sharing arrangements, testing whether or not the informal institution is flexible enough or incentivizing enough for groups to compromise and work together for a more significant long-term payoff.

Yet, it is the sustainability of these *informal* power-sharing arrangements that is most surprising in the Nigerian context of sacralized politics

---

[18] Grief and Laitin (634) contend that institutions may be more or less subject to change in response to endogenous parameter shifts or exogenous events depending on the self-reinforcing or self-undermining mechanisms of the institution itself. Hence, "If an institution reinforces itself, more individuals in more situations would find it best to adhere to behavior associated with it," such that "[w]hen self-reinforcing, exogenous changes in the underlying situation that otherwise would have led an institution to change would fail to have this effect."

and inter-religious violence. Although the local power-sharing institutions stem from informal, unwritten agreements to which no party is legally bound, the parties or leaders of ethno-tribal blocs (who would seemingly have many reasons to defect) have adhered to the agreements made as far back as the late 1970s. This finding calls attention to the "staying power" of informal power-sharing institutions and their capacity to mitigate disputes and quash external ethno-religious tensions that, in the northern Nigerian context, otherwise tend to spill over from surrounding LGAs. Some of the self-enforcing mechanisms include the networks of coordination and collaboration that derive from power-sharing arrangements, the potential costs of deviating from the precedent, and the opportunity for ethno-tribal groups to garner greater representation than they might otherwise achieve in an LGA.

In the following and final chapter, I conclude with reflections on the broader insights or contributions of this study to the understanding of ethnic conflict. I argue that this study of the role of religion in the communal violence of northern Nigeria and of the capacity of informal local power-sharing institutions to promote peace revises some of the fundamental assumptions made by the ethnic conflict literature in regard to the nature of ethnic conflict and institutions of democracy and representation.

# PART III

# CONCLUSIONS

# 9

# Conclusion

## THE RIDDLE

"The resolution of civil conflict is among the most pressing issues facing the world today," note Gates and Strøm (2007, 11), considering that such conflicts "account for the vast majority of armed struggles in the contemporary world and the vast majority of casualties from war." Indeed, the crisis of communal and religious violence in northern Nigeria is one of the biggest challenges facing Nigerian local and national leaders today. Unfortunately, however, the micro-dynamics of the violence and causal conditions are blurred in the media and in the cyclical discourse about who or what deserves the blame for the violence and how it can be resolved. The international media tends to fall into a standard refrain, seemingly propelled by a materialist bent in academic studies of ethnic conflict, that the violence is rooted in economic (land) disputes, whatever its religious dimensions. Other locals and scholars emphasize the failure of the Nigerian state and the crisis of weak political leadership. Digging deeper into questions about the actors involved, other theories highlight the importance of political entrepreneurs who see an opening and employ religious sentiments to galvanize the population for their own political ends. There is certainly no end to the blame Nigerians place on local leadership, and the conspiracy theories abound (some assuredly true) about politicians who pay poor, desperate youth to stir up trouble. Other scholars and students of colonial history, particularly of the Marxist persuasion, blame the British colonial project – its reification of identities, establishing boundaries and hierarchies between groups that never existed before and thereby dooming post-colonial politics to instability and ethnic conflict. These are debates that take place among local and national government figures, NGO activists, religious leaders, and traditional leaders and that reflect broader scholarly debates about the causes of ethnic conflict.

And then there is religion. Again, locals have their own opinions about the Muslim–Christian dimension that has come to characterize much of the communal violence in the north. To some, it is all about religion – a cosmic conflict between true religion and wrong religion, between good and evil, one religion seeking to uproot the other – in which the narrative of fighting and defending oneself has far greater stakes for adherents. Assertions concerning which religion is "good" or "evil" naturally depends on where one falls on the religious spectrum. To others, it has nothing to do with religion. Religion is merely a façade over exploitative economic and political interests, or the conflicts are primarily attributed to ethno-tribal indigenous-versus-settler contests.

All of these arguments and theories no doubt possess some traction. Disputes over land and resources, particularly with increased land pressures, are a problem and can lead to communal violence. As my data on communal violence from 1979 to 2011 show, however, cases reported as involving Muslims and Christians tend to be characterized by very different precipitating events and reported causes than ethno-tribal violence rooted in economic disputes, and they tend to take place in different locations. The two should not be conflated, otherwise the variation in and patterns of communal violence, as well as the possibilities for its resolution, will be misunderstood. As for the weakness of the Nigerian state, certainly the rampant corruption, inability to provide basic necessities to its population, the civil war from 1967 to 1970, and the succession of repressive regimes did not do the population any favors and have not promoted conditions for prosperity and security in Nigeria. Local elite – including politicians who marginalize one section of the community, employ divisive religious language, interfere in electoral outcomes, hire youth to do their dirty work, and rig the voting system – are a menace to local political stability and communal peace.

Yet, the weaknesses of the Nigerian state and local leadership are also not a sufficient condition for inter-religious or ethno-tribal communal violence. While these weaknesses characterize national and local political institutions on a broad scale, communal violence does not occur across all LGAs at the subnational level. Similarly, a focus on political entrepreneurs as the causal force behind identity-based violence has limits. Such actors cannot mobilize ethnic violence at their whim. It would do little good to attempt to mobilize groups along ethno-tribal or religious cleavages if other social, political, and historical conditions are not present that render those cleavages salient in the first place. Finally, while indirect rule and the divide-and-conquer politics of colonial powers did indeed create or enhance ethnic divisions and leave behind a legacy of instability in many countries, the colonial legacy did not preordain ethnic violence within states. As the case studies show, areas of Nigeria characterized by a similar colonial history and pattern of assimilation and integration are not equally prone to inter-religious violence.

This brings us to the significance of religious identity and religious change for the Muslim–Christian communal violence. One of the most important and most-taught pieces in graduate seminars addressing the saliency of different ethnic identities is David Laitin's (1986) story about Yorubaland in western Nigeria. For almost two decades, his study of the saliency of religion and tribe among the Yoruba has influenced the study of ethnicity and ethnic conflict. The question he asks is why, in a context of religious pluralism, is tribal identity politicized, but not religion? By the beginning of the 1980s in Nigeria, religious change in combination with political manipulation elevated religious identity to a politically exploitable category for Muslim and Christian elite, but religious difference did not become a major cleavage among the Yoruba of western Nigeria. This seemed counterintuitive. As Laitin observed, despite the politicization of religious identity in Nigeria and the potential gains for the Yoruba in the west to split along Muslim–Christian lines, religious identity did not become a salient political cleavage. Ancestral or ethno-tribal identity is a more salient ascriptive identity, he found, trumping religious identity and reducing the propensity for inter-religious violence among the Yoruba.

Among ethnic groups in the Middle Belt and north of Nigeria, however, religious identity has indeed *become* a salient and divisive political category since the 1980s, leading to recurrent and devastating inter-religious violence in some pluralistic communities. It is evident that emotions run deep when it comes to conflict in northern Nigeria, and God has been co-opted into it. The variation in communal violence across this region, therefore, raises an important puzzle for the field of ethnic conflict studies and understandings of the relationship between subnational ethnic – religious, in particular – violence and political institutions. Thus, I ask a similar question as Laitin, but flipped on its head: why has religion become politicized and the primary cleavage of communal violence in northern Nigeria? Further, why does inter-religious communal violence flare up in some pluralistic communities in the Middle Belt and not others under similar conditions? I argue that the theory presented in this study – about the nature of religious change and local power-sharing institutions – has important implications for understanding the role of identity in conflict not only in Nigeria, but also in other countries where ethnic groups often live in mixed communities and where the politics of identity is rife.

In general, those who argue that religion has nothing to do with the violence in northern Nigeria since the 1980s do not appreciate its centrality and likely have not spent much time in the field. The phenomenon of inter-religious violence in northern Nigeria is inseparable from the story of religious change in Nigeria since the 1970s. Plateau state, along with a number of other Middle Belt states, experienced a rapid conversion of its non-Muslim population to Christianity following the end of colonial rule with the removal of the barrier to missionary evangelism. The Pentecostal-charismatic revival that swept from south to north in the 1960s and 1970s could easily be constructed as a threat to the predominance of Islam in northern Nigeria where religion and politics have been integrally linked as far back as the rule of the Sokoto Caliphate. In Plateau state, Christianity was virtually non-existent at the beginning of the 20th century. Today, Plateau state is majority Christian, around 70 percent of the population.

Evangelistic crusades and fervor along with the establishment of countless new neighborhood Pentecostal churches and mega-churches all speak to the rapid religious change that has occurred in northern Nigeria and the potential for it to be perceived as a "threat" in the minds of Muslims. As Shedrack Gaya Best (2011, 33) observes,

Pentecostal Christianity has ... been accused of creating a rumbling effect, threatening other faiths in the process. Religious revivalism, a general upsurge in religionism and the resort to religious propaganda as evident in the proliferation of religious groups, places of worship, clerics, etc. and the links they maintain with external bodies (Tamuno 1993) are additional factors for the activation of fanatical religion and subsequent violent conflict.

While describing the political and economic dimensions of the religious crises in Nigeria, one peace activist in Jos commented that the Pentecostals/charismatics are "more pushy in their approach and among Muslims," but that

if you follow the preaching, across the divide, you find both Christian and Muslim preachers who bury political issues into their preaching and, by implication, preaching hatred, creating fear of the other, and to some extent encouraging people to rise up ... not to accept defeat of opponent – and whether by omission or commission ... that kind of preaching – to feel that spirit of being strong – are contributing ... to that kind of rivalry feeling.[1]

Similarly, the emergence of Islamic extremist movements in the north – evidenced in intra-Muslim riots and violence at the beginning of the 1980s and the emergence of the radical and deadly Boko Haram sect – also reinforces fears of an Islamic Jihad intent on wiping out Christianity in the north. As Best (2011, 33) notes, "Many have argued that the radicalisation of Islam, its provocative public preachings and statements attributed to some of its leaders and clerics helped to inflame Nigerian passions in the direction of religion." Boer (2003, 35) points out that the surge in Christianity in the Middle Belt region "has made Islam even more nervous, for it stakes its claims on the basis of an alleged continued majority," and "increasing nervousness spells greater volatility."

This religious change, analyzed in greater depth in Chapter 2, does not mean that religious violence is inevitable. Rather, the Christian religious resurgence and radicalization of Islam helps to explain why religious identity – its language, beliefs, and symbolism – is a salient category of belonging in Nigeria that can be co-opted for violence, as well as peace, and can blur the underlying political context of local communal disputes. In short, religion has become a powerful ascriptive identity, framing device, and symbolic mobilizer of communal violence since the 1970s. Religion should be taken seriously. At the same time, the roots of the conflict are deeper. Digging into the local politics of ethno-tribal and inter-religious violence or peace in various communities, one discovers that the politics of representation and rights is indeed the ailment that, left untreated, has created the space for religious identity politics and conflict to flourish into violence. The religious narrative and framing of conflicts, therefore, should be taken very seriously while at the same time considering the deeper dimensions or the underlying conditions.

This analysis should not imply that religion and, by association, religious adherents are inherently conflict-prone. Those who ascribe to this philosophy have not thought through the matter or history very carefully (see Cavanaugh 2009). Inter-religious clashes, even with the rapid growth of new forms of Christianity and radicalized Islam, are not inevitable. Despite the prevalence of cases of inter-religious violence since the 1980s, Nigeria presents an easy foil. If religious pluralism is as divisive as some assume, why is it that only some pluralistic communities experience inter-

---

[1] Anonymous(Z), interview by Laura Thaut Vinson, Jos, Plateau State, March 29, 2011.

religious violence and not all? Why is it that some of the very same communities known for inter-religious violence today were *at one point* peaceful and integrated communities, communities in which no thought was given to Muslims and Christians being close friends and sharing in one another's lives? As with other forms of identity, religious pluralism is not a sufficient condition for ethnic conflict. This is why the more important and driving question that I have sought to answer is *under what conditions* does religious identity become the fault line of communal violence? How is religious identity different from other forms of identity in its mobilizing properties and potential for violence?

## THE NEW THEORY OF POWER-SHARING

As a first step in my fieldwork, I had to construct a picture of the actual scope of the violence and its variation by building an original dataset of communal violence for northern Nigeria. I then began to dig deeper into the power-sharing or consociationalism literature and think through its applicability to the Nigerian context and conundrums. Despite the emphasis on an inclusive politics of representation as a solution to ethnic conflict and a guarantor of a stable peace following civil war, studies of consociationalism or power-sharing in a number of countries do not bear out Lijphart's initial findings and contentions, as discussed in Chapter 4. Indeed, I found myself befuddled by the theory's high hopes (unmet) in solving ethnic conflict when it seemed to have very little applicability to the reality and puzzle of communal violence in northern Nigeria. As it quickly became clear from living in Jos, local politics matters in a host of ways – in shaping who has access to education, employment, land, representation, and fundamentally, certification of indigenous status. The question, however, was *how* exactly politics matters and shapes the propensity for inter-religious violence. A power-sharing arrangement instituted at the national level in no way could accommodate all of the diverse ethnic interests and parties (with Nigeria's 250 or more ethno-tribal groups) and the concerns specific to local communities. However, this led me to pursue the theory that perhaps patterns of representation at the subnational level – that is, whether LGAs have a form of power-sharing – would shed light on why some pluralistic LGAs manage to maintain relative ethno-tribal and inter-religious peace while their neighbors flounder in the swells of communal divisions and violence. My research posits, then, that Lijphart's theory of power-sharing is not defunct. Rather, with some revision in the level and assumptions of the analysis, power-sharing can be an effective tool of conflict prevention.

Qualitative investigation and data gathered on election and appointment results in Plateau state and Kaduna state bore out this theory. The data and case studies show that LGAs in which local ethno-tribal leaders negotiated an informal power-sharing arrangement at the time of local government reforms in the 1970s (or upon creation of the LGA) have been far less prone to inter-religious violence. The rotation of the executive seats of a local government council from one administration to the next helps to defuse claims of inequality in representation. Local government power-sharing also provides a foundation for broader application of the power-sharing principle at the LGA level; by defusing the perception that local struggles are a product of inter-religious competition, power-sharing promotes more cooperative and collaborative relationships among community members and leaders and the establishment of other integrated and informal institutions to maintain peace or neutralize dangerous rumors. While informal power-sharing institutions established in the 1970s preceded the major politicization of religion in Nigerian national and local politics, power-sharing had the unintended but beneficial consequence of helping to quell subsequent religious tensions, since ethno-tribal and religious identities tend to overlap.

The first revision my research suggests, therefore, is that power-sharing is more effective at the local communal level rather than the national level. As noted above, ethno-tribal politics in Nigeria is largely local, although the disputes can play out on the national stage between leaders of the major ethno-tribal blocs as well. The key difference is that the local government-level disputes over access to rights, resources, and local representation cannot be solved by a national power-sharing arrangement. With over 250 ethnic groups and grievances that vary considerably from community to community at the subnational level, placing a few representatives of a very few of these ethno-tribal groups in positions of executive or legislative authority at the national level will hardly address the concerns of local, diverse constituents. National politics and policies certainly affect the lives of individual Nigerians throughout the country, but national-level power-sharing is too far removed from the local conflicts specific to the ethno-tribal groups involved.

The second revision is that the benefits of power-sharing are easier to recognize and sustain at the local level. Part of the difficulty of formal national power-sharing arrangements is that the incentives to abide by the arrangement are ambiguous, punishment for defection is difficult to enforce, and the lines of accountability to constituents are unclear (Helmke and Levitsky 2006). At the same time, a key incentive for power-sharing – achievable at the local government level – is the potential for greater representation and influence for even minority ethno-tribal groups. If electoral politics is a free-for-all, depending on how electoral alliances pan out, significant ethno-tribal groups in an LGA might not otherwise have the political clout to ensure meaningful representation. In this context, a divisive politics of identity can more easily thrive. In contrast, where the chairman and the vice-chairman of a local government council run on the same ticket and are not allowed to be from the same ward or ethno-tribal group, campaign rhetoric that emphasizes ethnic divisions for the purpose of mobilizing constituents is less likely to find a hearing and will be counterproductive. To be elected, the leaders have an incentive to maintain a united front.

The leaders of the major ethno-tribal groups in an LGA also have incentive to abide by the arrangement, as the minority groups may otherwise side with one powerful bloc over another in order to tip the electoral balance and gain a modicum of representation. In this scenario, the major ethno-tribal blocs risk being pushed out of contention for any significant leadership seat, which could cause tensions and identity politics to flare. In contrast, a power-sharing institution can more effectively represent the interests of the major ethno-tribal blocs by giving each a share or a turn in the leadership of the local government council, while the tiniest minorities in the local government still have a chance of controlling legislative seats through councillorship positions that are determined at the ward level. The establishment of local development areas can also channel development funds and appease minorities dominant in a particular ward. One should also not overlook the historical incentives for leaders to form power-sharing institutions in order to re-write the colonial pattern of political domination exclusive to one ethno-tribal group. In other words, Horowitz (2002, 23) is right in emphasizing the importance of the incentive structure:

When electorates are alert to ethnic issues, as they typically are, exhortations to leaders to compromise are likely to be futile in the absence of rewards for compromise. Attention needs to be devoted, therefore, to maximizing incentives for accommodative behaviour. For elected politicians, those incentives are likely to be found in the electoral system... Where electoral rewards are present, they can provide the motivation ethnic leaders otherwise lack, they can operate even in the presence of ethnocentrism, and they can offset electoral losses that leaders anticipate as a result of making concessions to other groups. Where these rewards are present, they typically operate by means of vote-pooling arrangements: the exchange of votes by ethnically-based parties that, because of the electoral system, are marginally dependent for victory on the votes of groups other than their own and that, to secure those votes, must behave moderately on the issues in conflict ... Where vote pooling takes place, as it did in Lebanon and Malaysia, it promotes pre-electoral coalitions, coalitions that need to comprise in order to attract voters across group lines.

This is the function of local government power-sharing institutions identified in some Middle Belt LGAs in Kaduna and Plateau state. These incentives and benefits described by Horowitz in the passage above (e.g., resources and investment in local development) can be felt and observed by local ethnic groups where power-sharing characterizes local government councils, in contrast to power-sharing at the national level.[2]

Of course, if the electoral incentives were obvious, one would expect to find power-sharing in all pluralistic communities of northern Nigeria. In this sense, it is not merely the electoral incentives that shape the equation. A range of social, political, and religious realities shape patterns of ethno-tribal group relationships. These realities will vary from community to community and can change over time. As evident from the paired comparison case studies, post-colonial communal relationships and incentives to seek cooperation or compromise are shaped by everything from patterns of migration and religious changes over time to exogenous political interventions and entrenchment of colonial-era exclusions. Hence, the investigation into the particular factors in any one LGA that prompt power-sharing will yield a slightly different story, but the principle insight remains; areas with power-sharing are less likely to experience internal communal inter-religious or ethno-tribal violence.

Hence, one additional and important finding of this study is that the path to power-sharing is not predetermined. There is no one path to power-sharing. For policymaker and activists, this should be an encouraging observation; policy decisions or strategic interventions *may* be able to change the political calculus and encourage power-sharing where it does not presently exist. Indeed, a lack of power-sharing was not inevitable in any one of the now violence-prone LGAs. An area with a more fragmented historical relationship between local ethno-tribal groups and Hausa-Fulani Muslims is not precluded from future power-sharing;

---

[2] If local government leaders fail to come through on their promises, this does not put the power-sharing institution in jeopardy; rather, they jeopardize their individual legitimacy, as a different member of their ethno-tribal group can contest the leadership position in the next election.

a colonial legacy of lack of assimilation and integration is not a sufficient condition for inter-religious or ethno-tribal violence and political deadlock. Thus, contemporary political events and decisions, including national intervention in local processes, have as much of a role to play in shaping the acceptance of a power-sharing arrangement. Jos is case in point, as the failure of the national government to recognize the significance of these historical and contemporary variables led to ineffective political intervention and, consequently, tragic and recurring violence. The deterioration of Jos into a case of recurring inter-religious violence was not, however, inevitable.

### IMPLICATIONS OF THE RELIGIOUS/SYMBOLIC DYNAMIC

Having highlighted many times in this study the importance of the symbolism of religion and religious belonging in the communal violence in northern Nigeria, here I address its relationship to instrumentalist arguments. From the data and accounts of inter-religious violence, I contend that religious identity and the symbolism of religious events can take on a powerful mobilizing capacity to the extent that manipulation of identity by political entrepreneurs – often treated as a necessary condition for social group mobilization – is not a necessary condition for violent mobilization to occur between Muslims and Christians in many cases. My findings suggest that, while elite politicization of religious identity may be central in the initial construction of divisive religious narratives, elite manipulation is neither a necessary nor sufficient condition for violence; merely symbolic religious events are sufficient to spark clashes in northern Nigeria.

Regarding the role of identity in political mobilization, Chandra (2006, 415) argues that it is "context rather than ... some intrinsic property of these [descent-based] attributes," that shapes the politics of identity. One need not peel back the layers of a particular identity in order to understand how it becomes a site of political contestation, according to this argument. Rather, a "descent-based" identity takes on political meaning in combination with another or other variables that essentially determine its political parameters. Chandra's work on whether ethnic identity matters leaves one with a vague sense that ethnicity matters but not really, because identity and the political form it takes is subject to the instrumental wheeling and dealing of elite or political entrepreneurs. This is the conclusion reached by Fearon and Laitin (2000) as well. Similarly, in Posner (2005; 2004) and Wilkinson's (2004) work, it is elite manipulation doing the majority of the work. Group identity is merely a latent category that, when called upon, will dress itself up in the appropriate political attire, and, when left to rest, will sleep. Absent elite manipulation, all one has is latent identity *sans* politics. Scholars who adopt a rationalist or instrumentalist view contend that identity is not itself violence-prone; rather, identity becomes a "thing" or site of contention when actors pursuing particular ends mobilize identity to achieve their goals (e.g., Wilkinson 2008; Posner 2004).

Other scholars are less assertive about the epiphenomenal nature of ethnicity. Some argue, for example, that instrumental mobilization of identity by elite politicians is, as Laitin (1986) observes, only one side of the Janus face of culture. Regarding culture and the construction of preferences, Laitin (1986, 50) argues, "Embedded in any religion are symbols that provide believers with a sense of the 'really real' and, hence, with what economists call 'preference functions.' Rational action can only be properly understood when preferences are known; culture helps set those preferences." At the same time, however, Laitin concludes that one must look at the political construction of a group identity in order to understand how it becomes a site of contestation. Culturalist or identity-based arguments according to Brubaker and Laitin (1998, 443) "can not explain why violence occurs only at particular times and places, and why, even at such times and places, only some persons participate in it. Cultural contextualizations of ethnic violence, however vivid, are not themselves explanations of it." As Gurr (2000) and Posner (2004) also argue, identity is a salient category, but the likelihood of mobilization depends on social and political conditions. That is, while identity cannot be mobilized if it does not hold some deep-seated significance for actors, identity itself does not explain political mobilization.

While I accept the argument that political elite or political mobilization is critical to the story of explaining how identity becomes a salient political category, I depart from these scholars in two key respects. First, like Laitin, I argue that the emphasis on elites overlooks the importance of change in identity categories – for example, with a religion's rapid growth or doctrinal shift. It would be inaccurate to argue that political manipulation is somehow *the* cause of the rapid growth of Christianity throughout the Global South and its subsequent politicization. If not for the religious phenomenon of the 1960s and subsequently – mass conversion and the socio-political consequences of the change itself – it is unclear how elites could have constructed a narrative or rationale for violent Muslim–Christian mobilization. If one accepts the premise that identities are not fixed, then attention to the changes in identity over time is essential to the story of its politicization. It does not mean that these changes are insulated from social, political, or economic events (indeed, religious beliefs and practices are always in conversation with socio-political realities and life experiences), but rather that one should not assume that an identity's inception as a political category is due simply to the conjuring of politically self-interested actors. As Varshney (2003, 88) notes concerning rational choice theory, the "standard rational-choice accounts assume that ethnicity can be seen instrumentally. They focus primarily on how leaders strategically manipulate ethnicity for the sake of power. This argument has an intuitive appeal because the behavior of many, if not all, political leaders can be cited in support." However, Varshney (2003, 88) goes on to note,

> presented in this form, the instrumental-rational argument about ethnicity runs into serious difficulty ... if the masses were only instrumental about ethnic identity, why would ethnicity be the basis for mobilization at all? Why do the leaders decide to mobilize ethnic passions in the first place? Why do they think that ethnicity, not the economic interest of the people, is the route to power? And if economic interests coincide with ethnicity, why choose ethnicity as opposed to economic interests for mobilization?

Hence, scholars should pay careful attention to the importance of how changes in identity over time impact which identity or identities are politically salient at any one time and how the attributes associated with the identity itself shape the possibilities for mobilization.[3] In sum, like Horowitz (1985, 105), "I presume instead that if elites pursue a policy of deflecting mass antagonisms onto other ethnic groups, such a policy must strike roots in mass sentiments, apprehensions, and aspirations in order to succeed" (see also Wickham 2004, 120; Schwedler 2006).[4]

---

[3] Regarding the ethnic and religious violence in Indonesia, Davidson (2008, 176) notes that other economic and political factors may have been more "integral to the violence" than ethnic or religious identities, but he shows how the "framing of the violence dramatically and meaningfully altered the riots' trajectories regardless of their root cause. Here religion or ethnicity was dominant."

[4] As Schwedler (2006, 152) asks, in light of the conditions, what are the *boundaries* of justifiable action constructed within an ideological framework? The formation and transformation of ideas evolves in tandem with socio-political events or changes, but not all action is ideologically justified at any particular point in time and certain beliefs may militate against certain types of mobilization. To understand the avenues of action opened up and closed off by religious identity, one must consider the boundaries articulated within the political theology of the group and by its leaders.

Second, while recognizing the importance of context and elite politicization of identity, I argue that elite manipulation or political entrepreneurs are not *always* necessary to the story. While elite may be key in the story of how religion becomes a politicized category, their active manipulation is neither a necessary nor sufficient condition for the mobilization of inter-religious violence (if not at time $t$, then at time $t+1$). In other words, as a particular identity assumes greater political significance, it is possible for that identity to take on a symbolic importance that does not require elite manipulation to mobilize or construct the narrative of communal violence.

The large number of cases of violence that spilled over from one location to another in the Middle Belt or northern Nigeria is indicative of the significance of shared religious identity in the mobilization of violence. In an incident of violence against one's co-religionists in Zangon-Kataf, for example, the perception of an affront to members of the religious group as a whole is often sufficient to spark inter-religious violence in other parts of northern Nigeria, especially the states of Kano, Kaduna, Bauchi, and Plateau. As noted in cases already discussed, retributive violence can occur in towns even a couple hundred miles away from the original incident. The mere fact of shared religious identity can provide the mobilizing impetus despite the fact that the subsequent location of violence is disassociated from the causes or precipitating events and ethno-tribal groups of the original incident.

~

As the above discussion highlights, elite mobilization of grievances is not a necessary or sufficient cause of communal inter-religious violence, particularly as communal violence and the narrative of us-versus-them becomes a more entrenched social phenomenon. In northern Nigeria, symbolic religious events or offenses are now seemingly sufficient to instigate inter-religious conflict without an organized and strategic premeditated elite mobilization. In the Nigerian case, the narrative has taken on a life of its own, as people have adopted the Muslim-versus-Christian lens through which to view the "other." Communal violence, therefore, need not require direct political engineering, and it can become self-perpetuating. This is why the violence can take on "spontaneity" and is seemingly unpredictable. At this stage, strategic molding by political elite is perhaps more of a necessary condition for *undoing* or deconstructing the stereotypes and narratives that perpetuate the conflict.

## BROADER IMPLICATIONS AND AREAS FOR FUTURE RESEARCH

Beyond this discussion of how scholars conceptualize the relationship between ideas and instrumentalist mobilization, these findings also have broader implications for the study of institutions and ethnic politics in pluralistic societies. In particular, it calls for a re-orientation of how scholars conceptualize the relationship between institutions and conflict, particularly in research on federalism and constitutional design, encouraging greater attention to subnational institutions and the role of informal institutions and rules in creating stronger communal relationships.

### The Study of Institutions and Conflict

Regarding the broader implications of this research for studies of institutions and their ability to accommodate group interests in pluralistic or post-conflict societies, greater attention is necessary to the design and effects of institutions beyond the national level. Building of strong institutions is certainly fundamental in pluralistic or post-conflict societies, but to the extent that policymakers and scholars are surprised at the failure of national-level power-sharing arrangements to create broader inter-ethnic peace, they should not be. Scholarly focus on national-level arrangements, including constitutional design (e.g., Kuperman 2015) and the conditions under which formal power-sharing (or its various individual mechanisms) fail or succeed is certainly worthwhile, but the analysis should not stop there. As the vast literature on the effectiveness of consociational or power-sharing institutions emphasizes, the adoption of executive power-sharing or an ethno-federal model is hardly the solution to intra-state conflict. The Nigeria case is particularly illustrative here. While ethno-federalism, for the most part, successfully reduced conflict at the center between the country's largest ethnic groups, it did not do so, and fundamentally could not do so, at the subnational level. Rather, it shifted the locus of conflict to subnational units where various ethnic groups now compete for the benefits of political power and representation. The larger take-away from this discussion, therefore, is that merely resolving the issue of political control at the center through consociational mechanisms such as federalism are insufficient to create a peaceful society. Decentralization or devolution of power is not a panacea.

Work on comparative federalism can, however, helpfully advance the study of the relationship between local representative institutions (or lack thereof) and ethnic cooperation or conflict. In what ways can states most effectively reinforce local power-sharing? Under what conditions do national and subnational institutions constructively reinforce one another? What other types of informal communal norms or institutions can reinforce or be reinforced by power-sharing? These are areas for further study that can be usefully explored among and beyond African states, as young democracies or struggling democracies, in particular, have increasingly adopted and experimented with decentralization or devolution to address ethnic competition and power struggles. As Horowitz (2004, 245) contends, "If peacemaking in divided societies is a term with any real content, that content must be cast in terms of institutions: structures and recurrent patterns of behavior that work to reduce conflict."

## Taking the Informal Seriously

This research also calls for greater attention to *informal* institutional arrangements initiated by local actors to address perceived suboptimal outcomes to formal rules. First, analyses limited to formal institutional arrangements will overlook important dynamics of informal subnational governance. There is no constitutional requirement or government mandate directing local government bodies in Nigeria to adopt power-sharing. Rather, these are institutional arrangements generated through local consultation among ethnic leaders who, taking into account local communal political dynamics and incentive structures after 1976 decentralization, found the trade-offs of a purely competitive electoral model to be less attractive than a more inclusive or accommodative model of democratic representation funneled through power-sharing. Focusing only on formal institutional arrangements and mandates would overlook what I have argued is the fulcrum of communal peace or conflict in the analysis of Nigeria's inter-religious violence.

Second, tunnel vision on national-level institutional design also overlooks the ability of communities to draw on their own systems of authority and traditions of conflict resolution to reinforce local conflict resolution or to react constructively to premonitions of future conflict. Especially in contexts where religious and traditional leaders or chiefs remain significant local actors and authorities (e.g., Baldwin 2014; 2015), and communal norms and culture are key organizing features of social life, informal rules or agreements are important for understanding the relationship between institutions and communal cooperation or violence.

Third, as the case studies in this book also demonstrate, informal power-sharing institutions have ramifications beyond their particular political strictures. Power-sharing provides a foundation for other informal communal mechanisms of conflict prevention and conflict resolution, helping to dispel fears that control over local politics is a zero-sum game. To facilitate more representative societies, this study argues for the importance of designing post-conflict institutions that draw on the potential of informal institutions and the dynamic capacities of communities.

These observations have implications for policymakers and mediators attempting to construct stronger post-conflict institutions, but this study also suggests new avenues for research. For example, while the power-sharing arrangements identified in this study were generated from the bottom-up, it is unclear whether top-down mandated subnational power-sharing might effectively accomplish the same task, especially where local incentives are weak. Are there ways in which the incentives can be structured and sources of local legitimacy employed to ensure such arrangements become self-enforcing? Exogenous intervention may be necessary depending on the stage of conflict (i.e., violence ongoing or in a stage of tenuous peace) or where incentives might otherwise be weak or organizational capacity lacking. These are dynamics for further study.

## Taking "Low-level" Communal Conflict Seriously

A final note on how scholars approach the empirical study of ethnic conflict. While communal violence can result in devastating loss of life, displacement, and destruction of homes and property, many cases of communal violence fall outside the purview of major studies of ethnic conflict. Yet, these studies draw sweeping conclusions about the incidence and nature of ethnic and religious conflict. The main reason for the exclusion of cases is the grain of the data used in large-$n$ studies. As discussed in Chapter 5, they generally exclude from their analysis the "small-scale" cases with lower numbers of deaths. While the loss of life associated with civil war violence is likely to be much greater in the short-term compared to incidents involving low-level communal violence, this observation should not lessen the importance of communal violence. Left unaddressed or unresolved over the long-term, the number of lives lost to communal violence can rapidly accumulate. Furthermore, just as national level disputes can destabilize the state, so too can subnational communal disputes where local institutions do not effectively represent communities. Violence can spill over into surrounding communities, particularly when, as in Nigeria, politics is sacralized and an attack against co-religionists in one location is viewed as an attack on the faith of adherents elsewhere and inspires retaliation.

Nigeria amply illustrates the broader security implications of communal violence. Inter-religious violence is certainly not viewed as a minor dispute between a few communities in the north. To the contrary, it has become a major regional and national political issue, illustrated particularly by the widespread flare-up of inter-religious violence in northern Nigeria in reaction to the 2011 presidential election results. Sidel (2006, 162) makes a similar observation about the ramifications of the Poso 1998 violence in Indonesia in which "only" hundreds were *injured* and places of worship and homes destroyed, noting,

> [T]he rioting also worked to heighten suspicion across the religious divide, to strengthen the boundaries and lines of authority within each religious community, and to sharpen the organization and instruments of violence on both sides. The displacement of hundreds of families whose homes were destroyed and the flight of hundreds more in the face of continuing intimidation and fear of further attacks created hundreds of Internally Displaced Persons (IDPs), mostly within Poso regency, and hardened both the pattern of segregation and the resolve for retribution among the local population.

The violence in Indonesia subsequently in 1998, 2000, 2001, 2003, and 2004 was broader in scale and intensity. Ultimately, the violence left more than a thousand dead, displaced tens of thousands, and constituted religious identities as the primary division (Sidel 2006, 162–167). In short, other cases also demonstrate that these small-scale cases can also propel or morph into the larger scale violence that destabilizes the state and finds its way into international headlines (and large-$n$ datasets with higher death thresholds).

This further points to the importance of not overlooking subnational institutions; conflict stemming from weak local institutions and non-inclusive representation can spill over and destabilize the state *from the bottom up*. Consequently, the field will benefit from work that further moves the study of ethnic politics and conflict beyond its focus on civil war and national-level institutions.

On a methodological level, while collecting data on smaller scale incidents of communal violence is certainly a herculean challenge, scholars should be careful in drawing conclusions about the micro-dynamics of ethnic violence from large-$n$ studies in which the criteria of ethnic violence is often a death threshold of hundreds and where the state is one of the primary parties to the conflict. Such criteria exclude a whole realm of communal violence involving non-state actors in which thousands of lives are ultimately destroyed. It is clear from the hundreds of cases of northern Nigerian communal violence that do not show up in major large-$n$ datasets – datasets that are nonetheless employed in major scholarly studies of ethnic conflict or civil war – that scholars are overlooking an important site of civil conflict, conflict with ramifications that can hardly be described as small. Thus, this study also seeks to encourage attention to the costs and benefits associated with the different methods we employ to study civil conflict.

## Not a Clash of Civilizations

The study of Nigeria's inter-religious violence also emphasizes the importance of religious change in global politics. The rapid growth of Christianity in northern Nigeria, particularly the Pentecostal-charismatic resurgence and its political theology, has led to new political expressions and forms of mobilization. This is not unique to Nigeria. Paired with the rapid growth of Islam globally, as well its own various political expressions, religious identity has become an important political category and basis for inter-group conflict within states. Religious identities, depending on their political theologies, can serve as a significant source of identity, which can be mapped onto local grievances in pluralistic societies.

Much work remains to be done to examine the dynamics and implications of this religious change and resurgence. The religious change occurring in countries across the Global South with the rapid growth of Christianity and Islam is rooted in various factors – for example, internal self-reflection and re-articulation of political theologies, socio-political and economic changes and failures, and the promises of hope and new opportunity represented by vibrant faith communities. While there is indeed debate over the causes of the Christian religious change, it is the homogeneity of its political theology across many countries with the Pentecostal-charismatic revival that is remarkable. The rise of the Pentecostal-charismatic variant of Christianity, in particular, involved a significant shift in the political theology of the Christian community; politics is no longer considered anathema, but rather political participation and godly council are seen as obligations of Christians for the righteous transformation of political rule.

Similarly, within Islam, political reform and revival movements have been important in the Muslim world, as struggles for self-rule and socio-economic development have led reformers to critically apply the teachings of Islam to the challenges of their time and to re-articulate the relationship between religion, society, politics, and individual spirituality. The effects of the revivalist movement since the 1970s and the call for a return to Islam in both personal and public life has led to new forms of religio-social engagement and divergent forms of political participation or protest ranging from the adoption of secular or western values, modernist calls for Islam as a comprehensive way of life, conservative rejection of the revivalist movement, and a violent radical interpretation of the call to return to and restore Islamic faith and political rule. The Maitatsine movement in Nigeria in 1980s, the rise of Boko Haram in the northeast, debates about the implementation of Sharia or Islamic law in the north, and the majority moderate Islam of the massive Muslim community in Nigeria reflects not only this variation, but also emphasizes the importance of religious change.

The political ramifications of the re-articulations of Christian and Islamic political theologies have been significant globally. While in some cases it may be relatively benign and democratic, in other cases, the shift in the teaching and strength of a religious bloc can create new socio-political tensions and incentives to politicize religious identity and contestation. The global phenomenon of religious resurgence or revival since the 1970s is playing out on many stages, including the Nigerian stage. The politicization of religious identity in national politics provided fertile ground for the increasing politicization of local ethnic identities and, ultimately, the rise of inter-religious communal violence. The religious resurgence in Nigeria over the past few decades has changed the nature of political relationships and debates, particularly in northern Nigeria.

The discussion of these modern political transformations stemming from the dynamic interaction of political theologies and socio-political realities emphasizes the importance of taking seriously the changing boundaries or forms of religio-political practice propelled by this religious change, as Nigeria exemplifies. As Snyder (2011, 4) summarizes, the religious resurgence has broad implications, shaping "who the actors in world politics are, what they want, what resources they bring to the tasks of mobilizing support and making allies, and what rules they follow," and it can be both reinforcing and undermining to state legitimacy.[5] Yet, as

---

[5] As Woodberry (2012, 269) also notes, "Religious groups are not merely interchangeable with any other organization – distinct theologies and organizational forms lead to distinct outcomes."

Philpott (2007, 505) observes, "Scholars have offered a bewildering array of explanations for the politics of religions: their theology, their national and ethnic identities, colonialism, their historical relationships to political authorities, their competition with other religions, their grievances, and a multitude of economic, political, and demographic factors." To make a meaningful contribution, future research must be able to bridge the theoretical and methodological inconsistencies of the extant research and develop testable hypotheses regarding the influence of religion or religious change in relationship to the constitution of different actors, forms of mobilization, and the state.[6]

As the Nigerian context emphasizes, religious identities can transcend other categories of ethnicity and extend the breadth of conflict. However, this is not a clash of civilizations argument. Rather, it highlights the importance of understanding the implications of religious change and ideas for patterns of conflict and articulation of grievances, while also exploring the conditions under which religious identity becomes the perceived basis of conflict in some places and not others. That is, in what *way(s)* do religious ideas and cleavages become tools for mobilization or conflict? The presence of religious differences or grievances is not a sufficient condition for religious violence.

---

[6] Religion has been overlooked in the international relations and comparative politics scholarship, and has only been gaining ground in the past five to ten years. Commenting on the role of religion in international and domestic politics, Ruth Marshall (2009, 14) observes, "The apparent growth in religious influences is likely due to the fact that analysts are only now noticing what was always there." As Bellin (2008, 316) argues, the dominance of realpolitik in international relations has resulted in a failure to "reckon with the power of religion as an independent variable, the noninstrumental aspect of religious behavior, and the malleability of religious ideas, as well as their differential appeal, persuasiveness, and political salience over time." Or, as Bellin (339) goes on to note, the "problem is not that the question of religion has been overlooked in international affairs so much as that it has been undertheorized." The analysis of religion has been largely left to other disciplines that "rarely undertake the kind of structured comparison that a political scientist would embrace – a comparison that can yield generalizable hypotheses about when ethno-religious difference is likely to spell transnational conflict or about which conditions foster the transnational contagion of religious terror" (Bellin 2008, 340). The same critique may be leveled at scholarship on communal inter-religious violence. Additionally, many of the studies on the impact of religious change are single-country case studies that do not adopt comparative analysis to contribute to theoretical and generalizable conclusions. Within the literature on the role of religion in the Third Wave of democratization in Latin America, most of the work is of a descriptive nature (e.g., Gill 2004, 44). Finally, the studies bring limited insight into the conditions under which religion is likely to be a significant force for mobilization, against whom, on behalf of what issues, and to what ends. Factors such as regime type or institutional structure do not often enter the analyses.

Considering the relationship between ideas and mobilization or radicalization, an important area of research in the scholarship on non-state conflict or ethnic violence focuses on the individual incentives and conditions that mobilize individual participation in inter-group violence. This research highlights, for example, the cohesiveness of group social ties (Weinstein 2005, Staniland 2012), ethnic belonging and mobilization of ethnic symbols (Kaufman 2001, Gagnon 1994), insecurity and fear (Horowitz 1985, de Figueiredo and Weingast 1999), the emotional benefits of responding to perceived injustices (Wood 2015), and various personal or private motivations individuals act on during the chaos of conflict (Kalyvas 2003). Research that focuses on individual and group incentives or psychology for mobilization is an important counterpoint to macro-level or state-level analyses, but the micro-dynamics of individual mobilization should also not overlook the informal and local institutional contexts that affect the strategic calculus of actors and their willingness to engage in costly mobilization. This book, therefore, speaks to this research as well, suggesting that the institutional dynamics of local representation are critical in shaping or structuring the incentives of individual to mobilize in the context of communal ethnic violence. That is, absent such institutions, fears and misperceptions may spiral, the bonds between groups may deteriorate, and perceived peaceful pathways to resolving group grievances may seem increasingly less feasible. In short, moving beyond the analysis of state-level institutions in explanations of civil conflict does not mean throwing out institutional analyses altogether; rather, it also requires taking into account the dynamics of local cleavages and the institutions that reinforce those cleavages or attempt to mitigate them.

## Parties and Power

Finally, another important area for further research is how party rules and leadership interact with the politics of local governance. Since party leadership is central in choosing which individuals will run under their party banner and in putting forward tribally mixed tickets, the internal calculus of party leadership and in relationship to party rules is an area for further exploration. What role do party leaders play in enforcing and upholding informal power-sharing rules? How does the fear of voter defection in the face of potential departure from power-sharing rules constrain party leadership to conform to power-sharing arrangements? These and other questions call for closer study of the interaction of party rules and actors with the informality of and incentives for local power-sharing, particularly in countries or contexts in which party control of local governments is more contested or where parties act essentially as ethnic parties (i.e., unlike Plateau state where party identification is more fluid and the party that controls the state governorship and its resources generally wins control of the majority if not all of the local governments in the state, whatever the ethnic affiliations of the local government leaders).

## GENERALIZABILITY

While Nigeria, specifically local governments in its northern region, is the subject of this study, the broader implications of the power-sharing theory and analysis are not confined to Nigeria or a particular set of local governments. That is, the theory and hypotheses this book explores are not about understanding the causes of conflict particular to Nigeria, per say, but about exploring a new theory of power-sharing in a context of ethnic pluralism and variation in the incidence of inter-religious violence while controlling for other important competing explanations, as discussed in detail in Chapter 8. The variation among local governments in Nigeria certainly provides this leeway to draw broader conclusions relevant for other pluralistic societies working to build stronger institutions that promote inter-ethnic cooperation and inclusivity. Nigeria is not the only country beset by communal violence, nor is inter-religious violence the only type of civil violence that can threaten the security of communities and the state. I do not claim, therefore, that the findings of this study have equal insight for *all* forms or types of intra-state conflict. Rather a number of different dynamics are important in considering the broader generalizability of the findings. These include the nature of the conflict, the timing of the adoption of power-sharing institutions, and the degree of autonomy or independence local governments have from state- and national-level actors or institutions.

First, regarding types of intra-state violence, some violence takes the form of secessionist movements, movements that seek to overthrow the state and the ethnic group in power, disputes over land and material resources, rebel movements derived from a small segment of the population, or radical Islamic movements – such as Boko Haram and its affiliates in northern Nigeria – that claim their cause is a religious battle to usher in an Islamic state. These movements can all vary in size, resources, and support among the population as well. As my communal violence data revealed, some cases of violence in northern Nigeria derive from a pattern of causal and precipitating events in which religious ideas, symbols, and actors are front and center, while in other cases the clashes are associated with disputes between farmers and cattle-herders over rights to grazing land. As my focus is on *communal* violence, I did not include in the analyses cases in which members of political parties rioted. I also did not include cases in which groups targeted state officials or the police. These types of violence and their relationship to local institutions (if at all) are beyond the scope of this study. I do not assume that all types of intra-state conflict are identical and can be solved or ameliorated by the same type or level of institutional measures. That is, conflicts rooted in disputes over national-level representation, abuse of power, dismissal of constitutional and electoral rules, and the like, are unlikely to be resolved by subnational power-sharing institutions. However, to the extent that such disputes inspire subnational mobilization along ethnic lines, the findings suggest that local-level representative institutions that are inclusive of local ethnic groups in key seats of representation are less prone to the manipulation of identity and ethnic violence that might flow from these impasses. Considering violence between *communally* defined groups within a defined political territory, issues of which groups are represented in local political office or who holds the reins of power are ubiquitous.

Second, the degree of actual influence or authority accorded local governments will also shape the extent to which power-sharing can play any significant role in promoting inter-ethnic cooperation. While this study argues that, to be effective, power-sharing at a local government level must share the central governing seats, the degree of actual power that national governments devolve to the local level can vary. Further, there can be variation in the degree of outside meddling by state or national government bodies or actors. Nigeria's states still wield significant control over the purse strings of local government units, despite the independence allocated in the constitution for local governments. Nonetheless, its local governments are still important sites of contestation, as discussed in Chapter 3. In cases where local government units are merely facades or have been deprived of any real governing power or influence, one would hardly expect local power-sharing to serve any meaningful function or purpose in dispelling inter-ethnic grievances. Of course, as noted in Chapter 4, power-sharing is unlikely to prove effective where a state does not also provide a basic assurance of regular and recurring local government elections. Without adherence to this basic democratic norm, providing local leaders with a stable time horizon, elites have little incentive to abide by a rotational power-sharing agreement. It is here, then, that scholars of comparative federalism can help advance the study of the conditions under which local power-sharing institutions are effective; not all forms of devolution are cut from the same cloth. To the extent that devolution imbues local governments with real power under democratic electoral norms, this study suggests that such institutions paired with power-sharing will be the most effective in providing communal stability and integration. In this vein, the adoption of federalism and decentralized institutions is unlikely to ameliorate ethnic tensions if it merely serves as a pretense of local representation and self-determination.

Finally, the timing of decentralization and devolution of power to local administrative units will also likely shape the effectiveness of power-sharing institutions. That is, because power-sharing cases in this study were largely adopted in the period following the 1970s decentralization reforms, they were functioning prior to the rise of inter-religious violence. It is an open question whether, if decentralization and power-sharing are pursued as a means to *resolving* ethnic conflict or violence (or in the aftermath of significant violence) in a particular locality, the necessary social and political foundation exists to effectively mitigate fears and address grievances. It is for this reason, as noted previously, that national-level incentives and reinforcement may be necessary to monitor the initial implementation of power-sharing institutions. This is an area for further research, however. For example, the effects of Kenya's 2010 constitutional change devolving power to 47 new political and administrative units or counties remain to be seen. Their creation came during a period of peace, but also in the aftermath of the 2007–2008 post-election violence. While the new devolution may help push conflict away from the center, the findings from this research suggest that the ability of the devolution to reduce conflict depends on whether the integrity of such institutions can be maintained and are imbued with real local authority or power or are merely tools of political elite and party manipulation.

In general, questions regarding the incentives for and sustainability of such institutions under different conditions related to timing and exogenous pressures, as well as the distributional effects on resource distribution, are important areas for further comparative research. Nonetheless, it is clear from the theory and findings that local power-sharing institutions should be a necessary component of peacebuilding and conflict resolution strategies in divided societies for inter-ethnic peace to be sustainable at a subnational level. As the case studies from northern Nigeria demonstrate, unlike their national-level variant, local power-sharing institutions can be sustainable and mitigate inter-religious violence even in the face of considerable pressure, including religious violence in surrounding areas.

## The Case of Indonesia and the Rise of Ethnic Conflict

At a minimum, this research highlights that – whether or not communities in many other countries have identical forms of power-sharing – local politics matters not only for stability within pluralistic communities, but also for the stability of the state as a whole. Other forms of locally-conceived institutional arrangements that help to manage ethnic relations in ethnically pluralistic countries, such as pacts, are open for further research. Like Jamie Davidson's (2008, 16) work on ethnic conflict in Indonesia, this study joins a growing body of work being done by scholars "who are reexamining group strife in subnational contexts" and who, "by moving below the national ... [have] shown that these [national] institutions, no matter how influential, fail to account for the incontrovertible variation of collective violence within states."[7]

Indonesian politics and the civil conflict that has plagued the country at various times since the colonial period highlight the broader application of this study and the potential for further research. Like Nigeria, colonialism and the use of indirect rule integrally shaped the politics of identity in Indonesia and the politicization of ethnic cleavages (Bertrand 2004, 32). In the post-colonial period, ethnic identities that were otherwise dormant became the basis for communal violence, as well as violence both exacerbated by and targeted against the state. Bertrand (2004, 1) notes that "between 1997 and 2002, at least 10,000 people were killed in ethnic violence throughout the archipelago."

A range of factors shaped the conditions conducive for the emergence of violence – violence that was propelled by Muslim and Christian identities and ethno-tribal Dayak, Malay, and Madurese identities. These factors included: institutional changes, shifts in national political regimes,

---

[7] One challenge for generalizability in this project is that the prevalence of local and informal power-sharing institutions in federal states in Africa and elsewhere in the Global South is unclear. Most evidence is anecdotal, and the empirical project of documenting and gathering all the necessary data is a considerable undertaking in both time and resources. Indeed, it is unclear how widespread subnational power-sharing is in Nigeria beyond Plateau and Kaduna. In focusing on these two states, however, I did not select to explore them *because* they contain cases of power-sharing. Rather, I focused on these two states because of the variation in communal violence they exhibit. Based on the findings in only these two states, then, it is possible to infer that power-sharing is not an uncommon phenomenon in Nigeria.

a weakened state, the emergence of identity-based national politics, missionary movements and religious change, major migrations and relocation of ethnic groups, and deep economic changes (Sidel 2006; Bertrand 2004; Davidson 2008). The Nigerian case and the Indonesian one share a vast number of similarities, and it is the effects of the changes over time in particular communities that help to explain the variation in communal violence – why it flared up at certain times and in certain places. Most important, I argue, is what the studies of Indonesian ethnic conflict suggest about the significance of institutional changes or decentralization in the 1990s for local political representation.

As with the decentralization that occurred in the 1970s in Nigeria, the 1990s Indonesian liberalization suddenly opened up a new political arena for Indonesians to contest for political representation. Prior to the 1990s, the central government ran a "homogenous government bureaucracy" based on allegiance to its directives enforced through the imposition of loyal civil servants and military officials (Bertrand 2004, 39). "Such bureaucratic and administrative structures," notes Bertrand (2004, 39), "eliminated institutional differences in various regions and were intended to reduce the diversity of the ethnic, cultural, or religious landscape in favor of the common characteristics of the Indonesian nation." In other words, the central government significantly circumscribed local democratic forms of participation and representation. Due to the convergence of a number of factors in the 1990s, the stability of the system began to show its cracks; secessionist movements in Aceh, East Timor, and Irain Jaya gained momentum and were crushed by the military, students mobilized against the Suharto regime, and both intra-religious ethnic conflict and inter-religious conflicts led to instability, loss of thousands of lives, and massive displacement of thousands (Bertrand 2004, 43).

As Bertrand (2004, 58) highlights, such decentralization can create new opportunities for democracy to grow, but it may also increase the potential for groups to mobilize on an ethnic basis:

Institutional change increased the potential for violence. In addition to the uncertainty surrounding the fall of Suharto, rapidly changing institutions opened up not only opportunities but also fears of further mobilization. When the Habibie government began to implement a law on regional autonomy in 1999, competition rose for the positions of district head and provincial governor. Under the new law, vast resources were decentralized to the districts and, therefore, became a source of intense competition. Dayak political elites, who had been frustrated at their loss of representation and control over resources, had a strong interest in winning many of these posts. They were also in a good position given the numerical advantages of the Dayak in Central Kalimantan.

The effects of decentralization in Indonesia and the subsequent clamor of ethno-tribal groups for new districts calls up the Nigerian experience of a proliferation of new LGAs to more than 700 before many were dissolved as illegal. Davidson (2008, 136) notes, "[o]ne of the unintended consequences of the decentralization program in Indonesia has been a race to redistrict administrative units ... [a]t the outset of decentralization, the number of districts in the country stood at 292; by 2003 it had rocketed to over 430" (see also Sidel 2006, 180–181, 187). The districts became a new site of contestation for control over resources and representation. Depending on how the lines of districts were drawn, one or another ethnotribal group could gain the majority and hold greater prospects for control. Groups could also attempt redress for past grievances or marginalization through contestation in the new local political arena.

The implications for the stability of communal relationships were devastating. The developments in provinces such as West Kalimantan, Davidson (2008, 136) notes, "had particularly deadly consequences" with the new incentives to mobilize, as well as new capacity to do so with the increased ethno-tribal political consciousness and organization that had developed in preceding years. In Pontianak, the site of major ethnic violence starting in 1999, riots over land disputes were the harbinger of later ethnic conflict between the Dayak and Madureses. Yet, Davidson (2008, 122) observes that even these disputes over control of land and the "overall aggressiveness of these mobilizations centered over the question of representation in *bupati* [district head] posts." In other words, political reforms and a new institutional arrangement heightened the politics of representation and the political saliency of identity and religion.

Along with the increasing presence and distinctiveness of Christian and Muslim authority at the local level and the overlap in economic and political interests, Sidel (2006, 155) observes that the *pogroms* of Central Sulawesi, Maluku, and Poso in the 1990s and the inter-religious violence of 1998–2001 were affected by the "approaching elections of 1999, decentralization, and the redrawing of administrative boundaries (*pemekaran*)." These events "create[d] tremendous uncertainty and anxiety along the local borders – and within the local hierarchies – of religious faith, not only among Islamic and Christian ecclesiastical establishments but also among rival Muslim and Protestant networks of local politicians, businessmen, gangsters, civil servants, and (active and retired) military and police officers" (Sidel 2006, 155).[8] The symbolic politics of indigeneity and Muslim/Christian identity, as in Nigeria, became the basis for political organization and for claims of marginalization and inequality in many communities (Duncan 2013).

While references to power-sharing in local communal politics are sparse in this literature, there is indication that, at least in a few cases, it has been central to the negotiation of group representation and peace in some Indonesian communities. In one instance in 1999, brief rioting and heightened tensions between the Dayak and the Malays occurred in response to a perceived liberty taken with the power-sharing agreement in place (although Madurese were ultimately the primary targets in later violence). Davidson (2008, 153) recounts the events as follows:

In October 1999 rancor over the selection of provincial representatives (*utusan daerah*) to the national People's Consultative Council (MPR) sparked a limited clash that both highlighted Malay-Dayak tensions and portended the October 2000 riots. There was understanding that the DPRD [Provincial/ District/City People's Representative Council] members would elect two Malays, two Dayaks, and one Chinese to reflect the province's ethnic composition (and political balance). The selection of Zainuddin Isman, a PPP activist and former *Kompas* correspondent, complicated matters, however. Dayaks rejected Isman, for, although he claims Dayak ancestry, he is a Muslim and thus considered

---

[8] See also pages 161 and 188. Noting the relationship between decentralization and the processes of religious change in Maluku, Sidel (2006, 172–174) observes: "Yet in perhaps somewhat less obvious ways, the shift to an open, competitive, and decentralized system of organizing power in Indonesia was also accompanied by heightened uncertainty and anxiety as to religious identities and structures of authority *within* the Muslim and Christian communities. Anthropological writings on the villages of Ambon, after all, stressed the persistence well into the Suharto era of religious beliefs and practices that transcended the Muslim–Protestant divide, patterns of enduring alliance (*pela*) and mutual assistance between villages of different official faiths, and understandings of local property and authority relations based on suprareligious customary law (*adat*) and aristocratic lineage. Ethnographic work on other parts of Maluku likewise revealed a broad spectrum of diversity and change in the religious beliefs and practices of those registered as Muslims and Christians in the province, with 'conversion' a recent and ongoing process for many official believers, even well into the 1990s. Patterns of migration to and within Maluku – especially by (Muslim) Butonese from Sulawesi – were cited by observers in the same period as increasing the diversity of religious practices and heightening the 'ethnicizing' tensions between both Christian and Muslim 'natives,' on the one hand, and immigrant 'outsiders,' on the other, over economic resources, property relations, village elections, and other issues. Against this backdrop, the dominant structures of power associated with Protestantism and Islam in Maluku, much like their counterparts in Poso, were haunted by rising doubts and fears as to their authority, identity, and coherence." See also Duncan 2013.

"Malay." Therefore, for some the tally was three Malays and one Dayak. Angered by such duplicity, dozens of Dayaks tried to storm the DPRD building ... The symbolic potency of the fracas far surpassed the actual fighting. Whereas it demonstrated that future Malay-Dayak disturbances remained a possibility, it also indicated that Pontianak's looming "ethnic" clashes would, in fact, mask elite politicking.

While this account above moves on to discuss the deadly ethnic violence that flared between ethnic groups in Pontianak the following year, the reference suggests that power-sharing was one *local* form of informal politics employed to maintain peace. Similarly, in another account, Davidson (2008, 150) notes that the DPRD sought to balance local leadership by electing both a Malay and a Dayak to the posts of *bupati* and vice *bupati* in Sitang, Ketapang, Kapuas Hulu, and Landak districts in the 2000 and 2001 elections. This is clear evidence of power-sharing in Indonesian local politics. Davidson (2008, 146) also makes references to the role of traditional pacts in preventing ethnic conflict in a number of cases.

No mention is made of the effectiveness or success of these agreements over the last decade, or their prevalence across Indonesia's many pluralistic communities (before or after periods of ethnic violence), but these cases suggest that power-sharing instituted by leaders at the communal level is not a phenomenon specific to Nigeria. How these power-sharing institutions came into being, the conditions under which elite opted or did not opt for them, and whether or how they have been effective in promoting communal peace is a subject for further investigation. In the case of northern Nigeria, at least, I find that local power-sharing institutions have been pivotal in preventing inter-religious tensions from spiraling into symbolic and deadly Muslim–Christian violence.

## CONCLUSION

Ultimately, I call for a re-evaluation of the applicability and effectiveness of power-sharing in resolving or preventing ethnic violence. The evidence from northern Nigeria clearly shows that power-sharing between Muslims and Christians of various ethno-tribal combinations has been essential to peace and stability in a number of communities. The case studies also highlight how *informal* power-sharing institutions can be a viable form of democratic representation, or, rather, how power-sharing can accommodate a more democratic ideal. Despite their informal construction, the institutional arrangement can develop self-enforcing mechanisms and maintain incentives for ethno-tribal elites to abide by the original understanding, such as we see in Bassa, Kanam, and Chikun LGAs. This does not mean that the power-sharing institutions are not subject to pressures. Exogenous shocks (e.g., inter-religious violence in other communities) or endogenous changes (e.g., demographic shifts) threaten the sustainability of power-sharing institutions or their capacity to maintain inter-religious peace. However, I find that, by and large, the LGAs with power-sharing are better able to avert inter-religious communal violence by providing a foundation and incentives for the religious, political, and traditional leaders to coordinate peacebuilding and negotiate tensions as they arise in response to these exogenous and endogenous changes.

In conclusion, scholars of ethnic conflict are unlikely to fully appreciate or capture the dynamics of civil conflict within states without looking at how rights and representation are negotiated at the local level. This is not to say that national politics, institutions, and events do not also affect the construction of communal identities and politics, but rather that these national-level factors are inherently in conversation with local political contexts. To only consider national-level variables in the unfolding of subnational communal violence will render the patterns, variation, and role of local identities and representation in subnational violence inexplicable, and the solutions to such conflicts will remain muddled.

# APPENDIX A

# GINI Index Measures by State in Northern Nigeria, Urban/Rural

TABLE A.1 *GINI Index Measure, Urban/Rural**

| State | 1985/1986 Urban | 1985/1986 Rural | 1992/1993 Urban | 1992/1993 Rural | 1996/1997 Urban | 1996/1997 Rural | 1998 Overall | 2004 Overall | 2007 Overall |
|---|---|---|---|---|---|---|---|---|---|
| Bauchi | 0.38 | 0.36 | 0.39 | 0.32 | 0.41 | 0.34 | 0.2994 | 0.4256 | 0.4782 |
| Benue | 0.53 | 0.39 | 0.37 | 0.38 | 0.54 | 0.42 | 0.3258 | 0.5528 | 0.545 |
| Borno | 0.39 | 0.36 | 0.37 | 0.38 | 0.38 | 0.36 | 0.2337 | 0.5177 | 0.3947 |
| Gongola | 0.46 | 0.36 | 0.35 | 0.4 | | | | | |
| **Kaduna** | **0.44** | **0.35** | **0.37** | **0.35** | **0.46** | **0.45** | **0.3837** | **0.5075** | **0.4226** |
| Kano | 0.43 | 0.34 | 0.35 | 0.33 | 0.43 | 0.34 | 0.7218 | 0.4967 | 0.4318 |
| Kwara | 0.45 | 0.36 | 0.38 | 0.42 | 0.42 | 0.43 | 0.5250 | 0.5386 | 0.4783 |
| Niger | 0.36 | 0.36 | 0.36 | 0.43 | 0.43 | 0.42 | 0.4327 | 0.5519 | 0.4619 |
| **Plateau** | **0.38** | **0.38** | **0.36** | **0.39** | **0.52** | **0.40** | **0.4334** | **0.5101** | **0.439** |
| Sokoto | 0.48 | 0.36 | 0.34 | 0.43 | 0.39 | 0.43 | 0.6652 | 0.6020 | 0.3253 |
| FCT | | | 0.39 | 0.39 | 0.64 | 0.47 | 0.5153 | 0.5779 | 0.4368 |
| Adamawa | | | | | 0.49 | 0.48 | 0.4009 | 0.7190 | 0.4696 |
| Jigawa | | | | | 0.11 | 0.32 | 0.3227 | 0.5711 | 0.4397 |
| Kebbi? | | | | | 0.26 | 0.42 | 0.5272 | 0.5605 | 0.4104 |
| Kogi? | | | | | 0.34 | 0.45 | 0.4054 | 0.5505 | 0.5555 |
| Taraba | | | | | 0.39 | 0.51 | 0.5217 | 0.5917 | 0.5118 |
| Yobe | | | | | 0.45 | 0.37 | 0.3842 | 0.5106 | 0.4503 |
| Nasarawa | | | | | | | 0.4148 | 0.5991 | 0.4665 |
| Zamfara | | | | | | | 0.3481 | 0.6076 | 0.3366 |
| Gombe | | | | | | | 0.3237 | 0.5080 | 0.4343 |
| Katsina | | | | | | | 0.4349 | 0.5245 | 0.4110 |

* Rural and Urban GINI Index data for 1985 to 1997 are from Aigbokhan (2000, 60–62). The overall 1985 and 2004 real income GINI scores are from Oyekale et al. (2006, 49). The GINI score for 2007 is from UNDP (2010, 148). Note: There are some data missing, as some territories were later split into different states. For example, Gongola became part of Borno.

290

# APPENDIX B

# GDP per Capita for Northern States, 2007

TABLE B.1 *GDP per Capita by State (2007), ($US)*

| State | GDP per capita |
|---|---|
| Adamawa | |
| **Bauchi** | 166.82 |
| Benue | 1,434.43 |
| Borno | 529.52 |
| Gombe | 352.35 |
| Jigawa | 996.01 |
| **Kaduna** | 707 |
| **Kano** | 683.76 |
| Katsina | 994.28 |
| Kebbi | 508.5 |
| Kogi | 147.01 |
| Kwara | 320.21 |
| Nasarawa | 1,226.65 |
| Niger | 1,687.79 |
| **Plateau** | 194.57 |
| Sokoto | 1,488.98 |
| Taraba | 141.78 |
| Yobe | 261 |
| Zamfara | 1,585.21 |
| FCT | 10,208.50 |

*Source:* United Nations Development Programme (2010, 138).

# APPENDIX C

# Economic Indicators for Northern States, 1998–2004

TABLE C.1 *Real Income Growth, GINI Change, and Poverty Incidence, 1998–2004*

| State | 1998–2004 % Growth in Real Income | 1998–2004 Absolute Change in GINI | 1998 Poverty Incidence | 2004 Poverty Incidence | 1998–2004 Difference |
|---|---|---|---|---|---|
| North West | −6.726 | 0.0256 | 0.6394 | 0.6623 | 0.0229 |
| Jigawa | −49.5846 | 0.2483 | 0.6967 | 0.8695 | 0.1727 |
| Kaduna | −1.4002 | 0.1239 | 0.3944 | 0.5219 | 0.1275 |
| Kano | 8.3016 | −0.2251 | 0.633 | 0.5243 | −0.1086 |
| Katsina | 3.3369 | 0.0896 | 0.6673 | 0.6557 | −0.0116 |
| Kebbi | −33.5611 | 0.0333 | 0.8151 | 0.8366 | 0.0215 |
| Sokoto | −9.7414 | 0.2839 | 0.6109 | 0.6652 | 0.0543 |
| Zamfara | 21.6864 | 0.2595 | 0.6647 | 0.5795 | −0.0853 |
| North East | 2.5 | 0.16 | 0.5379 | 0.5561 | 0.0182 |
| Adamawa | −57.0007 | 0.3181 | 0.4323 | 0.7838 | 0.3515 |
| Bauchi | 26.7332 | 0.1262 | 0.3351 | 0.2815 | −0.0536 |
| Borno | 45.0371 | 0.284 | 0.3103 | 0.3218 | 0.0115 |
| Gombe | 3.006 | 0.1843 | 0.5944 | 0.5987 | 0.0043 |
| Taraba | −13.6393 | 0.0701 | 0.5281 | 0.5843 | 0.0562 |
| Yobe | 81.236 | 0.1264 | 0.7871 | 0.5778 | −0.2093 |
| North Central | −27.2472 | 0.0932 | 0.3502 | 0.5106 | 0.1604 |
| Benue | −73.2798 | 0.227 | 0.0133 | 0.5733 | 0.56 |
| Kogi | −42.9619 | 0.1451 | 0.4644 | 0.5686 | 0.1042 |
| Kwara | 1.6092 | 0.0136 | 0.2702 | 0.3886 | 0.1183 |
| Nasarawa | −38.7319 | 0.1843 | 0.2694 | 0.6142 | 0.3447 |
| Niger | 15.335 | 0.1193 | 0.4859 | 0.4615 | −0.0244 |
| Plateau | −34.2122 | 0.0767 | 0.3069 | 0.4802 | 0.1733 |
| FCT | −42.1667 | 0.0626 | 0.2971 | 0.5983 | 0.3013 |

*Source:* Oyekale, Adeoti, and Oyekale (2006, 47).

# APPENDIX D

# Religious Affiliation in Asia

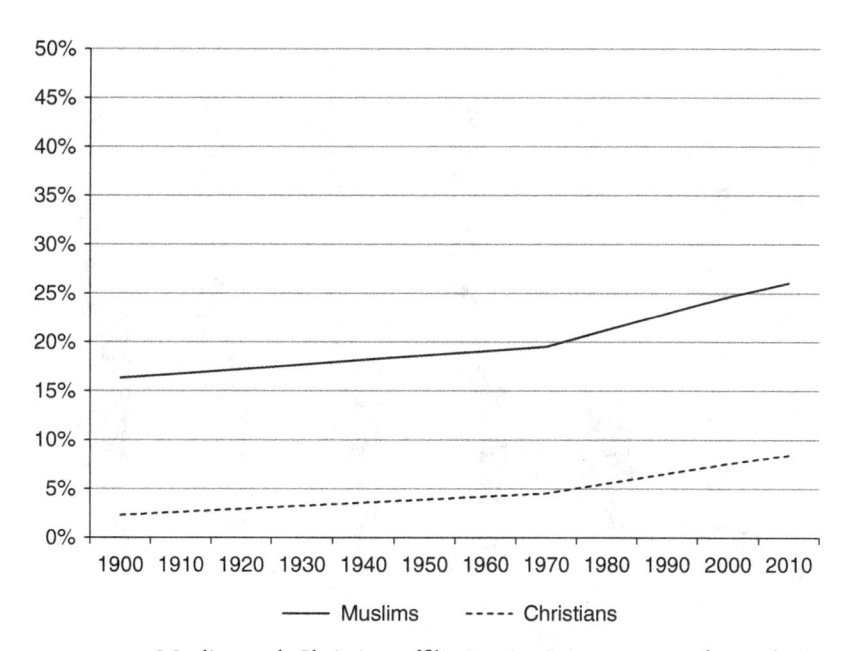

FIGURE D.1 Muslim and Christian affiliation in Asia, percent of population, 1900–2010
Source: Johnson (2007). Interpolated by author.

# APPENDIX E

# Christian Affiliation by Region

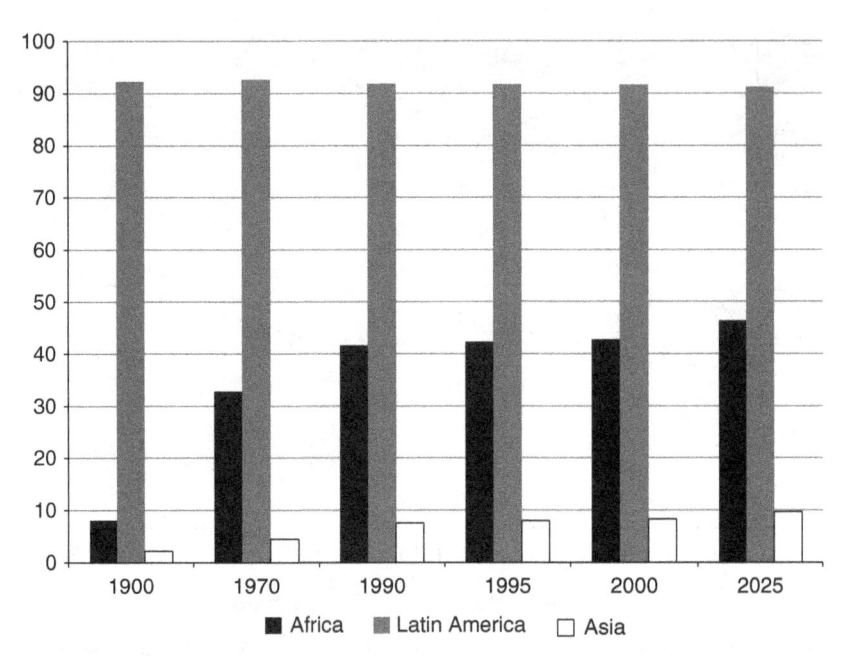

FIGURE E.1 Percent affiliated Christians in Africa, Latin America, and Asia, 1900–2025
Source: Barrett, Kurian and Johnson (2001).

# APPENDIX F

# Nigeria Cases of Violence Involving Religious Actors, 1979–2011*

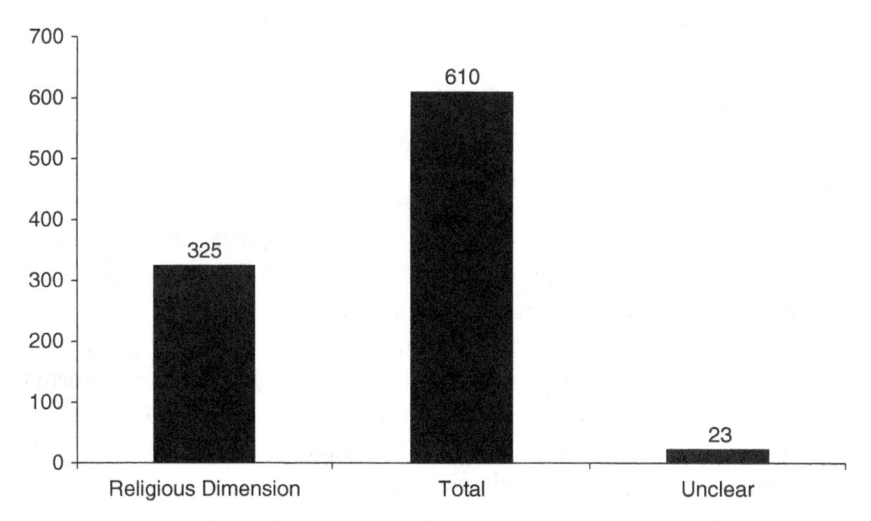

FIGURE F.1 Number of cases in which *any* religious group is noted as party to communal violence

* These are cases in which one of the groups party to the conflict is identified by their religious identity or as a religious group in general. In this sense, it is the most inclusive analysis, as it counts cases that are not inter-religious (e.g., clashing with police) and that are intra-religious.

# APPENDIX G

# Support for Collapsing of Cases into an Ethno-Religious Category

A Pearson's chi-square test and/or a two-sample test of proportions support the inclusion of cases in the Ethno-Religious category. The difference in proportions was not significant, $\chi^2$ (1, N = 129) = 1.77, $p$ = 0.18. A two-sample test of proportions shows that 93 percent of communal violence cases in which only religious identities are reported and 85 percent of cases that report both religious and tribal/communal identities are associated with a religious precipitating event. The proportions are not statistically different.

TABLE G.1 *Ethno-Religious Cases and Religious Precipitating Events, $\chi^2$*

|  | Other Precipitating Event | Religious Precipitating Event | Total |
|---|---|---|---|
| Religious ID only | 4 | 51 | 55 |
| Religious ID mixed | 11 | 63 | 74 |
| Total | 15 | 114 | 129 |
| Pearson chi$^2$(1) | | | |
| $\chi^2$ = | 1.7698 | | |
| $p$ = | 0.183 | | |

TABLE G.2 *Ethno-Religious Cases and Religious Precipitating Events, Test of Proportions*

|  | Mean | Standard Error | z | P>|z| | [95% Confidence Interval] | No. Observations |
|---|---|---|---|---|---|---|
| Religious ID only | .9272727 | .0350164 |  |  | .8586419    .9959035 | 55 |
| Religious ID mixed | .8513514 | .0413541 |  |  | .7702987    .932404 | 74 |
| Difference | .0759214 | .0541877 |  |  | -.0302846    .1821274 |  |
| under Ho: |  | .0570698 | 1.33 | 0.183 |  |  |

297

# APPENDIX H

# Support for Collapsing of Cases into an Ethno-Tribal Category

A two-sample test of proportions assesses whether there is a statistically significant difference in the means of ethno-tribal groups' associations to precipitating events of an economic or tribal nature. The test of proportions is not statistically significant, $p = 0.99$, with tribal and economic precipitating events associated with approximately 90 percent of communal violence associated with reports referring to the tribal identities of the actors only as opposed to those referring to both tribal *and* communal identities (e.g., Fulani cattle herders, Berom farmers). This analysis of their precipitating events supports the inclusion of these cases in a single ethno-tribal category.

TABLE H.1 *Ethno-Tribal Cases and Economic/Tribal Precipitating Events, Test of Proportions*

|  | Mean | Standard Error | z | P>\|z\| | [95% Confidence Interval] | | No. Observations |
|---|---|---|---|---|---|---|---|
| Tribal ID only | .9029126 | .0291733 | | | .845734 | .9600912 | 103 |
| Tribal ID mixed | .8969072 | .0308746 | | | .836394 | .9574204 | 97 |
| Difference | .0060054 | .0424774 | | | −.0772487 | .0892595 | |
| under Ho: | | .0424455 | 0.14 | 0.887 | | | |

299

# APPENDIX I

# Support for Disaggregating Ethno-Tribal and Ethno-Religious Categories

A simple two-sample test of proportions also confirms the disaggregation of the ethno-tribal and ethno-religious categories as a whole. Examining whether there is a statistically significant difference in the proportion of cases of ethno-religious versus ethno-tribal violence associated with religious precipitating events, the results show that there is a very statistically significant ($p$ = .000) difference. Indeed, 88 percent of ethno-religious cases and only 1 percent of ethno-tribal cases are associated with a religious precipitating event.

TABLE 1.1 *Ethnic Violence and Religious Precipitating Events, Test of Proportions*

|  | Mean | Standard Error | z | P>|z| | [95% Confidence Interval] | No. Observations |
|---|---|---|---|---|---|---|
| Ethno-religious | .8837209 | .0282237 |  |  | .8284036  .9390383 | 129 |
| Ethno-tribal | .015 | .0085951 |  |  | −.001846  .031846 | 200 |
| difference | .8687209 | .0295034 |  |  | .8108953  .9265465 |  |
| under Ho: | .0540571 | | 16.07 | 0.000 | | |

# APPENDIX J

# Ethno-Religious and Ethno-Tribal Violence and Population Data*

TABLE J.1 *Population and Communal Violence Figures, Middle Belt States (1979–2011)*

| State | Ethno-Religious | Ethno-Tribal | Unclear Cases | Cross-Border Ethno-Tribal | Population |
|---|---|---|---|---|---|
| Adamawa | 4 | 6 | 4 | | 3,178,950 |
| Bauchi | 36 | 4 | 2 | 1 | 4,653,066 |
| Benue | 0 | 53 | 4 | 16 | 4,253,641 |
| Borno | 10 | 12 | 4 | | 4,171,104 |
| FCT | 1 | 0 | 0 | | 1,406,239 |
| Gombe | 2 | 4 | 1 | | 2,365,040 |
| Jigawa | 9 | 3 | 0 | | 4,361,002 |
| Kaduna | 34 | 9 | 13 | | 6,113,503 |
| Kano | 16 | 1 | 4 | | 9,401,288 |
| Katsina | 7 | 18 | 0 | | 5,801,584 |
| Kebbi | 1 | 0 | 0 | | 3,256,541 |
| Kogi | 0 | 1 | 0 | 2 | 3,314,043 |
| Kwara | 8 | 7 | 1 | | 2,365,353 |
| Nasarawa | 0 | 25 | 1 | 2 | 1,869,377 |
| Niger | 9 | 1 | 2 | | 3,954,772 |
| Plateau | 49 | 49 | 20 | 5 | 3,206,531 |
| Sokoto | 2 | 2 | 0 | | 3,702,676 |
| Taraba | 1 | 22 | 2 | 9 | 2,294,800 |
| Yobe | 3 | 1 | 0 | | 2,321,339 |
| Zamfara | 3 | 1 | 0 | | 3,278,873 |
| Total | 195 | 219 | 58 | 35 | 75,269,722 |

* Population data are taken from the 2006 report of the Nigeria National Population Commission. Consistent with the coding of Ethno-Tribal and Ethno-Religious cases, "Unclear Cases" include those where one group was noted by its religious identity and the other group was "unclear" or noted by its tribal identity, or where one group is identified by its tribal identity and the other group is "unclear."

# APPENDIX K

# Precipitating Events and Cases of Ethno-Religious and Ethno-Tribal Violence, 1979–2011

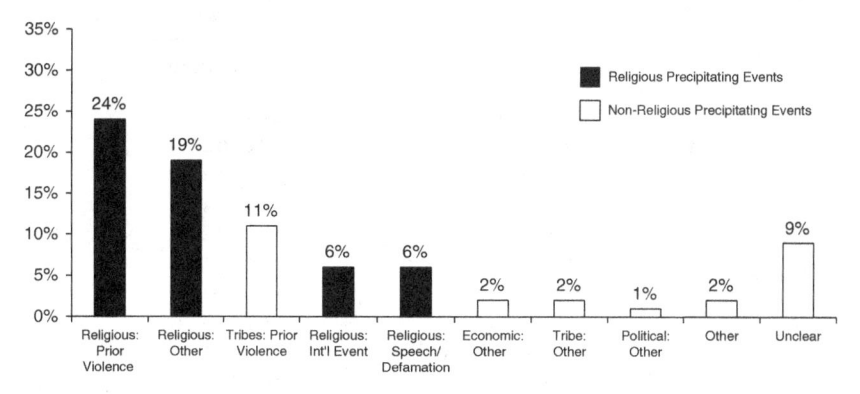

FIGURE K.1 Types of precipitating events in cases of *ethno-religious* violence

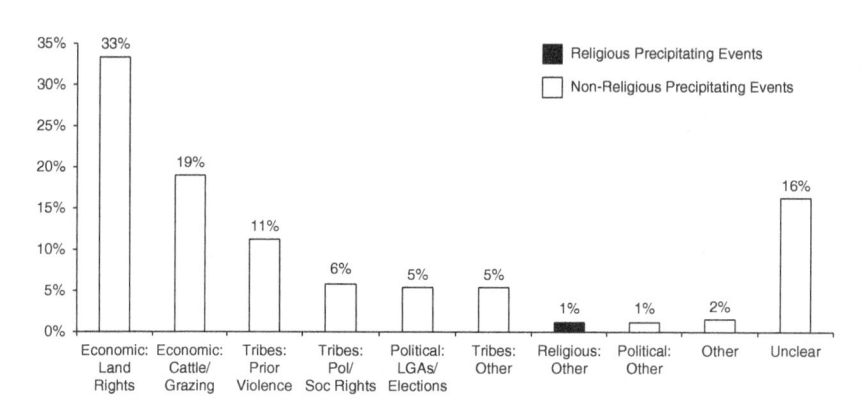

FIGURE K.2 Types of precipitating events in cases of *ethno-tribal* violence

# APPENDIX L

# LGA Population, Kaduna state, and Plateau state

TABLE L.1 *Kaduna LGAs Population Total*

|    | LGA | Total Population |
|----|-----|------------------|
| 1  | Birnin-Gwari | 258,581 |
| 2  | Chikun | 372,272 |
| 3  | Giwa | 292,384 |
| 4  | Igabi | 430,753 |
| 5  | Ikara | 194,723 |
| 6  | Jaba | 155,973 |
| 7  | Jema'a | 278,202 |
| 8  | Kachia | 252,568 |
| 9  | Kaduna North | 364,575 |
| 10 | Kaduna South | 402,731 |
| 11 | Kagarko | 239,058 |
| 12 | Kajuru | 109,810 |
| 13 | Kaura | 174,626 |
| 14 | Kauru | 221,276 |
| 15 | Kubau | 280,704 |
| 16 | Kudan | 138,956 |
| 17 | Lere | 339,740 |
| 18 | Makarfi | 146,574 |
| 19 | Sabon-Gari | 291,358 |
| 20 | Sanga | 151,485 |
| 21 | Soba | 291,173 |
| 22 | Zangon-Kataf | 318,991 |
| 23 | Zaria | 406,990 |
|    | Total | 6,113,503 |

*Source:* National Population Commission (2010, 21).

TABLE L.2 *Plateau LGAs Population Total*

| | LGA | Total Population |
|---|---|---|
| 1 | Barkin Ladi | 179,805 |
| 2 | Bassa | 189,834 |
| 3 | Bokkos | 179,550 |
| 4 | Jos East | 88,301 |
| 5 | Jos North | 437,217 |
| 6 | Jos South | 311,392 |
| 7 | Kanam | 167,619 |
| 8 | Kanke | 124,268 |
| 9 | Langtang North | 142,316 |
| 10 | Langtang South | 105,173 |
| 11 | Mangu | 300,520 |
| 12 | Mikang | 96,388 |
| 13 | Pankshin | 190,114 |
| 14 | Qua'an Pan | 197,276 |
| 15 | Riyom | 131,778 |
| 16 | Shendam | 205,119 |
| 17 | Wase | 159,861 |
| | Total | 3,206,531 |

*Source:* National Population Commission (2010, 41).

# References

"Niger Delta Avengers: Why We Are Crippling the Oil Sector." *TheNEWS*, May 27, 2016. Accessed May 27, 2016. www.thenewsnigeria.com.ng/2016/05/niger-delta-avengers-why-we-are-crippling-oil-sector/.

Constitution of the Federal Republic of Nigeria, Ch. 1, PII, Sec. 10.

Abbass, Isah Mohammed. 2014. "No Retreat No Surrender Conflict for Survival between Fulani Pastoralists and Farmers in Northern Nigeria." *European Scientific Journal* 8 (1):331–346.

Abdulsalami, Isa. 2001. "Jos Crisis Ignites Exodus." *Guardian*, September 16, 2001, 7.

Abdulsalami, Isa. 2008. "We Should Learn from the South Where Muslims and Christians Live in Peace." *Guardian*, December 20, 2008, 8.

Abdulsalami, Isa, Lemmy Ughegbe, and Kelechi Okoronkwo. 2008. "Sultan Cites Hunger, Poverty in Jos Crisis." *Guardian*, December 17, 2008, 1–2.

ACLED. "Dataset Comparison 2: All Country Years and a Focus on Nigeria and South Africa." www.acleddata.com/wp-content/uploads/2012/10/ACLED-Data-Comparison_Countries.pdf (accessed Oct 31, 2013)

Act!ionaid. 2008. *Middle Belt, Not Killing Belt!: The History, Dynamics, and Political Dimensions of Ethno-Religious Conflicts in the Middle Belt*.

Adebanwi, Wale. 2009. "Terror, Territoriality and the Struggle for Indigeneity and Citizenship in Northern Nigeria." *Citizenship Studies* 13 (4):349–363.

Adebanwi, Wale and Ebenezer Obadare. 2013. *Democracy and Prebendalism in Nigeria: Critical Interpretations*. New York: Palgrave Macmillan.

Adesoji, Abimbola. 2010. "The Boko Haram Uprising and Islamic Revivalism in Nigeria." *Africa Spectrum* 45 (2):95–108.

Adesoji, Abimbola. 2011. "Between Maitatsine and Boko Haram: Islamic Fundamentalism and the Response of the Nigerian State." *Africa Today* 57 (4):98–119.

Adeyi-Adikwu, Stevin. 1987a. "Government Orders Probe into Kafanchan Clash." *Guardian*, March 11, 1987, 1, 16.

Adeyi-Adikwu, Stevin. 1987b. "White Paper Lists Causes of Kaduna Riot." *Guardian* (Lagos), July 24, 1987, 1, 11.
African Development Bank. 2013. "MDG Report 2013: Accessing Progress in Africa towards Millennium Development Goals." Accessed December 18, 2013. www.afdb.org/fileadmin/uploads/afdb/Documents/Publications/Millennium_Development_Goals__MDGs__Report_2013.pdf
Afrobarometer. 2008. "Public Opinion and Local Government in Nigeria." *Afrobarometer Briefing Paper* (No. 53).
Agbaje, Adigun. 1998. "The Federal Character Principle and the Search for National Integration." In *Federalism and Political Restructuring in Nigeria*, edited by Kunle Amuwo, Adigun Agbaje, Rotimi Suberu, Georges Hérault, 101–120. Ibadan: Spectrum Books Limited.
Agbese, Andrew. 2011. "How I Resumed as Kanam LG Chair." *Daily Trust*, September 14, 2011. Accessed February 4, 2013. www.dailytrust.com.ng/index.php/politics/31939-how-i-resumed-as-kanam-lg-chair.
Aigbokhan, Ben E. 2002. "Poverty, Growth and Inequality in Nigeria." *AERC Research Paper*. Nairobi: African Economic Research Consortium.
Akhaine, Saxone. 1996. "Religious Crisis Claims More Lives in Zaria." *Guardian*, September 16, 1996.
Akpasubi, Jackson. 1990. "Plans to Make Councils Second-tier of Govt." *Guardian*, July 8, 1990, A2.
Alapiki, Henry E. 2005. "State Creation in Nigeria: Failed Approaches to National Integration and Local Autonomy." *African Studies Review* 48 (3):49–65.
Albert, Olawale. 1998. "Federalism, Inter-ethnic Conflicts and the Northernisation Policy of the 1950s and 1960s." In *Federalism and Political Restructuring in Nigeria*, edited by Kunle Amuwo, Adigun Agbaje, Rotimi Suberu, and Georges Hérault, 50–63. Ibadan: Spectrum.
Alesina, Alberto, Enrico Spolare, and Romain Wacziarg. 2000. "Economic Integration and Political Disintegration." *American Economic Review* 90 (5):1276–1296.
Alubo, Ogoh. 2009. "Citizenship and Identity Politics in Nigeria." Workshop on Citizenship and Identity Politics in Nigeria, Lagos: CLEEN Foundation/Ford Foundation.
Ammah, Rabiatu. 2007. "Christian-Muslim Relations in Contemporary Sub-Saharan Africa." *Islam and Christian-Muslim Relations* 18 (2):139–153.
Amnesty International. "Nigeria: Gruesome Footage Implicates Nigeria in War Crimes." *Amnesty.org*, August 5, 2014. Accessed July 20, 2016. www.amnesty.org/en/latest/news/2014/08/nigeria-gruesome-footage-implicates-military-war-crimes/.
Anonymous(A). Interview with Leader of a Local Women's Organization, group forum, November 10, 2011. Chikun LGA, Kaduna State, Nigeria.
Anonymous(B). Interview with a Traditional Ruler of Kanam LGA, October 13, 2011. Jos, Plateau State, Nigeria.
Anonymous(C). Interview with University of Jos Professor, September 14, 2011. Jos, Plateau State, Nigeria.

Anonymous(D). Interview with COCIN Pastor, April 15, 2011. Jos, Plateau State, Nigeria.
Anonymous(E). Interview with University of Jos Professor, September 7, 2011. Jos, Plateau State, Nigeria.
Anonymous(F). Interview with Local Scholar/Professor, March 1, 2011. Jos, Plateau State, Nigeria.
Anonymous(G). Interview with University of Jos Professor, April 4, 2011. Jos, Plateau State, Nigeria.
Anonymous(H). Interview with Religious Leader, June 3, 2011. Jos, Plateau State, Nigeria.
Anonymous(I). Interview with Former Member of Chikun's House of Assembly, November 9, 2011. Chikun LGA, Kaduna State, Nigeria.
Anonymous(J). Interview with Chikun LGA Local Leader, Forum Participant, November 10, 2011. Chikun LGA, Kaduna State, Nigeria.
Anonymous(K). Interview with a Former Chairman of Kanam LGA, October 18, 2011. Kanam LGA, Plateau State, Nigeria.
Anonymous(L). Interview with a Former Chairman of Kanam LGA, October 18, 2011. Kanam, Plateau State, Nigeria.
Anonymous(M). Interview with Community Leader in Bassa LGA, October 27, 2011. Bassa LGA, Plateau State, Nigeria.
Anonymous(N). Interview with Chikun LGA Local Peace Activist, October 10, 2011. Jos, Plateau State, Nigeria.
Anonymous(O). Interview with a Former Chairman of Kanam LGA. Kanam LGA, Plateau State, Nigeria.
Anonymous(P). Interview with Local Bassa LGA Chief, October 27, 2011. Bassa LGA, Plateau State, Nigeria.
Anonymous(Q). Interview with Local Bassa LGA Community Member, October 27, 2011. Bassa LGA, Plateau State, Nigeria.
Anonymous(R). Interview with Local Bassa LGA Muslim Chief, October 27, 2011. Bassa LGA, Plateau State, Nigeria.
Anonymous(S). Interview with Chikun LGA Local CAN and JNI Leaders, November 10, 2011. Chikun LGA, Kaduna State, Nigeria.
Anonymous(T). Interview with Local Bassa LGA Chief, October 27, 2011. Bassa LGA, Plateau State, Nigeria.
Anonymous(U). Interview with Bassa LGA Local Peace Activist and Teacher, October 27, 2011. Bassa LGA, Plateau State, Nigeria.
Anonymous(V). Interview with Christian Religious Leader, October 18, 2011. Kanam LGA, Plateau State, Nigeria.
Anonymous(W). Interview with Kanam LGA Local Political Administrator, October 19, 2011. Kanam LGA, Plateau State, Nigeria.
Anonymous(X). Interview with Group Forum Participant (1), November 10, 2011. Chikun LGA, Kaduna State, Nigeria.
Anonymous(Y). Interview with Group Forum Participant (2), November 10, 2011. Chikun LGA, Kaduna State, Nigeria.
Anonymous(Z). Interview with Local Peace Activist, March 29, 2011. Jos, Plateau State, Nigeria.
Anonymous(AA). Interview with Local Scholar, June 28, 2016, Jos, Plateau State.

Anonymous(AB). Interview with Local Scholar, June 28, 2016, Jos, Plateau State.
Arriola, Leonardo. 2009. "Patronage and Political Stability in Africa." *Comparative Political Studies* 42 (10):1339–1362.
Atran, Scott. 2003. "Genesis of Suicide Terrorism." *Science* 299 (5612):1534–1539.
Awolalu, Omosade J. 2001. "The Emergence and Interaction of Religions in Nigeria." *Journal of Religious Thought* 41 (2):7–18.
Ayoade, J. A. A. 1998. "The Ideology of Power-Sharing: An Analysis of Content, Context and Intent." In *Federalism and Political Restructuring in Nigeria*, edited by Kunle Amuwo, Adigun Agbaje, Rotimi Suberu, and Georges Hérault, 121–136. Ibadan: Spectrum Books Limited.
Azari, Julia R. and Jennifer K. Smith. 2012. "Unwritten Rules: Informal Institutions in Established Democracies." *Perspectives on Politics* 10 (1):37–55.
Baba, Yahaya T. 2015. "Executive Dominance, Party Control, and State Legislatures in Nigeria: Evidence from Three States in the Northwest Geopolitical Zone." In *African State Governance: Subnational Politics and National Power*, edited by Carl A. LeVan, Joseph Olayinka Fashagba, and Edward R. McMahon, 121–144. New York: Palgrave Macmillan.
Baca, Michael. "Farmer-Herder Clashes Amplify Challenges for Beleaguered Nigerian Security." IPI Global Observatory, July 16, 2015. Accessed July 20, 2016. www.theglobalobservatory.org/2015/07/farmer-herder-nigeria-buhari-abuja-fulani/.
Bakke, Kristin M. and Erik Wibbels. 2006. "Diversity, Disparity, and Civil Conflict in Federal States." *World Politics* 59 (1):1–50.
Baldwin, Kate. 2014. "When Politicians Cede Control of Resources: Land, Chiefs, and Coalition-Building in Africa." Comparative Politics 46 (3):253–271.
Baldwin, Kate. 2015. The Paradox of Traditional Chiefs in Democratic Africa. New York: Cambridge University Press.
Barnes, Andrew E. 2009. *Making Headway: The Introduction of Western Civilization in Colonial Northern Nigeria*. Rochester: University of Rochester Press.
Barnett, Michael N. and Janice Gross Stein. 2012. *Sacred Aid: Faith and Humanitarianism*. New York: Oxford University Press.
Barnett, Michael and Thomas Weiss. 2008. *Humanitarianism in Question: Politics, Power, Ethics*. Ithaca: Cornell University Press.
Barret, David, George Kurian, and Todd Johnson. 2001. World Christian Encyclopedia. New York: Oxford University Press.
BBCnews. 2011. "Nigerian Gunmen Kill Churchgoers in Zonkwa, Kaduna." *BBCnews*, November 4, 2011. Accessed February 7, 2013. www.bbc.co.uk/news/world-africa-15589201.
Bellin, Eva. 2008. "Faith in Politics: New Trends in Study of Faith and Pol." *World Politics* 60:315–347.
Bellion-Jourdan, Jerome. 2005. "Islamic Organizations: Between Islamism & Humanitarianism." *International Institute for the Study of Islam in the Modern World (ISIM)*.
Benedetti, Carlo. 2006. "Islamic and Christian Inspired Relief NGOs: Between Tactical Collaboration and Strategic Difference." *Journal of International Development* 18 (6):849–859.

Benthall, Jonathan. 2012. "'Cultural Proximity' and the Conjuncture of Islam with Modern Humanitarianism." In *Sacred Aid: Faith and Humanitarianism*, edited by Michael N. Barnett and Janice Gross Stein, 65–89. New York: Oxford University Press.

Berenschot, Ward. 2013. *Riot Politics: Hindu-Muslim Violence and the Indian State*. New York: Columbia University Press.

Berger, Peter L. 1999. "The Desecularization of the World: A Global Overview." In *The Desecularization of the World: Resurgent Religion and World Politics*, edited by Peter L. Berger, 1–18. Washington, D.C.: Ethics and Public Policy Center.

Berger, Peter L. 2008. "Secularization Falsified." *First Things: A Monthly Journal of Religion and Public Life* 180:23–27.

Bertrand, Jacques. 2004. *Nationalism and Ethnic Conflict in Indonesia*. New York: Cambridge University Press.

Best, Shedrack Gaya. 2011. "Religion, Conflict, and Peacebuilding: Conceptual and Theoretical Considerations." In *Religion and PostConflict Peacebuilding in Northern Nigeria*, edited by Shedrack Gaya Best. Ibadan: John Archers Publishers.

Binningsbo, Helga. 2005. "Consociational Democracy and Postconflict Peace: Will Power-Sharing Institutions Increase the Probability of Lasting Peace after Civil War." 13th Annual National Political Science Conference, Hurdalsjoen, Norway, January 5–7, 2005.

Blattman, Christopher and Edward Miguel. 2010. "Civil War." *Journal of Economic Literature* 48 (1):3–57.

Bleaney, Michael and Arcangelo Dimico. 2010. "How Different Are the Correlates of Onset and the Continuation of Civil Wars." *Journal of Peace Research* 48 (2):145–155.

Blench, Robert. 2004. *Natural Resource Conflicts in North-Central Nigeria: A Handbook and Case Studies*. London: Mandaras Publishing. Accessed July 20, 2016. www.rogerblench.info/Development/Nigeria/Pastoralism/Nigeria%20Conflict%20Book.pdf.

Boer, Jan H. 2003. *Nigeria's Decades of Blood 1980–2002, Studies in Christian-Muslim Relations*. Ontario: Essence Publishing.

Boix, Carles. 2008. "Civil Wars and Guerrilla Warfare in the Contemporary World: Toward a Joint Theory of Motivations and Opportunities." In *Order, Conflict, and Violence*, edited by Stathis Kalyvas, Ian Shapiro, and Tarek Masoud, 197–218. New York: Cambridge University Press.

Boone, Catherine. 2003. "Decentralization as Political Strategy in West Africa." *Comparative Political Studies* 36 (4):355–380.

Bornstein, Erica. 2003. *The Spirit of Development: Protestant NGOs, Morality, and Economics in Zimbabwe, Religion in History, Society and Culture*. New York: Routledge.

Brass, Paul R. 2006. *Forms of Collective Violence: Riots, Pogroms, and Genocide in Modern India*. Gurgaon: Three Essays Collectives.

Bratton, Michael and Nicolas Van de Walle. 1997. *Democratic Experiments in Africa: Regime Transitions in Comparative Perspective*. New York: Cambridge University Press.

Brubaker, Rogers and David Laitin. 1998. "Ethnic and Nationalist Violence." *Annual Review of Sociology* 24:423–452.

Bunte, Jonas and Laura Thaut Vinson. 2016. "Local Power-Sharing Institutions and Inter-religious Violence in Nigeria." *Journal of Peace Research* 53 (1): 49–65.

Campbell, John. 2011. *Nigeria: Dancing on the Brink*. 1st ed. Lanham: Rowman and Littlefield Press.

Campbell, John. 2016. "What Makes Boko Haram Run?" *Council on Foreign Relations*, May 5, 2016. Accessed July 20, 2016. www.cfr.org/nigeria/makes-boko-haram-run/p37838.

Casanova, José. 1994. *Public Religions in the Modern World*. Chicago: University of Chicago Press.

Cavanaugh, William T. 2009. *The Myth of Religious Violence: Secular Ideology and the Roots of Modern Conflict*. New York: Oxford University Press.

Cederman, Lars-Erik 2008. "Articulating the Geo-Cultural Logic of Nationalist Insurgency." In *Order, Conflict, and Violence*, edited by Stathis Kalyvas, Ian Shapiro, and Tarek Masoud, 242–270. New York: Cambridge University Press.

Cederman, Lars-Erik, Nils Weidmann, and Kristian Gleditsch. 2011. "Horizontal Inequalities and Ethnonationalist Civil War: A Global Comparison." *American Political Science Review* 205 (3):478–495.

Chandra, Kanchan. 2006. "What Is Ethnic Identity and Does It Matter?" *Annual Review of Political Science* 9:397–424.

Chapman, Thomas and Philip G. Roeder. 2007. "Partition as a Solution to Wars of Nationalism: The Importance of Institutions." *American Political Science Review* 101 (4):677–691.

Cheeseman, Nic. 2015. *Democracy in Africa: Successes, Failures, and the Struggle for Political Reform*. New York: Cambridge University Press.

Cheeseman, Nic and Blessing-Miles Tendi. 2010. "Power-Sharing in Comparative Politics: The Dynamics of 'Unity Government' in Kenya and Zimbabwe." *Journal of Modern African Studies* 48 (2):203–229.

Chesnut, Andrew. 2007. "Specialized Spirits: Conversion and the Products of Pneumacentric Religion in Latin America's Free Market Faith." In *Conversion of a Continent: Contemporary Religious Change in Latin America*, edited by Timothy Cleary and Edward Steigenga, 72–92. Piscataway: Rutgers University Press.

Chester, Lucy. 2008. "Factors Impeding the Effectiveness of Partition in South Asia and the Palestine Mandate." In *Order, Conflict, and Violence*, edited by Stathis Kalyvas, Ian Shapiro, and Tarek Masoud, 75–96. New York: Cambridge University Press.

Chukwuma, Innocent. 2009. "Preface." From the Citizenship and Identity Politics in Nigeria, Conference. Center for Law Enforcement Education in Nigeria (CLEEN) Foundation, Lagos, Nigeria. www.cleen.org/Citizenship%20and%20Identity%20Crisis%20in%20Nigeria.pdf.

Cleary, Edward L. and Hanna W. Stewart-Gambino. 1998. *Power, Politics, and Pentecostals in Latin America*. Boulder: Westview Press.

Collier, Paul and Anke Hoeffler. 1998. "On Economic Causes of Civil War." *Oxford Economic Papers* 50 (4):563–573.

Collier, Paul and Anke Hoeffler. 1998. "Justice-Seeking and Loot-Seeking in Civil War." World Bank, Washington, DC.

Collier, Paul and Anke Hoeffler. 2000. "Greed and Grievance in Civil War." *Policy Research Working Paper*: World Bank.

Collier, Paul, Anke Hoeffler, and Mans Soderbom. 2004. "On the Duration of Civil War." *Journal of Peace Research* 41 (3):253–273.

Collier, Paul and Nicholas Sambanis. 2005. *Understanding Civil War: Evidence and Analysis, Africa*. Washington, D.C.: The World Bank.

Crampton, E. P. T. 2004. *Christianity in Northern Nigeria*. 3rd ed. London/Plateau: African Christian Textbooks.

Crawford, Neta. 2003. "Just War Theory and the U.S. Counterterror War." *Perspectives on Politics* 1 (1):5–25.

Crook, Richard C. and James Manor. 1998. *Democracy and Decentralisation in South Asia and West Africa: Participation, Accountability and Performance*. New York: Cambridge University Press.

Crowder, Michael. 1978. *The Story of Nigeria*. London: Faber and Faber.

Davenport, Christian and Patrick Ball. 2002. Views to a Kill: Exploring the Implications of Source Selection in the Case of Guatemalan State Terror, 1977–1995. *Journal of Conflict Resolution* 46(3): 427–250.

Davidson, Jamie S. 2008. *From Rebellion to Riots: Collective Violence on Indonesian Borneo*. Madison: University of Wisconsin Press.

de Cordier, Bruno. 2008. "The 'Humanitarian Frontline,' Development and Relief, and Religion: What Context, Which Threats and Which Opportunities?" *Third World Quarterly* 30 (4):663–684.

de Cordier, Bruno. 2009. "Faith-based Aid, Globalisation and the Humanitarian Frontline: An Analysis of Western-Based Muslim Aid Organisations." *Disasters* 33 (4):608–628.

de Figueiredo, Rui J. P., Jr., and Barry R. Weingast. 1999."The Rationality of Fear." In *Civil Wars, Insecurity, and Intervention*, edited by Barbara F. Walter and Jack Snyder, 261–302. New York: Columbia University Press.

Diamond, Larry. 2008. "The Rule of Law Versus the Big Man." *Journal of Democracy* 19 (2):138–149.

Dinshak, Luka. 2008. "Conflict Escalation and the Effects of Conflict: The Case of Mikang Local Government Area, Plateau State." In *Causes and Effects of Conflicts in the Southern Zone of Plateau State, Nigeria*, edited by Shedrack Gaya Best, 87–112. Ibadan: John Archers Publishers.

Dixon, David. 1995. "The New Protestantism in Latin America: Remembering What We Already Know, Testing What We Have Learned." *Comparative Politics* 27 (4):479–492.

Donnelly, Jack. 2007. "The Relative Universality of Human Rights." *Human Rights Quarterly* 29 (2):281–306.

Duncan, Christopher R. 2013. *Violence and Vengeance: Religious Conflict and Its Aftermath in Eastern Indonesia*. Ithica: Cornell University Press.

Ebiede, Tarila Marclint. 2016. "Militants are Devastating Nigeria's Oil Industry Again." *Washington Post*, July 11, 2016. Accessed

July 20, 2016. www.washingtonpost,com/news/monkey-cage/wp/2016/07/11/militants-are-again-devastating-nigerias-oil-industry-heres-the-background-you-wont-find-elsewhere/?ct=t(July_15_20167_15_2016)&mc_cid=4eef89efdc&mc_eid=fb004b2640.

Egwu, Samuel. 1998. "Structural Adjustment, Agrarian Change and Rural Ethnicity in Nigeria." Nordiska Afrikainstitutet, Motala Grafiska.

Elaigwu, J. Isawa and Habu Galadima. 2003. "The Shadow of Sharia Over Nigerian Federalism." *Publius: Journal of Federalism* 33 (3):123–144.

Elbadawi, Ibrahim and Nicholas Sambanis. 2000. "Why Are There So Many Civil Wars in Africa? Understanding and Preventing Violent Conflict." *Journal of African Economies* 9 (3):244–269.

Ellingsen, Tanja. 2000. "Colorful Community or Ethnic Witches' Brew? Multiethnicity and Domestic Conflict during and after the Cold War." *Journal of Conflict Resolution* 44 (2):228–249.

Elshtain, Jean Bethke. 2003. *Just War Against Terror: The Burden of American Power in a Violent World*. New York: Basic Books.

Escriba-Folch, Abel. 2010. "Economic Sanctions and the Duration of Civil Conflicts." *Journal of Peace Research* 47 (2):129–141.

Esposito, John L. 1998. "Religion and Global Affairs: Political Challenges." *SAIS Review* 18 (2):19–24.

Esposito, John L. 1999a. *The Islamic Threat: Myth or Reality?* 3rd ed. New York: Oxford University Press.

Esposito, John L. 1999b. "Contemporary Islam: Reformation or Revolution?" In *The Oxford History of Islam*, edited by John L. Esposito, 643–690. New York: Oxford University Press.

Esposito, John L. 2002. *Unholy War: Terror in the Name of Islam*. New York: Oxford University Press.

Esposito, John L. 2011. *Islam: The Straight Path*. 4th ed. New York: Oxford University Press.

Ewokor, Chris. 2016. "The Niger Delta Avengers: Nigeria's Newest Militants." *BBC.com*. June 2, 2016. Accessed July 14, 2016. www.bbc.com/news/world-africa-36414036.

Falola, Toyin. 1998. *Violence in Nigeria: The Crisis of Religious Politics and Secular Ideologies*. Rochester: University of Rochester Press.

Falola, Toyin and Matthew Heaton. 2008. *A History of Nigeria*. New York: Cambridge University Press.

Fashagba, Joseph Olayinka. 2015. "Subnational Legislatures and National Governing Institutions in Nigeria, 1999–2003." In *African State Governance: Subnational Politics and National Power*, edited by Carl A. LeVan, Joseph Olayinka Fashagba, and Edward R. McMahon, 93–120. New York: Palgrave Macmillan.

Fearon, James D. 2004. "Separatist Wars, Partition, and World Order." *Security Studies* 13 (4):394–415.

Fearon, James D. and David D. Laitin. 1996. "Explaining Interethnic Cooperation." *American Political Science Review* 90 (1):715–735.

Fearon, James D. and David D. Laitin. 2000. "Violence and the Social Construction of Ethnic Identity." *International Organization* 54 (4):845–877.

Fearon, James D. and David D. Laitin. 2003. "Ethnicity, Insurgency, and Civil War." *American Political Science Review* 97 (1):75–90.

Ferris, Elizabeth. 2005. "Faith Based and Secular Humanitarian Organizations." *International Review of the Red Cross* 87 (858):311–325.

Fick, Maggie. 2016. "Militants Strike at Heart of Nigeria's Oil Industry." *Financial Times*, July 18, 2016. Accessed July 20, 2016. www.ft.com/cms/s/0/20641fc4-49d9-11e6-8d68-72e9211e86ab.html#axzz4Ez5Yjlyk.

Findley, Michael G. and Joseph K. Young. 2012. "Terrorism and Civil War: A Spatial and Temporal Approach to a Conceptual Problem." *Perspectives on Politics* 10 (2):285–305.

Fox, Jonathan. 2004a. "The Rise of Religious Nationalism and Conflict: Ethnic Conflict and Revolutionary Wars, 1945–2001." *Journal of Peace Research* 41 (6):715–731.

Fox, Jonathan. 2004b. "Religion and State Failure: An Examination of the Extent and Magnitude of Religious Conflict 1950–1996." *International Political Science Review* 25 (1):55–76.

Freston, Paul. 2004. "Evangelical Protestantism and Democratization in Contemporary Latin America and Asia." *Democratization* 11 (4):21–41.

Freston, Paul, ed. 2008. *Evangelical Christianity and Democracy in Latin America*. New York: Oxford University Press.

Freston, Paul. 2011. "Religious Pluralism, Democracy, and Human Rights in Latin America." In *Religion and the Global Politics of Human Rights*, edited by Thomas F. Banchoff and Robert Wuthnow, 101–127. New York: Oxford University Press.

Fujii, Lee Ann. 2009. *Killing Neighbors: Webs of Violence in Rwanda*. Ithaca: Cornell University Press.

Gaffey, Conor. 2016. "Biafra Protests Prompt Separation Anxiety in Nigeria." *Newsweek*, March 1, 2016. Accessed July 20, 2016. www.newsweek.com/nigeria-biafra-nnamdi-kanu-protests-432002.

Gagnon, V. P. 1994/1995. "Ethnic Nationalism and International Conflict: The Case of Serbia." *International Security* 19:130–166.

Galadima, Habu. 2009. "The Federal Republic of Nigeria." In *Global Dialogue on Federalism: Local Government and Metropolitan Regions in Federal Systems*, edited by Kincaid Nico and John Steytler. London: McGill-Queen's University Press.

Gaskill, Newton. 1997. "Rethinking Protestantism and Democratic Consolidation in Latin America." *Sociology of Religion* 58 (1):69–91.

Gates, Scott and Kaare Strom. 2007. "Power-Sharing, Agency and Civil Conflict." In *Power-sharing Agreements, Negotiations and Peace Processes*. Oslo: Center for the Study of Civil War.

Gettleman, Jeffrey. 2012. "At Least 15 Die in Kenya Church Attacks." *New York Times*, July 1, 2012. Accessed July 18, 2012. www.nytimes.com/2012/07/02/world/africa/at-least-15-dead-in-attacks-on-2-churches-in-kenya.html.

Gifford, Paul. 1998. *African Christianity: Its Public Role*. Bloomington: Indiana University Press.

Gill, Anthony. 1998. *Rendering under to Caesar: The Catholic Church and the State in Latin America*. Chicago: University of Chicago Press.

Gill, Anthony. 2002. "Religion and Democracy in South America." In *Religion and Politics in Comparative Perspective*, edited by Ted Wilcox and Clyde Jelen. New York: Cambridge University Press.

Gill, Anthony. 2004. "Weber in Latin America: Is Protestant Growth Enabling Consolidation of Democratic Capitalism?" *Democratization* 11 (4):42–65.

Gill, Anthony. 2005. "The Political Origins of Religious Liberty." *Interdisciplinary Journal of Research on Religion* 1 (1):1–33.

Gonyok, Charles K. and M. Y. Mangvwat. 1981. "The Hausa-Fulani and Their Lot in Jos – A Rejoinder." *Nigerian Standard*, October 12, 1981, 6.

Goshit, Z. D. and Ponfa Kums. 2007. "Land Conflicts in Plateau State since the 1980s." In *Historical Perspectives on Nigeria's Post-colonial Conflicts*, edited by Fwatchak Olayemi, Sati Akinwumi, and Okpeh Ochayi Okpeh, 228–238. Lagos: Unimark Limited.

Grief, Avner and David Laitin. 2004. "A Theory of Endogenous Institutional Change." *American Political Science Review* 98 (4):633–652.

Grim, Brian. 2013. "Restrictions on Religious Freedom: Measures and Implication." In *The Future of Religious Freedom: Global Challenges*, edited by Allen D. Hertzke, 86–104. New York: Oxford University Press.

Grim, Brian J. and Roger Finke. 2011. *The Price of Freedom Denied: Religious Persecution and Conflict in the 21st Century, Cambridge Studies in Social Theory, Religion and Politics*. New York: Cambridge University Press.

Gurr, Ted R. 1970. *Why Men Rebel*. Princeton: Princeton University Press.

Gurr, Ted R. 1993. "Why Minorities Rebel: A Global Analysis of Communal Mobilization and Conflict Since 1945." *International Political Science Review* 14 (2):161–201.

Gurr, Ted R. 2000. *Peoples versus States: Minorities at Risk in the New Century*. Washington, D.C.: United States Institute of Peace.

Gwamna, Je'adayibe Dogara. 2010. *Religion and Politics in Nigeria*. Bukuru: African Christian Textbooks.

Hallum, Anne. 2002. "Looking for Hope in Central America: The Pentecostal Movement." In *Religion and Politics in Comparative Perspective*, edited by Ted Wilcox and Clyde Jelen, 225–239. New York: Cambridge University Press.

Hart, Benedict. 1994. "The Battle for Jos North Chairmanship." *Guardian* (Lagos), April 27, 1994, 13.

Hart, Benedict, and David Oladimeji. 1994. "Curfew Declared in Jos over Violent Demonstrations." *Guardian* (Lagos), April 14, 1994, 1.

Hartzell, Caroline and Matthew Hoddie. 2003. "Institutionalizing Peace: Power Sharing and Post-Civil War Conflict Management." *American Journal of Political Science* 47 (2):318–332.

Hartzell, Caroline, Matthew Hoddie and Donald Rothchild. 2001. "Stabilizing the Peace after Civil War: An Investigation of Some Key Variables." *International Organization* 55 (1):183–208.

Hassner, Ron E. 2013. *War on Sacred Grounds*. New Haven: Cornell University Press.

Hausa-Fulani Elders' Forum. 2009. "Jos Ethno-Religious Crisis Is a Time Bomb Capable of Disintegrating Nigeria." *Guardian* (Lagos), January 14, 2009.

Hechter, Michaeland Nika Kabiri. 2008. "Attaining Social Order in Iraq." In *Order, Conflict, and Violence*, edited by Stathis Kalyvas, Ian Shapiro, and Tarek Masoud. New York: Cambridge University Press.

Hegre, Havard. 2004. "The Duration and Termination of Civil War." *Journal of Peace Research* 41 (3):243–252.

Hegre, Havard., Tanja Ellingsen, Scott Gates, and Nils Petter Gleditsch. 2001. "Toward a Democratic Civil Peace? Democracy, Political Change, and Civil War, 1816–1992." *American Political Science Review* 95 (1):33–48.

Helmke, Gretchen and Steven Levitsky. 2004. "Informal Institutions and Comparative Politics: A Research Agenda." *Perspectives on Politics* 2 (4):725–740.

Helmke, Gretchen and Steven Levitsky, eds. 2006. *Informal Institutions and Democracy: Lessons from Latin America*. Baltimore: Johns Hopkins University Press.

Hertzke, Allen D. 2013. *The Future of Religious Freedom: Global Challenges*. New York: Oxford University Press.

Hoddie, Matthew and Caroline Hartzell. 2010. *Strengthening Peace in Post-Civil War States: Transforming Spoilers into Stake-holders*. Chicago: University of Chicago Press.

Hoffman, Bruce. 2006. *Inside Terrorism*. New York: Columbia University Press.

Hoomlong, Katherine Naanzoem. 2008. "The Causes and Effects of Conflict in Shendam Local Government Area, Plateau State." In *Causes and Effects of Conflicts in the Southern Zone of Plateau State, Nigeria*, edited by Shedrack Gaya Best, 24–64. Ibadan: John Archers Publishers.

Horowitz, Donald. 1985. *Ethnic Groups in Conflict*. Berkeley: University of California Press.

Horowitz, Donald. 2001. *The Deadly Ethnic Riot*. Berkeley: University of California Press.

Horowitz, Donald. 2002. "Constitutional Design: Proposals versus Processes." In *The Architecture of Democracy: Constitutional Design, Conflict Management, and Democracy*, edited by Andrew Reynolds, 15–36. New York: Oxford University Press.

Horowitz, Donald. 2004. "Some Realism about Constitutional Engineering." In *Facing Ethnic Conflict: Toward a New Realism*, edited by Andreas Wimmer, Richard J. Goldstone, Donald Horowitz, Ulrike Jora, and Conrad Schetter, 245–257. Lanham: Rowman & Littlefield Publishers.

Human Rights Watch. 2001. "Jos: A City Torn Apart." Accessed August 2, 2010. www.hrw.org/node/76878.

Human Rights Watch. 2005 (May 25). "Revenge in the Name of Religion: The Cycle of Violence in Plateau and Kano States." Accessed August 30, 2011. www.hrw.org/en/reports/2005/05/24/revenge-name-religion-0.

Human Rights Watch. 2006 (April 26). "They Do Not Own This Place: Government Discrimination against 'Non-Indigenous' in Nigeria." Accessed April 8, 2012. www.hrw.org/report/2006/04/25/they-do-not-own-place/government-discrimination-against-non-indigenes-nigeria.

Human Rights Watch. 2007. "Criminal Politics, Violence, 'Godfathers' and Corruption in Nigeria." www.hrw.org/sites/default/files/reports/nigeria1007webwcover_0.pdf.

Human Rights Watch. 2009 (Nov 26). "Nigeria: Prosecute Killings by Security Forces." Accessed August 5, 2014. www.hrw.org/news/2009/11/26/nigeria-prosecute-killings-security-forces.

Human Rights Watch. 2010 (Jan 19). "Nigeria: Use Restraint in Curbing Jos Violence." Accessed August 2, 2010. www.hrw.org/news/2010/01/19/nigeria-use-restraint-curbing-jos-violence.

Human Rights Watch. 2011. "Nigeria Post-election Violence Killed 800." Accessed February 7, 2013. www.hrw.org/news/2011/05/16/nigeria-post-election-violence-killed-800.

Human Rights Watch. 2012 (Oct 11). "Nigerians Caught in the Crossfire." Accessed August 5, 2014. www.hrw.org/news/2012/10/11/nigerians-caught-crossfire.

Human Rights Watch. 2013 (Dec 12). "Leave Everything to God: Accountability for Inter-communal Violence in Kaduna and Plateau States, Nigeria." Accessed June 24, 2014. www.hrw.org/node/121280.

Human Rights Watch. 2014. "Nigeria: Escalating Communal Violence." Accessed July 14. www.hrw.org/news/2014/04/15/nigeria-escalating-communal-violence.

Humprheys, Macartan and Jeremy Weinstei. 2008. "Who Fights? The Determinants of Participation in Civil War." *American Journal of Political Science* 52 (2):436–455.

Idunwo, Sunny. 1999. "The Burden of Kafanchan History." *Guardian* (Lagos), June 5, 1999.

International Crisis Group. 2010. "Northern Nigeria: Background to Conflict." Accessed June 14, 2011. www.reliefweb.int/sites/reliefweb.int/files/resources/880F82BDF4CF7582C12577FF0050EB69-Full_report.pdf.

Isuwa, Sunday. 2011. "Post-election Violence Costs Kaduna N10bn.'" *Daily Trust*, December 14, 2011.

Jarstad, Anna. 2006. "The Logic of Power-Sharing after Civil War." Workshop on Power-Sharing and Democratic Governance in Divided Society, Center for the Study of Civil War, PRIO, Oslo, Norway, August 21–22, 2006.

Jarstad, Anna. 2008. "Former Enemies in Joint Governance." In *From War to Democracy: Dilemmas of Peacebuilding*, edited by Anna Jarstad and Timothy Sisk, 105–133. New York: Cambridge University Press.

Jarstad, Anna. 2009. "The Prevalence of Power-Sharing: Exploring the Patterns of Post-election Peace." *Africa Spectrum* 44 (3):41–62.

Jelen, Ted and Clyde Wilcox, eds. 2002. *Religion and Politics in Comparative Perspective: The One, the Few, and the Many*. New York: Cambridge University Press.

Jenkins, Philip. 2002. "The Next Christianity." *The Atlantic Monthly*, Oct 2002, 53–68.

Jenkins, Philip. 2002. *The Next Christendom: The Coming of Global Christianity*. London: Oxford University Press.

Jenkins, Philip. 2011. *The Next Christendom: The Coming of Global Christianity*. 3rd ed. New York: Oxford University Press.
Johnson, Carter. 2008. "Partitioning to Peace: Sovereignty, Demography, and Ethnic Civil Wars." *International Security* 32 (4):140–170.
Johnson, Todd, ed. 2007. *World Christian Database*. Leiden/Boston: Brill.
Johnson, Todd and Sun Young Chung. 2004. "Tracking Global Christianity's Statistical Centre of Gravity." *International Review of Mission* 93 (369):166–181.
Joseph, Richard. 1987. *Democracy and Prebendelism in Nigeria*. New York: Cambridge University Press.
Jung, Courtney, Ellen Lust-Okar, and Ian Shapiro. 2008. "Problems and Prospects for Democratic Settlements: South Africa as a Model for the Middle East and Northern Ireland." In *Order, Conflict, and Violence*, edited by Stathis Kalyvas, Ian Shapiro, and Tarek Masoud, 139–194. New York: Cambridge University Press.
Justino, Patricia. 2009. "Poverty and Violent Conflict: A Micro-level Perspective on the Causes and Duration of Warfare." *Journal of Peace Research* 46 (3):315–333.
Kalu, Kalu N. 2009. *State Power, Autarchy, and Political Conquest in Nigerian Federalism*. Lanham: Rowman & Littlefield Publishers.
Kalu, Ogbu. 2008. *African Pentecostalism: An Introduction*. New York: Oxford University Press.
Kalyvas, Stathis. 2003. "The Ontology of 'Political Violence': Action and Identity in Civil Wars." *Perspectives on Politics* 1 (3):475–494.
Kalyvas, Stathis. 2008. "Promises and Pitfalls of an Emerging Research Program: The Microdynamics of Civil War." In *Order, Conflict, and Violence*, edited by Stathis Kalyvas, Ian Shapiro, and Tarek Masoud, 397–421. New York: Cambridge University Press.
Kaufmann, Chaim. 1996. "Possible and Impossible Solutions to Ethnic Civil Wars." *International Security* 20 (4):136–175.
Kaufman, Stuart J. 2001. *Modern Hatreds: The Symbolic Politics of Ethnic War*. Ithica: Cornell University Press.
King, Charles. 2012. "Can There Be a Political Science of the Holocaust." *Perspectives on Politics* 10 (2):323–341.
Kukah, Matthew H. 2003. *Religion, Politics, and Power in Northern Nigeria*. Ibadan: Spectrum Books.
Kuperman, Alan J., ed. 2015. *Constitutions and Conflict Management in Africa: Preventing Civil War through Institutional Design*. Philadelphia: University of Pennsylvania Press.
Ladan, Muhammed Tawfiq. 1999. "The Role of Youth in Inter-ethnic and Religious Conflicts: The Kaduna/Kano Case Study." In *Inter-Ethnic and Religious Conflict Resolution in Nigeria*, edited by Ernest E. Uwazie, Isaac O. Albert, and Godfrey N. Uzoigwe, 97–111. Oxford: Lexington Books.
Laitin, David D. 1986. *Hegemony and Culture: Politics and Religious Change among the Yoruba*. Chicago: University of Chicago Press.
Lake, David A. and Rothchild, Donald. 1996. "Containing Fear: The Origins and Management of Ethnic Conflict," *International Security* 21 (2): 41–75.

Laremont, Ricardo Rene. 2011. *Islamic Law and Politics in Northern Nigeria*. Africa World Press.

Lauren, Paul Gordon. 2011. *The Evolution of International Human Rights: Visions Seen*. 3rd ed, *Pennsylvania Studies in Human Rights*. Philadelphia: University of Pennsylvania Press.

Lemarchand, Rene. 1972. "Political Clientelism and Ethnicity in Tropical Africa: Competing Solidarities in Nation-building." *American Political Science Review* 66 (1):68–90.

Lemarchand, Rene. 2006. "Consociationalism and Power Sharing in Africa: Rwanda, Burundi, and the Democratic Republic of Congo." *African Affairs* 106 (422):1–20.

LeVan, Carl A. 2011. "Power Sharing and Inclusive Politics in Africa's Uncertain Democracies." *International Journal of Policy, Administration, and Institutions* 24 (1):31–53.

LeVan, Carl A., Joseph Olayinka Fashagba, and Edward R. McMahon. 2015. *African State Governance: Subnational Politics and National Power*. New York: Palgrave Macmillan.

Lewis, Peter M. 2011. "Nigeria Votes: More Openness, More Conflict." *Journal of Democracy* 22 (4):60–74.

Lewis, Peter and Darren Kew. 2015. "Nigeria's Hopeful Election." *Journal of Democracy* 26 (3):94–109.

Lijphart, Arend. 1977. *Democracy in Plural Societies: A Comparative Exploration*. New Haven: Yale University Press.

Lijphart, Arend. 2002. "The Wave of Power-Sharing Democracy." In *The Architecture of Democracy: Constitutional Design, Conflict Management, and Democracy*, edited by Andrew Reynolds, 37–54. New York: Oxford University Press.

Lumsdaine, David H., ed. 2009. *Evangelical Christianity and Democracy in Asia*. New York: Oxford University Press.

MacLean, Lauren Morris. 2004. "Mediating Ethnic Conflict at the Grassroots: The Role of Local Associational Life in Shaping Political Values in Cote d' Ivoire and Ghana." *Journal of Modern African Studies* 42 (4):589–617.

Magesa, Laurenti. 2007. "Contemporary Catholic Perspectives on Christian-Muslim Relations in Sub-Saharan Africa: The Case of Tanzania." *Islam and Christian-Muslim Relations* 18 (2):165–173.

Mamdani, Mahmood. 1996. *Citizen and Subject: Contemporary Africa and the Legacy of Late Colonialism, Princeton Series in Culture/Power/History*. New Jersey: Princeton University Press.

Mangvwat, Monday Yakiban. 2011. "Historical Insights on Plateau Indigene-Settler Syndrome, 1902–2011." Workshop on Citizenship and Indigeneity Conflicts in Nigeria, Abuja.

Marostica, Matthew. 1998. "Religion and Global Affairs: Religious Activation and Democracy in Latin America." *SAIS Review* 18 (2):45–51.

Marsden, Lee. 2012. *The Ashgate Research Companion to Religion and Conflict Resolution, Religion and International Security*. Burlington: Ashgate.

Marshall, Ruth. 2009. *Political Spiritualities: The Pentecostal Revolution in Nigeria*. Chicago: University of Chicago Press.

Martin, David. 1990. *Tongues of Fire: The Explosion of Protestantism in Latin America*. Oxford: Blackwell.
Mead, Timothy M. 1996. "Barriers to Local-Government Capacity in Nigeria." *American Review of Public Administration* 26 (2):159–173.
Mehler, Andreas. 2009. "Peace and Power Sharing in Africa: A Not So Obvious Relationship." *African Affairs* 108 (432):453–473.
Miguel, Edward, Shanker Satyanath, and Ernest Sergenti. 2004. "Economic Shocks and Civil Conflict: An Instrumental Variables Approach." *Journal of Political Economy* 112 (4):725–753.
Miller, Donald E., Kimon H. Sargeant, and Richard Flory. 2013. *Spirit and Power: The Growth and Global Impact of Pentecostalism*. New York: Oxford University Press.
Mohamed, Charmain. 2006. "Justice in Jakarta." *Human Rights Watch*. Accessed July 30, 2010. www.hrw.org/en/news/2006/11/19/justice-jakarta.
Mueller, John. 2000. "The Banality of 'Ethnic War.'" *International Security* 25 (1):42–70.
Mukoro, Akpomuvire. 2003. "The Evolution of a Democratic Local Government System in Nigeria." *Journal of Social Science* 7 (3):171–179.
Musa, Gaiya. 2004. "Christianity in Northern Nigeria." *Exchange* 33 (4):354–371.
Mustapha, Abdul Raufu. 2003. "Ethnic Minority Groups in Nigeria – Current Situation and Major Problems." Commission on Human Rights: Subcommission on Promotion and Protection of Human Rights, Working Group on Minorities, Ninth Session, Queen Elizabeth House, University of Oxford, May 12–16.
Nasr, S. V.R. 1999. "European Colonialism and the Emergence of Modern Muslim States." In *The Oxford History of Islam*, edited by John L. Esposito, 549–600. New York: Oxford University Press.
National Population Commission. 2006. "Population and Housing Census of the Federal Republic of Nigeria: Priority Tables." Abuja: Federal Republic of Nigeria.
National Population Commission. 2010. "Federal Republic of Nigeria 2006 Population and Housing Census: Population Distribution by Sex, State, LGA, and Senatorial District." Abuja: Federal Republic of Nigeria.
Ndam, Lohdam, ed. 2001. *The Challenge of Developing Nigeria's Local Government Areas*. Jos: Mgbangzee Ventures.
Norris, Pippa. 2008. *Driving Democracy: Do Power-Sharing Institutions Work?* New York: Cambridge University Press.
Norris, Pippa and Ronald Inglehart. 2004. *Sacred and Secular: Religion and Politics Worldwide*. New York: Cambridge University Press.
Nwafor, John. 2002. *Church and State: The Nigerian Experience*. Frankfurt: IKO-Verlag Fur Interkulterelle Kommunikation.
Obayuwana, Oghogho and Musa Njadvara. 2011. "NEMA Reunites 20,000 Kaduna Violence Victims with Families." Guardian (Lagos), May 2, 2011, 7.
Ofuoku, A. U. and B. I. Isife. 2009. "Causes, Effects and Resolution of Farmers-Nomadic Cattle Herders Conflict in Delta State, Nigeria." *International Journal of Sociology and Anthropology* 1 (2):047–054.

Okpanachi, Eyene. 2012. "Ethno-Religious Identity and Conflict in Northern Nigeria: Understanding the Dynamics of Sharia in Kaduna and Kebbi States." Ibadan: French Institute for Research in Africa.

Ololade, Olatunji. 2011. "You Do Not Own This Land." *Nation*. Accessed February 7, 2013. www.thenationonlineng.net/2011/index.php/mobile/colu mnist/friday/olatunji-ololade/24452-you-do-not-own-this-land.html.

Olowu, Dele, and James S. Wunsch. 2004. *Local Governance in Africa: The Challenges of Democratic Decentralization*. Boulder: Lynne Rienner Publishers.

Osadolor, Osarhieme Benson. 1998. "The Development of the Federal Idea and the Federal Framework, 1914–1960." In *Federalism and Political Restructuring in Nigeria*, edited by Kunle Amuwo, Adigun Agbaje, Rotimi Suberu, and Georges Hérault, 34–49. Ibadan: Spectrum Books Limited.

Osaghae, Eghosa. 1998. *Crippled Giant: Nigeria since Independence*. Bloomington: Indiana University Press.

Osaghae, Eghosa. 2015. "Nigeria: Devolution to Mitigate Conflict in the Niger Delta." In *Constitutions and Conflict Management in Africa: Preventing Civil War through Institutional Design*, edited by in Alan J. Kuperman. Philadelphia: University of Pennsylvania Press.

Osaghae, Eghosa E. and Rotimi T. Suberu. 2005. "A History of Identities, Violence, and Stability in Nigeria." Working Paper No. 6, Centre for Research on Inequality, Human Security and Ethnicity (CRISE).

Osinubi, Tokunbo Simbowale and Sunday Osinubi Oladipupo. 2006. "Ethnic Conflicts in Contemporary Africa: The Nigerian Experience." *Journal of Social Science* 12 (2):101–114.

Ostein, Philip. 2009. "Jonah Jang and the Jasawa: Ethno-Religious Conflict in Jos, Nigeria." In *Muslim-Christian Relations in Africa*, edited by John Chesworth and Franz Kogelmann. February 18, 2011. www.sharia-in-africa.net/pages/p ublications/jonah-jang-and-the-jasawa-ethno-religious-conflict-in-jos-nigeria .php.

Oyediran, Oyeleye and Alex E. Gboyega. 1979. "Local Government and Administration." In *Nigerian Government and Politics under Military Rule 1966–79*, edited by Oyeleye Oyediran, 169–191. New York: St. Martin's Press.

Oyekale, A. S., A. I. Adeoti, and T. O. Oyekale. 2006. "Measurement and Sources of Income Inequality in Rural and Urban Nigeria." Session Paper, 5th PEP Research Network General Meeting, Addis Ababa, June 18–22, 2006.

Oyugi, Walter O. 2006. "Coalition Politics and Coalition Government in Africa." *Journal of Contemporary African Studies* 24 (1):52–79.

Paden, John N. 2005. *Muslim Civic Cultures and Conflict Resolution: The Challenge of Democratic Federalism in Nigeria*. Washington, D.C.: Brookings Institution Press.

Paden, John N. 2008. *Faith and Politics in Nigeria: Nigeria as a Pivotal State in the Muslim World*. Washington, D.C.: United States Institute of Peace.

Paden, John. 2012. *Postelection Conflict Management in Nigeria: The Challenges of National Unity*. Arlington: School for Conflict Analysis and Resolution, George Mason University.

Patterson, Eric. 2005. "Religious Activity and Political Participation: The Brazilian and Chilean Cases." *Latin American Politics and Society* 47 (1):1–29.

Pérouse de Montclos, Marc-Antoine. 2014a. "Nigeria's Interminable Insurgency? Addressing the Boko Haram Crisis." Chantham House: The Royal Institute of International Affairs. Accessed October 7. www.chathamhouse.org/publication/nigerias-interminable-insurgency-addressing-boko-haram-crisis.

Pérouse de Montclos, Marc-Antoine, ed. 2014b. *Boko Haram: Islamism, Politics, Security and the State in Nigeria*. Vol. 2. Leiden: African Studies Center; French Institute for Research in Africa.

Pew Research Center. "Religious Demographic Profile, Nigeria." Pew Forum on Religion and Public Life. Accessed October 3, 2009. www.pewforum.org/world-affairs/countries/?CountryID=150.

Pew Research Center. 2006. "Spirit and Power: A 10-Country Survey of Pentecostals." Washington, D.C.: The Pew Forum on Religion and Public Life. www.pewforum.org/2006/10/05/spirit-and-power/.

Pew Research Center. 2010. "Tolerance and Tension: Islam and Christianity in Sub-Saharan Africa." Pew Forum on Religion and Public Life. Accessed October 4, 2010. www.pewforum.org/download-the-full-report-islam-and-christianity-in-sub-saharan-africa.aspx.

Pew Research Center. 2012. "The Global Religious Landscape: A Report on the Size and Distribution of the World's Major Religious Groups as of 2010." In *Pew-Templeton Global Religious Futures Project*. Washington, D.C.: Pew Forum on Religion and Public Life. Accessed May 2013. www.pewforum.org/2012/12/18/global-religious-landscape-exec/.

Pew Research Center. 2015. "The Future of World Religions: Population Growth Projections 2010–2050." Pew Forum on Religion and Public Life. www.pewforum.org/files/2015/03/PF_15.04.02_ProjectionsFullReport.pdf.

Philpott, Daniel. 2004. "Christianity and Democracy: The Catholic Wave." *Journal of Democracy* 15 (2):32–46.

Philpott, Daniel. 2007. "Explaining the Political Ambivalence of Religion." *American Political Science Review* 101 (3):505–525.

Philpott, Daniel. 2009. "Has the Study of Global Politics Found Religion?" *Annual Review of Political Science* 12:183–202.

Piazza, James. 2009. "Is Islamist Terrorism More Dangerous?: An Empirical Study of Group Ideology, Organization, and Goal Structure." *Terrorism & Political Violence* 21 (1):62–88.

Plateau State of Nigeria. 2004. Plateau Resolves: Report of the Plateau Peace Conference (18th August–21 September 2004). Jos.

Posen, Barry. 1993. "The Security Dilemma and Ethnic Conflict." *Survival: Global Politics and Strategy* 35 (1):27–47.

Posner, Daniel N. 2004. "The Political Salience of Cultural Differences: Why Chewas and Tumbukas are Allies in Zambia and Adversaries in Malawi." *American Political Science Review* 98 (4):529–545.

Posner, Daniel N. 2005. *Institutions and Ethnic Politics in Africa*. New York: Cambridge University Press.

Quinn, Kevin, Michael Hechter, and Erik Wibbels. 2004. "Ethnicity, Insurgency, and Civil War Revisited." (Unpublished Paper). Seattle: University of Washington.

Ranger, Terance O. 2008a. "Afterward." In *Evangelical Christianity and Democracy in Africa*, edited by Terence O. Ranger, 231–241. New York: Oxford University Press.

Ranger, Terance O., ed. 2008b. *Evangelical Christianity and Democracy in Africa*. New York: Oxford University Press.

Reynal-Querol, Marta. 2002. "Ethnicity, Political Systems, and Civil Wars." *Journal of Conflict Resolution* 46 (1):29–54.

Roe, Paul. 1999. "The Intrastate Security Dilemma: Ethnic Conflict as a 'Tragedy'?" *Journal of Peace Research* 36 (2):183–202.

Rothchild, Donald and Philip G. Roeder. 2005a. "Dilemmas of State-Building in Divided Societies." In *Sustainable Peace: Power and Democracy after Civil War*, edited by Donald Rothchild and Philip G. Roeder. 1–25. Ithaca: Cornell University Press.

Rothchild, Donald and Philip G. Roeder. 2005b. "Power Sharing as an Impediment to Peace and Democracy." In *Sustainable Peace: Power and Democracy after Civil War*, edited by Donald Rothchild and Philip G. Roeder, 29–50. Ithaca: Cornell University Press.

Saideman, Stephen, David Lanoue, Michael Campenni, and Samuel Stanton. 2002. "Democratization, Political Institutions, and Ethnic Conflict: A Pooled Time-Series Analysis, 1985–1998." *Comparative Political Studies* 35 (1):103–129.

Sambanis, Nicholas. 2000. "Partition as a Solution to Ethnic War: An Empirical Critique of the Theoretical Literature." *World Politics* 52 (4):437–483.

Sambanis, Nicholas. 2001. "Do Ethnic and Non-ethnic Civil Wars Have the Same Cause?" *Journal of Conflict Resolution* 45 (3):259–282.

Sambanis, Nicholas. 2004. "Using Case Studies to Expand Economic Models of Civil War." *Perspectives on Politics* 2:259–279.

Sambanis, Nicholas and Håvard Hegre. 2006. "Sensitivity Analysis of Empirical Results on Civil War Onset." *Journal of Conflict Resolution* 50 (4):508–535.

Sambanis, Nicholas and Jonah Schulhofer-Wohl. 2009. "What's in a Line? Is Partition a Solution to Civil War?" *International Security* 34 (2):82–118.

Samuel, Obadiah, Chris Kwaja and Angela Olofu-Adeoye. 2011. "The Challenge of PostConflict Partitioning of Contested Cities in Northern Nigeria: A Case Study of Jos North LGA." In *Religion and PostConflict Peacebuilding in Northern Nigeria*, edited by Shedrack Gaya Best. Jos: John Archers Publishers.

Sayne, Aaron. 2013. "What's Next for Security in the Niger Delta?" United States Institute of Peace: Special Report, April 26, 2013.

Searcey, Dionne. 2016. "Nigeria Finds a National Crisis in Every Direction It Turns." *New York Times*, July 17, 2016. Accessed July 20, 2016. www.nytimes.com/2016/07/18/world/africa/nigeria-niger-delta-buhari-oil-militants.html?_r=0.

Schwedler, Jillian. 2006. *Faith in Moderation: Islamist Parties in Yemen and Jordan*. New York: Cambridge University Press.

Shah, Timothy Samuel. 2009. "Preface." In *Evangelical Christianity and Democracy in Asia*, edited by David H. Lumsdaine, vii–xx. New York: Oxford University Press.

Sidel, John T. 2006. *Riots, Pogroms, Jihad: Religious Violence in Indonesia*. Ithaca: Cornell University Press.

Sisk, Timothy. 1996. *Power Sharing and International Mediation in Ethnic Conflicts*. Washington, D.C.: United States Institute of Peace.

Snyder, Jack, ed. 2011. *Religion and International Relations Theory*. New York: Cambridge University Press.

Spears, Ian. 2000. "Understanding Inclusive Peace Agreements in Africa: The Problems of Power Sharing." *Third World Quarterly* 21 (1):105–118.

Spears, Ian. 2002. "Africa: The Limits of Power-Sharing." *Journal of Democracy* 13 (3):123–136.

Staniland, Paul. 2012. "States, Insurgents, and Wartime Political Orders." *Perspectives on Politics* 10 (2):243–264.

Steigenga, Timothy and Edward Cleary. 2007. *Conversion of a Continent: Contemporary Religious Change in Latin America*. Piscataway: Rutgers University Press.

Stein, Chris. 2016. "Farmer-Herder Conflict Rises across Nigeria." *Voice of America*, May 11, 2016. Accessed July 20, 2016. www.voanews.com/content/farmer-herder-conflict-rises-acrossnigeria/3326151.html.

Stinton, Diane. 2004. *Jesus of Africa: Voices of Contemporary African Christology, Faith and Culture*. Maryknoll: Orbis Books.

Straus, Scott. 2012. "Retreating from the Brink: Theorizing Mass Violence and the Dynamics of Restraint." *Perspectives on Politics* 10 (2):343–362.

Suberu, Rotimi T. 2001. *Federalism and Ethnic Conflict in Nigeria*. Washington, D.C.: United States Institute of Peace.

Suberu, Rotimi T. 2009. "Religion and Institutions: Federalism and the Management of Conflicts over Sharia in Nigeria." *Journal of International Development* 21:547–560.

Suberu, Rotimi T. 2013. "Prebendal Politics and Federal Governance in Nigeria." In *Democracy and Prebendalism in Nigeria: Critical Interpretations*, edited by Wale Adebanwi and Ebenezer Obadare, 79–102. New York: Palgrave Macmillan.

Suberu, Rotimi T. 2015. "Lessons in Fiscal Federalism for Africa's New Oil Exporters." In *African State Governance: Subnational Politics and National Power*, edited by Carl A. LeVan, Joseph Olayinka Fashagba, and Edward R. McMahon, 31–58. New York: Palgrave Macmillan.

Svensson, Isak. 2012. *Ending Holy Wars: Religion and Conflict Resolution in Civil Wars*. St Lucia, Queensland: University of Queensland Press.

Tamuno, Tekena N. 1998. "Nigerian Federalism in Historical Perspective." In *Federalism and Political Restructuring in Nigeria*, edited by 'Kunle Amuwo, Adigun Agbaje, Rotimi Suberu, and Georges Hérault, 13–33. Ibadan: Spectrum Books Limited.

Thaut, Laura. 2009. "The Role of Faith in Christian Faith-based Humanitarian Agencies: Constructing the Taxonomy." *Voluntas: International Journal of Voluntary and Nonprofit Organizations* 20 (4):319–350.

Thaut, Laura, Janice Gross Stein, and Michael Barnett. 2012. "In Defense of Virtue: Credibility, Legitimacy Dilemmas, and the Case of Islamic Relief." In *The Credibility of Transnational NGOs: When Virtue Is Not Enough*, edited by Peter A. Gourevitch, David A. Lake, and Janice Gross Stein, 137–164. New York: Cambridge University Press.

Thomas, Scott. 2005. *The Global Resurgence of Religion and the Transformation of International Relations: The Struggle for the Soul of the Twenty-first Century*. Edited by Yosef Lapid and Friedrich Kratochwil, *Culture and Religion in International Relations*. New York: Palgrave Macmillan.

Todd, Johnson, ed. 2007. *World Christian Database*. Edited by Brill. Leiden/Boston.

Toft, Monica Duffy. 2006. "Religion, Civil War, and International Order." BCSIA Discussion Paper 2006–03, Kennedy School of Government, Harvard University, July.

Toft, Monica Duffy. 2007. "Getting Religion? The Puzzling Case of Islam and Civil War." *International Security* 31 (4):97–131.

Toft, Monica Duffy, Daniel Philpott, and Timothy Samuel Shah. 2011. *God's Century: Resurgent Religion and Global Politics*. 1st ed. New York: W. W. Norton.

Trianello, Marisa. 2008. "Power-Sharing: Lessons from South Africa and Rwanda." *International Public Policy Review* 3 (2):28–43.

Tsai, Kellee S. 2006. "Adaptive Informal Institutions and Endogenous Institutional Change in China." *World Politics* 59 (1):116–141.

Tull, Denis M. and Andreas Mehler. 2005. "The Hidden Costs of Power-Sharing: Reproducing Insurgent Violence in Africa." *African Affairs* 104 (416):375–398.

Turaki, Yusufu. 1993. *The British Colonial Legacy in Northern Nigeria: A Social Ethical Analysis of the Colonial and Post-colonial Society and Politics in Nigeria*. Jos: Challenge Press.

Turaki, Yusufu. 1999. *Theory and Practice of Christian Missions in Africa: A Century of SIM/ECWA History and Legacy in Nigeria, 1893–1993*. Nairobi: International Bible Society Nigeria Press.

Turaki, Yusufu. 2010. *Tainted Legacy: Islalm, Colonialism and Slavery in Northern Nigeria*. McLean: Isaac Publishing.

Ukiwo, Ukoha. 2006. "Creation of Local Government Areas and Ethnic Conflicts in Nigeria: The Case of Warri, Delta State." CRISE West Africa Workshop, Accra, Ghana.

Umaru, Sani. 1981. "The Hausa/Fulani and Their Lot in Jos (2)." *New Nigerian*, October 18, 1981, 8–9, 12.

United Nations Development Program. 2010. *Human Development Report Nigeria, 2008–2009*. Abuja: UNDP.
United Nations Population Division. 2013. "World Population Prospects: The 2012 Revision, Key Findings and Advance Tables." United Nations Department of Economic and Social Affairs.
Uzoma, Rose C. 2004. "Religious Pluralism, Cultural Differences, and Social Stability in Nigeria." *Brigham Young University Law Review* (2):651–664.
Van de Walle, Nicolas. 2009. "Opposition Weakness in Africa." *Journal of Democracy* 20 (3):108–121.
Vandeginste, Stef. 2009. "Power-Sharing, Conflict and Transition in Burundi: Twenty Years of Trial and Error." *Africa Spectrum* 3:63–86.
Varshney, Ashutosh. 2002. *Ethnic Conflict and Civic Life: Hindus and Muslims in India*. New Haven: Yale University Press.
Varshney, Ashutosh. 2003. "Nationalism, Ethnic Conflict, and Rationality." *Perspectives on Politics* 1 (1):85–99.
Verdeja, Ernesto. 2012. "The Political Science of Genocide: Outlines of an Emerging Research Agenda." *Perspectives on Politics* 10 (2):307–321.
Voll, John Obert. 1999. "Foundations for Renewal and Reform: Islamic Movements in the Eighteenth and Nineteenth Centuries." In *The Oxford History of Islam*, edited by John L. Esposito, 509–548. New York: Oxford University Press.
Walker, Andrew. 2012. What Is Boko Haram? United States Institute of Peace. www.dev.usip.org/sites/default/files/SR308.pdf.
Walter, Barbara and Jack Snyder. 1999. *Civil Wars, Insecurity, and Intervention*. New York: Columbia University Press.
Wickham, Carrie. 2004. "The Path to Moderation: Strategy and Learning in the Formation of Egypt's Wasat Party." *Comparative Politics* 36 (2):205–228.
Wiktorowicz, Quintan and Karl Kaltenthaler. 2006. "The Rationality of Radical Islam." *Political Science Quarterly* 121 (2):295–319.
Wilkinson, Steven I. 2004. *Votes and Violence: Electoral Competition and Ethnic Riots in India*. New York: Cambridge University Press.
Wilkinson, Steven I. 2008. "Which Group Identities Lead to Most Violence? Evidence from India." In *Order, Conflict, and Violence*, edited by Stathis Kalyvas, Ian Shapiro, and Tarek Masoud, 271–300. New York: Cambridge University Press.
Wood, Elizabeth Jean. 2015. "The Emotional Benefits of Insurgency in El Salvador." In *The Social Movements Reader: Cases and Concepts*, 3rd ed, edited by Jeff Goodwin and James Jasper, 143–152. Malden: Wiley-Blackwell.
Woodberry, Robert. 2012. The Missionary Roots of Liberal Democracy. *American Political Science Review* 106(2): 244–274.
Woodberry, Robert and Timothy Samuel Shah. 2005. *World Religions and Democracy*. Edited by Larry Jay Diamond, Marc F. Plattner, and Philip J. Costopoulos, *A Journal of Democracy Book*. Baltimore, MD: Johns Hopkins University Press.
World Bank. 2011. "Data: The Latest African Development Indicators Are Now Available." Accessed December 18, 2013. www.data.worldbank.org/news/african-development-indicators-2011.

World Bank. 2013. "Nigeria: Overview." Accessed December 18, 2013. www.worldbank.org/en/country/nigeria/overview.

World Bank. 2017. *African Pulse, No. 15* (April 2017). World Bank, Washington, D.C. www.openknowledge.worldbank.org/handle/10986/26485

Wucherpfennig, Julian, Nils W. Metternich, Lars-Erik Cederman, and Kristian S. Gleditsch. 2012. "Ethnicity, the State, and the Duration of Civil War." *World Politics* 64 (1):79–115.

Yamsat, Pandang. 2011. *The Christian Becoming a Political Leader*. Bukuru: African Christian Textbooks.

# Index

Abduh, Muhammad, 51
ACLED. *See* Armed Conflict Location and Event Dataset
affiliated Christians, 44, 55
al-Afghani, Jama al-Din, 51
African Traditional Religion, 65
All Progressive Congress (APC), 246
Anglican Church Missionary Society, 63
APC. *See* All Progressive Congress
Armed Conflict Location and Event Dataset (ACLED), 134–135
assimilation. *See* cultural assimilation
associationalism, 242–243
Aytap people, 227

Babangida, Ibrahim, 79, 99
Bako, Abubakar, 132–133
al-Banna, Hasan, 51
Bassa region
  power-sharing in, 175–176
    during colonial period, 209–210
    comparative studies of, 172–173
    demographic factors for, 238
    incentives for, 208–211
    among indigenous peoples, 210
    religious violence in, 254
Bello, Ahmadu, 68–69
Berger, Peter L., 41
Biafran Civil War, 8, 25, 88
Boko Haram, 5, 17–18, 53, 57–58, 263
Bosnia and Herzegovina, power-sharing in, 113–114
Buhari, Muhammadu, 15

Burma, power-sharing in, 113–114
Burundi, consociationalism in, 113

CAN. *See* Christian Association of Nigeria
Central African Republic, ethnic violence in, 5–6
Chad, power-sharing in, 113–114
Chikun region
  power-sharing in, 174
    comparative studies of, 168–170
    demographic factors for, 239
    geographic context for, 203–204
    among Hausa-Fulani people, 203
    incentives for, 202–204
    religious violence in, 169–170, 250–253
Christian Association of Nigeria (CAN), 31, 66, 80–81, 241
Christian missionaries, 63–65
  education through, 66–69
Christianity. *See also* Pentecostal-charismatic Christianity
  affiliated Christians, 44
  in Middle Belt, 10–11
  Maitatsine riots and, 10, 57–58
  missionary education and, 66–69
  in Nigeria, by region, 294
  religious change through, 53–57
    for affiliated Christians, 55
    in church growth, 54–55
    through missionary education, 66–69
    in Pentecostal-charismatic variants, 47–48, 54, 69–71
  population growth of, 54

revival and expansion of, 41–42, 47–50, 71–73
  through geographical saturation, 43–44
  for Pentecostal-charismatic Christianity, 47–48
  political consequences of, 48–50
  political influence through, 48–50, 80–81
Christians. *See also* affiliated Christians; Muslims and Christians
  identity conflict with Muslims, 1–2, 10–11
Church Missionary Society (CMS), 63
Church of Christ in Nigeria (COCIN), 64, 70–71
civic associationalism, 2
clientelism, in LGAs, 102–103
CMS. *See* Church Missionary Society
COCIN. *See* Church of Christ in Nigeria
colonial period, in Nigeria
  in Bassa region, 209–210
  in Kanam region, 205
  LGAs during
    aggressive subnationalism in, 94–95
    Hausa-Fulani people in, 94–95
    Indirect Rule and, 94
    Native Authority system, 94, 95
    reform movements in, 94–95
  religious change during, 61–65
    arrival of Christian missionaries, 63–65
    under Indirect Rule, 61–63
    through protection of Muslim rule, 63–65
  Zangon-Kataf region during, 223–229
    elites in, 224
    under Indirect Rule, 223–224
colonialism
  Indirect Rule and, 61–63
  consequences of, 62–63
  power-sharing and, 26–28
communal riots, 21
communal violence, 2, 5–6
  from absence of power-sharing, 192
  contextual factors for, 7–8
    subnational politics, 7–8
  in Ghana, 6
  in Kanam region, 248–250
  in Kenya, 6
  methodological approach to, 32–35
    church growth data, 34–35
    ethnic violence dataset, 32–34

    power-sharing data, 34
    qualitative case studies, 35
    religious violence dataset, 32–34
  religious change as factor in, 42–43
  research on, 274–276
  riots compared to, 21
  in Tanzania, 6
comparative studies, for power-sharing, 167–173, 233–234
  of Bassa region, 172–173
  of Chikun region, 168–170
  of Jos North region, 168–170
  of Kanam region, 169, 170–172
  of Shendam region, 170–172
  of Zanga-Kataf region, 172–173
competition, within LGAs, 100–103
  numbers of LGAs as factor for, 101
  resource allocation as factor in, 100–101
consociationalism, 114
  in Burundi, 113
contestation, of democratic elections
  in LGAs, 100–103
  power-sharing and, 121–122
cultural assimilation, power-sharing and, 198–200
  in Shendam region, 220
Cyprus, power-sharing in, 113–114
Czechoslovakia, power-sharing in, 113–114

decentralization, of government
  through federalism, 84, 89–92
  in Indonesia, 284–285, 286
  in Kanam region, 206
  through LGAs, 25, 95–97
  power-sharing through, 25
  research on, 282
  in Zangon-Kataf region, 225–226
demographic patterns
  in power-sharing analysis, 163–164
    in Kaduna state, 155–156
  power-sharing influenced by, 238–240
    in Bassa region, 238
    in Chikun region, 239
    in Jos North region, 239
    in Kanam region, 239
*The Desecularization of the World* (Berger), 41

economic inequality, power-sharing influenced by, 243–245
ECWA. *See* Evangelical Church Winning All

elites, 88
  power-sharing among, historical framework for, 197
  in Zangon-Kataf region, 224
Eternal Love Winning Africa (ELWA), 70
Ethiopia
  power-sharing in, 113–114
  religious violence in, 6
ethnic belonging, 279
ethnic conflict. *See* ethnic violence
ethnic identity
  descent-based, 268–269
  elite politicization of, 271
  political parties and, 248
ethnic symbols, mobilization of, 279
ethnic violence
  Biafran Civil War and, 8, 25
  in Central African Republic, 5–6
  in Indonesia, 283–287
    decentralization of government in, 284–285, 286
    religious change as factor for, 286
  Jos North region, 28–30
  methodological approach to, 32–34
  in Myanmar, 5–6
  as national security challenge, 37
  power-sharing as solution for, 114, 119–120
  subnational variations in, 2
ethnicity, defined, 2
ethno-federalism
  power-sharing as, 109–110
  in research on institutional conflict, 272–273
ethno-religious violence. *See* religious violence
Evangelical Church Winning All (ECWA), 34–35, 55–56
extreme regionalism, in Nigeria, 87

FCS. *See* Fellowship of Christian Students
federalism
  comparative, 272–273
  in Nigeria, 85, 86–93
    centralization of power and, 89–92
    decentralization of power and, 84, 89–92
    extreme regionalism and, 87
    during First Republic, 86–88
    power-sharing and, 92, 109–110
    state creation and, 87, 90–91

Fellowship of Christian Students (FCS), 81
Fodio, Usman Dan, 57, 59

GDP. *See* gross domestic product
generalizability, of power-sharing, 280–283
Ghana, communal violence in, 6
GINI Index measures, 289–290
Global South, Pentecostal-charismatic Christianity in, 47–48
Goemai Christians, in Shendam region, 219–222
Gonyok, Charles, 214
gross domestic product (GDP), in Nigeria, 291
Guyana, power-sharing in, 113–114

Hausa Muslims, 185–186
Hausa-Fulani people, 9
  during colonial period, in LGAs, 94–95
  conversion to Islam, 59
  under Indirect Rule, 61–63
  in Jos North region, 169–170
  power-sharing for, 28–29, 156–159, 203
  in Zangon-Kataf region, 227
Human Rights Watch, 185, 188–189, 190–191
humanitarianism, religious change as influence on, 41–42

identity-based conflict. *See also* ethnic violence
  academic study of, 2–3
  between Muslims and Christians, 1–2
  in Nigeria, 11
    political actors' influence on, 14–17
    population demographics as factor for, 14
    in specific states, 13
    structural inequalities as factor in, 12–13
    weakness of state as factor in, 17–20
  structural inequalities as factor in, 12–13
India, religious violence in, 5
indigenous populations. *See also* Hausa-Fulani people
  in Jos North region, 213
  power-sharing among, 210
Indirect Rule, 61–63
  consequences of, 62–63
  in Kanam region, 204
  LGAs and, 94

# Index

Indonesia
  ethnic conflict in, 283–287
    decentralization of government in, 284–285, 286
    religious change as factor for, 286
  religious violence in, 5, 270
informal power-sharing, 115–122. *See also* local power-sharing
inter-marriage, religious violence and, 235
international human rights, religious change influenced by, 41–42
Iqbal, Muhammad, 51
Iraq, power-sharing in, 113–114
ISIS. *See* Islamic State
Islam. *See also* Muslims and Christians
  Hausa-Fulani people's conversion to, 59
  political reform and, 276–277
  religious change and, 57–58
    during pre-colonial period, 59
  revival of, 44–45, 50–53, 276–277
    in Nigeria, 31–32
    political consequences of, 51–53
    through reform movements, 51
  *ulama*, 51
Islamic extremism, 263
Islamic State (ISIS), 53

Jamaat-i-Islam, 51
Jama'atu Nasril Islam (JNI), 80–81, 181, 209
Jang, Jonah, 99, 249–250
Jarawa Muslims, in Shendam region, 219–222
Jema'a emirate system, 227
JNI. *See* Jama'atu Nasril Islam
Jonathan, Goodluck, 15, 109–110
Jos North region
  ethnic violence in, 28–30
  formation of, 215–216
  Hausa-Fulani people in, 169–170
  indigenous populations in, 213
  Muslim-Christian violence in, 242–243
  power-sharing in, 28–30, 212–218
    comparative studies of, 168–170
    consequences from absence of, 186–188
    demographic factors in, 239
  religious violence in, 169–170

Kaduna state, power-sharing in
  consequences from absence of, 191–192
  data analysis of, 142–146, 154–160
  data collection for, 144–146
  data interpretation, 155–160
  demographics in, 155–156
    in LGAs, 155–156, 159–160
    violence and, patterns of, 154
  data collection for, 144–146
  immigrant population in, 169
  population of, 304
  zone-based rotation, 156–159
Kanam region
  colonial rule in, 205
  communal violence in, 248–250
  decentralization reforms in, 206
  Indirect Rule in, 204
  Native Authority in, 204
  power-sharing in, 175
    in comparative studies, 169, 170–172
    democratization as factor in, 206–207
    demographic factors for, 239
    incentives for, 204–208
Kataf Christians, 185–186
Kenya
  communal violence in, 6
  constitutional change in, 282
Khan, Sayyid Ahmad, 51

Latin America, Pentecostal-charismatic Christianity in, 47–48
Lebanon, power-sharing in, 113–114
LGA. *See* local government area
Lijphart, Arend, 114
local government areas (LGAs)
  authority of, research on, 281–282
  clientelism in, 102–103
  during colonial period
    aggressive subnationalism in, 94–95
    Hausa-Fulani people in, 94–95
    Indirect Rule and, 94
    Native Authority system, 94, 95
    reform movements, 94–95
  competition within, 100–103
    numbers of LGAs as factor for, 101
    resource allocation as factor in, 100–101
  contestation for leadership within, 100–103
  creation of, 9–10
  decentralization through, 25, 95–97
  defined, 3
  election inconsistencies in, 99
  electoral interference in, 99

local government areas (cont.)
  ethno-tribal groups in, 266–267
  formalization of, 95
  mismanagement issues in, 102–103
  patronage in, 102–103
  during post-colonial period, reform movements in, 95–97
  power-sharing in, 21–23, 124–128, 229–231
    through decentralization, 25
    in Kaduna state, 155–156, 159–160
    mechanisms of, 176–183
    in Plateau state, 124–125, 147–153
    for religious violence, 162
    scope of, 124
  reform movements in, 93–100
    during colonial period, 94–95
    national-level interference as part of, 99–100
    during 1970s, 95–100
    during post-colonial period, 95–97
    state-level interference as part of, 97–98
local power-sharing, 115–122
  critiques of, 120–121, 122
  in heterogeneous societies, 118
  incentive systems in, 118, 119, 123
  institutional legitimacy through, 118–119
  logical foundations of, 115–122
  through resource allocation, 117–118
  as self-reproducing, 121
  top-down model of, 115
Lugard, Frederick, 61

Maitatsine riots, 10, 57–58, 277
Malaysia, religious violence in, 5
Mangvwat, M. Y., 214
Mato, Alhaji Sanusi, 216–217
Mawdudi, Mawlana, 51
methodology, for communal violence research, 32–35
  church growth data, 34–35
  ethnic violence dataset, 32–34
  power-sharing data, 34
  qualitative case studies, 35
  religious violence dataset, 32–34
Middle Belt, of Nigeria, 8–9
  Christianity in, 10–11
    Maitatsine riots and, 10, 57–58
    missionary education and, 66–69
  power-sharing in, 199
  during pre-colonial period, 60–61
minority representation, through power-sharing, 178–179
modernization theory, 46–47
Mohammad (Prophet), 52
Mohammed, Mallam Muktar Usman, 184
Mohammed, Murtala, 89
Mohammed, Samai'ila, 216
Molwus, Nde Alexander, 76
MSS. See Muslim Student Society
Muslim Brotherhood, 51
Muslim Student Society (MSS), 81, 132
Muslims
  Hausa Muslims, 185–186
  identity conflict with Christians, 1–2, 10–11
  Jarawa Muslims, 219–222
Muslims and Christians, tensions between, 78–81
  in Jos North, 242–243
  over creation of religious organizations, 80–81
  over OIC, 79–80
  over Sharia, 78–79
Myanmar
  ethnic violence in, 5–6
  religious violence in, 5

National Poverty Eradication Program, 184
Native Authority system, 94, 95
  in Kanam region, 204
Niger state, 200–201
Nigeria. See also colonial period; Middle Belt; pre-colonial period; religious change
  Boko Haram in, 5, 17–18
  Christian affiliation in, by region, 294
  church growth data for, 34–35
  communal violence in, 2, 5–6
  decentralization of government in, 84, 89–92
  economic clout of, 5
  economic indicators in, 292
  elites in, 88
  federalism in, 85, 86–93
    centralization of power and, 89–92
    decentralization of power and, 84, 89–92
    extreme regionalism and, 87
    during First Republic, 86–88
    power-sharing and, 92, 109–110

state creation and, 87, 90–91
GDP per capita in, 291
GINI Index measures in, 289–290
Hausa-Fulani people in, 9
  conversion to Islam, 59
  under Indirect Rule, 61–63
  power-sharing for, 28–29
identity-based conflict in, 11
  political actors' influence on, 14–17
  population demographics as factor for, 14
  in specific states, 13
  structural inequalities as factor in, 12–13
  weakness of state as factor in, 17–20
Islam revival in, 31–32
LGAs in
  creation of, 9–10
  defined, 3
national-level manipulation of local politics in, 19
in OIC, 31, 66, 241
Operation Safe Haven in, 20
PDP in, 76, 91
political party identity in, 248
population growth in, 5
Sharia in, 31
Sokoto Caliphate in, 59, 60–61
state formation within, 9
  under federalism, 87, 90–91
violence in, historical context for, 8–11
  in post-colonial era, 9–10
  in pre-colonial era, 9–10
  religious changes as influence on, 10–11
weak political leadership in, 259–261
Nigeria Social Violence Project, 136
Non-State Conflict Dataset, 134–136

Obasanjo, Olusegun, 89
OIC. *See* Organization of Islamic Conference
Onaiyekan, John, 82
Operation Safe Haven, 20
Organization of Islamic Conference (OIC)
  Muslim and Christian tension over, 79–80
  Nigerian membership in, 31, 66, 241

patronage, in LGAs, 102–103
PDP. *See* People's Democratic Party

peacebuilding, through power-sharing, 179–181, 192–193
Pentecostal-charismatic Christianity, 45, 46
  expansion of, 47–48, 54, 69–71
  in Global South, 47–48
  in Latin America, 47–48
  political influence of, 48–50
  revival of, 47–48, 69–71, 73–74
  social status through participation in, 48
  in Uganda, 48
  in Zambia, 48
People's Democratic Party (PDP), 76, 91, 246
  in Shendam region, 220–221
the Philippines
  power-sharing in, 113–114
  religious violence in, 5
Plateau state, power-sharing in, 124–125, 217–218
  consequences from absence of, 189–191
  data analysis of, 147–153
    between cattle-herders and farmers, 151–152
    data collection for, 142–146
    data interpretation, 149–153
    in LGAs, 147–153
    violence and, patterns of, 147–148
  population of, 305
political parties
  ethnic identity and, 248
  power-sharing and, 246–248
    electoral bodies controlled by, 246
    federal structure as factor in, 247
    political godfathers in, 246–247
post-colonial period, in Nigeria
  LGAs during, reform movements in, 95–97
  power-sharing in, 199
  violence in, historical context for, 9–10
  Zangon-Kataf region during, 226–227
power-sharing, 21–30, 264–268. *See also* comparative studies; Kaduna state; local power-sharing; Plateau state
  adoption of, 24–30
  colonial history as factor in, 26–28
  demographic balance in, 24–25
  alternative hypotheses for, 255–256
  associationalism and, 242–243
  in Bassa region, 175–176
  during colonial period, 209–210
  comparative studies of, 172–173

power-sharing (cont.)
    demographic factors for, 238
    incentives for, 208–211
        among indigenous peoples, 210
    in Chikun region, 174
        comparative studies of, 168–170
        demographic factors in, 239
        geographic context for, 203–204
        among Hausa-Fulani people, 203
        incentives for, 202–204
    civic integration and, 242–243
    collaboration among groups through, 21–22, 179–181
    consequences from absence of, 183–192
        communal violence as, 192
        in Jos North region, 186–188
        in Kaduna state, 191–192
        in Plateau state, 189
        religious violence as, 184–192
        in Shendam region, 188–189
    consociationalism and, 113, 114
    contestation of democratic elections and, 121–122
    demographics as factor in, 238–240
    displacement of population and, 243
    economic inequality as factor in, 243–245
    electoral incentives for, 238–240, 267
    electoral representation through, 266
    ethnic conflict reduction through, 114, 119–120
    as ethno-federalism, 109–110
    external interferences in, 128
    federalism and, 92, 109–110
    through fixed representation model, 23–24
    forms of, 23–24
    generalizability of, 280–283
    among Hausa-Fulani people, 28–29, 156–159, 203
    historical framework for, 197–200
        cultural assimilation as part of, 198–200
        among elites, 197
        political integration as part of, 198–200
    through inclusive decision making, 112
    informal, 115–122
    in Jos North region, 28–30, 212–218
        comparative studies of, 168–170
        consequences from absence of, 186–188
    demographic factors in, 239
    in Kanam region, 175
        comparative studies of, 169, 170–172
        democratization as factor in, 206–207
        demographic factors for, 239
        incentives for, 204–208
    in LGAs, 21–23, 124–128, 229–231
        through decentralization, 25
        in Kaduna state, 155–156, 159–160
        mechanisms of, 176–183
        in Plateau state, 124–125, 147–153
        for religious violence, 162
        scope of, 124
    limitations of, 111–114
    mechanisms of
        in LGAs, 176–183
        minority representation through, 178–179
        perceptions of fair play through, 177–178
        politicization of ethnicity constrained by, 177
    methodological approach to, 34, 35–38
    in Middle Belt region, 199
    at national level, 111–114
    in Niger state, 200–201
    through partitioned decision-making, 112
    peace through, 25–26
    peacebuilding through, 179–181, 192–193
    political incentives for, 199
    political parties and, 246–248
        electoral bodies controlled by, 246
        ethnic identity and, 248
        federal structure as factor in, 247
        political godfathers in, 246–247
    in post-colonial period, 199
    prior peace history as factor in, 236–237
    religious change and, rate of, 240–241
        among religious groups, 21
        religious implications of, 268–271
        religious violence and, 182–183, 193–195
            data analysis of, 161–163
        in religiously homogeneous communities, 201
    rotation model for, 23, 125–126
        seat-based, 125–126
        ward-based, 126
    second-generation problems with, 119
    in Shendam region, 219–223
        in comparative studies, 170–172

consequences from absence of, 188–189
among Goemai Christians, 219–222
among Jarawa Muslims, 219–222
lack of cultural assimilation, 220
SPEED data, 26
static model for, 126–128
seat-based, 126–127
ward-based, 127–128
at subnational level, 117
symbolic implications of, 268–271
among tribal groups, 21
unsustainable experiments in, 113–114
in Zangon-Kataf region, 223–229
in comparative studies, 172–173
power-sharing, data analysis of, 142–160
through comparative studies, 167–173
of Bassa region, 172–173
of Chikun region, 168–170
of Jos North region, 168–170
of Kanam region, 169, 170–172
of Shendam region, 170–172
of Zanga-Kataf region, 172–173
demographic patterns, 163–164
in Kaduna state, 155–156
for ethno-religious violence, 161–163
for ethno-tribal violence, 161–163
interpretation of, 145–146
in Kaduna state, 142–146, 154–160
data collection for, 144–146
data interpretation, 155–160
demographics in, 155–156
in LGAs, 155–156, 159–160
violence and, patterns of, 154
zone-based rotation, 156–159
in LGAs
in Kaduna state, 155–156, 159–160
in Plateau state, 147–153
for religious violence, 162
patterns in, 146
in Plateau state, 147–153
between cattle-herders and farmers, 151–152
data collection for, 142–146
data interpretation, 149–153
in LGAs, 147–153
violence and, patterns of, 147–148
statistical support in, 164
types of, 146
pre-colonial period, in Nigeria. *See also* colonial period

Middle Belt during, 60–61
religious change during, 58–61
arrival of Islam, 59
national cohesion as result of, 60–61
national fragmentation as result of, 60–61
violence in Nigeria during, 9–10

al-Qaeda, 53

reform movements, in LGAs, 93–100
during colonial period, 94–95
national-level interference as part of, 99–100
during 1970s, 95–100
during post-colonial period, 95–97
state-level interference as part of, 97–98
religion, revival of, 41–43
causes of, 47–53
for Christianity, 41–42, 47–50, 71–73
through geographical saturation, 43–44
for Pentecostal-charismatic Christianity, 47–48, 69–71, 73–74
political consequences of, 48–50
political influence of, 48–50, 80–81
for Islam, 44–45, 50–53, 276–277
in Nigeria, 31–32
political consequences of, 51–53
through reform movements, 51
modernity and, 41
modernization theory for, 46–47
secularization thesis for, 46–47
religious affiliation, in Asia, 293
religious change, 53–78
through Christianity, expansion of, 53–57
for affiliated Christians, 55
in church growth, 54–55
through missionary education, 66–69
in Pentecostal-charismatic variants, 47–48, 54, 69–71
population growth of, 54
during colonial period, 61–65
arrival of Christian missionaries, 63–65
under Indirect Rule, 61–63
protection of Muslim rule, 63–65
communal violence as result of, 42–43
democracy and, 41–42
global context for, 43–47
humanitarianism influenced by, 41–42
as independent nation, 66–74
in Indonesia, 286

religious change (cont.)
  international human rights regime
    influenced by, 41–42
  through Islam, expansion of, 57–58
  during pre-colonial period, 59
  politics of, 74–78
  during pre-colonial period, 58–61
    arrival of Islam, 59
    national cohesion as result of, 60–61
    national fragmentation as result of,
      60–61
  research on, 276–279
  War on Terror and, 41–42
religious identity
  as divisive political category, 261–262
  tribal identity as proxy for, 234–236
religious violence. See also communal
    violence
  in academic scholarship, 286
  in Bassa region, 254
  by case, 1979–2011, 295
    association between religious
      precipitating events, 296–297, 301,
      303
    ethno-tribal category, 298–299,
      300–301, 302
  causes of, 30–32
  in Chikun region, 169–170, 250–253
  datasets on, 134–142
    ACLED, 134–135
    construction of, 137–142
    newspaper sources in, 140–142
    Non-State Conflict, 134–136
    review of, 134–136
    SCAD, 134–135
  defined, 2–3
  in Ethiopia, 6
  identities of groups involved in, 138
  in India, 5
  in Indonesia, 5, 270
  inter-marriage and, 235
  in Jos North region, 169–170
  during Kafanchan incident, 132–133
  local factors for, 6–7
  in Malaysia, 5
  methodological approach to, 32–34
  in Myanmar, 5
  as national security challenge, 37
  in the Philippines, 5
  power-sharing and, 182–183, 193–195
    data analysis of, 161–163

  in Shendam region, 222–223
  in Thailand, 5
research, on institutions and conflict,
    272–283. See also comparative
    studies; methodology
  on communal conflict, 274–276
  decentralization of power and, 282
  ethno-federalism in, 272
  generalizability of, 280–283
  for informal institutions, 273–274
  for intra-state violence, 280–281
  on LGA authority, 281–282
  on party rules, 279–280
  on power-sharing, 279–280
  religious change in, 276–279
rotation power-sharing, 23, 125–126
  seat-based, 125–126
  ward-based, 126

SCAD. See Social Conflict in Africa Dataset
SCIA. See Supreme Council for Islamic
    Affairs
seat-based power-sharing
  in rotation model, 125–126
  in static model, 126–127
second-generation problems, with power-
    sharing, 119
secularization, modernity as influence on, 41
secularization thesis, for revival of religion,
    46–47
Shagari, Alhaji Shehu, 99
Sharia law
  Muslim and Christian tension over, 78–79
  in Nigeria, 31
Shendam region
  PDP in, 220–221
  political redistricting in, 221
  power-sharing in, 170–172, 219–223
    consequences from absence of, 188–189
    among Goemai Christians, 219–222
    among Jarawa Muslims, 219–222
    lack of cultural assimilation and, 220
  religious violence in, 222–223
SIM. See Sudan Interior Mission
Social, Political, and Economic Event
    dataset (SPEED) data, 26, 237
Social Conflict in Africa Dataset (SCAD),
    134–135
Sokoto Caliphate, 59, 60–61
SPEED data. See Social, Political, and
    Economic Event dataset data

# Index

Sri Lanka, power-sharing in, 113–114
static power-sharing, 126–128
   seat-based, 126–127
   ward-based, 127–128
Sudan, power-sharing in, 113–114
Sudan Interior Mission (SIM), 63–64
Sudan United Mission (SUM), 64
Supreme Council for Islamic Affairs (SCIA), 80–81

Tanzania, communal violence in, 6
Thailand, religious violence in, 5

Uganda, Pentecostal-charismatic Christianity in, 48

violence. *See also* communal violence; ethnic violence; religious violence
   communal, 2
   in Nigeria, historical context for, 8–11

War on Terror, religious change and, 41–42
ward-based power-sharing
   in rotation model, 126
   in static model, 127–128

Yamsat, Pandang, 76–77
Yar'Adua, 109–110

Zambia, Pentecostal-charismatic Christianity in, 48
Zangon-Kataf region
   during colonial period, 223–229
   elites in, 224
   under Indirect Rule, 223–224
   decentralization reforms in, 225–226
   Hausa-Fulani people in, 227
   during post-colonial period, 226–227
   power-sharing in, 223–229
   in comparative studies, 172–173